THE NATIONAL
URBAN LEAGUE
1910-1940

WEISS, Nancy J.   The National Urban League, 1910–1940.   Oxford, 1974.   402p   map   tab   bibl   73-90366.   12.50.   ISBN 0-19-501765-X

This thoroughly researched, heavily documented, *post-partum* Friedel-directed dissertation is a chronicle that should be on the shelf of all libraries that provide more than superficial knowledge of black history.   Blacks were a major part of the urbanization of the U.S. between the wars, and the Urban League was one of the major organizations that monitored and aided their transition from agrarian to urban. Replete with primary source quotations, this tracing of Urban League development from 1910 to 1940 illuminates the general urban history of the nation.   A scholarly monograph written for the graduate or undergraduate, it should serve as a springboard to additional research, as well as a reference at the high school level.   The less intensive Guichard Parris and Lester Brooks, *Blacks in the city; a history of the National Urban League* (CHOICE, Apr. 1972), is a better general history (Weiss stops at 1940).   But the scholarship of Weiss, her insights into the relations between leaders, and her consideration of Urban League development in the context of national movements and interpretations make it a better stimulus for future study.

THE NATIONAL URBAN LEAGUE 1910-1940

NANCY J. WEISS

New York • Oxford University Press • 1974

Map design by David Lindroth

Copyright © 1974 by Oxford University Press, Inc.
Library of Congress Catalogue Card Number: 73-90366

Printed in the United States of America

To my Mother and Father

PREFACE

In studying the history of black people since 1900 we are accustomed to thinking of two major peaks. Everyone knows about the controversy between Booker T. Washington and W.E.B. Du Bois over ideology and tactics. And our own experience with the civil rights movement reminds us of its origins in the years following World War II. What happened between those two peaks is much less familiar. In the last decade, studies of the Garvey Movement, the early years of the NAACP, the formation of urban ghettos, and the explosion of racial violence have contributed importantly to filling the gap. This book is an effort to close it further.

The first half of this century was the seedtime of racial reform, a period when blacks and whites, separately and in concert, experimented with tactics and structures and developed the organizations that have carried the struggle for equality down to the present day. The history of the first three decades of the National Urban League is part of the history of race relations in those years. It documents the development of an interracial approach to racial advancement, and it shows how the attitudes and practices of white employers, labor unions, and government officials affected the lives of blacks in American cities.

The history of the Urban League in this period is also part of the history of urban black communities. It documents the aspirations and experiences of blacks new to the cities, and it illustrates the kinds of programs and services that had to be generated to meet their needs. It provides a perspective on black Americans at a critical juncture in their transformation from a predominantly agricultural peasantry to a predominantly urban proletariat.

The history of the Urban League between 1910 and 1940 is also a vehicle for some understanding of the larger national context that called forth and continually reshaped the organization's purposes and programs. It speaks to the place of racial reform in progressivism, to the impact of World War I on American society, to the persistence of social concern in the 1920s, to the response of voluntary agencies to the Depression, to the role of minorities in the politics of the New Deal, and to the history of American labor practices. Additionally, it shows how little attention, except in times of crisis and national need, America was paying to black problems in the decades before the civil rights movement began in earnest.

The history of the Urban League is necessarily an organizational history, but in this respect, because of the sources, it has some significant limitations. The National Urban League Papers are notably thin in certain areas because considerable correspondence and printed material was destroyed indiscriminately when the League moved its headquarters office in the early 1950s. The papers of a few League officials help to fill in some of the gaps, but here, too, there are serious limitations. The personal correspondence of one of the League's co-founders, Ruth Standish Baldwin, stored at the home of her daughter, disintegrated in a flood of the Delaware River in the 1950s. The papers of her son, William H. Baldwin, secretary of the League during the course of this study, contain almost no mention of his relationship with the organization. Similarly, the papers of Charles S. Johnson, the first director of research and editor of *Opportunity*, are exceptionally unrevealing about his role in the Urban League. Mrs. Eugene Kinckle Jones, Jr., has the unfinished autobiography of her father-in-law, the League's executive secretary, but she refuses to make it available for scholarly consultation. Similar problems apply to the early records of Urban League affiliates; the papers of the Chicago Urban League, for example, were destroyed by fire. Few of the other important affiliates have preserved any material at all from this period; where such information does exist, it usually consists of fragmentary board minutes and published reports.

This means that it is impossible to deal adequately with many of the questions one ought to raise about the organizational history of the Urban League. We do not know, for instance, how the executive secretary functioned in relation to the executive board and its chairman. Nor do we know how the actual decision-making process worked. Where did policy originate: in the board or in the executive staff? Did the board always agree to whatever Eugene Kinckle Jones wanted to do? Or did they agree because Jones, realizing their views, never pushed them too far? How did the board divide on critical policy questions?

The paucity of source material means that none of these important problems can be analyzed with any depth and sophistication. It also means that it is virtually impossible to cast any significant light on the role of Urban League affiliates in shaping League policy. It is clear that local Leagues, though autonomous, usually followed program guidelines set forth by the national office. But it is not at all clear how they in turn may have influenced the direction of the national organization.

Despite these limitations, the records do reveal much of importance about what the Urban League did. This study will demonstrate how the League adapted for blacks the employment and welfare services already offered foreign- and native-born whites by settlement houses, charitable agencies, and immigrant aid societies. And it will show where the League pioneered and refined tools of interracial teamwork, research and investigation, and professional social work training to help reach some sort of rapprochement between blacks and the cities. It will attempt to trace the changing context of the League's efforts during its first three decades and at the same time to emphasize the underlying continuity of the organization's concerns. In so doing, it may add some perspective to the contemporary self-examination of vehicles for racial advancement, and it may help to sharpen our perception of the historical roots for the continuing plight of urban blacks.

ACKNOWLEDGMENTS

One of the special pleasures of completing this book is the opportunity to thank the many generous people who helped to see it to fruition. Through the good offices of John Hope Franklin, the National Urban League granted me access to its records in the Library of Congress before they were officially opened for research. John C. Broderick, assistant chief of the Manuscript Division, and Joseph D. Sullivan, Jr., archivist and manuscript librarian, consistently cooperated in helping me to use the collection before it had been completely processed. In addition, I am indebted to the staffs of the following libraries for making it possible and pleasant to work in their collections: Amistad Research Center and Race Relations Department, Fisk University (now at Dillard University); Arthur A. Schomburg Collection, New York Public Library; Erastus Milo Cravath Library, Fisk University; Firestone Library, Princeton University; Free Public Library, Newark, New Jersey; Historical Society of Pennsylvania; Houghton Library, Harvard University; Moorland Foundation, Howard University; Michigan Historical Collections, University of Michigan; National Archives; Oral History Research Office, Columbia University; Quaker Collection, Haverford College Library; Social Welfare History Archives Center, University of Minnesota; Sophia Smith Collection, William Allan Neilson Library, Smith College; State Historical Society of Wisconsin; Tuskegee Institute; University of Chicago Library; Urban Archives Center, Temple University; Western Reserve Historical Society, Cleveland. For permission to consult and to quote from letters in their possession, I am grateful to the Rockefeller Family Archives, the Carnegie Corporation of New York (for the Carnegie Corporation Archives), and Herbert Aptheker (for the Papers of W. E. B. Du Bois). The directors of the Baltimore, St. Louis, and Englewood, New Jersey, Urban Leagues kindly allowed me to examine records still held by their organizations.

Urban Leaguers and their families and colleagues graciously shared with me memories and records that added important information and a lively sense of contemporaneity to the documentation in library collections. William H. Baldwin's keen interest, introductions to other Urban Leaguers, and thoughtful review of the dissertation on which this book is based kept me informed and enthusiastic about the task at hand. I am indebted also to William M. Ashby, Roger N. Baldwin, Lester B. Granger, Mrs. George E. Haynes, Edward S. Lewis, Guichard Parris, Mrs. Ira De A. Reid, and Mrs. L. Hollingsworth Wood. Henry Lee Moon sharpened my perspective by giving me the point of view of an official of the NAACP. I gained additional information from correspondence with David P. Agnew, Lloyd K. Garrison, James H. Hubert, Ralph W. Jackson, Richard J. Mack, Floyd Nichols, Sarah H. Pope, Marion Walton Putnam, Arthur Sachs, Virginia Schoellkopf, and Melvina Squires. For answering my inquiries about Urban Leaguers, I am further indebted to staff members of the alumni associations of Amherst College, Stanford University, and Yale University; the public libraries of Englewood and Atlantic City, New Jersey; the Haviland Records Room, Society of Friends, New York City; the Family Service Association of Greater Middletown, Connecticut; the Metropolitan Life Insurance Company, New York City; and the Starwood Corporation, Cincinnati.

My research assistants and former students, Richard P. Cheston, R. Mark Dare, William V. Engel, and Anthony Murry, helped significantly to move this study to its conclusion. I am grateful for grants for research and manuscript preparation from the Shelby

Cullom Davis Center for Historical Studies and the University Research Board of Princeton University. Elizabeth Campbell and Helen Wright cheerfully typed the final manuscript, and Roberta Blaché expertly assisted in the preparation of the index. My editors at Oxford University Press, Sheldon Meyer and Caroline Taylor, skillfully guided the transformation from typescript to published book.

Most of all, I owe an incalculable debt to my teachers, colleagues, and friends who read this work in various drafts and inspired and sustained its author during the long months of research and writing. Arthur Mann introduced me to the study of history over a decade ago and has been an unfailing source of encouragement and wise counsel ever since. Frank Freidel supervised this study in dissertation form with welcome patience and consistent good humor and launched me on my professional career with a healthy balance of laissez-faire and careful direction. Arno J. Mayer pushed me to take a critical look at my assumptions and to build a more rigorous analytical framework. James M. McPherson shared with me his own work in race relations and provided invaluable advice and support at every stage of this project. Arthur S. Link read the final manuscript with the practiced eye of a professional editor. August Meier gave it the benefit of his incomparable knowledge of the history of organizations for racial advancement.

The dedication is an imperfect expression of appreciation to my parents for understanding at difficult times, practical assistance of all kinds, and the unswerving conviction that I could do it when I sometimes thought I couldn't. It is easy to take such things for granted, but it would be infinitely harder to manage without them.

N. J. W.

Princeton, New Jersey
February 1974

CONTENTS

PART THREE: 1929–1940

PART ONE

1910 -1918

1 THE ORIGINS OF RACIAL PROTEST AND REFORM,

1890–1905

The history of modern racial reform movements begins shortly before 1890. The last decade of the nineteenth century and the first two of the twentieth—a period marked on one end by the enactment of the first Jim Crow car law in Florida, in 1887, and on the other by the Chicago race riot of 1919—saw political, economic, and social changes that would define the status of blacks in the United States and the contours of "the Negro problem" for most of the next half-century. These years were also the period in which blacks articulated competing philosophies of racial advancement that would influence racial activity for decades to come. Finally, it was during this period that whites and blacks together forged the organizational apparatus that would carry the struggle for equality down to the civil rights movement of the 1950s and 1960s.

I

The most striking development of the late 1890s and early 1900s from the point of view of race is the explicit establishment, through law and custom, of a separate and unequal status for blacks in the United States. The comparative fluidity of race relations in the era of Reconstruction deteriorated by the end of the century into increasingly rigid segregation and discrimination, so that the 1890s and early 1900s marked what Rayford W. Logan has called "the nadir of the Negro's status in American society." Where some doubt and leeway had previously existed, state laws and city ordinances enacted in those decades spelled out provisions for racial separation in nearly every sphere of daily life. The tide of Jim Crow legislation began with the disfranchisement of blacks in most southern states and spread to encompass proscriptions against racial mixing in transportation facilities, public institutions, places of public accommodation, employment, and housing. The new laws often simply confirmed long-honored customs, and the prohibitions on paper frequently represented only a part of the segregation and discrimination actually practiced.

Sanctions for Jim Crow came from varied quarters: the Supreme Court, in a series of decisions including the *Civil Rights Cases* of 1883 and culminating in 1896 in *Plessy* v. *Ferguson*, which upheld the legality of separate-but-equal; the imperialistic spirit of the age, with its romanticized notion of the white man's burden and its less romantic Social Darwinist notion of Anglo-Saxon superiority by might; and the newest teachings of biologists, anthropologists, sociologists, and historians (further popularized by novelists and journalists), who advanced scholarly "proof" of the inferiority of the darker races.

Jim Crow also found congenial surroundings in national politics. Threaded through the story of blacks and political parties and movements after Reconstruction is a common theme of betrayal. As the radical Republicans who had pushed for emancipation and the Fourteenth and Fifteenth amendments died, and the party as a whole became absorbed in economic objectives, the cause of black rights lost its standing as a major party priority. The Democratic Redeemers who overthrew the Reconstruction governments in the 1870s believed that Negroes were inferior, but they also felt a paternalistic responsibility to protect them, so that under their tenure Negroes continued to enjoy some of the gains won during Reconstruction. But the "redneck" politicians who succeeded the Redeemers in the 1890s brought a tone of outright racism into southern politics. Even the Populists, who had flirted with an alliance of blacks and poor whites for political advantage, soured on racial cooperation as they made blacks the scapegoats for their party's political misfortunes. The progressives, too, had a largely negative record on the issue of race. Progressivism in the South, as C. Vann Woodward has described it, was for the most part "for whites only." Most northern progressives shared to some degree the racial assumptions of their generation, and blacks benefited less from the political, economic, and social reform movements of the early twentieth century than any other group in society.

The dearth of political support for real racial equality extended even to the most reform-minded occupants of the White House. President Theodore Roosevelt was a Social Darwinist who believed that "as a race, and in the mass, the [blacks] are altogether inferior to the whites." [1] He also felt, however, that individual blacks should have an equal chance with whites according to their qualifications. Accordingly, he appointed blacks to federal offices in the North as well as the South, often over the strong resistance of southern whites. Roosevelt's appointments policy, his reliance on the advice of Booker T. Washington, and his strongly stated opposition to lynching seemed at first to indicate that Negroes would have a place in the Square Deal. But during his second term Roosevelt alienated many blacks by certain actions, especially his summary discharge of three companies of black infantrymen who refused to inform on their fellows who had allegedly shot up the town of Brownsville, Texas. Black dissatisfaction with Roosevelt became even stronger when the Progressive party refused to seat Negro delegates from the South in its 1912 convention or to consider an equal rights plank drafted by W. E. B. Du Bois.

Nor was President Taft particularly attractive from a black point of view; while he named a few Negroes to government posts, he more often abided by his inaugural promise not to appoint to federal office anyone whom white Southerners found objectionable. Woodrow Wilson, the first native of the South to be elected to the presidency since the Civil War, had the worst record of any of the progressive presidents on the issue of race. Despite campaign promises of justice and fair dealing for blacks, Wilson and his cabinet further slashed already meager black patronage and established a policy of officially sanctioned segregation in the federal departments in Washington. The President, who believed in the social separation of the races and who was fond of telling "darky" stories at cabinet meetings, maintained in the face of strong protests that the Jim Crow arrangements were "to their [Negroes'] advantage." [2]

Some statistics underscore the plight of blacks in the early twentieth century. Close to nine-tenths of all those who were employed in 1890 earned their living in agriculture or domestic and personal service; the same was true for just over four-fifths of the employed blacks in 1910. Three-quarters of all black farmers were tenants or sharecroppers. Negro children in 1910 were less likely than whites to be in school, and the rate of illiteracy in the black population, though cut almost in half between 1890 and 1910, was still six times that of whites. The per capita expenditure for teachers' salaries in fifteen southern states and the District of Columbia was $10.32 for each white child, but only $2.89 for each black. Lynching, though on the decline in absolute terms after 1892, became an increasingly brutal and sadistic crime perpetrated more and more exclusively against Negroes. The average annual number of lynchings fell from 188 in the 1890s to 93 in the 1900s and 62 in the 1910s; but whereas whites accounted for 32 per cent of the lynch victims in the 1890s, they were only 9 per cent of those killed in the 1910s. During the decade 1898–1908, serious race riots broke out in Wilmington, North Carolina; New York; New Orleans; Atlanta; and Springfield, Illinois.[3]

II

Out of the intensified segregation, discrimination, and repression of the 1890s and early 1900s grew the organized efforts of blacks for racial advancement. The circumstances of the period shaped the direction that racial reform would take. In response to widespread white disaffection from the black cause in the years after Reconstruction, black leaders embraced a philosophy of self-help and racial solidarity. Some still advocated protest, publicity, and legal action, but others, disillusioned by the political process, turned to economic improvement, education, and moral uplift as paths to racial progress.

In the context of this emphasis on self-help and racial solidarity, it made sense that efforts to protest the denial of black rights should be couched in terms of racial separatism. T. Thomas Fortune, the founder of the Afro-American League, aptly explained the logic of not relying on the good offices of whites: "We think it has been thoroughly demonstrated," he wrote in 1887, "that the white people of this country have determined to leave the colored man alone to fight his battles. . . . There is no dodging the issue; we have got to take hold of this problem ourselves, and make so much noise that all the world shall know the wrongs we suffer and our determination to right those wrongs." [4]

By the end of the nineteenth century there was some precedent, particularly in the Negro convention movement, for organized protest. Negro conventions met irregularly from 1830 to 1890 to protest against slavery, segregation, and discrimination, consider proposals for emigration, and encourage racial progress through racial solidarity, education, vocational training, economic advancement, and moral uplift. But the conventions were sporadic, lacking in continuity, plagued by divided leadership and disagreement over strategy, and relatively ineffectual.

There were two major attempts in the late nineteenth and early twentieth centuries to create a permanent national apparatus for black protest. The first was the Afro-American League (later the Afro-American Council), founded in 1890 by T. Thomas Fortune. The second, the Niagara Movement, grew out of a meeting of black leaders called by W. E. B. Du Bois in 1905. Both subscribed to an ideology of agitation and protest, although the Council ultimately moderated its rhetoric when it came under the control of Booker T. Washington. In his address to the founding convention of the Afro-American League, Fortune defended agitation, even revolution, as necessary and legitimate tools to achieve black rights. It was "time to begin to fight fire with fire. . . . It is time to face the enemy and fight inch by inch for every right he denies us." [5] A similar conviction led W. E. B. Du Bois, then a professor of sociology at Atlanta University, and William Monroe Trotter, militant editor of the Boston *Guardian*, to break with the accommodationist leadership of Booker T. Washington. Whereas Washington eschewed social equality and political activism (at least in public) and urged blacks to concentrate on the development of education and economic self-sufficiency, Du Bois and Trotter insisted on immediate equality— social, economic, and political—and urged agitation to reach these goals.

Both the Afro-American Council and the Niagara Movement used similar methods—influencing public opinion and seeking court action in cases of denial of black rights—that reflected the militant ideologies of their founders; both sought an end to segregation and discrimination, full manhood suffrage, equal access to public accommodations and educational opportunities, equitable treatment before the law, and legislation to enforce the Fourteenth and Fifteenth Amendments. Neither accomplished very much, due largely to lack of funds and mass support, organizational inexperience of their leaders, buffeting in the ideological conflict between the accommodationist forces of Washington and the more radical ones of Du Bois and Trotter, and, ultimately, the anomaly of separatist efforts to secure integration. Nevertheless, the methods and concerns of the Niagara Movement, if not of the Council, laid the pattern for the most durable protest organization of the twentieth century, the National Association for the Advancement of Colored People.[6]

Despite the all-encompassing claims of their programs, the Afro-American Council and the Niagara Movement dealt primarily with the denial of black political and civil rights and focused their efforts chiefly on the South. This emphasis made sense, since nine-tenths of the black population lived in the South, and since anyone in that period would certainly have pointed to Jim Crow and racial violence as the most obvious, important dimensions of the Negro problem. With this emphasis, however, the protest organizations neglected the special problems of blacks in cities, especially in the North.

III

At the same time that political developments were fashioning a status for blacks that was explicitly separate and unequal, migration patterns of blacks themselves began to reshape and nationalize the Negro problem. After the Civil War, Negroes began to move in substantial numbers to urban centers of the South and, as early as 1880, black migrants showed up with increasing frequency in cities outside the South. Although in 1900 nine-tenths of the nation's 8,833,994 Negroes still lived in the South, by the turn of the century New York and Philadelphia both had Negro populations exceeding 60,000 and Chicago's was just over 30,000. While one-fifth of all Negroes lived in urban communities (2500 or more) in 1890, more than a quarter did so in 1910. More dramatic is the fact that over three-quarters of Negroes in the North lived in urban areas in 1910, a concentration that was higher than that of foreign-born whites.[7]

Contemporary observers commented on the emergence in major cities of definable Negro neighborhoods. "New York has its 'San Juan Hill' in the West Sixties, and its Harlem district of over 35,000 within about eighteen city blocks," Negro sociologist George Edmund Haynes noted in 1913. "Philadelphia has its Seventh Ward; Chicago has its State Street; Washington its North West neighborhood, and Baltimore its Druid Hill Avenue. Louisville has its Chestnut Street and its 'Smoketown'; Atlanta its West End and Auburn Avenue." [8] The urbanization of the black population had begun well before the Great Migration of World War

I; and with urbanization came the development of black ghettos and new dimensions of racial problems.

According to scholars, black and white, who, around the turn of the century, began to study patterns of urban adjustment among black masses, northern city life was far from smooth. Prejudices of white employers and labor as well as lack of industrial training forced most Negroes to earn their livelihood as unskilled laborers and servants. The strong participation of black women in the labor market, chiefly as domestics, meant that their children were left during the day and sometimes at night without adult supervision. Schools were shabby, teachers inadequate, and children were generally denied decent places to play. The housing available to blacks was most often poorly maintained, and high rents made taking in lodgers an economic necessity. The presence of these outsiders contributed to the instability of family life, while the proximity of saloons, brothels, and gambling halls made it difficult to maintain standards of morality and discipline. The cities commonly neglected their Negro districts, giving the residents little police protection and sanitation services. Predictably, crime, juvenile delinquency, disease, and infant mortality were well known to urban Negroes.[9]

Unlike many of their contemporaries, writers who documented the plight of blacks in northern cities did not explain it as a function of innate racial inferiority. Instead, they held that Negroes were where they were because of inefficiency and lack of training; because the cities short-changed them on education, sanitation, and health services; because whites disliked, distrusted, and exploited them. All of these causes were susceptible to improvement through organized social reform.

The challenge of improving the living and working conditions of urban Negroes called forth a separate organizational apparatus directed specifically at city problems, and different from the protest organizations in methods as well as central concerns. Though the NAACP was the heir of the Niagara Movement, the National Urban League grew out of this second reform tradition.

Ironically, the urban racial reform movement shared a strong philosophical bond with Booker T. Washington, who repeatedly warned blacks to resist the temptations of the cities, urging them instead to "Cast down your bucket where you are"—on the land in the rural South. Washington, principal of Tuskegee Institute, was the major prophet of racial progress through economic improvement and moral uplift. Although he engaged in covert political action, the Tuskegee educator took a public stance that deprecated political activism and stressed self-help, industrial education, economic accumulation, and the cultivation of morality as the proper paths to racial advancement. He preached a Puritan ethic of thrift, industry, and morality, and he advised blacks to recognize the dignity of manual labor, since "the masses of us are to live by the productions of our hands." "It is at the bottom of life we must begin," he said, "and not at the top." Washington also imposed safe limits on Negroes' aspirations: "In all things that are purely social we [Negroes and whites] can be as separate as the fingers, yet one as the hand in all things essential to mutual progress." [10]

Despite Washington's insistence that blacks belonged in the rural South, his ideology came to have a remarkable applicability to movements for urban racial reform. Like Washington, urban racial reformers subordinated attainment of political and civil rights to the more immediate goals of moral and economic progress. They emphasized vocational training, education, and moral uplift in the work they undertook to help blacks adapt to the rigors of city life. Their major concerns were to find jobs and decent housing for urban Negroes, educate and equip them for productive work, improve health and sanitation in Negro districts, and provide playgrounds and wholesome recreational outlets.

The earliest efforts to aid city Negroes were offshoots of charity, church benevolent, and settlement movements. Blacks staffed and supported old-age homes, orphanages, hospitals, reformatories, kindergartens, day nurseries, and refuges and rescue homes

for women. The spirit of self-help and racial solidarity that in-
spired early protest organizations also typified some of these philanthropic and protective ventures. While some were financed
principally by funds raised among Negroes, many of the more
ambitious projects were joint enterprises, largely staffed and promoted by Negroes but supported by white philanthropy. Negro
churches, which sponsored boys' and girls' clubs, kindergartens,
homemaking classes, and employment bureaus, were responsible
for much of the organized social service work undertaken for the
race. Several cities had Negro YW and YMCAs, and a few had
settlement houses especially for blacks. Some white settlements
welcomed Negroes along with immigrants; others, like Henry
Street in New York and the College Settlement in Philadelphia,
opened separate branches in Negro neighborhoods.[11]

The most extensive, nationally influential efforts to aid urban
Negroes developed in New York City. The city's black population increased by half between 1900 and 1910, making New York
the home of the largest black population outside the South.
There was only a tiny middle class; more than nine-tenths of
black New Yorkers held positions as laborers or in domestic and
personal service. The limited economic opportunities available to
black men forced their wives into the labor market in large numbers; 59 per cent of black women in the city in 1900 held jobs as
compared to 27.2 per cent of the foreign-born and 24.6 per cent
of the native-born white women. New York had the lowest percentage of Negro home ownership in any urban community with
a black population of 2500 or more in 1910. The death rate of
blacks in the city was more than one and one-half times that of
whites in 1900 and 1910; the discrepancy was even greater for infants. Black children in 1910 attended school in almost the same
proportion as whites, but black illiteracy was still twelve times
that of native-born whites.[12]

Yet this alone is not a sufficient explanation for New York's
prominence in racial reform movements. Blacks in other cities
suffered from similar disabilities and disparities. In 1900 Philadel-

phia had more blacks than New York, and the percentage of blacks in the total population of Philadelphia, Pittsburgh, Cincinnati, or Boston was higher than that of New York in 1900 and again in 1910.[13] In addition to a large black community, New York had other features which made it a likely source of racial reform. A large, ever-expanding immigrant population meant that the city had a range of philanthropic and protective organizations that could easily be copied and adapted to blacks. Moreover, as a financial, professional, religious, educational, and communications center, the city had a significant white population interested in philanthropy and reform. As the largest city in the country, New York was a magnet for young men and women, particularly settlement workers, who were interested in a laboratory for practical social service. New York experienced the problems of urbanization earlier and more intensely than other cities. Social justice movements flourished in New York during the Progressive Era. Thus a climate conducive to reform, combined with the problems of a growing black ghetto, produced a wide range of social service efforts among Negroes.

One of the earliest of these was the New York Colored Mission. Established by Quakers as a religious organization, it became an active social service agency in the 1880s and 1890s. The Mission ran an employment bureau and a nursery school, a boys' club and a night school; it provided temporary lodgings and meals for newcomers; and it offered the services of social workers, visiting nurses, and doctors. At the turn of the century, the Protestant Episcopal Mission Society opened St. Cyprian's Parish House and Chapel on San Juan Hill. It offered Negroes vocational training, an employment bureau, instruction in homemaking, a soup kitchen, a visiting nurse, and recreational activities. In 1892 the Children's Aid Society started the Henrietta Industrial School for Negro children, followed by the Henrietta Evening Trade School for adults in 1909. In 1895 the New York Kindergarten Association began a Free Kindergarten Association for Colored Children, which sponsored home visiting, a kindergarten, a library, and boys', girls', and mothers' clubs. Housing bureaus worked to clean up Negro slums, and the city Board of Health held special classes in tuberculosis prevention and sanitation. A Negro Fresh Air Committee began providing playgrounds and summer camps in 1905. There were several settlement houses and Negro Y's. Groups like the Professional and Business Men's Social Club and the Young Men's Industrial League helped Negroes advance in the professions, trades, and business.[14]

But the scope and resources of organizations like these were too limited. Racial problems, in the city and the nation, required a much broader, better organized attack. The founders of the National Urban League had just such a movement in mind.

2 FORERUNNERS OF THE URBAN LEAGUE

Responding to the plight of blacks in the city, racial reformers in 1905 and 1906 founded two New York-based organizations that anticipated much of the work of the National Urban League and eventually merged to form its nucleus. Their titles explain their functions—the National League for the Protection of Colored Women and the Committee for Improving the Industrial Condition of Negroes in New York.

I

For Frances A. Kellor, who founded the National League for the Protection of Colored Women (NLPCW), attention to the plight of Negro women in the urban centers of the North was part of a concern about the orderly social adjustment of minorities in America. Born in 1873 into a well-to-do middle-class white family in Columbus, Ohio, Miss Kellor attended the University of Chicago as an undergraduate and earned a law degree at Cornell in 1897. She then enrolled at Chicago as a graduate student in sociology, but left there in 1902 to go to the New York School of Philanthropy for training in social work, which she would make her life's career.[1]

As a social investigator and responsible muckraker, Frances Kellor was an archetypal reformer of the progressive tradition.

She concentrated her efforts on the second-class citizens of the Progressive Era: immigrants and blacks. As an official of the North American Civic League for Immigrants and as secretary of New York Governor Charles Evans Hughes's Immigration Commission in 1909, she argued for a national distribution system designed to avoid unemployment and overcrowding among the newcomers and to enable them to take advantage of available industrial opportunities. Her concept of a comprehensive immigration policy included information and educational services for aliens and protection in the courts and against unscrupulous exploitation. Her efforts culminated in 1910 in the establishment in New York of a State Bureau of Industries and Immigration, where she served as chief investigator.[2]

The principles by which Frances Kellor sought to reform immigration policy also applied to her work with blacks. She first came to public notice as a student of blacks in the United States when she wrote a series of articles analyzing criminality among Negroes—one of the earliest sociological studies of racial problems. Her findings disputed the popular belief of European criminal sociologists in the existence of a "criminal type." Environment, not heredity, she held, explained an individual's susceptibility to criminality. Thus Negroes were likely to commit crimes not because of racial defects, but because of the influence of social factors—concentration in the unskilled laboring class, unstable domestic life, lack of wholesome recreational and social outlets, inadequate education, and so on.[3] Her location of the roots of social disorganization among Negroes in environment rather than in innate racial traits was characteristic of post-Social Darwinist progressive thought.

Miss Kellor returned to the problem of how environment influenced black behavioral patterns through an investigation of city employment agencies that she undertook as a fellow of the College Settlement Association. Her report of her findings, *Out of Work*, described the "brutal and humiliating" treatment of employees in agencies housed in crumbling tenements, linked with saloons, brothels, and gambling centers, and governed by dishonesty and extortion. Most alarming of all, Miss Kellor discovered that many offices served as fronts for "disreputable houses." Lured North by "false representations regarding wages and employment," unsuspecting girls were "met at the stations and wharfs and kept at the offices until sold." "They are often threatened," she wrote, "until they accept positions in questionable places and are frequently sent out without knowing the character of their destination." [4] Women of all races fell prey to the perils of supposed domestic employment, but Negroes, unaccustomed to the ways of the city, were particularly vulnerable.

Indignant at the conditions she discovered, Frances Kellor joined with other reformers to organize the Inter-Municipal Committee on Household Research, a multicity investigative effort designed to inquire into methods of employment agencies, conditions of domestic work, and laws affecting employers and employees. "We are . . . studying negro employment agencies and lodging houses with the special desire of understanding and suppressing negro importation from the South under undesirable conditions," she wrote W. E. B. Du Bois in 1905.[5] The Committee created bureaus of information in Boston, New York, and Philadelphia to furnish lists of reliable employment agencies, job opportunities, boardinghouses, training schools, and social centers.

In 1905, with Miss Kellor as general director, the Inter-Municipal Committee organized associations in New York and Philadelphia to protect Negro women. "They aim," she explained, "to prevent helpless, friendless, penniless, inefficient Negro women from being sent North by irresponsible agencies," since women who came North without definite plans for respectable jobs and reputable places to stay were likely to be forced into prostitution. To help those who did migrate, the associations hoped to station matrons at the various ports, "to secure separate steerage accommodations and stewardesses on board ship," and to establish "respectable lodging houses and . . . training schools" in northern cities.[6] In their work the new groups conferred and to

some extent cooperated with local agents of the Travelers' Aid
Society.[7] This was an ambitious program for two local associations to handle alone; effective control of "the present nefarious
traffic in negro women" was well beyond their range. "Local
work unaffiliated with a national movement is useless," Miss Kellor pointed out, "for if you drive the traffic out of one city it
simply goes to another. We have to compete with an organized
system, and only organized work will do that." [8]

In 1906, Miss Kellor and her associates established the National
League for the Protection of Colored Women. Its purposes
echoed those of the local associations: "first to check the emigration of Negro women from the South," and, second, in the case
of those who did emigrate, to protect them during the journey
north, to direct them "to proper lodgings in the strange city and
to assist them in finding suitable employment and wholesome
recreation." [9]

Such services were not entirely new to New York. In 1897,
Victoria Earle Matthews, daughter of a Georgia slave, founded
the White Rose Mission and Industrial Association on the Upper
East Side. The Association provided travelers' aid, employment
advice, and temporary lodgings for working girls new to the city.
The White Rose Home developed into a settlement house with
classes in sewing, cooking, and simple arts and crafts, as well as a
kindergarten and mothers' club.[10]

Frances Kellor's new League sought to do on a national scale
what Victoria Matthews had begun in New York. The northern
city was a hostile environment for black women. Employment
opportunities were generally limited to domestic service, and
good positions were hard to come by without references and
training. It was equally hard to find safe recreation and decent,
low-cost lodgings. And the moral risks were well known. The
League tried, first, "to prevent colored girls from coming North
at all, unless they are sure of finding work and have some
training." [11] It enlisted southern ministers, teachers, editors and

others in a campaign to warn these women of "the dangers and difficulties" of "the journey to and the life in the North." [12]

"But," League officials readily acknowledged, "many of them will come, and something must be done for them"—and this comprised the heart of the League's work.[13] "Something" began in the South with publicity concerning life in the North and requirements of the journey ahead. League officials crusaded for improved conditions on board the steamers coming north. Travelers' aid agents met the boats and trains at Memphis, Norfolk, Baltimore, Philadelphia, and New York. Their "rescue work" involved protecting girls from unscrupulous men and "disreputable houses," making certain that they knew where they were bound and had enough money to get there, and directing them to safe lodging places and reliable employment agencies. The League sponsored recreational and social clubs, employment information services, and programs of basic vocational education. It opened a temporary home for the newcomers in Philadelphia, while it co-operated in New York with the Colored Mission, the White Rose Home, the Brooklyn YWCA, and other shelters.[14]

In addition to Frances Kellor, the National League for the Protection of Colored Women included among its white leaders prominent advocates of urban social reform. As might be expected in an organization that concerned itself with the protection of women, women accounted for five of the eight white members of the executive committee.[15] They came from middle-class families of means; natives of the Middle Atlantic and New England states, they lived in New York and Philadelphia, where the first associations for the protection of Negro women had been established in 1905. They were philanthropist-reformers whose interest in racial problems stemmed from family and religious influences. Elizabeth Walton, a staunch Quaker, was the daughter of abolitionists; Ruth Standish Baldwin's husband was a trustee of Tuskegee Institute and an official of the General and Southern Education Boards. Some of them, like Mary E. Dreier, president of the Women's Trade Union League and a vigorous promoter of woman suffrage, were actively involved in the woman's movement of the late nineteenth and early twentieth centuries. Although they were not college women (with the exception of Mrs. Baldwin), they expressed in their civic activities the conviction, commonly associated with educated women of that day, that women of means should find purpose and fulfillment by devoting their lives to constructive service and reform.

By contrast, the six male leaders of the NLPCW were businessmen and professionals, five of them college graduates, three of them holders of graduate degrees. The whites were Alfred Manierre, a lawyer; William Jay Schieffelin, a drug merchant and manufacturer; and the Rt. Rev. Frederick J. Kinsman, a professor of church history, all New Yorkers. The blacks were Eugene P. Roberts, a doctor in New York; Fred R. Moore, national organizer of the National Negro Business League and subsequently editor of the New York *Age;* and the Rev. Henry L. Phillips, rector of an Episcopal church in Philadelphia. Their religious backgrounds predisposed them to protective work, and the NLPCW fit logically into their interests in conservative racial reform. For example, Schieffelin was president of the Armstrong Association and a trustee of Hampton and Tuskegee Institutes; Manierre, as a temperance reformer, felt strongly about the evil influence of saloons and brothels; Moore, a close associate and sometime agent of Booker T. Washington, had a particular interest in curbing black migration from the South.

II

Several of these same men and women participated in the Committee for Improving the Industrial Condition of Negroes in New York (CIICN), which prefigures the National Urban League both in the interracial support it attracted and in the industrial program it promoted. Its primary purpose was to expand employment opportunities for the city's Negroes. The idea of an industrial organization to assist New York Negroes had originated with William H. Baldwin, Jr., president of the Long Island Rail Road, whose widow, Ruth Standish Baldwin, was one of the founders of the Committee on Urban Conditions in 1910. Baldwin had called "a private conference regarding the condition of the Colored people in New York City" at the Mount Olivet Baptist Church on January 4, 1903. Those attending included W. E. B. Du Bois; Wallace Buttrick, secretary of the General Education Board; Felix Adler, the Ethical Culture leader; William H. Brooks and C. T. Walker, Negro pastors of St. Mark's Methodist Episcopal Church and Mount Olivet Church; Negro manufacturer Samuel R. Scottron, and William L. Bulkley, the first Negro principal in the consolidated New York City school system.[16]

The conferees discussed the needs of the city's Negroes, but they did not take any action. Rather, as Scottron recalled, "we indulged the hope that something would surely be done soon along those lines." [17] It lay with one of their group, William L. Bulkley, to become the leader of the movement for industrial opportunity. In Bulkley's view, it was tragic for students to leave school only "to open doors, run bells or hustle hash" for the rest of their lives.[18] In order to give blacks a chance at "one of the fundamentals of our constitution—*the right to work; opportunity to work; encouragement to work* in any sphere in which one may be useful," Bulkley developed a system of industrial education that resulted in the birth of the CIICN.[19]

Bulkley himself had clearly broken with the traditional educational-employment pattern reserved to Negroes. Born a slave in South Carolina in 1861, he attended a log cabin school in Greenville and was graduated in 1882 from Claflin University in Orangeburg, where he later taught Latin and Greek. He worked his way through two years of graduate training at Wesleyan University (Connecticut), studied in France and Germany, and in 1893 received a Ph.D. in ancient languages and literature from Syracuse University. He joined the New York City school system in 1890 and in 1899 was named principal of P.S. 80, a predominantly black institution on West Forty-first Street, in the heart of the Tenderloin. A decade later, he became the first Negro principal of a predominantly white school (P.S. 125) in the city's history.[20]

Under Bulkley's leadership, P.S. 80 became a model of "the school [as] a social centre for the parent and the child." [21] Five nights each semester, families gathered there for lectures on proper school behavior, health, nutrition, sanitation, and other problems; for exhibits of handicrafts and classroom work; and for evenings of music, discussion, and refreshments. Bulkley organized a kindergarten for children of working mothers, and in 1906 he opened an evening school which offered industrial and commercial training for Negroes over sixteen years of age.[22] Visiting school board members praised it as "the most successful evening school that had ever been established in New York." [23]

Its graduates offered equally impressive testimonials. The school "opened my eyes to new fields of usefulness and has given me new hope of becoming that which I did not dream of a few years ago," one woman wrote. "It has taught me a trade by which my earnings have not only been increased a hundredfold, but which will enable me to make an independent living the rest of my life." "Of course I had a little knowledge of millinery before entering there," another volunteered, "but not enough to branch out on my own resources"; after a term at the evening school, however, she began "a very successful business" in Asbury Park, "and this year have to move in more spacious quarters. . . . Your evening school is one of the greatest things ever brought about by man for the colored people." [24]

Bulkley hoped to expand his school's services into a program to meet the problems of the Negro population of the entire city. "The condition of possibly 75,000 people," he said in 1906, "forces itself upon our attention, if not from a humanitarian standpoint, certainly from one of self-interest. . . . It is impossible for those increasing thousands of black humanity to settle in the city and find wholesome housing conditions or helpful vocations." [25] Lack of economic opportunity, he pointed out, would "stifle laudable aspirations, provoke discouragement and invite all the evils that an idle brain can conceive." [26]

Blacks were at the bottom of New York society, Bulkley believed, because they were second-class citizens in the New York City marketplace. They were kept there by unreasoning racial prejudice and discrimination, forces they could counter only by the most painstaking persuasion, protest, and education. But they were also kept there by their own vocational ignorance and inefficiency, obstacles they could do something about.

Fighting this economic slavery required two tacks: enabling Negroes to learn useful trades and opening up "avenues for the utilization of those trades." Bulkley's industrial classes had begun, on a limited scale, to meet the first objective. In a series of local meetings, he explained the need for a new industrial committee to meet the second.[27] Social worker Mary White Ovington reported that Bulkley approached the Charity Organization Society with his problem in March 1906. Paul U. Kellogg, editor of the COS magazine *Charities*, learned of Bulkley's work, "and the next thing a meeting was called of prominent colored folk and a few white people to see if anything definite could be done to improve the economic condition of the Negro in New York." At this same time, the Armstrong Association, which supported Hampton Institute in Virginia, was thinking of inaugurating work among blacks in New York. William Jay Schieffelin, president of the Association, joined the group called together at the instigation of Bulkley and Kellogg, "and was interested at once." [28] In May 1906 some sixty Negro and white New Yorkers met at Schieffelin's home to organize the CIICN.[29] Its primary goal was to be " 'economic opportunity' "—"a square deal" for all citizens "in the matter of getting a livelihood." [30]

In its emphasis on industrial education, the CIICN closely reflected the racial ideology of Booker T. Washington. Yet Washington looked with some suspicion on the new organization, perhaps because of its links with his rival, W. E. B. Du Bois. Du

Bois, but not Washington, had been included in William H. Baldwin, Jr.'s 1903 conference on Negro conditions in New York. When Du Bois agreed to speak in Brooklyn under the auspices of the CIICN in 1907, CIICN secretary Samuel R. Scottron reminded him of his close association with the organization. Asking Du Bois to discuss the work envisioned by the initial conferees, Scottron observed: "You undoubtedly had Mr. Baldwin's confidence, and know, possibly, more than any of us now here of his conclusions." [31] In addition to Scottron, Mary White Ovington kept Du Bois informed of the activities of the new industrial committee.

Du Bois's personal connections with the CIICN need not have been the only source of Washington's suspicions. The Committee's main founder, William L. Bulkley, was an avowed supporter of Du Bois and of full and immediate equality for Negroes. Washington urged his political deputy, Collector of Internal Revenue Charles W. Anderson, to attend CIICN meetings to prevent "Bulkley and his crowd" from "get[ting] hold of this important organization." [32] From his seat on the CIICN's executive committee, Anderson provided Washington with a reliable listening post. Soon after the organization was founded, he assured Washington that "our friends have control of the movement. . . . I hope for good results." [33]

Washington's "friends" on the CIICN were part of a distinguished group, for the Committee attracted some of the most prominent professionals, businessmen, and reform leaders, Negro and white, in New York City.* [34] "So far as is known," *Charities* editorialized, "the committee is unique as a compact working body in which representatives of progressive elements among both white and colored populations meet on an equal footing." [35] Schieffelin accepted the chairmanship and used his considerable prestige to enlist influential associates to work for the new organization. As he wrote one of them, "There are seventy thousand

* For more detailed information about the educational backgrounds and professions of CIICN members, see Tables A.1 and A.2, Appendix.

Negroes in New York and we ought to feel a responsibility concerning them." [36]

White men and women who answered the call were, like Schieffelin, representatives of an upper-middle-class urban elite. Of the 55 white founders and members of the CIICN (48 men, 7 women) who have been identified, 16 were businessmen, 33 were professionals, and the remaining 6 were philanthropist-reformers. They were, in the main, natives of large cities in the Northeast; of the 49 whose birthplaces are known, 18 came from New York City alone, while another 16 were born in the other Middle Atlantic states or New England; all told, more than half came from cities of over 100,000 population. All of them lived or worked in New York City during their membership on the CIICN. Most of them were Protestants, and more than two-thirds had British names, while about one-fifth could trace their ancestry to Germany. Whereas less than 3 per cent of their contemporaries (their average age at the time of the CIICN's founding was forty-four) had ever enrolled in college and only about 1 per cent had actually graduated,[37] almost three-quarters of the men and women involved in the CIICN went to college, while close to two-fifths had earned one or more graduate degrees.

It made sense for these men and women to support the CIICN. They came from a class of patrician reformers. Some of them, like Oswald Garrison Villard, grandson of abolitionist William Lloyd Garrison, had old family credentials in the field of racial advancement. Some, like Mary White Ovington and Lilian Brandt, were social workers who devoted their professional lives to helping blacks and immigrants. Some were concerned about vocational training by virtue of their own jobs. Mary Schenck Woolman, for example, was director of the Manhattan Trade School for Girls; Charles Russell Richards headed the department of manual training at Teachers College, Columbia University; William Henry Maxwell was superintendent of the public schools of Greater New York; Matthew J. Elgas was superintendent of evening schools; and P. Tecumseh Sherman was state

commissioner of labor. Others, like Schieffelin, philanthropist
James G. Phelps Stokes, and shoe manufacturer Charles E. Bige-
low, were supporters of industrial education for Negroes as trustees of Hampton and Tuskegee Institutes and the General and
Southern Education Boards. Several, like George McAneny,
Grosvenor Hyde Backus, and May Hurlburt, were officials of the
Hampton-sponsored Armstrong Associations. The majority were
directors of settlement houses and charitable and civic improvement organizations.

Brought up in the Protestant ethic, these men and women believed in productive work, and they preferred to encourage gainful employment for blacks in New York than to sustain them
through white charity. As professionals and owners of their own
businesses they could advocate improved employment opportunities without experiencing the fears and prejudices of lower-class
whites who saw blacks as competitors for their jobs. Moreover,
insofar as supporting the CIICN meant embracing Booker T.
Washington's prescription of thrift, self-help, and industrial education for the black masses, it hardly bespoke racial radicalism.
Most enlightened whites of this period applauded Washington,
particularly insofar as he explicitly disavowed social equality for
blacks. Thus it was possible to see the CIICN as an instrument of
a conservative philosophy of race relations as well as a vehicle for
racial reform. For every Villard or Ovington on the committee,
there were also racial conservatives, like *World's Work* editor
Walter Hines Page or General Education Board executive secretary Wallace Buttrick, who continued to defer to the influence of
southern white supremacy.

Nor could most of the nineteen black members of the CIICN
have been defined as radicals. There was at least one notable supporter of the Niagara Movement: Reverdy C. Ransom, the Boston minister. But a number of the blacks, such as Anderson; T.
Thomas Fortune and Fred R. Moore, both editors of the New
York *Age*; manufacturer Samuel R. Scottron; and attorney Wil-
ford H. Smith were in fact close friends and associates of Booker

T. Washington. Moore, for example, was for several years national organizer of Washington's National Negro Business League, and in 1904 Washington made him editor of the *Colored American Magazine*. Smith represented Washington in a suit against William Monroe Trotter of the Boston *Guardian*, and he was the lawyer for the Alabama test cases on disfranchisement and jury discrimination which Washington secretly financed.[38] Another committee member, Roscoe Conkling Simmons, was Washington's nephew by marriage.

As a group, the blacks involved in the CIICN were the Talented Tenth of the Negro race—doctors, lawyers, educators, newspaper editors, ministers, and businessmen. Of those 14 whose educational backgrounds are known, 8 attended college, and 6 held graduate degrees. Two-thirds of those whose birthplaces are known came from the South, an interesting commentary on the sectional origins of black leadership in this period. Their credentials clearly sustained the judgment of the New York *Age* that the CIICN had attracted "many of the strongest and best white and black citizens in the city." [39]

The work of the CIICN was far-ranging. It joined the NLPCW in appealing to southern newspapers, churches, and schools to discourage migration to the North, where Negroes were already settling "faster than they can be assimilated and adjusted to surrounding conditions." [40] In this respect the Committee paralleled the social justice progressives who worked for immigration restriction on the ground that it was impossible to try to reduce poverty, disease, and illiteracy or to wipe out slums when these were fed by a steady stream of newcomers unfamiliar with city life.

In New York the CIICN sought to make Negroes aware of vocational opportunities and to encourage them to train for skilled trades. And it hoped to educate whites about black capabilities and enlist their help in improving industrial conditions for blacks. At the urging of the CIICN, the Board of Education opened more night schools in Negro areas. The regular public school curriculum expanded to incorporate new trade classes, and a new summer industrial center taught women techniques of millinery, flower-making, and dressmaking.

The Committee set up its own vocational exchange in Harlem and cooperated with other employment agencies to find job openings for Negroes. It compiled a list of skilled mechanics, organized them into a trade association, and helped them crack the employment barrier in contracting firms like the City and Suburban Homes Company. The CIICN sponsored associations of Negro porters, elevatormen and hallmen, and chauffeurs to encourage fellowship, raise their standards, and improve their working conditions. Hoping to improve conditions in tenement houses, it set up a housing bureau in Harlem and offered lectures on landlord-tenant rights and obligations. In an effort to stimulate Negro-owned and operated businesses, it gave advice and loans to contractors and small tradesmen. The Committee cooperated with and helped sustain such organizations as the Armstrong Association, the White Rose Home, and the National League for the Protection of Colored Women, joining in the latter's travelers' aid efforts at the steamship docks.[41]

Both the CIICN and the NLPCW raised the level of sophistication of the social service efforts among blacks in northern cities. Yet the CIICN never had a paid professional staff, neither organization had an established method of fund-raising, and the programs of both were too narrowly defined to permit a coordinated approach to the full spectrum of urban racial problems. A third organization, the Committee on Urban Conditions Among Negroes, would seek to remedy some of these deficiencies, and would join with the CIICN and the NLPCW to form the National Urban League.

3 TOWARD CONSOLIDATION: THE COMMITTEE ON URBAN CONDITIONS AMONG NEGROES

The Committee on Urban Conditions, founded in 1910, drew on the personnel and programs of the CIICN and the NLPCW. But it went beyond them in important ways, and in so doing it laid the immediate foundations for the National Urban League. Although the Urban League itself actually came into being in 1911 with the consolidation of the three organizations, it has always claimed the year of its birth as 1910, when the Committee on Urban Conditions was formed. Moreover, the men and women who created the Committee are generally recognized as the founders of the League. Thus the history of the Committee on Urban Conditions is in fact the story of the founding of the National Urban League.

Two people credited with organizing the Committee on Urban Conditions typify the central ideological strains on which the Urban League was based. George Edmund Haynes, a black sociologist, spoke for the first strain: the professionalization of social service and the importance of scholarly investigation as the basis for practical reform. Ruth Standish Baldwin, a patrician white reformer, represented the second: an enlightened conservative philosophy of racial reform, strongly influenced by Booker T. Washington.

I

Born in Pine Bluff, Arkansas, in 1880, George Haynes attended schools in Arkansas, Alabama, and Tennessee, and was graduated from Fisk University in 1903. He then enrolled as one of the few black students at Yale, where he waited tables and tended furnaces to meet his graduate school expenses. Haynes studied sociology with the famous exponent of Social Darwinism, William Graham Sumner. He received an M.A. from Yale in 1904 and was offered a scholarship to continue his studies in theology at the Yale Divinity School. But he was helping to support his widowed mother, who was a domestic servant, and his younger sister, who was ready to enter Fisk's preparatory division. To earn money for her tuition, he took a job as traveling student secretary of the International Committee of the YMCA. Haynes took graduate courses at the University of Chicago during the summers of 1906 and 1907, and the following year he entered Columbia to study sociology and social administration. As a part of his program Haynes took courses and eventually lectured at the New York School of Philanthropy (later the New York School of Social Work). He became the first Negro graduate of the School in 1910, and, two years later, he was the first Negro to receive a Ph.D. from Columbia.[1]

When George Haynes was going to graduate school, sociological studies by blacks of conditions of black life were only in their infancy. W. E. B. Du Bois had pioneered the scholarly investigation of black problems in his study of Philadelphia Negroes, which was published in 1899. Du Bois explained his innovative methods of study at the 1897 meeting of the American Academy of Political and Social Science. He was, he said, "dividing the prospective scientific study of the Negro into two parts: the social group and his peculiar social environment." He "proposed to study the social group by historical investigation, statistical measurement, anthropological measurement and sociological interpretation."[2] Without "intelligent and discriminating research" into Negro problems, "the labors of philanthropist and statesman" would, he felt, "continue to be, to a large extent, barren and unfruitful." [3]

Du Bois moved from Philadelphia to Atlanta University to take charge of its work in sociology and its conferences on the Negro problem. Atlanta University publications based on those conferences illuminated Negro health and mortality, urbanization, efforts for social betterment, businessmen and artisans, college graduates, schools and churches, and crime. Du Bois's efforts to build "an increasing body of scientifically ascertained fact, instead of the vague mass of the so-called Negro problems" made Atlanta "the only institution in the world carrying on a systematic study of the Negro and his development, and putting the result in a form available for . . . scholars." [4]

The work George Haynes did as a graduate student followed the pattern that Du Bois had established. As a fellow of the New York School of Philanthropy's Bureau of Social Research, Haynes participated in a major study of migrations to urban centers, which was undertaken "as a basis for pioneering some kind of public employment-finding agency." Edward T. Devine, director of the School and of the project, asked him to investigate Negro migration. He became absorbed not only in the causes and process of migration, but in its effects. What kind of life could Negroes expect when they settled in northern cities? Haynes developed his findings into a doctoral dissertation, *The Negro at Work in New York City*, which was published in 1912 by the Columbia University Press.[5]

When Haynes undertook his study, most people believed that blacks would "remain anchored to the soil" in rural areas.[6] His investigations convinced him, however, that blacks, like whites, were "coming to the city to stay." The same kinds of necessities and desires made whites and Negroes alike seek out the growing industrial and commercial centers. "We may as well recognize," he wrote, ". . . that the Negro population of our towns and cities will continue to increase and become permanent." [7]

The cities offered the migrants a dismal reception. Haynes knew first-hand that Negroes suffered from economic discrimination in the South. Working in a variety of summer positions during his years at Fisk, he had had personal experience with the differentials in jobs available to Negroes and to whites, and he had seen Negroes forced into menial positions under less qualified white supervisors.[8] During his first year in New York, he went to work for the CIICN to help secure jobs for Negro graduates of public schools and vocational courses. Under the CIICN's auspices, he interviewed "about forty employers in building trades and about twenty in manufacturing establishments" to find out how their Negro employees (if any) were getting along, and whether firms that had no Negro workers would consider hiring some. This experience taught him about the attitudes of northern employers toward Negroes—findings borne out in his own study of employment opportunity in the city.[9]

According to Haynes, it was hard enough for anyone brought up in the country to fit gracefully into patterns of city living. But for Negroes, still saddled with a heritage of subservience, whether dictated by law or by tradition, there were special obstacles. Their own inefficiency and lack of skill combined with racial prejudice on the part of white workers and employers to force the large majority of Negroes into domestic and personal service. In Haynes's view, it was all part of a discouraging cycle; opportunities remained closed because Negroes so rarely had "the *chance* to acquire the skill and experience" they needed to move up. High rents and low wages sent wives and mothers into the labor market in disproportionate numbers, left their children unsupervised, and brought the disruptive influence of lodgers into the family home. Adequate housing and wholesome recreation, sanitation and health, morality and family discipline were early victims of an economic system unable (or unwilling) to offer Negro men decent jobs at a living wage.[10]

Anyone who paused to reflect could readily see that the newly urbanized Negro population constituted a problem—not only for the Negroes themselves, but for the entire community. But prevailing attitudes toward blacks were inadequate to cope with the situation. Convinced that blacks were a southern rural problem, "economic, educational and political leaders" believed "that their improvements should emphasize land-ownership and farm life," concentrating on agricultural training.[11]

Haynes had a different idea. Recognizing the permanency of an urban Negro population ill-prepared to meet the strains of northern city life, he believed that it was up to Negro and white leaders to ease the adjustment migrants had to make. Difficulties of blacks in the city were "solvable by methods similar to those that help other elements of the population," he argued. "The problem alike of statesman, race leader, and philanthropist" was to understand the segregation and discrimination arising from the migrations and "to co-operate with the Negro in his effort to learn to live in the city as well as the country." [12]

What Haynes had in mind was not a new organization, but an educational movement designed to bring existing welfare organizations to include blacks in their social service efforts. He wanted to generate in them a moral consciousness of their obligation to help the community overcome deprivation and discrimination and live up to the true meaning of justice and democracy.[13] He wanted Negro educational institutions to "begin training social workers and other leaders," and he wanted existing agencies to cooperate with and hire these professionals "to help newcomers . . . learn to live in town." But his ideas were too far advanced for most of his contemporaries; his faith that organized interracial cooperation might accomplish economic and social justice "struck leaders as a dream." [14]

Haynes talked with his former associates at the YMCA about the possibility of the Y sponsoring a project for training Negro social workers in southern colleges. They felt, however, that such work was beyond the YMCA's traditional program responsibilities. Haynes then went to see two women active in the National League for the Protection of Colored Women—Frances A. Kellor and Ruth Standish Baldwin.[15]

II

While the story of the Urban League's origins is in large part the story of George Edmund Haynes, it is also the story of the Baldwin family, and the League's development must in considerable measure be traced to a man who died well before its founding, but who left to the unborn organization a legacy of concern and conviction—and a determined, socially conscious wife and son.

William Henry Baldwin, Jr., was a Yankee who traced his ancestry through seven generations to Henry Baldwin, who migrated from England before 1640 to settle in North Woburn, Massachusetts.[16] For generations, Baldwins had made their careers in commerce, industry, and farming, until William Henry Baldwin, Sr., who had prospered as a dry goods commission merchant, abandoned business for public service, becoming president of the Boston Young Men's Christian Union in 1868. The Union was "a downtown center for adult education, recreation and social service" that "antedated the YMCA." [17]

Born in Boston in 1863, Baldwin, Jr., went from Roxbury Latin School to Harvard, from which he was graduated in 1885. He had just entered law school there when Charles Francis Adams asked President Eliot of Harvard to recommend six promising young men for careers with his Union Pacific Railroad. Baldwin began his railroad years as a clerk in the auditor's office at Omaha. He progressed rapidly, becoming assistant vice president of the line in 1890. When Jay Gould won control of the Union Pacific the following year, Baldwin joined the Flint and Père Marquette Railroad. Subsequently serving as a vice president of the Southern Railway Company, he succeeded Austin Corbin as president of the Long Island Rail Road in 1896, a position he held until his death from cancer in 1905.[18]

"The only Democratic back-slider" in a family of "free-think-ing and independent, moderately well-to-do, Unitarians and re-spectable Republicans," Baldwin was distinguished not only as a successful businessman but as an active reformer and civic leader.[19] "To enumerate the various educational, charitable and social movements in which he was interested," his associates eu-ologized, "is practically to make a catalogue of recent reform movements in New York City." [20] At the turn of the century he was chairman of the Committee of Fifteen, a muckraking reform group that inveighed against Raines Law Hotels,* prostitution, gambling, and other corruption allegedly linked with Tammany government.[21] Among his other activities, he was a member of the New York Charity Organization Society and of local and na-tional child labor committees, a director of the Armstrong Asso-ciation, a trustee of the University Settlement, the Peoples' Insti-tute, and Smith College, and a prominent spokesman for civil service reform.[22]

Baldwin was among the leading northern white patrons of southern education. He became actively interested in problems of educating both whites and Negroes in the South during his ten-ure with the Southern Railway. "The education of one class without a corresponding opportunity for another class is, of course, out of the question," he once explained. "So long as the negro is down, the white man will stay down. Eight million ig-norant negroes must be an eternal drag on their white neigh-bors. And those neighbors, if ignorant, will not permit the negro to prosper unless they too are educated and prosper." [23] Baldwin served as a trustee of the Southern Education Board and was the first chairman of the Rockefeller-supported General Education Board. He became a close personal friend and trusted adviser of

* These "hotels" were a dodge used by saloonkeepers to get around an 1896 New York State liquor tax law. Under the so-called Raines Law, saloons were prohibited from selling liquor on Sunday, but hotels (defined as estab-lishments of at least ten rooms, with a kitchen and dining room) were free to dispense liquor at will. Saloonkeepers took out hotel licenses and ran houses of prostitution adjacent to their barrooms.

Booker T. Washington. "I almost worship this man," Mary White Ovington once heard him say.[24] The admiration was mutual; Washington wrote that, with the exception of General Samuel C. Armstrong of Hampton Institute, he had probably "learned . . . more" from Baldwin "than from any other" man.[25] As a trustee and financial consultant to Tuskegee Institute for more than ten years, Baldwin was "perhaps more active than any other man in helping . . . Washington to achieve that measure of success which he has had in raising funds and increasing the efficiency of his school." [26]

Baldwin's stand on the race issue faithfully echoed that of Booker T. Washington. Like Washington, he rejected social equality for Negroes: "Social recognition for this generation, at least," he told the American Social Science Association in 1899, "is denied,—properly so, naturally so. Any attempt to force it merely complicates the situation and injures the cause of the black man." He felt—again like Washington—that it was a mistake to make political and civil equality the immediate priority. Blacks should be patient; their rights would come "just as rapidly" as they were "worthy to receive them." [27] Industrial education was the proper means to racial progress. In sum, he urged blacks to "Avoid social questions; leave politics alone; continue to be patient; live moral lives; live simply; learn to work." [28] And he advised that "the greatest opportunity for a successful life lies in the Southland where you were born, where the people know you and need you, and will treat you far better than in any other section of the country." [29]

Baldwin was a vigorous advocate of Booker T. Washington's system of industrial education as it had developed at Tuskegee, partly because he believed that men ought not to be denied their "chances to get on and up," but also because it was in his self-interest as a railroad executive to develop a supply of skilled black labor in the South.[30] His statements often had the ring of racial conservatism. He once said, for example, that "distinctions of color in the South are right and proper," and he had definite ideas about the kind of education and work most Negroes were fitted for.[31] He took it for granted that blacks would "willingly fill the more menial positions, and do the heavy work, at less wages," while whites would handle "the more expert labor." [32] "It is a mistake to be educated out of your necessary environment," he admonished blacks; "it is a crime for any teacher, white or black, to educate the negro for positions which are not open to him." He even criticized Washington's decision to enroll his daughter at Wellesley.[33] "I do not mean to say that the negro is not capable of higher education," he explained. "There is a percentage of the negro race that can take higher education, and should have it; for example, those who show themselves competent to become teachers or professional men. But I am talking about this great black mass of poor, poverty-stricken negroes who are at the bottom." [34] Equivocal positions like these are hard to square with Washington's judgment that Baldwin was "more genuinely interested . . . in the success of the Negro people" than anyone he had ever met. Even Washington recognized that Baldwin's public statements made him sound like a racial conservative; in an apologia for the man he respected so much, Washington explained, "Persons who knew him only slightly, after hearing him express himself on the race question, gained the impression that he was not in full sympathy with the deepest aspirations of the Negro people. But this impression was mistaken." [35]

So many of Baldwin's concerns foreshadowed tenets later central to the National Urban League. He advised Negroes to remain in the South and participate in that section's industrial development, for the northern city promised slums, a high death rate, vice and exploitation, and hostility from organized labor. Baldwin considered the Negro race, on the whole, to be "ill-prepared for these perils"—a view whose practical consequences motivated much of the work of the Urban League.[36] He felt that the best way to encourage southern sympathy for Negro education was to show the benefits such training would bring—"to have colored graduates scattered everywhere in the South doing

their part well as teachers, traders, farmers, foremen, or professional men, was the one way to convince reasonable men." [37]
Years later, League leaders would rely on the example of a single
successful Negro worker to influence employers' hiring practices
and students' vocational aspirations. Industrial training and employment opportunity, so central to the League's program, found
in Baldwin an early and persuasive advocate. Baldwin, "unlike
many other Northern philanthropists," editor T. Thomas Fortune wrote, "believed not only in educating the head, heart and
hand of the Afro-American people but in keeping wide open the
door of opportunity for them in the industrial and business avenues controlled by him or in which he had a voice." [38] Beyond
the obvious merit of industrial education for the individual Negro worker and for the economy at large, he saw it as a vehicle
for expanding a common ground of interracial cooperation and
understanding. For it was cooperation and common values that
would hold out hope for peace between the races in America.
This faith in the power of interracial cooperation, in the importance of bringing together blacks and whites of good will in an
effort beneficial to both races, would be cited time and again by
the leaders of the National Urban League as the distinctive, fundamental principle of their organization.

Baldwin died before any of the constituent organizations of the
Urban League had been founded, but League-related literature
holds him responsible for the 1906 meetings that resulted in the
CIICN. While his death in January of the preceding year makes
this impossible, he had in fact initiated meetings toward a similar
end four years earlier. Although no direct action resulted from
Baldwin's 1903 conference, many of the participants were actively involved in setting up the CIICN in 1906. Moreover, despite the time lag, they credited Baldwin with originating the
idea of such an organization. "The development of the committe
is in a sense the fulfillment of a plan long cherished by the late
William H. Baldwin," the CIICN's introductory pamphlet
claimed.[39] When W. E. B. Du Bois came to New York to speak

under the auspices of the CIICN in 1907, Samuel R. Scottron, the Committee's secretary, asked that he be sure "to say something as to *Mr. Baldwin's intentions to provide for the Negroes of New York City, and of their needs,* before he died." [40] The CIICN was formed, Scottron told Du Bois, "to carry on the work at that time planned by Mr. Baldwin." [41]

William Baldwin also influenced the unborn Urban League through his wife, who took up the reform causes for which her deceased husband had labored. The daughter of Samuel Bowles, editor of the Springfield (Massachusetts) *Republican,* Mrs. Baldwin was born in Springfield in 1865. Much of her life centered around near-by Smith College, from which she was graduated in 1887. For two years preceding her marriage in 1889 she was secretary to the president of Smith, L. Clark Seelye. She also taught briefly in the English Department. She became the College's first regularly elected woman trustee, serving on the board for twenty-five years.[42] "The things that she would stand for," President William Allan Neilson commented at the time of her resignation in 1932, "were so obviously the wise things, the generous things, the just things, the liberal things, the noble things, that even the administration could never oppose them. They dominated the deliberations of the Board of Trustees and sometimes even regenerated its members." [43]

Despite her nearly lifelong semi-invalidism, Mrs. Baldwin devoted much of her time to organizations for social justice. She replaced her husband on what became the Committee of Fourteen, acting as director of its research efforts. Concerned about the exploitation and corruption of young women, she served as chairman of the National League for the Protection of Colored Women and as vice president of the New York Probation and Protective Association.[44]

Some of Mrs. Baldwin's concerns were less predictable for a woman of her background. "She shared my radicalism in her more respectable way," her civil libertarian nephew Roger has said. "She became a member of the Socialist Party and a supporter of the many pioneering movements of labor and the left." [45] During World War I she remained a staunch pacifist. In the years before her death, she was an adviser and patron of the Highlander Folk School in Monteagle, Tennessee, a labor school in the southern mountains designed "to train rural and industrial leaders for a new social order [and] to conserve and enrich the indigenous cultural values of the mountains." [46]

Embodying wisdom, dignity and grace—indeed, "the best of everything in the old New England tradition" [47]—Mrs. Baldwin was "absolute" in "her allegiance to principle." [48] "She was the highest type of what used to be called a liberal," Smith's President Neilson said when she died. "She was highly tolerant of all kinds of people, and believed that human personality blossoms and ripens by being allowed to have free play." [49] Her philosophy was perhaps best summarized in a letter she wrote to the director of the Highlander Folk School, which places her squarely in the tradition of the best Progressive Era reform thinking:

> Man the individual isn't very moral any way yet—when he improves I dare to believe that collective man will improve somewhat too. . . .
>
> It will never be a *perfect* world—with *perfect* justice—but it can be a lot better, so we'll just keep "inching along" towards that better.
>
> Even illusions about those I love and trust—I cherish but few. I love them for what they strive to be not for what they actually are— & I hope they love me that way in return—"What I strove to be & was not comforts me." [50]

III

Ruth Standish Baldwin and her colleague, Frances A. Kellor, readily agreed with George Haynes's ideas about the importance of preparing Negroes for urban life and educating them for social service. They were ready with concern, leadership, and good contacts; he supplied the professional know-how for a viable plan of action. "Seeing eye-to-eye," he explained, "we soon joined hands to pioneer the urban movement." [51] The logical vehicle for implementing Haynes's ideas seemed to be the CIICN, which had already appointed a special subcommittee to consider enlarging its program. It was Mrs. Baldwin's idea to make Haynes executive secretary of the Committee and to incorporate his ideas into its plan of work. She arranged for him to present the findings of his studies to interested members of the CIICN and the NLPCW. Surprisingly, however, the CIICN turned down the proposal for expansion of its responsibilities. "Miss Kellor, Mrs. Baldwin and I were stunned," Haynes recalled. *"The original idea had collapsed."* [52]

Haynes and Mrs. Baldwin resolved to form their own organization, and at a meeting on May 19, 1910, at the New York School of Philanthropy, the Committee on Urban Conditions Among Negroes was formally launched. Its founding, *The Crisis* said, marked "a new era in the handling of the city problem as it affected the Negroes." [53]

Five members of the Committee on Urban Conditions came from the CIICN, while six (three of them also on the CIICN) had been active in the NLPCW. The principal founders of both of those groups, Frances Kellor and William L. Bulkley, belonged to the new organization. George Haynes's academic ties accounted for several of the Committee's new members. Edwin R. A. Seligman, one of his economics professors at Columbia, accepted the chairmanship of the organization. Among the other new members were two more Columbia faculty with whom Haynes studied, Felix Adler, professor of social and political ethics, and Edward T. Devine, professor of social economy and former director of the New York School of Philanthropy. From the School came its associate director, Roswell C. McCrea, and another economist and former classmate of Haynes, Edward E. Pratt.

In all, 18 men and 7 women—19 whites and 6 blacks—directed the efforts of the Committee.[54] Like the CIICN, its white members came from the upper-middle-class urban elite. They were Northerners and city dwellers by birth; primarily Protestants, but also Quakers, Unitarians, and Ethical Culturists; and nearly all from families with British names. They, too, were unusually well-educated—more than half held graduate degrees—and two-thirds earned their living as professionals, while the rest were businessmen and philanthropist-reformers. The strong representation of professional social workers and social work educators had a profound influence on the direction of the Committee's efforts. More than any of its predecessors, the Committee embodied in its work the practical application of economic and social intelligence as a tool for reform.

The blacks on the Committee were natives of the South who had become pillars of New York's black professional community. Four had attended graduate school and three held graduate degrees. They were the leading citizens of black New York's upper class: Adam Clayton Powell, Sr., pastor of the Abyssinian Baptist Church; Fred R. Moore, editor of the New York *Age*; Eugene P. Roberts, physician-in-charge at St. Cyprian's Baby Clinic, inspector for the city health department, and lecturer on baby care in the city school system; and William L. Bulkley, school principal and founder of the CIICN.

Much of the new Committee's plan of work was by that time conventional—seeking improved housing, health and sanitary services, and recreational facilities in Negro neighborhoods; protecting Negro women from exploitation; helping Negroes to improve their skills and find better jobs. But the Committee on Urban Conditions, reflecting the influence of Haynes and the other professional sociologists and economists among its leaders, went beyond the scope of the CIICN and the NLPCW in at least three respects. Its practical activities were to be based on "*research* for facts about the movement of white and Negro populations to the cities; living and working conditions among Negroes in those cities." It sought "*educational opportunity* for training of Negro social workers, and social science education for

Negro leaders in other walks of life to prepare them for leadership in urban centers." And it proposed to " [*secure*] *openings for
trained Negro workers* in existing welfare agencies and [to in-
duce] such agencies to include Negroes in the community they
served." The Committee promised to survey and coordinate social
agencies already at work and to create new organizations where
necessary.[55]

Accepting an invitation to join the Fisk University faculty,
George Haynes went to Nashville in 1910 to develop a department of sociology at the university and to organize a pioneering
program for training Negro social workers. He agreed with
Committee and university officials to spend most of the academic
year at Fisk with an assistant running the Committee's New York
office, and to return to New York in May or June, 1911, to complete the organization of the work there. Thereafter, he would be
based in Nashville and would come to New York every six
weeks or so to supervise the Committee's activities. The Committee hired Emanuel W. Houston, a graduate of Atlanta University
with some background in teaching and urban social research, as
a fellow and part-time executive assistant for the New York office. Houston's work proved unsatisfactory, however, and the
Committee's executive board dismissed him at the end of March
1911.[56] Haynes proceeded unsucessfully to " [poll] the Negro
colleges in search for one with training to serve as his assistant,"
and "then looked for students, or graduates with 'aptitudes' toward social work." [57] He finally learned of Eugene Kinckle
Jones, a twenty-five-year-old graduate of Virginia Union and
Cornell Universities, who was teaching mechanical drawing at a
Louisville high school. Jones was a tall, light-skinned young man
with fine features and a carefully trimmed moustache. The son of
two college professors, he had originally enrolled in engineering
because of his love of mathematics. But he recognized that prospects for jobs for black engineers were not hopeful, and he decided instead to study the problem of Negro unemployment.[58]
At Cornell he earned a master's degree in sociology and wrote his

thesis on "the evidences for progress of the American Negro since emancipation." He had "an alert mind, a sober judgment, much diligence and ability as a student," his professor wrote. "He is thoroughly gentlemanly in bearing and conversation, has ability as well as training in research work and could meet people of both races tactfully and easily." [59] These qualities suited him perfectly for racial diplomacy. On April 10, 1911, Jones became the first full-time New York-based secretary of the Committee on Urban Conditions.

Operating on a budget of $2500 during its first year, the Committee on Urban Conditions conducted a survey of conditions in Harlem, took over fresh air work among New York City Negroes, operated a summer camp for Negro boys, and opened a playground for children in Harlem. It collected information on the work and facilities of some twenty societies and institutions dealing with Negroes. Its work, according to the Cleveland *Gazette*, had been "peculiarly successful." From its inception, however, it had intended to avoid duplication of all-too-limited efforts in behalf of blacks and to stimulate new efforts to meet neglected needs. To promote the most efficient cooperation possible among agencies interested in blacks, the Committee set out to merge with the CIICN and the NLPCW.[60]

Representatives of the three organizations met in April and recommended that "a consolidation be brought about" whereby the Committee on Urban Conditions would cease to exist, while the NLPCW and CIICN would become partially autonomous subcommittees of the new agency.[61] But securing agreement on a new constitution posed some problems. The CIICN seemed to be the main stumbling block; in August George Haynes wrote one of its leaders, Samuel H. Bishop, that he had "been working over that constitution." "Would it please you for a conference," he asked, ". . . to come to an understanding about this matter? We are really holding back in pushing some things about our work awaiting the results of this union." [62] Sections of the constitution dealing with cooperating organizations, officers, and committees were revised to conform with resolutions adopted by the Industrial Committee, but the CIICN held out for additional changes. The proposed constitution gave the executive board of the National League on Urban Conditions "power of supervision and recommendations as to the general plans, policies, budgets, and financial appeals" of the existing organizations.[63] "Supervision" seemed to the CIICN to presage unwelcome encroachment on its autonomy, and it suggested that the word be changed. "I doubt whether that would be agreed to by either the Protective League or the Urban Committee," Haynes wrote, his patience beginning to wear thin, "since the word 'control' and other words of the same paragraph have been eliminated to satisfy the Industrial Committee." "I sincerely hope," he added, "that this constitution will be adopted as now revised, and that the Industrial Committee will be entirely satisfied with the conditions of our union." [64]

The CIICN finally accepted the terms for consolidation in September 1911, with the proviso that the Committee on Urban Conditions not go out of existence, but continue to do local work in New York "and thus be not a rotten borough but one of the three integrating societies." "I am very glad of this," Bishop told Haynes, "and am sorry personally that the Industrial Committee has delayed the consummation of so desirable an end." [65] Members of the Committee on Urban Conditions recognized that the CIICN regarded the union as "an experiment" which it would try for a year to see if the three could really work together.[66] On this somewhat shaky footing, the consolidated National League on Urban Conditions Among Negroes was finally born on October 16, 1911.

The new organization drew favorable reviews. "Effective social agencies consolidate for the purpose of doing a more constructive work for improving conditions among Afro-Americans," the Pittsburgh *Courier* announced.[67] The merger of "three such useful societies," [68] organizations that had done such "a great work," seemed to the Cleveland *Gazette* to mark a "new departure in social work." [69] These comments reflected high hopes for the new League's success; it was, the *Afro-American* predicted, the beginning of a "new chapter in social uplift," or, in the words of the national social work magazine, *The Survey*, "a new stage in constructive social work among negroes." [70]

Given the racial climate of the day, it may seem paradoxical that the Urban League should have aroused such positive expectations. In predicting a successful future for the new organization, one black newspaper attributed its confidence to a particular feature of the new League: its "representative membership," a membership encompassing "all points of view and various sections of both the white and colored communities." [71] The *Gazette* hit on an important point. The make-up of the League's membership in many respects determined its fortunes. Moreover, it established the League's credentials as a vehicle for progressive reform.

4 PROGRESSIVISM AND RACIAL REFORM: THE NAACP AND THE NATIONAL URBAN LEAGUE

The National Urban League, like the NAACP, was an authentic product of the Progressive Era in which it was founded. The ties of these organizations to progressivism lay both in tactics and in personnel. The methods they adopted in their fight for racial advancement were those that progressives followed; and the men and women they recruited shared to a remarkable degree the principal characteristics of the "progressive profile." [1]

This linkage between progressivism and racial reform is in some ways paradoxical. Blacks ranked low among the popular causes of the period, and progressivism in politics, as we have seen, went hand-in-hand with outright racism. But there was more to progressivism than a racist political movement. It was also a complex of social justice movements that paid some positive heed to the problems of blacks. Led by intellectuals, social workers, philanthropist-reformers, and others, the social justice movements strove to improve the living and working conditions of the exploited and disadvantaged in urban America. It is no doubt true that many social justice progressives shared to some degree the racial prejudices of their generation. It is also true, on balance, that blacks benefited less than any other group in American society from standard progressive reforms. But racial reformers belong in the ranks of social justice progressives, and the organizations they founded are among the most important institutional legacies of the era of reform.

I

The membership of the National Urban League, according to the Cleveland *Gazette*, "includes many persons socially prominent in New York together with a company of serious-minded colored people" * [2] The *Gazette* had good reason to be impressed by the social standing of the whites who concerned themselves with racial advancement. However, it neglected to notice their impeccable credentials in the field of reform. The whites who served on the boards of the Urban League and the NAACP during the 1910s were progressives in that they participated as individuals in a wide range of municipal reform movements. They were progressives, too, in that they came primarily from the Anglo-Saxon Protestant, upper-middle-class, urban elite.

The reform interests of the NAACP and Urban League board members read like a catalogue of social justice progressivism. They were suffragettes and settlement house workers. They advocated pacifism and immigration restriction. They developed and executed plans for the reorganization of municipal government. And they campaigned for child labor, factory, and housing reforms.

As a group, these white racial reformers were somewhat older than the average progressive, for the Urban League and the NAACP understood the advantage of enlisting men and women of established professional and civic standing in a cause as controversial as racial advancement. Though political progressives were usually under forty, and settlement house residents often in their twenties when they first began their work, the average age at

---

* For more detailed information about the educational backgrounds, places of residence, and professions of racial reformers in the 1910s, see Tables A.3, A.4, and A.5, Appendix.

which members joined the board of the Urban League was forty-one, and of the NAACP, forty-six.

Products mainly of post-Civil War America, these men and women grew to maturity during Reconstruction and its aftermath and during the racial reaction of the 1890s. Most of the racial reformers came from environments in which their personal experience with blacks would probably have been relatively limited. Like the progressives, they were, in Alfred D. Chandler, Jr.'s, words, native-born "city men of the upper middle class." They came primarily from families of means, many of whom were old-stock Americans; about three-quarters had British family names, and over a fifth could trace their origins to Germany. At a time when just over 90 per cent of the black population lived in the South,[3] 81 per cent of the Urban Leaguers and 84 per cent of the NAACP board members whose birthplaces can be identified were born in the New England, Middle Atlantic, and North Central states.* This concentration is predictable, since these states had been centers of abolitionist activity, and since southern whites—those most likely to be directly familiar with blacks—had almost always been unreceptive to racial reform. Nor is it surprising that few of the racial reformers came from other countries. While 16.3 per cent of white Americans in 1910 were foreign-born,[4] only 6.3 per cent of the Urban League's board and 8 per cent of the NAACP's were born abroad. Most first-generation immigrants were so busy struggling to cope with their new surroundings that they had little time or inclination to turn to reform. As a rule, too, they had strong prejudices against blacks, both because of a desire to feel superior to at least one ethnic or racial group in their new country, and because blacks were potential competitors in the labor market.

* Of the thirty-two white Urban Leaguers whose birthplaces can be identified, twelve were born in New York, two in other Middle Atlantic states, six in New England, six in the North Central region, four in the South, and two abroad. Among twenty-five white NAACP board members, the comparable figures are eight, two, two, nine, two, two.

Racial reform was unlike other progressive movements in the geographical concentration of its white leaders. Although political progressivism was strong in all parts of the country, racial reform, like abolitionism, was a product of the North. But whereas abolitionism had flourished in the New England and North Central states, racial reform among whites was concentrated almost exclusively in New York. The home of 5.2 per cent of the nation's population in 1910, New York claimed three-quarters of the white Urban Leaguers and four-fifths of those on the board of the NAACP.[5] None of the racial reformers lived in the West, only two in the South, and just a handful in the old abolitionist centers of New England and the North Central region. Like the New Yorkers, the others lived in large cities—Boston, Chicago, Philadelphia, Washington, Cincinnati, Atlanta, and New Orleans. It made sense for the League and the Association to look to the cities for their white board members. The changes they sought to effect required the cooperation if not the active support of the economic and political leaders of the country. They also needed the allegiance of powerful publicists if they were to get their cause before the country, and the talents of distinguished lawyers if they hoped to win victories in the courts. And all of these were men of the big cities.

But living in cities was not enough to give men and women a firsthand acquaintance with racial problems. The fashionable Upper East Side addresses of board members like Paul D. Cravath or Mrs. Haley Fiske were far removed in distance as well as lifestyle from the crowded black neighborhoods of Harlem and San Juan Hill. There had to be other influences that predisposed these men and women toward racial advancement.

Few of the racial reformers recorded their reasons for taking up the cause of black rights. From their common backgrounds, however, come clear strands of influence that must have contributed to their interest in racial problems. Chief among these are family tradition, religious affiliation, and political belief.

Many of the most prominent racial reformers bore the strong

stamp of their abolitionist heritage. The father of Elizabeth Walton, one of the principal leaders of the Urban League, had been an officer of the 54th Massachusetts Regiment of black soldiers during the Civil War. Her mother taught in Negro schools in the South and founded a free kindergarten for Negro children in New York. Upon her mother's death, Miss Walton took over her work in various movements for Negro welfare.[6] Oswald Garrison Villard, a founder of the NAACP, was the grandson of the abolitionist William Lloyd Garrison. Acutely conscious of his heritage, Villard sought to make his New York *Evening Post* "a worthy follower of the 'Liberator.'" For him the connection between the old abolitionism and the new struggle for racial advancement was explicit: "If in this cause of human rights I do not win at least a portion of the epithets hurled at my grandfather in his battle, I shall not feel that I am doing effective work."[7] His colleague Mary White Ovington, like Villard a leader in both the NAACP and the CIICN, also felt strongly the influence of her abolitionist parents and grandparents; as she told Villard, "you and I were brought up on stories of heroism for a cause, and dreamed dreams of doing something ourselves some time."[8] The Negro question "ought to interest anyone as a 'problem,'" Ruth Standish Baldwin's son wrote Villard, "& it ought to interest me especially on account of my traditions."[9] The abolitionist influence is apparent in many other cases: for example, Paul D. Cravath's father, an official of the American Missionary Association, was a founder and president of Fisk University, and A. S. Frissell's brother was principal of Hampton Institute. Following the pattern their forebears established, the racial reformers of the early twentieth century held scores of positions as trustees of Negro educational institutions, settlement houses, and welfare organizations.

Religious influences also contributed to the concerns of the racial reformers. While Protestant churches in the United States had been ambivalent on the question of race, the rise of evangelicalism in the early nineteenth century fostered a social concern and radicalism in certain northern churches that contributed to the development of abolitionism. Liberal denominations, particularly Presbyterians and Congregationalists, were very much involved in the abolitionist movement and in freedmen's education after the Civil War. The abolitionist legacy in these churches persisted into the Progressive Era. At the same time, they were strongly influenced by the social gospel, as was the Episcopal Church. The social gospel turned the attention of American Protestants to the evils of industrial society. Reacting to the crime, poverty, disease, squalor, and exploitation that were becoming integral parts of urban life, many Christians began to concentrate not on otherworldly salvation of the individual, but on the redemption of the social order here on earth. The social gospel also took root among Unitarians, a liberal denomination long devoted to social reform, and Quakers, the religious group with the oldest and most forthright commitment to the cause of black equality. Both of these denominations had played leading roles in the antislavery movement, and their involvement in racial reform continued well after the Civil War was over.[10]

Most of the racial reformers belonged to the denominations most strongly influenced by abolitionism and the social gospel. Like the progressives, they were predominantly Protestant, and nearly all of the Protestants among them belonged to the higher status Episcopal, Presbyterian, and Congregationalist churches. In addition, many of the leading figures in the NAACP and the Urban League were Unitarians or Quakers.* There were enough Quakers on the board, a local executive secretary recalled, "to run interference for [Eugene Kinckle] Jones no matter what play he called." [11] One of them spoke directly to the influence of his

---

* Of twenty-eight white Urban Leaguers whose religious affiliations are known, fifteen were Protestant, none Catholic, three Ethical Culturist, three Jewish, four Unitarian, and three Quaker. The chances are good— on the basis of business and professional standing, clubs, etc.—that most of the eight unidentified Urban Leaguers were Protestant. No precise information is available for the NAACP board, but it appears that it was very much like the Urban League.

religious background on his involvement in racial reform. John T. Emlen, founder of the Armstrong Association in Philadelphia and a longtime member of the Urban League board, taught black children in a Quaker Sunday School in Germantown after he was graduated from college. When he realized their lack of opportunities for recreation, he began a boys' club. He had taken a degree in architecture, but his experiences in Germantown, he later wrote, "made me feel that I could be more useful in the world in doing work for Negroes than as an architect." [12]

Like Unitarians and Quakers, Jews were heavily overrepresented among the racial reformers in comparison to their share of the total population.* Strongly influenced by nineteenth-century liberalism and socialism as well as by religious tradition, Jews in the United States were champions of social justice, civil liberties, and civil rights. Most of the Jewish racial reformers were second- and third-generation German Jews, many of them from the great German Jewish banking families. For some, concern for the rights and welfare of blacks was part of a concern for the minority status of Jews as well; for others, it seemed preferable to channel efforts for social justice toward blacks instead of the masses of eastern European Jewish immigrants, from whom they were separated by ideology and religious tradition as well as social class.[13] Her "interest in the colored race," Ella Sachs Plotz said, "was early aroused" by her grandfather, Marcus Goldman, "who was always a great admirer of Booker T. Washington and often told me, as a child, of incidents in his life." On a trip to Tuskegee in 1915, she met Ruth Standish Baldwin and learned of the Urban League's work. "Ever since then I have worked heart and soul for the colored people to help create a better understanding between the white and black races." [14]

The Urban League's board included an equal proportion of practicing Jews and Jewish-born members of the Ethical Culture

* Together these three denominations comprised almost half of the Urban Leaguers whose religious affiliations are known. They accounted for less than 1 per cent of the church members in the United States.

Societies. As Felix Adler, a longtime Urban Leaguer and leader of the New York Society for Ethical Culture, explained, his religion sought to spiritualize social reform and betterment movements. Ethical Culture taught its followers to look at "the man at the bottom" as "an object not primarily of pity, but rather of respect." [15] Such views fitted neatly with participation in racial reform.

Several of the most influential board members of the NAACP and the Urban League were self-declared Socialists. Despite a 1901 convention resolution affirming economic and social justice for blacks, the Socialist party showed some ambivalence on the race issue during the early part of the Progressive Era. In the late 1910s, however, the party became bolder in its championship of blacks and tried to assert some leadership in the fight for racial justice. It was, Mary White Ovington believed, "the only party that has any Democracy about it." Much of the early hesitation stemmed from a reluctance to alienate white labor. But for leading Socialist intellectuals like the NAACP's Charles Edward Russell, John Haynes Holmes, and William English Walling, there was never any doubt that socialist theory demanded political and economic, if not social, equality for blacks. The Socialists were among the most advanced egalitarians in the ranks of racial reform.[16]

Women in the NAACP and the Urban League had reasons of their own to engage in racial reform. They accounted for about a quarter of the whites in the two organizations, and their participation reflected their changing status in American society. The first generation of college women in the United States came of age shortly before the Progressive Era. Their exposure to higher education left them with a strong motivation to do something useful with their lives. "We have in America a fast-growing number of cultivated young people who have no recognized outlet for their active faculties," wrote Jane Addams, a member of the NAACP board. "They hear constantly of the great social maladjustment, but no way is provided for them to change it, and their uselessness hangs about them heavily." [17] This sense of use-lessness sent many middle- and upper-class young women into the settlement movement to satisfy their "longing to know life at its barest and hardest, to grapple with cold physical facts, to stand on a common footing with those who have no special advantages." [18] Seeking personal fulfillment while responding to pressing social problems, they embraced the full range of progres-sive social justice movements, including the movement for racial reform.

Higher education must have had a strong influence on both men and women racial reformers. Most progressives were unusu-ally well-educated,[19] and the board members of the NAACP and the Urban League were no exception. Nearly three-quarters of them had enrolled in college, and the large majority had earned their degrees. Half of them went on to pursue graduate studies in American and European universities, and many held one or more advanced degrees. By comparison with their contemporaries, they represented a marked educational elite. While they were in col-lege and graduate school, they were exposed to the social gos-pel and the "new" academic disciplines of economics and sociol-ogy, all of which asserted the positive power of man to effect changes in his social environment. Such a curriculum often in-spired young college graduates "to do something for suffering humanity." As one young reformer summed up the impact of his education, "I came alive, I felt a sense of responsibility to the world, I wanted to change things." [20]

Most of the racial reformers used their education as the basis for professional careers. Three-quarters of the Urban League's board and four-fifths of the NAACP's were professional men and women. The NAACP, which relied chiefly on legal action and public protest, included a large number of lawyers and publicists. The concentration of educators, social workers, and philanthropist-reformers on the Urban League's board reflected the organiza-tion's strong interest in vocational education, social work train-ing, and social service. Predictably, there were markedly fewer businessmen among the racial reformers than among the progressives. A variety of factors—the refusal of labor unions to open their ranks to blacks; the reluctance of white employees to work side by side with (or under the authority of) blacks; popular convictions regarding the untrustworthiness and limited abilities of black workers; and the prevalent belief that white customers would react negatively to black employees and salespeople—restrained businessmen from participating in large numbers in the work of racial advancement. Nor did the NAACP and the Urban League draw on the working classes; their boards included no white collar workers, skilled craftsmen, or laborers, no one employed in agriculture, and only one trade union organizer.

This collective portrait blurs the considerable difference in ideology between those who supported the Urban League and those who joined the NAACP. Equally important, there was a significant range of ideology and opinion within each board. But the Urban League was weighted much more heavily toward the right, and the most advanced members of the NAACP were considerably more radical than their counterparts in the League. The conservative wing of the Urban League board included Jacob W. Mack, a shirt manufacturer; Mrs. Haley Fiske, the wife of the president of the Metropolitan Life Insurance Company; Adrian Van Sinderen, a corporation executive; William G. Willcox, an insurance executive; Republican National Committee chairman Charles D. Hilles; A. S. Frissell, chairman of the board of the Fifth Avenue Bank; and seven lawyers.*

There was a range of opinion even within this group, but there was an even greater distance between them and such Urban Leaguers as John Haynes Holmes, Roger N. Baldwin, and Sophonisba Breckinridge (all of whom were pacifists, as were Ruth Standish Baldwin, Elizabeth Walton, and L. Hollingsworth Wood). Holmes, for instance, was a Unitarian clergyman and a So-

---

* Paul D. Cravath, Nicholas Danforth, Wilder Goodwin, Victor H. McCutcheon, Oliver C. Reynolds, George H. Richards, and George W. Seligman.

cialist with a keen interest in social questions. He was an ardent supporter of the rights of labor, equality for women, and social justice. Roger Baldwin was a social worker and civic reformer in St. Louis who went to jail during World War I for refusing conscription. In 1917 he moved to New York to head the American Union Against Militarism, which later became the American Civil Liberties Union. Miss Breckinridge, a social worker and educator, was dean of the Chicago School of Civics and Philanthropy and secretary of the Immigrants' Protective League.

The range of opinion among members of the NAACP board was even more marked. Its more conservative adherents, mainly lawyers,* stood in considerable contrast to women reformers such as Mary White Ovington, a social worker with Socialist sympathies, or Jane Addams, the founder of Hull House.† Even further to the left were Socialist intellectuals like William English Walling and Charles Edward Russell.

To an extent, the left wing of the Urban League board overlapped with the right wing of the NAACP. Some people found it possible to support both. As Roger Baldwin put it, "method and timing divide all reformers, and however deplorable their quarrels seem, they sift out the practical. Or, from a detached view, one holds the goal line while the others carry the ball." Accordingly, Baldwin explained, he had "long supported both the 'radical' NAACP and the 'conservative' National Urban League, not always on friendly terms, but with closer association with the Urban League in my more accustomed old role as a social worker." [21] In a few cases, the same person sat on both boards.‡

* Moorfield Storey, onetime president of the American Bar Association; Charles Nagel, Secretary of Commerce and Labor in the Taft administration; Elbridge L. Adams, Thomas Ewing, Jr., Albert Pillsbury, and Wilson M. Powell.
† Other prominent women reformers on the board were Florence Kelley, secretary of the National Consumers' League; Lillian Wald, head resident of the Henry Street Settlement; and Gertrude Barnum, general arbitrator and publicity agent of the International Ladies Garment Workers Union.
‡ This was true of John Haynes Holmes and four blacks, William L. Bulkley, Howard University dean Kelly Miller, and two ministers, Adam Clay-

The ideological diversity within and between the two organizations shows up even more clearly among their black board members. It was in their interracial composition that the Urban League and the NAACP differed most significantly from the progressives. Both organizations shared the common guiding principle of interracial cooperation; they believed that both races should work together on an equal footing to secure common ends. Nevertheless, blacks accounted for a much smaller percentage of the racial reformers than whites did. This stemmed in large part from the fact that few blacks had the financial resources and leisure to enable them to devote themselves to reform. Those who did serve on the boards of the organizations for racial advancement were a *Who's Who* of Negro America for their day. They were generally older than their white colleagues—the average age at which blacks joined the Urban League board in the 1910s was fifty, for the NAACP, forty-eight—and nearly all of them had been born in the South during the era of the Civil War and Reconstruction.* While none of the whites in the NAACP and only about 6 per cent of those in the Urban League actually lived in the South during their tenure on the boards, about 38 per cent of the black board members of the NAACP and 45 per cent of the black Urban Leaguers still lived in southern states.

These blacks had become leaders of the black business and professional communities in New York and other major cities, North and South. They were the success stories of black America: doctors, lawyers, ministers, educators, businessmen, and publicists, four-fifths of whom had gone to college, more than half of whom held graduate degrees. They were even a more marked educa-

---

ton Powell, Sr., pastor of Harlem's Abyssinian Baptist Church, and William H. Brooks, pastor of St. Mark's Methodist Episcopal Church in New York. George Cleveland Hall, a black surgeon who sat on the board of the National Urban League, was a member of the Chicago branch of the NAACP.

* Only one of eleven black Urban Leaguers whose birthplaces are known was born outside the South. Among twenty black NAACP board members, four were born in the North, two abroad, and the others in the South.

tional elite than their white counterparts; during the years 1876–95, the period when most of them were of college age, the total number of Negroes who graduated from college was only 1563.[22] While these black leaders were not always wealthy, their exceptional educational backgrounds and occupations marked them as distinguished members of the tiny Negro upper-middle and upper classes—a group that typically scorned lower-class lifestyles, imitated the values and culture of white middle-class America, and exhibited a "conservative . . . outlook on life." [23]

Both the NAACP and the Urban League drew on the same educational and occupational groups. On closer inspection, however, there were some significant differences in occupational patterns between the two organizations. More than half of the Urban Leaguers were educators, a fact explained partly by the League's emphasis on vocational training. But the affiliation of large numbers of educators with the League rather than the NAACP is also attributable to the allegiance of most educators in this period to the accommodationist approach of Booker T. Washington. Dependence on white philanthropy, the influence of white churches, and the prevalent faith in industrial education all promoted a certain conservatism among black educators. Black lawyers, on the other hand, especially in the North, believed in the primacy of civil and political rights and took a leading role in more radical protest efforts. Thus they joined the NAACP but not the Urban League. The NAACP also drew a significantly larger proportion of black ministers. Whereas leaders of the mass churches, particularly in the South, tended to be conservative, the better educated northern ministers in the higher status denominations were more likely to oppose Booker T. Washington and to espouse protest.[24]

As the fact that they shared four black board members should indicate, there was at least some minimal ideological convergence between the NAACP and the National Urban League. The NAACP included some blacks who had mixed loyalties in the

Washington–Du Bois controversy, and the Urban League included those who believed in protest as well as those who favored
accommodation. But while there was a range of opinion within
both organizations, the blacks who belonged to the NAACP
were, as a group, clearly the more radical of the two. Most members of the Urban League board fell within the Washington
camp * or straddled the fence between accommodation and protest.† The only black board member known to have been an outspoken anti-Bookerite was John Hope, president of Morehouse
College and a participant in the Niagara Movement.

The NAACP included no avowed supporters of Booker T.
Washington, but in addition to the five men who were affiliated
with both organizations, others with divided allegiances included
Mary Church Terrell, the first president of the National Association of Colored Women, and A. M. E. Zion Bishop Alexander
Walters, a former president of the Afro-American Council. What
distinguished the NAACP most strikingly from the Urban
League, however, was its strong concentration of radical black
leaders who rejected accommodation and insisted upon outspoken
protest and agitation to achieve immediate equality.‡ [25]

II

This alignment of black board members according to accommodation and protest underscores the ideological difference between
the Urban League and the NAACP. The NAACP bore the clear

---

* For example, Washington himself; his wife, Margaret Murray Washing-
ton; Fred R. Moore, publisher and editor of the New York *Age;* and
Washington's successor as principal of Tuskegee Institute, Robert R.
Moton.
† For example, Kelly Miller, George Cleveland Hall, William H. Brooks,
Adam Clayton Powell, Sr., and William L. Bulkley.
‡ Mainly veterans of Niagara, this group included Du Bois; Ida Wells-Bar-
nett, the noted antilynching crusader; Dr. N. F. Mossell, founder and su-
perintendent of Frederick Douglass Hospital in Philadelphia; J. Milton
Waldron, a Baptist minister with Socialist sympathies; George W. Craw-
ford, a New Haven lawyer; and C. E. Bentley, a dentist in Chicago.

philosophical imprint of W. E. B. Du Bois; the Urban League's ideological roots were less carefully defined, but on balance they could be traced to the influence of Booker T. Washington.

Washington's relationship to the Urban League is more ambiguous than it might logically seem. The case for aligning him with the organization rests on surprisingly limited but nonetheless suggestive evidence. The first indication would be Washington's close professional cooperation and personal friendship with William H. Baldwin, Jr. Baldwin's widow brought to the founding of the League the influence of her husband's views on race relations. Moreover, she, too, developed a close personal rapport with Washington and his family. In 1906 she told Oswald Garrison Villard that her commitment "to aiding . . . in the work for Negroes in New York City" stemmed from conversations with Washington around the time of her husband's death.[26] Years later Eugene Kinckle Jones recalled that Mrs. Baldwin told him that Washington had "suggested [the] idea" of forming the Urban League to her but had "declined to serve on [the] Board." [27] L. Hollingsworth Wood, longtime president of the League, called Washington "one of our founders," [28] and when Jones described the "outstanding characters in the [Urban League] movement," Washington's name headed the list.[29]

Both Ruth Standish Baldwin and George Haynes were effusive in their admiration of the Tuskegee educator. "He really is the very biggest man on the whole 'job.'—& the sanest & best poised person I know," Mrs. Baldwin wrote.[30] Haynes concurred: "I quite agree with you about his being undoubtedly the biggest man we have in the Southern situation today, probably the only man of first water the South has produced since colonial days." [31] Both of them wrote Washington on several occasions indicating their hopes of conferring with him on aspects of the work of the new National League on Urban Conditions. Yet documentary evidence that such consultations actually took place is surprisingly slim. The only practical assistance Washington is known to have offered in the early months of the organization was "a list of New York people who in my opinion would be interested in the work that you are doing." [32]

But Washington was much more closely identified with the League than the dearth of correspondence might suggest. He finally joined its executive board in 1915, but the behind-the-scenes negotiations leading up to his formal election are considerably more revealing than the fact of his membership. Fred R. Moore, Washington's close associate and himself a member of the board, had been urging that the Tuskegeean be added to the League's directors, and in February 1914 Ruth Standish Baldwin wrote George Haynes that she had met with Washington to discuss the matter. "Mr. W— agreed with Mr. Wood & me," she told Haynes, "that this is *not* the psychological moment for him to do so & stands ready to help the work along in any & every way he can. He will come on later if it seems wise." [33] Just what was wrong with that particular moment remains a mystery, but the nature of the discussion between Washington and Mrs. Baldwin indicates that he was interested in and sensitive to the fortunes of the Urban League. The appropriate "psychological moment" apparently arose within a matter of months; a death during the summer of 1914 created a vacancy on the board, and Moore again proposed that Washington be elected.[34] This time he agreed, and he served until his death in November of the following year. His wife succeeded him on the board, as did Robert R. Moton, his successor as principal of Tuskegee Institute.

The second argument for associating Booker T. Washington and the Urban League derives from policy and doctrine. Although it devoted its principal efforts to blacks in cities, the League grew out of organizations that subscribed to Washington's advice to Negroes to make their lives in the rural South. In its emphasis on training, the League implemented Washington's favorite theme. The organization shared with him an awareness that Negroes really were starting from the bottom; Washington's talk of teaching Negroes to use toothbrushes and to sleep between sheets foreshadowed the League's efforts to educate migrants in the most rudimentary practices of northern urban life. In a speech to blacks in New York which he gave under the auspices of the Urban League in 1915, Washington echoed the League's litany for newcomers to northern cities. "Any man who begins at the bottom and succeeds is bound to receive recognition from his fellowmen," he said. "As a race we are entitled to a place in society and politics and those rights will come quicker if we work together. Never be discouraged. . . . Get into your professions, take advantage of your night schools, labor is honorable, idleness is disgraceful." And, he continued, "If you have a strong, vigorous, healthy body, do not ruin it by frequenting drinking places, gambling establishments and dance halls. . . . Practice thrift; start a bank account to-morrow, if it be only a dollar." [35]

The Tuskegee educator and the Urban League also shared a common assessment of priorities. The "fundamental proposition," George Haynes maintained, was "the issue of wages and working conditions. You give him [the Negro worker] wages and proper working conditions, and he is bound to come up in all other things." [36] civil and political rights, the League believed, would have little meaning to a jobless Negro mired in urban squalor. It was concentration of interracial effort "on the most fundamental elements of race status: —economic standing, physical and mental well-being"—that would bring about "internal group improvement." [37] Or, as Washington explained, "while the Negro should not be deprived by unfair means of the franchise, political agitation alone [will] not save him. . . . Back of the ballot he must have property, industry, skill, economy, intelligence, and character. . . . No race without these elements [can] permanently succeed." [38]

Washington may even have been responsible for the Urban League's conception of interracial cooperation. In the League movement, George Haynes said, whites were "to be asked to work WITH Negroes for their mutual advantage and advancement rather than working *for* them as a problem." [39] Or, as Ruth

Standish Baldwin summed it up in a phrase that appeared for many years on each sheet of Urban League stationery, "Let us work, not as colored people nor as white people for the narrow benefit of any group alone, but *together*, as American citizens, for the common good of our common city, our common country." [40] Washington also preached the interdependence and common destinies of the white and black races, and he told blacks that racial progress depended on cooperation with whites. Even his rhetoric foreshadowed the Urban League's: in 1890, he wrote, "the disposition on the part of many of our friends to consult *about* the Negro instead of *with*—to work for him instead of *with* him is rather trying and perplexing at times." [41]

These common bonds were no doubt responsible for Washington's willingness to "endorse" the Urban League's work "most strongly and heartily." [42] And yet the links between the educator and the organization were not entirely solid. The absence in his own records and writings of any indication of his involvement in the work of the Urban League raises some doubt about the depth of his sympathy for the organization. Because of its brevity, his membership on the executive board may have been largely a formality. Washington's preoccupation with implementing the Tuskegee ideal may understandably have limited the personal attention he extended to the Urban League.[43] Moreover, despite their philosophical similarities, their practical concerns were actually quite different. While Washington dealt primarily with the agricultural Negro of the rural South, the League was involved with the problems of blacks who migrated to cities, especially in the North. These factors help to explain why Washington was never the guiding force in Urban League affairs that W. E. B. Du Bois proved to be for the NAACP.

III

The racial ideologies of Washington and Du Bois played a central part in shaping the tactics and programs of the Urban League and the NAACP. Both organizations were concerned that blacks be accorded the full responsibilities and opportunities of first-class citizenship. The NAACP, like Du Bois, believed that ensuring recognition and free exercise of the legal rights of Negroes was the most important task at hand. The Urban League, on the other hand, more in the spirit of Washington, wanted to make certain that Negroes would be prepared, through having a stake in the nation's economy and a mastery of the perils of city life, to assume the burdens and rewards of being a citizen.

The two organizations divided between themselves the great tasks in the work of racial understanding. The founders of the Committee on Urban Conditions were careful to inform the fledgling NAACP of their "plans to form a national organization in the fields of employment and of philanthropy," and they took pains to avoid any overlapping of efforts.[44] George Haynes met with Du Bois in 1910 to discuss the objectives and programs of the two organizations, and Du Bois wrote Haynes that the NAACP intended "to co-operate with and forward" the work of the Committee on Urban Conditions, and "to avoid all unnecessary duplication." While "the condition of the colored people in New York and the agencies for their relief and uplift" would have been "a natural matter of study" for the NAACP, Du Bois acknowledged that the Committee on Urban Conditions had pre-empted the field.[45]

In February 1911, representatives of the NAACP and the Committee on Urban Conditions met and agreed that the two organizations should cooperate without overlapping in their work. The NAACP would "occupy itself principally with the political, civil and social rights of the colored people," while the Committee on Urban Conditions would deal "primarily with questions of philanthropy and social economy." To keep each other informed, the two organizations would "interchange monthly reports on their activities and plans." [46]

The NAACP had included widened industrial opportunities for Negroes among its original program objectives, and the decision to steer clear of "social service and employment" came as something of a shock. "Some of us gasped at having so large a field of 'advancement' taken out of our program," NAACP founder Mary White Ovington recalled, "but nothing could have been more fortunate." The NAACP "could not have raised money for 'philanthropy' as successfully as an organization with a less militant program." Moreover, "securing employment" was "a business in itself." Accordingly, "the two national organizations divided the field, working together from time to time as action demanded." [47]

In seeking integration and equal rights for blacks, the NAACP worked chiefly through political and legal channels and advocated public protest and agitation as legitimate, indeed essential, tools for influencing policy. During its first decade, the Association used private lobbying and public protest in an unsuccessful effort to overturn the Wilson administration's policy of segregation in government agencies and discrimination in federal appointments. It began a long series of court tests to secure the enforcement of the Fourteenth and Fifteenth amendments, and it won some victories with a Supreme Court decision in 1915 outlawing grandfather clauses in state voting requirements and another in 1917 prohibiting residential segregation by city ordinance. It launched a decades-long campaign against lynching and provided legal assistance for victims of racial violence and Jim Crow justice. The organization initiated efforts to stop discrimination in education and professional activities. Sometimes its goals required a tactical retreat to an endorsement of separate-but-equal, as in its successful efforts to open military officers' ranks to Negroes, which resulted in separate training camps.

The Urban League concerned itself primarily with seeking employment opportunities for blacks and providing social services to ease the process of urbanization. Its efforts during its corresponding first decade were much quieter and less controversial than those of the NAACP. It sought jobs and decent housing for migrants and counseled them on behavior, dress, sanitation, health, and homemaking. It trained Negro social workers and placed them in community service positions as family caseworkers, probation officers, settlement house workers, supervisors of day nurseries and boys' and girls' clubs, travelers' aid workers, and others. The League unsuccessfully petitioned the American Federation of Labor to end lily-white union policies. And it conducted scientific investigations of conditions among urban Negroes as a basis for practical reform. While the NAACP dealt in protest and agitation, the Urban League's tools were primarily those of negotiation, persuasion, education, and investigation.

A perhaps apocryphal but apt anecdote reports that the Urban League liked to describe itself as "the State Department" of Negro affairs, terming the NAACP "the War Department." [48] Their differences were a matter of direct action versus investigation and diplomatic persuasion, of immediatism versus gradualism. As the two organizations readily acknowledged, there was ample room for both approaches. Joel Spingarn, chairman of the board of the NAACP, complimented his Urban League counterpart, Hollingsworth Wood, on a conference on migration that the League sponsored in 1917: "I am glad, very glad, that you are doing just this sort of thing, in your own way, and not in mine," he wrote, "for no one realizes more than I that there is a place for both ways." Or, as John R. Shillady, the executive secretary of the NAACP, told an Urban League conference in 1918, "You are dealing from one angle, and we are dealing from another, . . . but we are all on the same job." [49]

Whether of war or diplomacy, the tactics of both the NAACP and the Urban League came straight from the progressive mold. The laborious process of investigation, publicity, protest, education, legislation, and court action duplicated the methods of the progressives and their predecessors in their campaigns for social justice and economic and political reform.[50] The Urban League's development of scientific social investigation of conditions of city life is a case in point. It aligned the organization with those reformers who insisted on ascertaining the facts as a basis for sensible social reform. A dedication to scientific investigation typified most reform movements of the Progressive Era. An accurate perception of social need, rather than mere emotional or sentimental fervor, was to be the motivation for social change. It was what Robert Bremner has called "a factual generation"; as muckraker Ray Stannard Baker explained his craft, "facts, facts piled up to the point of dry certitude, was what the American people then needed and wanted." The Progressive Era was dominated by realism, by an effort to discover the truths of life as it was actually lived. Research was an essential prerequisite to reform, investigation an indispensable prelude to action. ⅝ ⅛ The scientific study of Negro conditions was still a very recent phenomenon when the Urban League was founded; indeed, George Edmund Haynes, writing in 1912, found it appropriate to justify his approach in *The Negro at Work in New York City*, explaining, "What has been done was done in the search for truth, that the enthusiasm of reform may be linked with the reliability of knowledge in the efforts to better the future conditions of the city and the Negro." [52]

Like their methods, the values and assumptions of the racial reformers revealed the strong influence of progressivism. Their goal was not to overturn the American system, but to win a place in it for blacks. They wanted to take American democracy at its word, and they saw the promises of the American Creed as broad enough to include American Negroes. Unlike radical protest movements, they set out to win their objectives within the democratic process—the NAACP through political and legal channels, the Urban League through economic and social institutions and power centers. Both the NAACP and the League reflected the Progressive Era's determination to cast off shackles denying the individual the opportunity for advancement according to his ability. The Urban League summed up its concept of opportunity in its longtime slogan, "Not Alms, But Opportunity." The League's role, unlike that of old-style benevolent organizations, was not to provide charity, for well-meant alms or paternalistic handouts would make little dent in the causes of the urban Negro's *malaise*. Believing that the obstacles to socio-economic progress among Negroes lay not in their own innate deficiencies but in the way whites treated them, the League determined to create conditions of economic opportunity that would enable Negroes who took advantage of them to achieve their rightful places in urban society.

An emphasis on opportunity rather than alms was common to racial reformers. It had been voiced two decades earlier in terms nearly identical to the Urban League's by William Lloyd Garrison, Jr. Addressing a meeting of charitable organizations on methods of bettering the lot of slum Negroes, Garrison said in 1893: "It is justice, not charity, that the victims of our social misrule demand of us. Opportunity, not alms, is craved. . . . It is eradication not relief we aim at." [53]

John F. Kennedy once observed that the word "crisis," written in Chinese, "is composed of two characters: one represents danger and one represents opportunity." [54] The NAACP titled its magazine *Crisis*, thus summing up its view of the racial situation in America; the Urban League, by calling its publication *Opportunity*, expressed an optimism that "the Negro problem" could be eased substantially if only whites could be persuaded to give Negroes a chance.

Finally, the racial reformers and the progressives shared a common dedication to the realization of justice. For the progressives, justice was defined in economic and social terms. For the NAACP and the Urban League, it meant an end to segregation and discrimination, and the substitution of a situation in which black Americans could enjoy the rights and opportunities guaranteed them under the Constitution. As George Haynes expressed it, justice—"the foundation in the adjustment of relations between nationalities and races"—meant "that every individual should have an opportunity for physical, mental and moral development to the limit of his capacity. It waives the question of superiority and inferiority of individuals or races and vouchsafes to

all the chance for self-realization. It means equal opportunity." [55]
It meant, in short, squaring American democracy with its Enlightenment origins.

Making the democratic system work and freeing the individual
for the fullest possible personal development were central tenets
of Progressive Era thought. Many who held them concluded,
however, that they excluded Negroes, and that racism was perfectly consistent with the broadened opportunities, political democracy, and social justice of the progressive movements. Here
the racial reformers disagreed. The way it treated Negroes was,
in their view, the fundamental test of American democracy. The
Urban League's concern, Ruth Standish Baldwin maintained, was
neither parochial nor self-serving; rather, working for improved
living conditions for urban Negroes was "part of the larger problem of developing a more wholesome community life in general
and a sounder national democracy." When she and her colleagues
sought "to better conditions among the *Negroes* of Harlem or
San Juan Hill or Brooklyn," Mrs. Baldwin explained, they sought
"also to make a better New York City for *everybody* to live in,
and to help in some measure towards a truer realization of the
ideals of sound community living in our great Republic." [56]
Urban Leaguers and NAACP members alike shared with Ray
Stannard Baker an awareness of "the utter absurdity and impossibility of limiting a democracy," and a conviction "that if the
negro does not fit into our present sort of democracy, it is not the
negro who is wrong, but the democracy. The final test of any
democracy is its humblest citizen." [57]

Urban Leaguers would spend decades measuring the American
democracy against the treatment it accorded to blacks. Usually
they found it wanting. Their efforts to fit blacks into the American system and the system's all but total imperviousness to significant change frame the history of the Urban League during its
first thirty years.

5 TRAINING BLACKS FOR
URBAN SOCIAL SERVICE

The constitutional objectives that the Urban League set for itself indicated both the range and the vaguely defined nature of its responsibilities. Whereas the NAACP could pursue concrete goals like antilynching legislation or the overturn of Jim Crow, the League found itself with a general mandate "to promote, encourage, assist and engage in any and all kinds of work for improving the industrial, economic, social and spiritual conditions among Negroes." [1]

Carrying out this mandate required trained personnel. When the Urban League was founded, social work as a profession was in its infancy; social work for blacks, and more particularly, black social workers, were even less common. Hence the League addressed itself immediately to filling this void.

Private philanthropy had satisfied the earliest desires to help those unable to care for themselves; personal benevolence seemed consistent with the gentleman's obligation to his less successful fellow citizen. Influenced by laissez faire and Social Darwinism, most Americans in the latter half of the nineteenth century subscribed to the belief that the poor and the socially maladjusted were unable to keep up because of personal shortcomings. While the rich thought social differentiation should exist, they recognized an obligation to alleviate the most blatant human miseries.

In the 1880s the charity organization movement began to sup-

plant individual almsgiving as the most widely accepted approach
to social improvement. Its central principles included investigation, cooperation and coordination among community welfare
services, adequate standards of relief, and substitution of "friendly
visiting," or personal contact between rich and poor, for the traditional impersonality of almsgiving. The charity organization
movement fostered the development "of a more broadly social"
approach to the causes of poverty and misfortune; as charity
agents gathered factual information about their clients and grew
to know them personally, they came to recognize that economic
and social factors other than personal frailty could be involved in
their distress.

By the end of the nineteenth century the prevailing perception
of the causes of social ills had shifted to an indictment of a hostile
economic and social environment rather than individual weakness. This new view, embraced by social justice progressives,
went hand in hand with an emerging faith in the power of social
reform. Instead of accepting existing conditions as the irreversible
plan of a mechanistic universe, progressives insisted that the organized application of human intelligence could go a long way toward accomplishing positive change. And in their dedication to
scientific method and technical investigation, they came to believe that the attack on social ills could best be led by those with
special professional competence.[2]

Whereas the main qualifications for "friendly visitors" had
been class affiliation, compassion, and a desire to serve, the new
profession of social work required technical training. In 1898, the
New York Charity Organization Society opened a six-week Summer School in Philanthropy, with a curriculum of lectures, visits
to agencies and institutions, and field work under the Society's
auspices. In 1904 the program expanded to a full academic year,
and in 1910 it became a formal two-year course of study. In the
meantime, other schools were organized, including the Chicago
School of Civics and Philanthropy, the Boston School for Social

Workers, and similar institutions in Philadelphia, Baltimore, and St. Louis.[3]

In its early years, social work was a profession primarily for whites. Before the founding of the Urban League, blacks had come to the attention of the National Conference of Social Work on only two occasions: in 1887, the conference considered the problems of Negroes and Indians; and, in 1908, the assembled social workers discussed Negro health.[4] While articles about blacks appeared occasionally in *The Annals of the American Academy of Political and Social Science*, the October 7, 1905, issue of *Charities* devoted to "The Negro in the Cities of the North" was the only effort of a leading social work publication to deal in any depth with the problems of blacks.[5]

Blacks were no better represented in the ranks of social workers than among the subjects they studied. Although black churches, women's clubs, and other secular agencies engaged in a wide range of social welfare activities, their leaders rarely had the benefit of professional social work training. At the turn of the century the New York Charity Organization Society hired the first black woman to be employed as a professional family caseworker. In 1910, when George Haynes became the first Negro graduate of the New York School of Philanthropy, he could cite only two other trained black social workers in the entire country.[6] Haynes's count may have been too modest, but he was not far from the mark. Instead of assigning black professionals to cope with urban problems, most people, he said, assumed that anyone could learn from intuition and experience to understand the "most serious social conditions." "Love for children and a sentimental kindness," Mary White Ovington wrote, seemed to "constitute the requisites for work among the poor." [7]

But "inefficient and inexperienced enthusiasts" were ill-prepared to grasp the growing dimensions of the Negro problem.[8] The migrations, beginnings of ghettos, and social complications that followed made it essential to train blacks for urban social service. "The Colored worker knows and understands the psychology of the migrant," John C. Dancy, director of the Detroit Urban League, insisted. "He has a warm sympathy that cannot and does not carry with one of another race." [9] "Our experience," a member of the national staff agreed, "has proven that no person can get as close to a Negro, sympathize with and get his confidence as a Negro." [10] "Nine out of ten" white social workers, a founder of the Atlanta School of Social Service later argued, "either insist on the standards of family and social life which they consider those of normal white people; or they believe that because their clients are Negroes they cannot be expected to have much in the way of standards." [11] What Negroes needed, George Haynes felt, was "more and better trained leadership"; according to "group psychology and common sense," the "most direct way of influencing the customs and habits of a people" was to give them "teachers and exemplars of their own kind." [12]

When he became executive secretary of the Committee on Urban Conditions in 1910, Haynes also joined the faculty of Fisk University in order to organize a department of social science to train black social workers. Fisk, he hoped, "would lead the way for the Negro college to grapple with the city problem as Tuskegee and Hampton are working at the rural condition." [13] The department began functioning during the 1910–11 academic year. Haynes taught the key course on urban conditions among Negroes. For special lectures he called on "experts on social problems," among them Roger N. Baldwin, who, for several years, came to speak on delinquency and probation.[14] By 1913 the social science curriculum included one introductory and one advanced course in economics, a sociology course that combined classroom study with field investigation and practical work, and a course on Negro history for juniors, to be followed in the senior year by Haynes's course on the Negro problem.[15]

From the time he arrived in Nashville, Haynes began to work out plans for establishing a training center for Negro social work-

ers. His hopes were realized in the fall of 1914 with the opening
of the Bethlehem Training Center under the auspices of the
Urban League, Fisk University, and the Woman's Missionary
Council, M. E. Church, South. The program combined classroom
study at Fisk with field work in juvenile courts, in Negro neighborhoods, and at Bethlehem House, a settlement created by the
three cooperating institutions and supported by the Woman's
Missionary Council. Bethlehem House opened in the fall of 1913
as an extension of a kindergarten and sewing school that had been
conducted by the Council. It offered clubs, classes, and other activities typical of settlement houses.[16]

The academic part of the training program included courses in
"Social Ideals of the Bible," "History and Principles of Religious
Education," "Principles of Sociology," "Playground and Recrea-
tion Methods," "Statistics and Method of Community Study,"
"Practical Sociology," "Negro History and Problems of Negro
Life," and "Domestic Science" or "Manual Arts."

The Center produced probation officers, settlement workers,
kindergarten directors, executive secretaries of social betterment
and civic organizations, institutional church workers, church and
charity visitors, home and foreign missionaries, and secretaries of
religious organizations. "The special aim of this training," the
Urban League explained, "is to link the growing enthusiasm and
knowledge of educated Negro youth with the pressing needs of
the toiling thousands of the Negro people." [17]

The experiment at Nashville in effect pioneered professional
social service training for Negroes. "Several Schools of Philanthropy are open to Negro students," Haynes told the Conference
on Charities and Correction in 1911, "but these institutions are
out of the reach of nearly all of them." Those few courses in economics and sociology available at Negro colleges, he felt, were
"scarcely more than class room discussions, often remotely relating to conditions among Negroes." [18] Bethlehem Center, he
hoped, would be a model for similar programs at these schools.
By and large Haynes was right about curriculum; at Talladega,

for example, sociology was taught in one year-long course covering "General Principles, Biblical Teaching and Practical Sociology." [19] But he did not give sufficient credit to Atlanta University's sociology department which W. E. B. Du Bois organized in 1898. Seniors in Du Bois's course on "Social Reform" received a thorough grounding in principles of sociology and devoted a full term to studying social and economic conditions among blacks and methods of reform.[20] And the Atlanta University Studies, the first of which was published in 1896, had pioneered scientific sociological research on aspects of Negro life. Though there is no evidence that Haynes consulted either Du Bois or his successor, Augustus Dill, about their work at Atlanta, he did attend some of the Atlanta University Conferences from which the studies grew.[21]

Despite its prominence in sociological research, Atlanta was not at that time training professional social workers. "So it is safe to say," Haynes concluded, without much exaggeration, "that, until we started . . . there had been no definite training for social work offered anywhere for Negro students and no arrangements existed to connect them when prepared with the serious conditions among our people in cities." [22] Haynes's programs, as Fisk officials had hoped, made the university "the champion of the most up-to-date movement for the uplift of the Negro." [23]

Haynes's efforts in Nashville fitted into a three-part plan to enlist blacks in social work and to relate black colleges to urban black communities. The first stage—"preparatory instruction and training in the Negro college"—involved developing the social science department at Fisk, encouraging other southern Negro colleges to incorporate instruction in economics and sociology in their curricula, and sending League staff to Negro colleges and educational and religious organizations to lecture on migrations, city problems, and organized methods of betterment. The second—"selecting . . . promising students and providing them with the opportunities for further professional study and practical experience among their own people in cities"—led to the Bethlehem Training Center, scholarships for students at the Negro colleges affiliated with the Urban League, a special fellowship program, and Urban League cooperation in founding the Atlanta School of Social Service in 1920. The third part of the plan—"the organization of social betterment work in the cities where these trained people may use their ability for social uplift"—comprised the core of the Urban League's practical program.[24]

During its earliest years, the Urban League offered material aid to potential urban leaders through scholarships for students at black colleges that had affiliated with the Urban League movement. These colleges, which included Howard, Virginia Union, Talladega, Morehouse, and Paine, had agreed to develop social science courses, along the lines of those Haynes had established at Fisk, and to cooperate with the League in furthering its educational objectives. In return, the League earmarked funds for four $50 scholarships (a year's tuition, room, and board at a black college at that time cost $100 to $150) to enable upperclassmen interested in careers in social work to pursue a year of study in the field at their undergraduate institutions.[25] In December 1913 the League changed the scholarship program into a social science scholarship contest, open to all students in economics and sociology at the affiliated schools. Students competing for a first prize of $50 and a second of $25 submitted examinations, essays, and book reviews on designated topics. The League discontinued this contest in 1915, however, because of insufficient interest among the students and the poor quality of the papers submitted.[26]

The Urban League's social science scholarships for undergraduates were a failure. It had more success, however, with a fellowship program to enable promising young Negroes to pursue advanced studies at designated schools of social work. Nine men and eight women held fellowships during the 1910s, thirteen of them at the New York School of Philanthropy and four at Fisk.[27] The League covered the fellows' living expenses, and in most instances, the schools waived tuition payments. Fellows in New

York gained practical experience by working with the League and the Charity Organization Society, while those in Nashville did field work in conjunction with Bethlehem House and other local betterment movements.[28]

For example, Ellie A. Walls, one of the League's first two fellows, enrolled at the New York School of Philanthropy during 1911–12, the year following her graduation from Fisk. Her fellowship consisted of free tuition plus a $35-per-month living stipend. The League arranged for her to live at the Lincoln Settlement, where her room rent was waived in exchange for some work at the settlement house. During the summer before her classes began, Miss Walls worked for the Urban League in New York, where her projects included research on convalescent care for Brooklyn Negroes and a study of "ways and means for care of delinquent Colored girls and women in Manhattan and Brooklyn." During the academic year, she was assigned for field work to the United Charities as a caseworker.[29]

The League designed a separate program of "broken" or part fellowships for young people with some prior advanced training or social work experience who hoped to qualify for positions within the League movement. The fellowships enabled them to work for a short time under supervision in an Urban League office in order to gain on-the-job experience.

Following their academic training, all fellows were expected to devote at least one year to social work. While there was no requirement that this work be done under the auspices of the Urban League, perhaps a third of the fellows at one time or another worked in the League movement. Fellows pursued careers as "Urban League executives, probation and parole officers, family case workers, girls' and boys' club supervisors, specialists in mental hygiene, directors of recreational activities in connection with play-grounds for public schools and secretaries for the Y.M.C.A. and Y.W.C.A." The League did not even require that its fellows remain in social work; its goal was simply to train urban leaders who would work toward improving the status of blacks.[30]

The League solicited candidates for fellowships by sending announcements of the program to the press, interested national organizations, and administrators, professors, and students at white and Negro colleges alike. Candidates were expected to have completed a college course or its equivalent. In awarding fellowships, the League evaluated applicants on the basis of academic abilities, "general personality," "capacity for executive duties and for leadership," "general intelligence on current affairs," and "ability, knowledge of, and fondness for outdoor sports and recreation." [31]

The Urban League fellowships for the first time enabled young Negroes to bring professional know-how to bear on their efforts to help urban communities solve their problems. The record of the program in the 1910s was mixed. Finding jobs was not always easy; Ellie Walls, faced with the necessity of supporting her invalid mother, became a public school teacher in Houston, because social work was "unpaid" and "almost unheard of" in Texas at that time. One or two of the League's fellows, among them Chandler Owen, the editor of the Socialist *Messenger*, became outspokenly critical of their former benefactors. On balance, however, the program marked the beginning of an important achievement, and the fellows who remained in social work found their training in social work theory invaluable to the practical work they later undertook. Forrester B. Washington, a fellow at the New York School of Philanthropy in 1915–16 who later became director of the Atlanta School of Social Work, best summed up the importance of the training the Urban League had made possible. Thanks to his graduate education, Washington explained, "I didn't enter the profession, as had many in those days (and some since) depending on a 'gift of gab' to convince the public that they were, (or are) social workers." [32]

Creating a program to train black social workers was the Urban League's most important accomplishment during its earliest years. Its corollary was putting blacks to work in practical social service projects.

6 FINDING A FOOTING

The program to train black social workers was the Urban League's most innovative effort during its first years. Fulfilling its general mandate was more difficult, because its charge was as vaguely defined as it was broad. How could such an organization best promote "any and all kinds of work for improving the industrial, economic, social and spiritual conditions among Negroes"? It needed to chart a course at once consistent with its resources and faithful to its aspirations. Learning to live with the tension between limited capabilities and overwhelming needs was one of its earliest challenges.

The first years were necessarily a time of experimentation. The League would continue the social service programs of its constituent organizations and copy others from charitable and immigrant aid societies. But the absence of a long perspective sometimes made it difficult to distinguish the frivolous from the essential; inexperience often meant diffusion of effort. The same held true when it tried to give meaning to its status as a national movement. Setting priorities and structuring its operations preoccupied the League as it began its work.

I

The League's most basic problem was to put itself on a firm financial footing. It never raised money easily, nor did it attract a large group of benefactors. Its initial budget, for the fiscal year

1912, was under $15,000; five years later, it had increased by
about 60 per cent. From its founding until 1918, its largest single
contribution in any twelve-month period was only $3500.[1]

The League's income came primarily fron a tiny group of
wealthy philanthropists: John D. Rockefeller, Jr., Julius Rosenwald, and Alfred T. White. These men, Hollingsworth Wood
recalled, together with Ruth Standish Baldwin and some un-
named "others," "united in making this experiment possible." [2]
From the first, the single most important name in the League's financial picture was unquestionably Rockefeller. John D. Rockefeller, Jr., had developed a close association with William H. Baldwin, Jr., through the General Education Board, and the relationship
carried over to Ruth Standish Baldwin after her husband's death.
Hollingsworth Wood credited Mrs. Baldwin with persuading
Rockefeller to make the first of many incentive/matching fund
pledges in 1912. Characteristically, she disclaimed the responsibility, attributing the Rockefeller promise "largely . . . to the impression Mr. Haynes made upon him." [3] Nevertheless, her contacts would have inclined Rockefeller to give Haynes a hearing.
As secretary and later president of the League, William H. Baldwin III "always felt welcomed" at Rockefeller's offices, he recalled; "I didn't always get the money I wanted," he said, "but I
always got understanding, encouragement and sound advice." [4]

Personal ties must have facilitated securing financial assistance
from the Rockefellers, but supporting the League was also consistent with their other commitments. Laura Spelman Rockefeller
came from a family of abolitionists; her parents' home in Ohio
had been a station on the Underground Railroad. John D. Rockefeller, Sr., shared his wife's concern for Negroes. His support for
Negro education began in 1882 when two missionary school-
teachers interested him in the female seminary they had begun in
Atlanta. The family's gifts made possible the development of
Spelman College, named for Mrs. Rockefeller and her parents.
Rockefeller made important contributions to Hampton and Tuskegee Institutes, and he founded the General Education Board to
channel northern money into southern education.[5]

From 1912 to 1918 John D., Jr., gave the Urban League $21,-
000, or an average of $3000 a year, making him the organization's
largest single contributor. Typically, he promised only a portion
of the money outright; the remainder depended on raising larger
sums from other sources.[6] The League's second largest contributor was Julius Rosenwald, the Chicago philanthropist who owned
Sears, Roebuck. The League was as logical a philanthropy for
Rosenwald as it was for Rockefeller. His cousin and close friend,
Paul J. Sachs, was a member of the League's executive board, and
it was Sachs who interested him in Negro problems and acquainted him with the Urban League. Rosenwald was extremely
impressed with Booker T. Washington, whom he met in 1911.
Washington's autobiography and a biography of William H.
Baldwin convinced him to contribute to Tuskegee, where he became a member of the board of trustees. Rural education in the
South became his major philanthropy. Through the Rosenwald
Fund he spent $3 million to build rural schoolhouses, train teach-
ers, improve Negro colleges and universities, develop health services, and provide fellowships.[7] His purpose in these benefactions,
he said, was to promote "better American citizenship"; uplifting
blacks, he felt, would benefit whites as well.[8] He gave the Urban
League $2000 annually.[9]

The League's third major donor, Alfred T. White, was a
Brooklyn-born merchant who built the first successful improved
tenement houses in New York in 1876. That same year he also
built the first seaside home for summer relief of poor children.[10]
He was an important benefactor of Hampton, and of Tuskegee,
where the main girls' dormitory bore his name. "From the very
beginning," Robert R. Moton said, he was "one of Dr. Washington's warmest and most helpful friends." [11] Each year White and
his sisters gave the Urban League $1500.[12]

For some years these three gifts accounted for more than 40
per cent of the League's annual budget. The NAACP's support
was much more broadly based; by 1918, in fact, the bulk of it
came from small contributions. In 1919, when the League recorded 793 gifts, the NAACP counted more than 62,300.[13]

The League's dependence on a few individuals tied it closely to their views. It made it especially susceptible to fluctuations in the economy and individual giving patterns; "unsatisfactory business conditions" in 1914 left the League "sorely in need of funds in a year when so many people are either cutting us down or cutting us out entirely," Paul Sachs told Julius Rosenwald.[14] Equally important, the meager sums the League raised limited the work it could undertake. The "financial stringency" in 1914 was so acute that it had to forgo printing its complete annual report.[15] New employees were sometimes hired on monthly contracts, since "failure to raise the budget" might "necessitate a curtailment of the work." [16] Such constraints bore heavily on the League's social service programs and its ability to develop affiliates in the years before the Great Migration.

II

Although the Urban League had envisioned itself as "a promoting and coordinating agency rather than a direct service agency," the needs of urban blacks brought it actively into direct service as well. The League's social service projects in the 1910s continued the work already begun by its constituent organizations during the previous decade. "Preventive" or "protective" work comprised one area of emphasis. The League employed one travelers' aid worker in New York, two in Norfolk, and one in Philadelphia to meet boats and trains and to handle "the customary cases of direction, relief, recovery of baggage and protection from unscrupulous men." [17] In addition, League staff members offered personal counsel, shelter, and employment assistance to women new to the city. Southern steamship agencies distributed cards directing strange travelers to the League's workers; Eugene Kinckle Jones even found a traveling lecturer-entertainer who agreed to include the League's card in his moving picture show.[18]

The League's reach, however, was limited. From October 1911 through January 1912, the travelers' aid workers handled 69 cases in New York, 151 in Norfolk, and 49 in Philadelphia; from May through August of 1913, the New York and Norfolk workers dealt with 554 cases at the docks and stations.[19] These were only a tiny fraction of the number of blacks coming north; moreover, the League fell far short of organizations like the Illinois Immigrants' Protective League, which aided over 5000 newcomers at Chicago's Dearborn Station in 1911 and more than 40,000 in 1913.[20] The Travelers' Aid Society took over the Urban League's work in New York in 1915 and hired a Negro woman as a travelers' aid worker; in 1916 the same thing happened in Philadelphia.[21]

The League initiated Big Brother and Big Sister programs that brought delinquent or potentially delinquent youngsters under the influence of mature, responsible adults through regular personal contact. Such work, the League hoped, would save black children "from falling into the clutches of the law." [22] By 1916 Negro Big Brothers and Sisters in New York were supervising annually more than 500 boys and girls under the age of sixteen who had been reported to the juvenile court. In that year, the national Big Brother and Big Sister movement agreed to pay the salaries of the Urban League's workers.[23]

Other preventive work included home visiting in cases of truancy and "incorrigible" behavior, the organization of neighborhood unions, "individual case work with girls on the verge of lives of immorality," and the promotion of girls' clubs and "wholesome and instructive amusements." Boys' and girls' workers met each month under Urban League auspices to exchange information and plan joint efforts, including the formation of neighborhood clubs.[24] The Court of General Sessions in New York appointed the League's probation worker as one of its regular probation officers—the first Negro to hold such a position. Since existing state and private institutions failed to care for the needs of Negro delinquents, the League cooperated with Utopia Neighborhood House in establishing and running a temporary detention home for delinquent Negro girls, and it urged the State to provide additional accommodations for blacks at the Hudson and Bedford Reformatories.[25]

The second phase of the League's social service efforts came under the heading of "general welfare." Here the organization concerned itself with the daily lives of urban Negroes—their behavior, health, housing, and recreational opportunities. Its workers counseled Negro families new to the city on the most elementary matters of behavior, dress, sanitation, health, and homemaking. In emergencies it provided food and clothing for the needy. A housing bureau, operating from the League's Harlem office, certified apartment houses it judged to be "respectable and clean," where "decent and discriminating" tenants might "be assured of dignified and refined associations," and it distributed lists of approved dwellings to migrants seeking a place to live. "Respectable strangers" in the city for a short time could come to the bureau for a list of reliable boarding houses.[26] The bureau tried to "protect tenements and neighborhoods from tenants of disreputable character" and to investigate exorbitant rents. League officials encouraged tenant-landlord cooperation, enforcement of safety and health regulations, and adequate housing inspection in Negro neighborhoods.[27]

The welfare of black children was of special concern. In addition to its Big Brother and Sister work, the League sponsored boys' and girls' clubs at churches, settlements, and schools, and persuaded the City Parks Department to establish a public playground in Harlem. In cooperation with the Negro Fresh Air Committee, the League ran a summer camp for twelve- to sixteen-year-old boys in Verona, New Jersey, until white Fresh Air Funds agreed in 1916 to take over the work among Negroes. Each season 150 boys enjoyed the camp's facilities for two weeks. Between 1913 and 1916, the League sent some 3000 Negro mothers and children on one-day beach outings administered by the Association for Improving the Condition of the Poor.[28]

Cooperating with the National Negro Business League, the Urban League conducted annual National Negro Health Weeks, using publicity, lectures and demonstrations, clinics, and other vehicles for health education in an effort to reduce the disproportionate incidence of disease among Negro adults and the high rate of infant mortality.[29] In 1915 it opened a convalescent home, Valley Rest, in White Plains for Negro patients in cooperation with the Burke Foundation, which funded the venture. By 1916 Valley Rest had cared for 220 black women, and provisions were being made to include men and children.[30]

The Urban League's earliest social service efforts were uneven in quality and far from adequate to redress the repressive effects of urban life. But even these fledgling efforts drew favorable reviews in the black press. Thanks to the work of the Urban League, according to the Pittsburgh *Courier*, "the spirit of better conditions among us along all lines has been kindled anew." [31] The Urban League's influence, the *Afro-American* agreed, "is being felt to good advantage." [32] The important point is not that the League's efforts were inadequate, but that they were pioneering; they represented a series of "firsts" for blacks, whose needs in these areas had previously been neglected or recognized only in the most haphazard fashion. The Urban League "deserves recognition and respect for what it has done to . . . promote Negro welfare," the *Southern Workman* felt; ". . . it can be seen how great a need is being met by this organization." [33] Eugene Kinckle Jones described the advances the League made as pilot projects undertaken "to convince larger social work agencies that work among Negroes should be integrated with their other activities." The League was always "happy to transfer programs" to other agencies once it was sure that they would treat blacks fairly.[34]

III

The Urban League's social services closely approximated the programs of immigrant aid societies. Organizations such as the Immigrant Protective League (established in 1908), the Association for the Protection of Jewish Immigrants (1884), the Hebrew Immigrant Aid Society (1902), and the Baron de Hirsch Fund (1890) worked for the social and industrial adjustment of immigrants in

the same ways that the Urban League eased the adjustment of
Negroes to cities. They sponsored travelers' aid and temporary
shelters, employment bureaus, and settlement houses to meet social and recreational needs. They also offered technical and trade
education and instruction in English language and American citizenship.[35]

Immigrant aid societies were not the only models for Urban
League programs. Many of the League's efforts also duplicated
services provided by settlement houses. Settlements offered educational and social clubs, recreational facilities, kindergartens and
day nurseries, vocational training and guidance, classes in child
care, homemaking, and handicrafts—all of which served important social needs of the predominantly immigrant settlement
neighborhoods. Settlement workers carried on campaigns for
public playgrounds, improved health and housing conditions,
protection of working women and children, and better employment bureaus. The probation worker at Jane Addams's Hull
House in Chicago became the first probation officer of the Cook
County juvenile court when it was established in 1899.[36]

The Urban League shared considerable common ground with
the settlement movement. Both were interested in acculturation
—the settlements that of immigrants new to America, the Urban
League that of Negroes new to cities. Both were motivated not
by the sense of *noblesse oblige* central to charity societies, but by
a belief in the interdependence of socio-economic classes. Both
accepted the progressive premise that carefully ascertained facts
must precede philanthropy or reform. One of the objectives of
Hull House, for example was "to investigate and improve the
conditions in the industrial districts in Chicago." [37]

Yet the settlements were much more active than the Urban
League in promoting reform. Many settlement workers were
never entirely sure "whether they sought to adjust the child and
the immigrant to society, or whether they meant to transform society to meet the needs of their pupils." [38] The Urban League
was generally preoccupied with adjusting Negro migrants to

urban life as it existed. While settlement workers were among the leaders pressing for progressive legislative reform, the Urban League tried to change private practices rather than laws.

Here the Urban League differed most markedly from other reform organizations of the Progressive Era. Most progressives focused on legislation as the vehicle of social change. Were women and children being exploited in industry? Progressives sought factory and child labor legislation to protect them. Were immigrants crowded into dangerous and insanitary housing? Progressives sought tenement house laws to enforce minimal standards of decency and safety. Were large corporations monopolizing private industry? Progressives sought antitrust legislation to reform them.

The NAACP fitted this traditional progressive pattern in its court work and efforts to secure legislation making lynching a federal crime. But the Urban League in its early decades eschewed the legislative process. It never considered seeking congressional action to make equal employment opportunity the law of the land, or to give blacks access to a wider range of housing, or to give them the right to use public parks and playgrounds. Instead, it tried to change individual practices in different businesses or cities by private, individual persuasion. If blacks were denied access to public recreational facilities, the Urban League would start its own playground and hope to persuade the city to take responsibility for its operation. If an employer treated his black employees shabbily, the League would dispatch a welfare worker to try to adjust their differences. If a company was reluctant to hire blacks, the Urban League would try to press for an opening for one particularly capable applicant. In many ways theirs was a more difficult approach that inevitably had limited results; at the same time, however, it avoided the necessity of building a popular coalition for a generally unpopular cause.

This emphasis on private practices rather than public laws set the Urban Leaguers apart from the settlement workers and most of their progressive colleagues. The League's concerns also differed from those of the settlements in two other important ways.

One was a matter of sequence. While the settlements were created in part to give trained workers a laboratory where they
could put their theories to work on practical social problems, the
Urban League, faced with practical problems all too readily at
hand, had to develop trained workers who could deal with them.
The other difference was one of constituency. Urban Leaguers
differed from some of their Progressive Era colleagues in that
they held the conviction that broadened economic opportunities,
social justice, and the rhetoric of American democracy belonged
equally to whites and blacks. Although there were a few settlement houses especially for blacks, the settlement movement
served a primarily immigrant constituency. Some settlements deliberately excluded blacks; others, as neighborhood institutions
founded in immigrant neighborhoods, never touched them. Because settlements and charitable agencies such as the Charity Organization Society rarely dealt with blacks, it fell to the Urban
League to adapt their programs and methods and create new ones
to fill the void.

IV

These social service projects comprised the heart of the National
Urban League's practical work in the years before the Great Migration. The League was also trying to find jobs for blacks, but
its employment efforts in these early years were so limited that
they scarcely deserve mention. The national office found 31 positions in New York during a four-month period at the end of
1911, 37 in a different four-month period in 1913, more than 200
in 1914, and by 1916 some 308 jobs during an entire year. When
jobs in the private sector were unusually scarce, as in the winter
of 1915, the League helped by running a city-authorized workshop for 774 unemployed Negro men.[39] The League's industrial committee sponsored rudimentary labor organizations—
associations of elevator men and hallmen, chauffeurs, mechanics,
and public porters—to stimulate a sense of identity with a par-

ticular occupation and to encourage high standards of performance.[40] In Philadelphia the Armstrong Association placed 309 workers in 1911–12; 497 in 1912–13; 455 in 1913–14; and 583 in 1914–15. But more than 80 per cent of the jobs found from 1912 to 1915 were in domestic service and unskilled labor.[41] The employment work was limited partly because of lack of resources and inexperience within the Urban League itself, and partly because a growing supply of immigrant labor combined with traditional prejudices to make employers unsympathetic to hiring blacks. All this would change with the Great Migration and the First World War.

In its earliest years, the Urban League had similar difficulties in establishing itself as a national organization. A network of travelers' aid agents inherited from the National League for the Protection of Colored Women established contacts for the League in such cities as Baltimore, Philadelphia, Norfolk, and Memphis.[42] While these workers could not sustain the range of programs the Urban League attempted in New York, they still provided nuclei for the development of more sophisticated local organizations. Some cities already had agencies compatible with the purposes and philosophy of the Urban League; like the Armstrong Association in Philadelphia and the St. Louis Committee for Social Service Among Negroes, many of them eventually became affiliated with the League. Other cities had no existing base in social service or employment, and they were fresh territory for organizing; after the League's founding. George Haynes and Kinckle Jones devoted what time they could to stirring up interest in local Urban Leagues by correspondence and personal visits.

Within a year of its founding, the League claimed branches in Philadelphia, St. Louis, Memphis, and Nashville, with travelers' aid workers in Baltimore and Norfolk. Almost two years later Savannah and Augusta had been added to the list, but Memphis had already folded. By 1915 Urban League affiliates in Savannah, Augusta, Atlanta, Nashville, and Louisville conducted clubs and classes for mothers and children, travelers' aid work, kindergartens, health campaigns, playgrounds, and relief efforts. Philadelphia had both an Association for the Protection of Colored Women, which handled travelers' aid and probation work, and an Armstrong Association, which ran an employment bureau and fostered organizations of mechanics, chauffeurs, engineers, stenographers, and other artisans. In St. Louis, the affiliated Committee for Social Service was equally advanced in its investigation of industrial conditions, plans for an employment agency, and success in securing a state-run home for delinquent Negro girls.[43]

Of necessity the League kept its early affiliates in loose reins. When the St. Louis Committee for Social Service expressed fears that affiliation with the Urban League would encroach too much on its independence, George Haynes assured Roger Baldwin that an affiliate would enjoy "full local autonomy" as well as "a large share of participation in the affairs of the National League." [44] Such autonomy was probably the only way to encourage other organizations to move under the Urban League umbrella. It was also the practical result of limited funds and staff at the national headquarters. The work of these affiliates did not measure up to the work in New York City. Absorbed in initiating the work in Nashville and New York, severely limited in finances, and staffed only by two trained professionals, the Urban League could hardly have been expected in these years to devote its meager resources to an ambitious program of organizing on the local level —nor immediately to succeed in the cities it did attempt to reach.

Some of the cities the Urban League approached admitted frankly that they were not ready to sustain a League affiliate. Others put together haphazard organizations that folded sooner or later. For any hope of survival, they would have needed constant support and supervision from the national office— attention the Urban League did not have the resources to give. Ruth Standish Baldwin cautioned George Haynes against trying too quickly to make the Urban League a *de facto* national movement. "We are attempting work in too many places & affiliating with colleges too rapidly," she wrote. "Our whole tendency is *ex*tensive rather than *in*tensive & I do not believe it a healthy tendency at all." [45]

Whether healthy or not, the black press applauded the League's progress. It was accomplishing "much good," the Baltimore *Afro-American* felt.[46] The branches, the Cleveland *Gazette* agreed, were "doing a beneficent work among our people." [47] Yet the League spread itself thin, and most of the affiliates it tried to found collapsed before the decade was out. With the exception of the social work fellowship program and some practical work in New York City, its first years produced no lasting accomplishments. By the time of the First World War, then, the Urban League was floundering: it was trying unsuccessfully to put itself on a national footing; it had made almost no progress toward improving employment opportunities for blacks; and in its local social service work it imitated established charitable and immigrant aid societies.

Much of the League's original mandate remained unfulfilled. This was due in part to the newness of its efforts. Partly, too, it could be attributed to the context in which the organization operated. When that context changed with the onset of the war and the Great Migration, it gave the Urban League a sharper focus and established it as a viable national movement.

7 THE GREAT MIGRATION

The migration of blacks to northern cities during World War I had a critical effect on the fortunes of the Urban League. More important, it altered black demographic patterns, both in its immediate impact in selected cities and in the precedents it set for the large scale urbanization of blacks in America.

I

The Great Migration brought perhaps 300,000 to 400,000 Negroes northward in the space of three years. It began in 1915 and continued into 1919, but its peak years were 1916–18. It was, most writers have agreed, another phase of the constant movement of Negro peoples during the preceding thirty to forty years. But whereas the earliest migrations had been directed primarily toward the South and West, this one focused on the cities of the North and East. Earlier migrants had moved primarily to less populated areas with better economic prospects. The migrants of World War I also sought economic advantages, but in densely packed cities where competition was keen. Previously, blacks had tended to move short distances within the South or across the Mason and Dixon line, with the majority of migrants coming from border states like Maryland, Virginia, and Kentucky. The wartime migrations, by contrast, "were frequently long-distance moves from the far South." [1]

The Great Migration was distinguished, too, by its volume and intensity. Between 1910 and 1920, the number of southern-born Negroes living in the North increased by more than 300,000, "which was more than the aggregate increase of the preceding 40 years and six times the previous average decennial increase." [2] In 1910 89 per cent of the nation's Negroes lived in the South, but the figure had decreased to 85.2 per cent a decade later. According to the 1910 census, before the wartime migration began, 27.4 per cent of the nation's 9,827,763 blacks lived in urban areas (defined as communities of 2500 or more), as compared with 48.7 per cent of the white population. [3] In 1920, urban centers claimed 34 per cent of the Negro population of 10,463,131. Part of this growth is attributable to the general trend toward urbanization in American society. The 1920 census revealed that, for the first time, more than half of all Americans lived in urban areas. Among whites the proportion of urban population was close to 53 per cent. But the black population explosion in northern cities must have had its own special driving force. The black population of Chicago, for example, increased more than seven times as fast as the white population in that city between 1910 and 1920. In Detroit and Cincinnati, the black rate of growth outpaced the white by roughly six to one. [4] And while the unusual urban population boom was peculiar to blacks, it also singled out the industrial centers of the North. While the dozen southern cities with more than 25,000 Negro inhabitants in 1920 witnessed a Negro population increase of 20.1 per cent over the decade 1910–20, the rate of increase in their twelve northern counterparts was over three times as high. [5]

The wartime migrants were mainly young adults of twenty to forty-five, people who were best suited by age to take advantage of economic opportunities. At first, the majority were men, either single or without their families. These were primarily unskilled or semiskilled workingmen responding to the new job openings in northern industries. In addition, there were "floaters and ne'er-do-wells" attracted by tales of easy work, high wages, and free transportation. Single women migrated in search of opportunities in domestic service. Later on, laborers began to leave the South with their families, and relatives came north to join men already established in new jobs.[6] "I am a Man of family," "I am 31 yrs. old have a very industrious wife, no children," "am 27 years of age . . . have a wife," the letters of inquiry began to read.[7]

"Of course they are not the best Negroes who leave the South," the *Christian Recorder* said in the summer of 1916. ". . . The best Negroes do not need jobs on railroads as section hands. They were not the best white people who left Europe to come to America. But as a rule they were vigorous, active, ambitious men and women, and if well treated they will equal the best we've got here; for all of us are immigrants." [8] As the migration progressed, lawyers, doctors, artisans, and skilled workers began to move north in greater numbers, establishing professional and business careers among the masses already transplanted. Generally, the migrations were on an individual basis, but sometimes entire neighborhoods or congregations decided to migrate as a group, seeking perhaps to fortify themselves with shared friendships, traditions, and understanding against the cold unfamiliarity of the North. "A club of 108 good men wants work," one correspondent wrote. "Could 300 or 500 men and women get employment?" another asked. Others repeated the message: "there are more than 250 men desire to come north"; "I can bring you all the men that you need"; "Friends will go, too." [9]

II

Contemporary writers devoted article after article to pinpointing the forces that brought Negroes north. Most agreed that these should properly fall into two categories of motives: one set, comprised of "pushing" forces, pertained to long-standing conditions in the South. The other—"pulling" forces—arose from circumstances in northern cities that were occasioned by the war.

The contributory, or "pushing" influences, describe the countless indignities in the lives of southern blacks. Blacks themselves gave the most poignant accounts of what those lives were like. "I want to get my famely out of this cursed south land," wrote a man from Greenville, Mississippi; "down here a negro man is not good as a white man's dog." "We are humane but we are not treated such," a correspondent from Daphne, Alabama explained. Instead, "we are treated like brute by our white here we don't have no privilege no where in the south." [10]

The lack of "privilege" meant, in the first instance, denial of the franchise and segregation in every form of public accommodation. It meant grossly inadequate schooling: schoolhouses that white superintendents admitted were "miserable beyond all description," teachers who were, in the main, "untrained" and "incompetent." [11] Even when he and his neighbors in Grabow, Louisiana paid poll taxes and state and parish taxes, one man complained, "we cannot get schools. . . . Causes me to be disgusted at the south." A college-educated teacher in Lexington, Mississippi, contrasted his teaching situation—150 pupils, for a salary of $27 a month—with that of whites with 30 students who were paid $100; "The Superintendent under whom we poor colored teachers have to teach," he lamented, "cares less for a colored man than he does for the vilest beast. . . . I am so sick I am so tired of such conditions that I sometime think that life for me is not worth while and most eminently believe with Patrick Henry 'Give me liberty or give me death.' " [12]

The all-pervasive atmosphere of hate and discrimination made the South intolerable for many blacks. "Would like to get where we would be able to have a chanse in the world and get out from among all the prejudice of the southern white man," a resident of Monroe, Louisiana, explained. This was a view in which many concurred; as a man from Mobile put it, "There is nothing here for the colored man but a hard time which these southern crackers gives us." Countless men and women shared what a Memphian called his "long[ing] for liberty." [13]

Many blacks felt that their very lives were at stake. Courts and law enforcement officials meted out Jim Crow justice. In the North, in the view of the white Montgomery *Advertiser*, blacks felt that "they don't arrest fifty niggers for what three of 'em done." [14] Even more important, lynching at the hands of an enraged mob was an ever-present threat. A resident of New Orleans expressed his desire to go north to escape "the Lynchman's noose and torchman's fire." In Macon, Georgia, it seemed that blacks were "shot down here like rabbits for every little orfence." "Our southern white people are so cruel," a man from Palestine, Texas, wrote, "we collord people are almost afraid to walke the streets after night." [15] "Is any one surprised that Negroes are leaving . . . by the thousands?" the *Southwestern Christian Advocate* asked. "The wonder is that any of them remain. They will suffer in the North. Some of them will die. . . . [But] any place would be paradise compared with some sections of the South where the Negroes receive such maltreatment." [16]

Dreadful as these conditions were, they were far from new when World War I began. The 1910s brought special economic conditions and opportunities that helped turn longstanding grievances and discontent into active migration.

Needless to say, blacks in the South had never enjoyed good jobs or high wages. During World War I, however, their economic status became even more precarious. A labor depression in 1914 and 1915 reduced daily wages to seventy-five cents or less. The boll weevil invaded in 1915 and 1916, ravaging the cotton crop in Louisiana, Mississippi, Alabama, Georgia, and Florida in particular. Serious flooding hit the same area in the summer of 1915. Crop failures and plummeting cotton prices caused planters to cut off credit and dismiss their sharecroppers and tenant farmers. The resulting excess of labor depressed already low wages. Many Negroes found themselves jobless and homeless.[17]

Segregation and discrimination may have made life in the South intolerable, but these economic developments made it all but impossible. "Compared with other things to which we have almost become resigned," a correspondent from Keatchie, Louisiana, explained, "the high cost of living coupled with unreasonably low wages is of greatest concern. We have learned to combat with more or less success other conditions, but thousands of us can bearly keep body and soul together with wages 60, 75, and $1.00 and meat at 19, flour $10 and $12 per bbl and everything else according." "We are forced to go [north]," a man from Newbern, Alabama, agreed, "when one things of a grown man wages is only fifty to seventy five cents per day for all grades of work. He is compelled to go where there is better wages and sociable conditions, believe me." Whether from Florida, South Carolina, Mississippi, or Alabama, the message was the same: "Wages here are so low can scarcely live"; "Owing to conditions (here) in the south one is hardly able to eke out an existence on the paltry salaries allowed by our white friends." In sum, "our chance here is so poor." [18]

Chances in the North, however, were suddenly opening up. War production stimulated northern industry at the very time that the traditional sources of industrial labor were being cut off. The war brought with it a reverse flow of immigrants returning to defend their homelands. Immigration dropped from 1,200,000 in 1913 and 1914 to just over 326,000 in 1915 and 110,000 in 1918.[19] Eventual legal restriction of immigration combined with the military draft to take industrial workers out of the factories. Moreover, remaining white workers sought higher-paid positions in munitions plants. For the first time, significant numbers of common factory jobs were open to Negro workers.

"Negro women are leaving the kitchen and laundry for the workshop and factory," William M. Ashby, executive secretary of the New Jersey Negro Welfare League, reported during the war. The new employees filled "places made vacant by the shifting of Hungarian, Italian, and Jewish girls to the munitions plants." [20] This unique opening of industrial opportunity, for black men as well as women, was perhaps the single most important factor explaining the timing of the Great Migration.

Once the movement started, it became self-generating. Success-

ful migrants returning south for a visit or writing to friends and
family left behind told amazing stories of newfound wealth and
freedom. Some northern industries sent labor agents south with
promises of free transportation and waiting jobs. In 1916, for example, the Pennsylvania and Erie Railroads gathered up train-
loads of blacks for a free ride to railroad jobs in the North. Such
wholesale recruiting indirectly benefited other industries; of some
12,000 black laborers brought north by the Pennsylvania Railroad, all but 2000 left for better-paying jobs once they arrived in
Pennsylvania. Smaller concerns followed suit; the National
Hosiery and Underwear Manufacturers of Philadelphia, to name
one, brought black girls north to work in their knitting mills.[21]

The northern Negro press (notably the Chicago *Defender*) encouraged Southerners to migrate by running enticing advertisements of jobs at hitherto unheard of wages and by editorializing
on the advantages of life in the North. "THE BARS ARE BEING LET
DOWN in the industrial world as never before in the history of this
country," one *Defender* editorial proclaimed. ". . . Will the great
mass of toilers take advantage of this golden opportunity?"[22]
Typical headlines read, "Good-bye, Dixie Land"; "Thousands
Leave Memphis"; "Still Planning to Come North"; "Northbound
Their Cry."[23] Ads promised "Good pay, good working conditions"; "Good steady employment"; "More positions open than
men for them."[24] The *Defender* was so outspoken in its encouragement of the exodus that some southern cities tried to block its
distribution among local Negroes. Nonetheless, its circulation in
1918 was two and a half times what it had been before the migration began. The paper became something of a *cause célèbre*
throughout the South; in Mississippi reading the *Defender* was
seen as a mark of intelligence, and "old men who did not know
how to read would buy it because it was regarded as precious."[25]

III

The Urban League itself contributed to the momentum of the
migration, both by sending blacks to the tobacco fields in the

Connecticut River Valley and, more generally, by advertising for laborers in northern industries. World War I saddled Connecticut's tobacco-growing industry with a serious labor shortage. No longer able to rely on a constant supply of immigrant workers, the tobacco planters first recruited women from New York, but they proved to be "of the worst type," with the result that they "demoralized" Hartford. Following this "blunder," the Connecticut Leaf Tobacco Association decided late in 1915 to experiment with Negro labor. In the interests of finding "the proper class of people," the Association called on the Urban League to supply the workers its planters needed. "Their purpose," a spokesman was careful to point out, was "not to import Negroes in order to cheapen the labor, but rather to provide steady sources of labor." [26]

The Association wanted 500 Negro families for permanent employment and 2000 students to work during the July and August harvest season. The tobacco corporations would sustain the students' transportation expenses and supply room and board for the summer. "The wages are good. The housing conditions are excellent and the corporations making the request are reliable," Urban League secretary William H. Baldwin wrote in notifying the executive board of a special meeting to consider "the advisability of our undertaking the task of supplying these corporations with such labor." [27] The League decided to go ahead with the project, and by the end of the summer it had sent 200 permanent workers and over 500 students to Connecticut. The experiment proved a success, thanks largely to "the efficient and able manner" in which the League handled it, the Tobacco Association said. The Negro students were "giving satisfaction," and the tobacco growers planned to rehire them the next year.[28]

The students returned not only the next season, but in 1918 as well. The Urban League cooperated with Negro colleges in selecting summer workers (many of whom were found through ads in the *Defender* and other black newspapers), arranging for their transportation, and supervising them on the job. The responsibilities of coordinating the employment program required that the National League hire an additional worker. The Tobacco Association reimbursed the League for his salary, for newspaper advertising and other miscellaneous expenses, and for meals and transportation for workers en route to Connecticut. Beyond this, however, the League made no special charges for its services, on the reasoning that "we were helping our boys as much as we were aiding the . . . Tobacco Corporation." [29]

On balance, the tobacco growers remained satisfied with the performance of their new Negro employees. There were occasional points of irritation; "To be honest and fair with you," F. B. Griffin, the president of the Association, wrote Eugene Kinckle Jones in 1918, "our Negro boys have not come out anywhere as good as in previous years." Of 122 whom his company had brought north that summer, 7 had joined the army and 33 had "simply left." "We go to work and make arrangements to board and feed and care for them, advance them money with which to get up here, and then they start out looking for other jobs. Especially if they have paid up their fair [*sic*], they think that all obligations on their part to stay until October 1st have expired immediately." But Griffin agreed with his fellow planters that he would be willing to take on Negro students the following summer.[30] "We consider the connection a valuable asset," the manager of the Tobacco Association wrote in thanking the League for its services, "and we hope next season we will be able to do business again with you." [31]

By the following year, however, the war was over and the employment situation had changed. Both parties felt that the Connecticut tobacco experiment had come off creditably, but for revealingly different reasons. The Tobacco Association pointed out that theirs was an essential industry, and that each Negro student had rendered "patriotic services" by working in the fields during the summer. For blacks, however, there was more at stake than an opportunity to aid the war effort. The New York *Age* had recognized the challenge from the beginning; while the employ-

ment of Negro students "solved the labor problem from an economic standpoint," the *Age* pointed out, it also "served to give
the white people of this section of the country an insight into the
character and development of the Negro race which they could
have secured in no other way." [32]

The Urban League's success in sending black laborers to the
Connecticut tobacco fields led some of its spokesmen to claim
that it had fathered the entire Great Migration. As the Rev.
Adam Clayton Powell, Sr., saw it, "the rush began" once news of
the tobacco workers' good fortune spread through the South.
And the Connecticut experiment led directly to recruitment of
black workers by railroads and large corporations. Behind it all
stood the Urban League, "largely responsible," in Powell's words,
"for the great migration movement." [33]

IV

Such an interpretation ignores the complex interaction of multi-
ple factors that created the Great Migration, and it exaggerates
the Urban League's influence in sustaining it. It is certainly true,
however, that the League played a significant role in bringing migrants north. As a "carpenter and inside trim man" from Macon,
Georgia, wrote to "Mr. Hill as director" of the Chicago Urban
League, "I am reading of a peace in the Chicago Defender saying
when in need of a job apply to you. Of course I am in need of
work." The *Defender* advised its correspondents to contact the
League for advice on moving to Chicago. Letters "To the Urban
Committy" came from all parts of the South: "i seen in the defender that you are interested in the well fair of the colored people those of the class that is interested in them selves and coming
to the north for a better chance"; "I noticed an article in the Chicago Defender that officers and members of your organization of-
fier to assist any member of the race to secure steady employment
in small cities near Chicago"; "I seen where you are in need of
men and are also in the position for firms to seek you. I see where

you are in the lines of work for the betterment of the race." [34]

The *Defender* and other leading black newspapers carried ads placed by the League and its affiliates telling of employment opportunities in the North. Promises of "$3.60 Per Day," good housing facilities, nine-hour working days, and "advancement in pay and position for intelligent, efficient workmen" could not help but be attractive.[35] A league notice in the *Defender* for moulders and machinists in Detroit brought replies from as far away as Alabama, Georgia, and Florida, generally not from men experienced in these trades, but from those promising that they would be quick to learn. Each inquiry was eventually answered—but with some caution. "We have been swamped with letters from the South regarding employment . . . ," the Detroit Urban League executive told a typical correspondent. "There is plenty of work up here, but on the other hand, the cost of living is high and the demand for labor is not steady and for this reason, we cannot guarantee jobs to any one outside of Detroit." [36]

How many prospective migrants such advice may have deterred cannot be calculated. Those who were eager to go north captured the momentum and impetus behind the movement in letters written to family and friends and to newspapers in response to advertisements. The North represented freedom, dignity, and opportunity—in short, a better life. A young man from Houston seeking "to Better his Standing" wrote that he "wanted to leave the South and Go and Place where a man will Be any thing except A Ker." "I will gladly take position in northern city or county where a mans a man," a New Orleans resident echoed. The letters were both pathetic and optimistic, poignant and confident. "I am a man that would like to get work in some place where I can elevate my self & family," a Mobile correspondent explained. For a black man in Charleston, the North promised "opportunity and chance of advancement as far as my ability is capable." Like many others, an Alabamian wanted "to get where i can put my children in schol." Southern blacks sought "a chance to get work," "any kind of honest labor," "a good

position where I can earn a good liveing." "I am not coming to
live on flowry Beds of ease," wrote the head of a New Orleans
family, "for I am a man who works and wish to make the best
I can out of life." His law school education, a sixty-three-
year-old Memphian was quick to point out, had "not swelled" his
head. "I can perform janitors duties, tend bar, or grocery store, as
clerk," he wrote. "I am willing to do almost anything I can do
that there is a dollar to it." [37]

Those who migrated wrote home in dazzling terms describing
the opportunities they found. "I was promoted on the first of the
month," a new Chicagoan boasted. "I was made first assistant to
the head carpenter when he is out of the place I take everything
in charge and was raised to $95. a month." From Dixon, Illinois,
came a report of a raise "to three dollars a day for ten hours—
eleven hrs. a day $3.19 . . . [and] for night work $3.90." [38]
Daily wages for unskilled labor in the North often equalled
weekly wages in the South.[39] From East Chicago, Indiana, a migrant wrote, "Never pay less than $3.00 per day or (10) hours.
. . . Piece work men can make from $6 to $8 per day. . . . People are coming here every day and are finding employment.
Nothing here but money and it is not hard to get." From Cleveland: "me and my family makes one hundred three darlers and 60
cents every ten days." [40] A "star molder" in a Chicago foundry
who had left Kentucky in 1910 corroborated the views of the
newer arrivals: "make as much as any man in the place. . . .
There is more chance here to learn a trade than in the South. I
live better, can save more, and I feel more like a man." [41]

Statistics bear out the enthusiasm these migrants expressed over
their newfound economic opportunities. In Philadelphia the
Armstrong Association's placements more than doubled from 583
in 1914–15 to 1413 in 1915–16; the following year the number climbed to 2019, and in 1917–18 the Association located
2382 jobs.[42] The most striking result of the migration was the decline of domestic and personal service as the major source of
employment for blacks in the city. In Chicago, for instance,
the percentage of gainfully employed Negroes engaged in

manufacturing grew from 15 in 1910 to 36 in 1920, while the percentage of those in trade rose from 5 to 19. At the same time, the percentage in domestic and personal service dropped from 60 to 28. The effects of the migrations become even more apparent in the records of individual companies; for example, 62 manufacturers, employing 1346 black workers in 1915, had hired 10,587 by 1920.[43] In Pittsburgh the number of blacks employed by twenty of the largest industrial plants grew from 2550 prior to 1916 to 8325 by the summer of 1917. Attractive wages went hand in hand with industrial opportunity; 95 per cent of more than 500 migrants interviewed in Pittsburgh in 1917 were earning more than $2.00 a day, while in the South only 44 per cent of them had attained that wage level.[44]

Life outside the South had other advantages, too. A Philadelphia newcomer who found economic security ("$75 per month" plus "enough insurance to pay me $20 per week if I am not able to be on duty") summed up the noneconomic benefits that made the North so attractive: "dont have to mister every little white boy comes along I havent heard a white man call a colored a nigger you no now—since I been in the state of Pa. I can ride in the electric street and steam cars any where I get a seat. . . . and if you are first in a place here shoping you dont have to wait until the white folks get thro tradeing." "Oh, I have children in school every day with the white children," an Indianan added almost as an afterthought.[45] The North meant "freedom of speech and action," "no lynching or Jim Crow." "You can live without fear," a migrant told the Chicago Commission on Race Relations.[46] A newcomer in Chicago expressed best of all why it felt so good to be out of the South. "I should have been here 20 years ago," he wrote home late in 1917. "I just begin to feel like a man. It's a great deal of pleasure in knowing that you have got some privilege. My children are going to the same school with whites and I dont have to umble to no one. I have registered—Will vote the next election and there isnt any 'yes sir' and 'no sir'— its all yes and no and Sam and Bill." [47]

But the North was not an untarnished pot of gold. All too few

migrants realized that attractive wages went hand in hand with
high-priced living—"they give you big money for what you
do," a Pittsburgher reported, "but they charge you big things for
what you get." Housing was at a premium; as one migrant wrote,
"The people are Begging for some whears to sta." [48] In Philadelphia, an investigator reported, space was so tight that press accounts spoke of Negroes "herded together like cattle." [49] In Pittsburgh, half of the single male migrants interviewed lived four or
more to a room. Rooming houses frequented by migrants were
generally "unsanitary" and "dilapidated," with sagging plaster,
broken windows, inadequate light and ventilation, and little or no
indoor plumbing. Among migrant families, housing conditions
were equally poor; 77 of 157 families investigated lived in one
room each, and of the 47 who lived in three or more rooms, 38
were forced to take in lodgers to make ends meet. "The rents paid
for such quarters," an investigator noted, "are often beyond belief." [50] In Chicago it was the same story: the most common Negro dwellings were in varying stages of serious disrepair, while
"the lodger evil" was so widespread that 62 per cent of 274 families studied had taken in paying boarders.[51]

In addition to problems of physical shelter, migrants often con-
fronted a threatening moral climate and social environment.
Cleveland, for instance, struck one newcomer as "a fine place to
make money," but "one of the worst places in principle you ever
look on in your life." It was almost impossible, he found, to raise
children "like they should be" in a city "crowded with the lowest negroes you ever meet. . . . all kinds of loffers. gamblers
pockit pickers you are not safe here to walk on the streets at
night you are libble to get kill at eny time." "I like the money
O.K.," a Pittsburgh correspondent recorded, "but I like the
South betterm for my Pleasure this city is too fast for me." [52] A
stockyards laborer who migrated from Mississippi soon learned
that Chicago was not the "wide open . . . friendly and free" city
he first thought. "It seems that there is more discrimination and
unfriendly feeling than I thought. I notice it at work and in public places." [53]

Overcoming these rough spots required professional help—the kind the Urban League's social work efforts were designed to provide. But helping newcomers cope with their new social and moral circumstances was only part of the job. The widely touted economic heaven was not accessible to everyone, and it was not guaranteed to last. Individual employers had to be convinced that Negroes could do the job; companies had to be persuaded to match the high wages and fair treatment some Negro workers enjoyed. And the workers themselves had to be helped to adjust to the expectations of their employers, both in technical performance and in general behavior.

The migrations created great opportunities for blacks, and they also posed important challenges for the Urban League. They pushed the League to become a national movement, and they forced it to perfect its programs.

8 THE URBAN LEAGUE RESPONDS

The migrations provided an opportunity for a full-scale testing of the program outlined by the Urban League's founders. They created a laboratory for the development of the organization's practical work, and they acted as the catalyst in its expansion into a national movement. In 1915 the League and its affiliates had spent just under $45,000; by 1920 their total annual expenditures were about $145,100.[1] The increase came about because of the migrants.

I

In the League's view, the newcomers were "at once both the despair and the hope of many a Northern city." The migrations would have dreadful social consequences if these blacks were "permitted to pack themselves into overcrowded colonies and drift into disease and crime through sheer ignorance of how to live and how to find work and hold a job in the North." But the influx could have hopeful results if the newcomers were "taken hold of upon their arrival and . . . taught how to become independent, productive citizens at a time when effective labor is at a premium."[2]

Despite the drawbacks to the resettlement of hundreds of thousands of Negroes in northern ghettos, the migration had its positive aspects. As the League's president pointed out when the executive board first discussed the migration, the movement "might be used to effect two results: first, to improve the conditions under which Negroes existed in the south . . . and second, to grasp the opportunities in the north for new fields of labor." [3]

Job opportunities were one kind of challenge confronting the Urban League. Perhaps equally pressing was the matter of the general acculturation of those who came to fill them. The northern Negro press urged responsible individuals and agencies to help the migrants adjust to their new homes. "What they need is that every church and social worker help them," the *Christian Recorder* stated. ". . . Get these Negroes in your churches; make them welcome; don't turn up your nose and let the saloon man and the gambler do all the welcoming." "A heavy responsibility rests upon every colored leader . . . to take an especial interest in their newly arriving brethren," the New York *News* agreed. "You must teach them not to take their liberty to be ladies and gentlemen for license to degrade themselves and their race here. . . . Urge them to get steady work and settle down. Urge them not to forget the simple life that they lived down home. Urge them to become good citizens and better parents. Urge them to go to church, to lead patient Christian lives, and all will come out well in the end." [4]

Responding to these urgings and to its own perceptions of the need for action, the Urban League invited representatives of employers (for example, the Erie Railroad, Pennsylvania iron and steel foundries), labor, government agencies, churches, welfare groups, schools, the press, and other interested organizations to a conference on Negro migration in New York in January 1917. Beyond explaining the causes and consequences of the migration, the purpose of the conference was to impress upon the assembled leaders the importance of aiding the migrants' adjustment to the urban environment, and to consider the most effective methods for such assistance.[5]

Despite the migration of "unprecedented numbers" that would

continue to increase in volume, the conferees agreed that the "great mass" of Negroes would remain in the South, making it essential that southern whites and Negroes reach a better common understanding. They proposed the formation of organizations to promote interracial goodwill, to study the socio-economic needs of southern Negroes and develop agencies and activities to meet them, and to improve the industrial efficiency of Negroes and the conditions under which they worked. Similar organizations in the North would fulfill the same responsibilities, acquaint migrants with common public services and facilities, and teach them the rudiments of life in the North—dress and personal habits, behavior on the job, the dangers of "unscrupulous or vicious persons" and "questionable resorts." [6] In effect, the conference endorsed the expansion of the Urban League idea.

A spokesman for the Boston NAACP tried unsuccessfully to amend the conference resolutions so as to encourage Negroes to migrate until such time as the South should grant them full legal, political, and civil rights and protection. This effort reflected the view of the NAACP's *Crisis*, which held that the only opportunity for Negroes was in the North, and which supported migration as a vehicle for advancement and a way of protesting against lynching and disfranchisement.[7] The conference, however, neither endorsed nor condemned the migration; instead, as the Baltimore *Afro-American* reported approvingly, "they resolved and rightly to accept the migration as a fact and to devote their energies to bettering the conditions that have resulted from it." [8]

Despite the urging of the press, the Urban League never engaged in resettlement of Negroes to relieve congestion in urban areas, nor did it promote any planned distribution of migrants to match available employment and desirable living conditions. And, unlike organizations aiding Jewish immigrants, it did not encourage Negro migrants to take up agricultural pursuits. Perhaps some kind of planned resettlement of migrants would have alleviated some of the problems Negroes encountered in cities; yet the Urban League felt that its main responsibility was to work with migrants where they were, and not to tell them where to go.

Prudence dictated that the League try to exercise at least some very minimal stabilizing influence. In a letter distributed to the black press at the height of the migration, Eugene Kinckle Jones urged "right-thinking Negroes . . . to discourage the wholesale migration of shiftless people," since "indolent, inefficient men," quick to lose their jobs, would only "become a burden to the Northern communities and bring reproach and humiliation to thrifty colored citizens in communities where white people [had] not hitherto considered Negroes undesirables." On the other hand, as Jones was careful to point out, migrants who were "sober and responsible" and who knew "how to give an honest day's toil" could secure and hold "good positions." [9] This kind of balancing summed up the Urban League's stance.

Following the example of the National League for the Protection of Colored Women, the Urban League sent potential migrants information about northern city life, warned them of the dangers ahead, and set out to help those who resolved nonetheless to come north. The League stationed travelers' aid workers at critical points along the journey.[10] It issued public notices—for example, a warning that "at the Piers in New York, Philadelphia and Baltimore a large number of crooks, thieves, pretenders, and labor agents hang out to greet the colored brother from the South," who was likely to be "robbed and left absolutely penniless in a strange city without friends." "If relatives do not meet you," the notice continued, "ask a policeman to direct you" to the Urban League office. Cards distributed in southern cities reiterated the importance of knowing "exactly where you are going" and of being met in the North by "some trustworthy person" to avoid getting "confused and lost in the great crowds at the piers and railroad stations," adding that migrants should be sure to get in touch with "responsible" Northerners before setting out from the South. And they urged travelers to take along warm clothing, "even during the summer." [11]

II

In order to carry on its work with the migrants, the Urban League had to expand quickly. The need for social welfare and employment services led to a flood of applications from cities eager to establish League affiliates.[12] Between 1916 and 1919 the League added thirteen new affiliates, most of them in major industrial magnets like Chicago, Cleveland, Columbus, Detroit, Milwaukee, Newark, Pittsburgh, and St. Louis. In 1918 the League had a total of twenty-seven affiliates.[13]

The NAACP, by contrast, had 310 branches with 88,292 members within a decade of its founding.[14] The primary reason for the relatively few Urban League affiliates was the League's insistence that all affiliates be staffed by paid professionals; those of the NAACP were almost all volunteer groups and thus much more easily assembled.[15] But it was also true that the Urban League had neither the personnel nor the money to devote to the work of national expansion. The initial policy was to have executive secretaries of affiliates in large cities "assist in organizing smaller neighboring cities."[16] T. Arnold Hill shouldered the assignment of organizing the western field while holding down two successive full-time jobs—first as executive secretary of the Chicago Urban League, and then, after 1925, as director of the National Department of Industrial Relations. Jesse O. Thomas took over the southern field in 1919, but the requirements that affiliates be governed by interracial boards handicapped progress in organizing the South.

The National Urban League adopted formal terms of affiliation governing local Urban Leagues in May 1918.[17] Affiliates were expected to incorporate in their constitutions the principles governing the National Urban League and to implement them in practical activities according to the particular needs of the local community. One requirement was the establishment of interracial executive boards. The "standard program" for local work began with an investigation of black living conditions. The next step

Urban League Affiliates, 1919

SOURCE: Organizations Affiliated with the National Urban League — Year 1919, NUL Papers

was to determine which problems could "be met by coordinating existing agencies," and which would require "new machinery." While the League provided program guidelines, affiliates were free to tailor their work to local conditions.[18]

The *raison d'être* for the new affiliates was to help migrants adjust to northern cities. Most often, blacks arrived in the North with high expectations but without a job or a place to live. "The danger" in this, as some migrants themselves explained, was that it was all too easy to get "among the wrong class of people"—people eager "to take advantage of the ignorance of newcomers." [19] Completely ignorant of the North, "thousands of unattached young women flocked to Newark," the executive there recalled. Without so much as a YWCA to turn to, "They simply stood out and alone without a buffer of any sort." [20] How to reach these newcomers before they were led astray was the first hurdle a local Urban League had to overcome. Some of them might have read League ads in the *Defender* or heard about the organization, perhaps through their pastor in the South. But the odds were against a migrant finding the League on his own initiative. Instead, the League had to go to the migrants to make itself known.

A critical time to locate migrants was immediately upon their arrival in the city. Black employees at railroad and bus stations distributed cards directing "New Comers to Detroit" to the League's offices for help in finding "employment and . . . decent lodgings FREE of charge." The Chicago League's travelers' aid worker gave out 10,000 informational cards in the League's first eight months of operation. Urban Leagues also went directly into black neighborhoods. "Club women" volunteering for the Chicago affiliate carried "verbal advice" and "card[s] of admonition" to "the homes of . . . the southern people." A special police officer, appointed at the Detroit League's instigation to work among migrants, gave out information about its services. The League covered churches and popular places of amusement, both of which would immediately attract newcomers to the city. At a

Detroit movie theater patronized by blacks, the operator ran lantern slides stating "that employment and other services [could] be secured free at the office of the League." Pastors prefaced Sunday sermons with a few words about the organization.[21] In Newark, April 1, 1917, became "Negro Welfare League Sunday," when local churches invited League representatives to the pulpit to speak briefly about its work.[22]

The needs of the newcomers spanned a broad spectrum. Where would they live? Until they found jobs, how would they get money for food? Coming from the South, where would they find winter clothes? In a complex urban society, how would a poorly educated, often illiterate population get along?

Some of these needs were best met by charities, but few private charities in the 1910s concerned themselves with blacks. Some would have been the province of public welfare, but it was years before a comprehensive welfare system existed. The Urban League eschewed the role of relief-giving agency, but the lack of alternatives sometimes meant that it had to step into the breach. "If someone came to our office at five o'clock on a winter day and said, 'I got no coal' or 'I got no food in the house,' we didn't say that was a matter for the Associated Charities," the former executive of the New Jersey League recalled. "We had to find a way to get meat and coal to them. We did practically anything without ever losing sight of the principles and purposes for which the League was founded." [23] Thus his League solicited donations of food as well as old clothes that could be refurbished by a sewing committee of well-to-do volunteers. In cases of extreme need, where aid was unavailable elsewhere, the organization distributed food, garments, and even monetary relief.[24] But relief was only peripheral to the League's principal tasks: finding jobs, housing, and recreational opportunities for blacks, and overseeing the most elementary aspects of their behavior.

The pressure of an exploding black population combined with the constraints of residential segregation to make decent, inexpensive housing extremely hard to come by. As a stopgap measure the

Detroit Urban League set up cots in its community center for a few of the newest arrivals. It arranged with some factories to guarantee payment of the migrants' first weeks' bills at restaurants and boardinghouses. It investigated and kept a list of empty houses and furnished rooms, which was made available to new-comers and to factories employing blacks. The League persuaded two of the largest foundries in the city to build low-priced homes near the plant for their black workers. And, in an ingenious effort, it bought up leases of disorderly houses ordered closed by the police and had them taken over by manufacturers for rental to blacks in their employ.[25] In Newark the Negro Welfare League compiled a list of people willing to take lodgers and houses avail-able for rental by blacks. In the tradition of the League for the Protection of Colored Women, it ran its own home for black working girls.[26] In Springfield, Massachusetts, the executive of the Dunbar Community League arranged for a "generous phil-anthropist" to buy a block of eight apartments, which the League managed and rented to black families at reasonable rates.[27] Women volunteers in Chicago inspected accommodations that were to be inhabited by the newcomers.[28]

The Urban League attached great importance to the provision of adequate recreational opportunities.[29] The black migrant needed wholesome amusements; otherwise, cast adrift as he was from "the restraining influence of his family [and] friends," he would surely succumb to the temptations of "vicious attractions entirely new to him." In this respect, however, the cultural offer-ings made available to immigrants at settlement houses did not provide the right model. "The hard-working laborer recently from a rural section of Alabama cannot be attracted away from saloon or pool-room with art lectures or literary forums or even the facilities of the average Y.M.C.A.," the head of the Detroit Urban League pointed out. Recreation that would satisfy such a man had to be "active and practical, to a certain extent primitive. If he does not get it under wholesome conditions, he will seek it under evil ones." The Urban League's solution was to set up weekly ten-cent newcomers' community dances and to organize baseball and basketball teams and other athletic activities, some of them in industrial plants that employed blacks. Proceeds from the dances supported scouting activities for children of the newcomers.[30] The Negro Welfare League in Newark organized monthly parties "for the Strangers" and persuaded the Board of Education to open a school building in a black neighborhood to be used as a social center on Friday evenings. There the migrants found games, sports, and musical activities under the League's supervision.[31]

III

The Urban League's work with blacks in the cities extended to the most basic level of manners and morals. In the tradition of Booker T. Washington, it began at the very bottom in its efforts to mold black migrants. "Use the toothbrush, the hairbrush and comb, and soap and water freely," the St. Louis League instructed.[32] In the League's view, men and women fresh from the rural South could not be expected to adapt automatically to the accepted standards of hygiene and behavior in the urban North. Migrants told the Chicago Commission on Race Relations that "getting used to climate and houses," "adjustment to city customs," and "getting used to the ways of the people" were the main difficulties confronting newcomers in Chicago.[33] The same was certainly true in other cities. As the Detroit Urban League pointed out, "Habits of dress and behavior which are perfectly alright in a small town . . . are perniciously conspicuous in a community like Detroit." [34] "Be clean, ladies and gentlemen," the Chicago *Defender* admonished in a representative editorial in March 1917; "water is cheap and deportment should be at a discount; avoid loud talking, and boisterous laughter on streetcars and in public places." [35] There was at least a touch of black bourgeois condescension in the *Defender*'s prescriptions for the "careless and indifferent members of the Race." [36] But the Urban

League took essentially the same view: "The need for cleaner streets, well kept houses, better deportment, more attention to personal hygiene and stricter conformity to other civic requirements was never so apparent and urgently necessary as now," the Chicago League reported in 1918. Accordingly, in its dealings with migrants, the organization constantly stressed "the necessity for strict application to duties, punctuality, efficiency and proper deportment." [37]

The Urban League followed through on this concern for proper standards (in short, standards commonly accepted by middle-class whites and blacks alike) in a variety of ways. Through mothers' clubs and home visiting, migrants were instructed about methods of housekeeping as well as diet and clothing appropriate to a northern climate. Staff workers and volunteers in Chicago carried the League's message "to the homes of the unenlightened." [38] The "friendly visitor" of the Negro Welfare League in Newark handed out cards "with a few terse hints as to the care of house and health." [39] The League cooperated with the local Board of Health in writing and distributing a circular on "essential rules of health" which would "suggest to them [newcomers] things which would enable them to more quickly fit themselves in new environment." [40] The special police officer selected by the Detroit Urban League reminded newcomers congregating in the streets "not to make a nuisance of themselves by blockading sidewalks, boisterous behavior and the like." [41] Public meetings in Chicago "served to welcome the strangers," but they also "offered an opportunity for general advice, health talks, and admonition." [42]

A group of "earnest race men" affiliated with the Urban League and local churches established a "Dress Well Club" in Detroit "to create a better impression of the Negro by attention to dress, personal appearance and public behavior." In leaflets, the club urged blacks to hold to high standards in order to avoid intensifying "prejudice, race friction and discrimination." Proper deportment was especially critical under circumstances of interracial contact: "Don't carry on loud conversations or use vulgar or obscene language in street cars, streets, or in public places," the Urban League admonished. "Don't be rude and ugly to people on the streets. Be courteous and polite and thereby keep out of trouble." "Don't make lots of unnecessary noise going to and from baseball games." [43]

Appearance was as important as behavior. The Newark Negro Welfare League spoke of its responsibility "to enlighten new comers in adjusting themselves in new conditions; wearing proper clothing especially." [44] "Don't crowd inside of a street car filled with people in your dirty, greasy overalls," the Detroit League admonished. "Wear regular street clothes when you go into the streets. . . . Don't sit in front of your house or . . . [in] public places with your shoes off. Don't wear overalls on Sunday. . . . Try to dress neatly at all times, but don't be a dude or wear flashy clothes. They are as undesirable and as harmful as unclean clothes." To underscore the point, a pamphlet of "Helpful Hints" printed contrasting pictures of a black woman seated in front of her house. The sloppily dressed, "disorderly" woman slouched on a stoop littered with papers, with a broom propped behind her in the doorway. Her "neatly clothed and orderly" counterpart sat primly on the steps, holding a folded newspaper in her lap. [45]

Detroit's "Helpful Hints" had their counterparts in other Urban Leagues. St. Louis' pamphlet, *A New Day*, explained the rationale behind the behavior it prescribed. Proper behavior in public was simple "decency"; cleanliness "promotes health" and "means longer life." A neat appearance "wins others' appreciation." The Chicago affiliate issued placards with the telltale question "Which?" printed under pictures "graphically contrasting good and bad habits of living." Instead of Detroit's "Don'ts," Chicago substituted a positive "pledge of conduct" directed toward the same results. [46]

Some of this advice may sound fatuous, but it was geared to very real contemporary conditions. For instance, the Chicago Commission on Race Relations found evidence of white reaction against the "ill-smelling clothes" of black laborers, their "loud laughing and talking," their "uncivilized" behavior on street-cars.[47] No matter how trivial such matters may seem, the Urban League was addressing itself to actual sources of interracial tension.

The lessons inherent in the Urban League's advice touched every aspect of time-honored middle-class virtues. The people it prized, the Armstrong Association announced, exhibited "skill, faithfulness, honesty, sobriety and cleanliness."[48] Migrants were admonished to "Get a job at once" and to be "on time, industrious, efficient and sober" in order to hold it. "Buying on the installment plan" was a mistake; opening a savings account showed good sense.[49] In Newark each friendly visitor taught her charges "Provident Savings."[50] "Your banker will gladly show you how to invest," St. Louis volunteered.[51] It was important to learn thrift and foresight: "Save some of [your money] for extra clothing and fuel for the winter and to take care of your family and yourself when sickness comes," Detroit instructed.[52] In Cleveland the Negro Welfare Association sponsored savings and thrift competitions, while in Newark the Negro Welfare League held "Food Conservation" meetings.[53] In the spirit of the progressive efficiency movement, Cleveland taught "economy of . . . time and energy."[54] Active church membership and school attendance rounded out the litany: going to church was one's "duty," while going to school bred "self-respect."[55] Following these prescriptions redounded to the benefit not only of the individual migrant, but of his entire race. And many of the migrants knew it; "on the whole," the Armstrong Association found, "these people have come to us determined to attempt the standards of life which we offer them."[56]

IV

This effort of the middle class to mould the behavior of the migrants after its own image was clearly a one-way process. There was never any hint that the black bourgeoisie had anything to learn from its newly arrived neighbors. Nor was there much tolerance for diversity in value systems or lifestyles. In George Haynes's view, the migrants' "susceptibility to guidance, their respectful submission to authority, and their eagerness to adapt themselves to the order and routine of industry and life of the communities" they entered provided "significant evidence of moral progress" within the race.[57]

In part the concern for "civilizing" the migrants expressed the traditional attempt of racial reformers to instill in lower-class blacks or immigrants the Puritan values of thrift, industry, sobriety, and piety.[58] It revealed the sense of superiority that some middle-class blacks felt toward the migrants—as George Haynes described them, "these inefficient, groping seekers for something better." [59] It demonstrated a hard-headed recognition that the unintentionally uncouth, raucous behavior of "ignorant and rough-mannered" migrants sometimes resulted in racial friction.[60] But it also betrayed the embarrassment of the black bourgeoisie and its fear that white distaste for the conduct of the migrants would lead to a reaction against the entire race. As a black civil engineer in Chicago put it, "We all suffer for what one fool will do." [61]

There was ample precedent for this reaction in the experiences of earlier immigrant groups. Well-established German Jews in New York saw the mass migration of Eastern European Jews in the last decades of the nineteenth century as a threat to their "hard-won respectability." "The thoroughly acclimated American Jew . . . ," the *Hebrew Standard* explained in 1894, "stands apart from the seething mass of Jewish immigrants . . . and looks upon them as in a stage of development pitifully low." Put off by the dress, language, ceremonials, and behavior of the newcomers, many German Jews shunned them. Others, however, worked through social service and charitable agencies to "civilize" them in their own image. In the 1880s and 1890s Jewish schools and agencies offered vocational instruction, English classes, and training "in the amenities, cleanliness, and the practical home and industrial arts." [62] Nevertheless, the worst fears of the German Jews came true. By the early part of the twentieth century the upsurge of Jewish immigration had bred an increase in anti-Semitism, and even the oldest Jewish families began to experience social exclusion and discrimination in jobs and housing.[63]

Just as "distinctions between 'the better class of Jews' and the others collapsed beneath the pressure of numbers," so the mass migration of blacks to northern cities jeopardized the standing of long-established black residents.[64] As the NAACP's field secretary summed it up, the "immediate effect" of the migrations on northern Negroes was to "set [them] back, at least in present happiness." They began to experience "discrimination and humiliation where [they] never knew it before. [They] began to be unlawfully segregated—barred from eating and drinking places, theatres, parks, beaches, and other public resorts." [65]

In Philadelphia, for example, the "relatively small population of Negroes of culture, education and some financial means . . . had always enjoyed the same social and educational facilities as the whites and courteous treatment from them." But with the rapid increase in the black population, drawn largely from "a group of generally uneducated and untrained persons, these privileges were withdrawn." The migration accelerated efforts to segregate schools and places of public accommodation. The rowdy behavior of some of the newcomers reflected badly on the black population as a whole. Understandably, long-time black residents blamed the migrants for what they saw as a setback to racial progress.[66]

Much of the blame was probably warranted, but it was easily overstated. "Old Settlers" in Chicago were correct in saying that the migrants had "made it hard for all of us," but it was an exaggeration to say that in the "good old days" before World War I "there wasn't any difference shown in color at all." Race relations were certainly better before the migration than after it, but even then they were far from perfect. No matter how different things really were, it was important that older black residents believed that the newcomers "brought discrimination with them." [67]

Just as it had in the case of the German Jews, this attitude among established blacks produced two reactions: some "stood aloof" from the newcomers, while others tried actively to reform them.[68] The Urban League chose the latter approach. It consciously described its work with the migrants in terms of Americanization efforts for immigrants, though it felt that it had the easier task.[69] "The Negro . . . needs help only in securing the opportunity to embrace American advantages," George Haynes explained. "He does not have to forget foreign customs and foreign loyalties for he is not a naturalized but a natural-born American citizen." [70]

The Urban League's concern for "civilizing" the migrants doubtless included a measure of altruism. But in large part it stemmed from realistic self-interest. As the Detroit League put it, "If we don't help the Negro immigrant . . . we are going to see a rapid growth in discrimination, segregation etc. The impressions of a race depend upon the impressions created by the individual of that race." [71]

Probably the most important reason for the emphasis on standards related to employment. "Get a job, get there on time, be regular, master it, dignify it, do better than the other man," the St. Louis Urban League urged; "this breaks down prejudice." [72] A major obstacle to employment opportunities for blacks was the common assumption among employers that blacks were by nature lazy, shiftless, stupid, and unreliable. If there was to be any hope of expanding job opportunities in industries, it was imperative that blacks hired during the war emergency not behave in such a way as to confirm these views. It was also true, however, that most blacks from the rural South had had little experience to prepare them to adapt quickly to the routine expected in northern industries. When the Bush Terminal Company in Brooklyn integrated its dock workers, an Urban League investigator found that "irregular old habits accquired in the lazy industrial system of the South and the Islands" helped make the new black employees "more unreliable, unsteady and inefficient." [73] "Adjustment to working conditions," one migrant told the Chicago Commission on Race Relations, seemed to be a major difficulty confronting newcomers to that city.[74] Thus the Urban League tried especially hard to keep new employees on their toes.

"No person was sent out to work," the executive of the Detroit League recalled, "until he had given a pledge to stick to his job, to be punctual, to avoid pay-day lay-off, to be pleasant, and to maintain good health habits." [75] A representative from the Negro Welfare League worked part-time at Newark's Municipal Bureau of Labor to advise job applicants on better appearance and proper behavior on the job.[76] Urban Leagues persuaded small industries as well as giants like Dodge, Armour, and U.S. Steel to hire Negro welfare workers to ease the transition to an integrated work force. They adjusted disputes and gave black workers pointers on their performance; they also advised management on policies of recruitment, recreation, and housing that would promote "a better efficiency and esprit de corps." [77] Eugene Kinckle Jones traveled to spread the League's influence beyond its affiliates. On a typical trip to Buffalo, he advised the American Brass Company "on methods to be used to get more regularity in attendance and efficiency in the men," and he urged the employees "to be more prompt and regular in attendance, more guarded as to their health and moral life, more efficient in their labor and more friendly toward their fellow workmen." [78]

League staff members visited factories for lunch-hour pep talks on the virtues of good manners, proper conduct, cleanliness, punctuality, and efficiency on the job. His objective, the Newark executive explained, was "primarily to make these men conscious of their duty to their employers in this, our great industrial opportunity." [79] In Detroit the speakers circulated cards entitled "Why He Failed." Not surprisingly, the unsuccessful worker "watched the clock," "was always behind," "was not ready for the next step," and failed to "put his heart in the work." [80] Such a message, the Baltimore *Afro-American* felt, was "good advice, not only to workmen from the South, but to workmen from the North." [81]

The need for such instruction applied even to categories of employment traditionally most accessible to blacks. Affiliates sponsored days' workers' classes to train migrant women in the fundamentals of cooking, laundering, and housekeeping—"things which simple as they seem these women do not know how to perform thoroughly or with dispatch at the present time." "We are not trying to keep colored people in domestic service," the Detroit League explained, " . . . but in this particular case, the women can do nothing but domestic work. We want to help them to make as much as possible in this so that they can fit themselves and their children for better things." [82]

The point was hammered home again and again: unless they made "the best possible impression," blacks could not expect to keep their jobs.[83] The future of the individual worker was only part of what was at stake, for his performance reflected inevitably on the race as a whole. "Every colored man and woman who makes good in a job of any kind," the Detroit Urban League pointed out, "creates opportunity for others of the race." [84] "RE-MEMBER," the Chicago Urban League wrote to new employees of firms hiring blacks for the first time, "THAT THE RACE, IN THIS NEW WORK, IS ON TRIAL IN YOU." [85]

V

The Urban League, the Chicago *Defender* declared, was "doing wonders to help the working class." [86] The *Southern Workman* called the organization's efforts on behalf of the migrants "its chief and best work." "By its persistent efforts and effective methods," the magazine said, the Urban League was "establishing itself as a very valuable national medium for reaching helpfully all phases of the urban Negro's needs." [87] But the League's success is nearly impossible to measure. For the NAACP such measurement came more easily, since court decisions rendered or legislation passed could be assessed with some certainty as victories or defeats. Had the Urban League done well to organize a handful of sports teams? Or had it failed because it never touched most of the migrants who frequented pool halls and brothels? Was it progress to secure decent housing for employees of one company when tens of thousands of blacks remained in decaying tenements?

Even in the area of employment, ostensibly the simplest to quantify, any satisfactory measurement is extremely hard to come by. There are no reliable statistics for Urban League job placements on a national level, and local records are at best fragmentary. In Detroit, where the black population was estimated at 25,000 to 35,000 early in 1918, the Detroit Urban League claimed to have placed over 10,000 Negroes in jobs during 1917 and more than 12,000 during 1919.[88] In Chicago, where there were about 70,000 gainfully employed Negroes in 1920, the Urban League succeeded in placing 1792 workers in 1917; 4500 in 1918; 14,000 in 1919; and 15,000 in 1920. The employers included Swift, Armour, General Can, International Harvester, and Inland Steel.[89]

Such statistics sound impressive, but they lack any meaningful interpretive framework, cannot be verified, and should, therefore, be read with caution. Evidence from Cleveland and Newark suggests something about the ratio of job placements to job seekers; of 920 applicants for work during a six-month period in Cleveland in 1918, 782 were "suitably placed." [90] In June 1918 the New Jersey Negro Welfare League placed 58 of its 72 job applicants; in October and November of the following year, it found positions for 213 of 299 job seekers.[91] But such statistics are far from complete, and they yield no information as to the proportion of job seekers who may never have thought to contact the Urban League.

Generalizing from such shaky data is a hopeless task. By the end of 1920, the Urban League reported a nine-year total of

64,452 placements through the national office and the affiliates, many of these in positions "never before held" by blacks.[92] Assuming that these placements represented 64,452 different people, all of whom still held their jobs in 1920, that might mean, at most, that the League was responsible for close to 8 per cent of the positions held by gainfully employed Negroes in nonagricultural occupations outside the South in that year.[93] But none of these assumptions can be made with any reliability.

Nor can we be certain that the Urban League was doing very much to move blacks out of the servant classes. The Detroit Urban League placed 1000 workers in "employment other than unskilled labor" over a twelve-month period at the peak of the migration.[94] But in Philadelphia close to 90 per cent of the Armstrong Association's placements from mid-1915 to mid-1918 were still in domestic service.[95] Indeed, in 1917–18, at a time when industry was opening its doors to black workers, the Armstrong Association listed only 78 "factory" jobs—less than 2 per cent of all of its placements.

Even in instances where industrial placements were made, it is difficult to evaluate the League's influence in opening up the jobs. In 1919, League literature claimed, 135 industrial plants in various parts of the country employed Negroes for the first time, thanks to the urging of Urban League affiliates.[96] But these firms faced wartime labor shortages, and their decisions to hire blacks were probably as much (if not more) the product of self-interest as the result of the Urban League's importunings. At the very least the League functioned as a conduit, a means by which labor and seekers after labor could be brought together profitably. No doubt it helped to persuade some employers that it was safe to take the gamble of hiring blacks. Impressionistic contemporary evidence speaks favorably of the League's impact; the Chicago Commission on Race Relations, for example, stated that the local League affiliate placed "more Negroes in employment than any other agency in Chicago." [97] But the times gave the League's efforts a critical advantage, so that it is virtually impossible to tell where employment progress is attributable to the organization's work.

The real test for the Urban League still lay ahead. It was comparatively easy to find jobs for blacks when industries were desperate for workers. But when the war was over and labor was no longer in short supply, what would happen to the employment picture? The "normalcy" of the next decade, not the special circumstances of the war and the Great Migration, would provide a clear measure of the League's skill and influence.

9 RESTRUCTURING A NATIONAL MOVEMENT

Before the Urban League could face the challenges of the postwar decade, it had to resolve internal controversy over the structure of its executive leadership and the direction its programs should take.

I

George Haynes and the man he chose as his assistant, Eugene Kinckle Jones, could not have been more dissimilar. Haynes's mother worked as a domestic to support her son and daughter; Jones was the son of two college professors. Haynes grew up in Pine Bluff, Arkansas; Jones lived in Richmond, where he attended a private academy. Jones was "a very diplomatic operator," a long-time board member recalled; "people liked him and he liked people." Haynes, he felt, "was a less competent administrator." Jones was "smooth" and "persuasive"; Haynes tended to be "more contentious. He took a position and argued it and stood by it and I think people found him a little difficult to move." [1]

These differences were reason enough for Haynes to be jealous of his protégé. And with the Urban League headquartered in New York but officially directed by a college professor based in Nashville, there was also cause for friction. George Haynes came to New York whenever possible, but he had no hand in the day-to-day operations of the office, which Jones supervised. It was not uncommon for him to be informed by mail of decisions taken by the executive board.

Haynes was not always treated in a manner befitting the organization's chief executive officer. L. Hollingsworth Wood— secretary of the League and from the beginning one of its most influential white members—apparently did not know his executive secretary well enough to avoid addressing him as "Haines." In 1915 Haynes was forced into a protracted correspondence with Wood and assistant treasurer Victor H. McCutcheon— not over League policy, but over permission to buy a $21 file cabinet with a lock for his office.[2] While the League paid Haynes a flat $800 annually (Fisk paid the remainder of his salary), Jones's salary rose from $1500 in 1912–13 to $2500 in 1917–18. Over the next four years it doubled.[3]

While Haynes expressed concern over the delineation of his authority,[4] his presence at and preoccupation with Fisk worried the League. According to Haynes's biographer, his chief interest had always been the work at Fisk rather than the National Urban League. He had intended to remain in New York only long enough to get the League off the ground with secure financial support—at most, he thought, for a period of two years. Thereafter, he would devote more attention to Fisk. Within five years after the initial arrangement, he expected to give almost all his time to the university. Haynes's plans were clearly spelled out in his negotiations with Fisk, and officials of the university understood his priorities. As one of them told the president, Haynes's time in New York would give him experience for "inaugurating and carrying on similar work at Fisk." But there is no indication that he made his intentions plain to the Urban League, which understandably felt uneasy about the division of his efforts.[5]

At the instigation of Ruth Standish Baldwin, the League created a special committee in February 1912 to study the disposition of Haynes's time, since she felt that the New York work demanded more of his attention. "I am not satisfied with the

national accomplishment or outlook," Mrs. Baldwin wrote
Haynes in January 1914. "It really is awfully hard having your
chief energies absorbed by your college work! Yet at present, at
any rate, I do not see how it can be avoided." A little more than
a week later, she reiterated the point: "It is . . . a growing disad-
vantage that our director is in Nashville & all the working members of the com[mittee] in New York! It has got to be very
seriously discussed when you come on." She also admonished him
that his trip north ought to include "a frank talk" with Wood
"about any matters on which you are not quite in unison, if
such there are." [6]

The real problem went well beyond the physical separation of
director from headquarters. While Haynes was at Fisk, Jones was
building an organizational structure in New York and winning
the loyalties of its members. Most important, he and the board
were emphasizing lines of work that began to diverge perceptibly
from Haynes's ideas about the course the Urban League should
follow. Haynes was primarily interested in working with liberal
arts colleges to develop trained urban Negro leadership. He believed that other organizations should take responsibility for practical social service programs. Under Jones's influence, however,
the emphasis of the Urban League centered more and more heavily on the extension of direct social welfare and service programs.[7]

The conflict between Haynes and Jones surfaced in 1916, in a
dispute over the League's priorities. Haynes thought that the
League ought to be concentrating on the development of New
York and Nashville as models of what could be accomplished
through interracial cooperation. By engaging in comparable "educational work" and "practical field work," the two centers would
prove the adaptability of the League's program to conditions peculiar to each geographical region. Later, the League could send
trained workers to direct similar programs in cities throughout the country. But it was folly, particularly in the South, to attempt to create interracial committees and programs of work

"before the demonstration [had] created a belief of its possibility and [had] shown correctly what [could] be done."

What Haynes saw happening, though, was an increasing investment of League time and money in the establishment of affiliates—and with this a widening "topical division between the educational work and the practical field work." Given the scarce resources at the League's disposal, it hardly made sense to him to devote so much attention to the extension of "practical betterment" before a strong base for training qualified workers had been established.

Haynes's distress grew out of genuine philosophical convictions. He opposed an organizational structure in which he and Jones would divide their authority according to function rather than region. Separating "training of workers" from "practical betterment" seemed to him to contradict "the best thought of modern education," which was "to prevent as far as possible the break between the practical life of the world and the preparation for that life." [8] But he also felt that the League's work in Nashville was being slighted. With New York "well on its feet," he told Hollingsworth Wood, he had believed that Nashville would be the next priority. The growing attention to traveling supervision and field work, combined with continued financial neglect of the South, led him "to fear that the case [was] different." [9] In 1914–15 the League had budgeted $750 for the southern headquarters and $8237 for national work. The next year Jones and Haynes recommended $4450 for Nashville and $8800 for New York but the executive board approved budgets of $1100 and $8320, respectively. For 1917–18 Haynes said that he needed $5425 to run the southern headquarters. The League gave him $1950, while it appropriated $10,360 for national work.[10]

It was time to reach a clear understanding of "where Nashville and Fisk stand in the League's plans . . . ," Haynes wrote. "I shall be glad if it may be determined what we have meant by Nashville as Southern Headquarters and training center." [11] After all, the work in Nashville had been his major contribution to the

Urban League movement. When it got short shrift, he could hardly help feeling that he, too, was being edged out of the picture.

Haynes lost his argument on behalf of northern and southern demonstration centers, but not without an intraorganizational struggle. Previously, Jones had held the title of assistant and then associate director of the League. Early in 1916, the League designated both Jones and Haynes as executive secretaries. On April 11, 1917, the steering committee confirmed the plan Haynes had protested against so vigorously by naming him educational secretary, with Jones as full-time executive secretary in New York.[12]

Haynes expressed his discontent with the decision to members of the executive board. During the summer a subcommittee of the board reopened the matter and solicited written statements from Haynes and Jones "as to the most effective organization of the [League's] work." [13] Both men attended a meeting in August with half a dozen board members and an outside mediator to settle the issue. They confirmed the division of work between Jones as executive secretary and Haynes as educational secretary, but they also provided for a rough regional division of responsibility.[14]

This understanding eased the situation sufficiently for Haynes to remain as educational secretary—at least temporarily. His influence in the League, however, reached a low ebb. Haynes was not included among the Negro leaders negotiating with the executive council of the American Federation of Labor—a group of which Eugene Kinckle Jones was a key member. Haynes found it necessary to write to R. R. Moton for "advice as to what steps to take" to be allowed to attend their April 1918 conference.[15]

In January 1918, the Urban League's conference on Negro labor called on the Department of Labor to appoint "one or two competent Negroes . . . to serve as assistants . . . in adjusting and distributing Negro labor to meet war and peace needs." Other Negro leaders and organizations joined in urging that the

Department pay special attention to the role of the Negro worker in meeting the industrial needs occasioned by the war.[16] As a result of these requests, Labor Secretary William B. Wilson agreed to appoint a special adviser on matters relating to blacks. On May 1, 1918, George Haynes, on leave from both the Urban League and Fisk, assumed his responsibilities as the Labor Department's Director of Negro Economics.[17] Eugene Kinckle Jones told the Secretary of Labor that Haynes was "a wise selection." [18]

Haynes's responsibilities in Washington did not solve the problem of his relationship with Jones. "Their inability to get on together" seemed to be hurting the League. At the same time, Haynes tangled with the Chicago Urban League, which felt that he was trying to take over its employment offices. In the summer of 1919, the steering committee asked Haynes to resign as educational secretary. "After some shifting back and forth," Haynes submitted his resignation "with the request that it be passed upon by the Executive Board." But Hollingsworth Wood considered another debate on the matter inadvisable. With new staff members handling the League's educational and southern work, and with Haynes fully occupied at the Labor Department, there was no point in continuing his affiliation with the League. "A long wrangle before the Board" would serve only to demean Haynes in the eyes of its members.[19]

Haynes never came back to the Urban League. When the Harding administration discontinued the Division of Negro Economics in 1921, he joined the Federal Council of Churches as head of its new department of race relations, a position he held until 1947. Accepting an invitation to attend the Urban League's fiftieth anniversary dinner in September 1960, Haynes admitted to public relations director Guichard Parris that he had not set foot in the National League's headquarters for over forty years.[20]

The solidification of Urban League leadership in Jones's hands instead of Haynes's made sense in light of their positions and the pressures of contemporary events. Jones's authority evolved out of day-to-day dealings with his staff and the problems at hand.

To many Urban Leaguers in New York, Haynes was a distant, unknown figure. Jones, whom they saw regularly, logically evoked their loyalty. As the Baltimore *Afro-American* observed, with unintended irony, "the success of the League . . . is due in large measure to the fact that Dr. Haynes found men like Mr. Eugene Kinckle Jones and others to carry on the work." [21]

II

The migration of World War I made it imperative that the Urban League turn toward national expansion. The needs of newly arrived Negroes in Chicago, Detroit, Pittsburgh, and other industrial centers were too immediate to allow the luxury of waiting for "demonstration" organizations in New York and Nashville to prove themselves. The conditions that the Urban League had been created to meet in New York were being magnified across the country. Of necessity, the League began to re-evaluate its operations and to gear itself for truly national work. It appointed a special committee to take stock of the League program. "Instead of confining ourselves . . . to the training of a comparatively few Negro social workers and to organizing social work in a comparatively few centers," the committee concluded, "our efforts should reach practically every city of any size, north and south." [22] This mandate for national expansion guided the League's development over the next decade.

In January 1918 the League called a conference of board and executive staff representatives of the national organization and affiliated bodies to consider ways of standardizing its work. A product of this conference was the standard program of work for local affiliates.[23]

At this time the National League took two additional steps, one of form and the other of substance, which made 1918 a turning point in its history. The first involved its name. When the three New York committees (NLPCW, CIICN, Committee on Urban Conditions) had merged in 1911, there had been some discussion over the proper title for the new organization. George Haynes had written Roger Baldwin inquiring about the choice of the name for his St. Louis Committee for Social Service Among Negroes. Had they debated whether to use "Colored people" or "Negroes"? Haynes wondered. He told Baldwin that the New York group was considering "Social Service League Among Colored People." [24] The name finally adopted—the National League on Urban Conditions Among Negroes—was a logical extension of its constituent, the Committee on Urban Conditions.

Before long people became dissatisfied with the cumbersome new title (which never managed to contract into a set of easily recognizable initials like "NAACP"). For several years changes were suggested and then postponed. "I think Nat[ional] Negro Social Service League the best solution," Ruth Standish Baldwin wrote Haynes in 1914. Hollingsworth Wood "thought the 'Urban' would best be kept & suggest[ed] National Urban League for Negroes." [25]

Mrs. Baldwin's assurance that "We'll try to come to some decision soon" proved illusory, for it took four years before the League adopted Wood's suggestion in modified form. The committee studying the League's program and structure recommended in January 1918 that its name be shortened to "National Urban League for Negroes," a change endorsed by the conference on standardization, which favored simply "National Urban League." At its February meeting a sharply divided executive board balked at the change, four members supporting "National Urban League" and five insisting that "Negro" be retained in the name of the organization.[26] Later that year the League's Columbus conference recommended shortening the name to "National Urban League," with each affiliate known as "(name of city) Urban League," and with the words "for social service among Negroes" printed in small type under the title. This formula finally won executive board approval.[27]

The final substantive change effected during 1918 separated the Urban League's work in New York from the national office.

Formerly, the local phases of the League's work had been supervised by a subcommittee of the national board. Administratively, however, the New York work belonged to the national organization and the workers were members of the national staff. By 1918 both the national and the local work had expanded sufficiently to require the creation of an autonomous New York affiliate. Accordingly, the programs were separated, and James H. Hubert came from the Brooklyn Urban League to be executive secretary of the new New York Urban League. The funds of the New York and National Leagues were not completely separated until two years later, but, for the purposes of program and administrative operation, the New York League was an independent entity beginning in 1918.[28]

The changes that the Urban League sustained during 1918 held profound meaning for the future direction of the organization. Its first years had been a time of testing and experimentation. Its executive direction had been divided with ambiguities in the allocation of responsibilities. The relationship of affiliated local bodies to the national organization had become hopelessly jumbled. Because of its responsibility for local work in New York, the National Urban League had been hindered in the development of a national perspective and program of work. And the programs it did pursue on the local level were largely repackaged versions of social welfare efforts carried on by the Charity Organization Society, immigrant settlement houses, and Negro agencies as old as the New York Colored Mission and the White Rose Industrial Association.

By 1918 all of these circumstances began to change. George Haynes joined the Department of Labor and left Eugene Kinckle Jones in command of the League. The affiliates became a streamlined system of local organizations with a standardized program of work, and the Urban League committed itself to the expansion of a national movement. The migrations created circumstances under which George Haynes's gradualist emphasis on training of qualified workers could not remain the primary focus of the

League; pressing social service and employment needs suddenly had to be met in urban centers across the country. By divesting itself of its local responsibilities in New York, the National League freed itself to develop strong programs in social science research and industrial relations. After the creation of the New York affiliate, social service programs became more and more exclusively the province of the growing body of local Urban Leagues. With its newly defined emphasis on employment opportunities, the National Urban League at last began to set its direction as a truly national organization.

PART TWO

1918-1929

10 ENTERING THE POSTWAR DECADE

The migrations and the war had created new opportunities and obligations for the National Urban League, and new hopes for the Negroes it sought to serve. The large-scale opening of better and more diversified jobs meant chances for better health, housing, food, and clothing. But the migrations and the war also had a negative side. The migrants suffered traumas of adjustment to conditions in urban ghettos and slums. Concurrently, changes in population and employment resulted in tensions in the older, established black communities of northern cities and in the larger white world. The migrations ensured, in Ray Stannard Baker's words, that blacks would become "more and more a national rather than a sectional problem." [1]

I

The race riots during and after World War I illustrated the accuracy of Baker's prophecy. Racial violence exploded in Houston, Philadelphia, Chester, Pennsylvania, and East St. Louis, Illinois, in 1917, and during the "Red Summer" of 1919 a rash of more than twenty outbreaks plagued cities north and south. Just as a riot over a lynching in Springfield, Illinois, in 1908 had set in motion the thinking and meetings that had resulted in the founding of the NAACP, so these new riots intensified the need for Urban League affiliates in cities across the country.

The Urban League played only a limited role in conjunction with the riots. Following the violence in East St. Louis, the Rotary Club moved to establish a local branch of the Urban League in the hope of diminishing racial tensions. It was defunct within a few years, however, due largely to the waning of white support for social welfare programs for blacks.[2]

In Chicago, the only riot-torn city that already had a League affiliate, the organization worked during the course of the turmoil to relieve suffering and restore calm. The League helped the Red Cross distribute food to needy families, and, when the violence made it too dangerous for blacks to get to their jobs in the stockyards, its headquarters served as an improvised pay station where they could collect their wages. The League provided a channel of communication between whites and blacks at the height of the tensions. It blanketed black neighborhoods with circulars exhorting people to stay off the streets and out of trouble, and it organized citizens' committees to help in maintaining order. As the violence subsided, the League's offices recorded claims of injuries and property damage to help the innocent victims sue for compensation. The League joined in urging Governor Frank O. Lowden to appoint the Chicago Commission on Race Relations, and its research director, Charles S. Johnson, served as the Commission's associate executive secretary. George Cleveland Hall, the League's vice-president, was one of the Commission's six black members. Johnson played a critical role in the Commission's study of the causes of the riot. The Chicago Urban League placed its files at the Commission's disposal, and the League's "original emphasis . . . on fundamental studies as the basis for action," Johnson said, "found emphasis" in the Commission's work.[3] The Urban League, said Governor Lowden, knew "exactly what to do and what to advise and consequently our task was made an easy one." [4]

From the Urban League's perspective, the lesson of Chicago and East St. Louis was that other cities should establish League affiliates to head off their own racial violence. Indeed, Eugene

Kinckle Jones later reflected that the founding of the Detroit Urban League had prevented a riot there.[5] "The race riots," the National Urban League declared, following the Chicago riot, ". . . are solemn warnings to our country of the dangers that we are facing in our own body politic. They emphasize anew the fact that after all, human relations can only be satisfactory when founded on conditions which are based on justice and equality." [6] In an appeal to mayors and "responsible citizens" of northern industrial centers, Hollingsworth Wood pointed out the explosive potential of "thousands of untrained men and women unused to city ways" who were forced to live under conditions which were "a positive danger to the community in health and morality." Out of ignorance, many of them became strikebreakers "and thus . . . incurred the suspicion and in some places open opposition of organized labor." [7]

The factors that had fed racial hostilities included "inadequate housing" for blacks in Chicago, "improper industrial conditions" in East St. Louis, and "racial distrust" growing out of racial separation in Washington. Here the League drew an obvious lesson: "Only by improving the housing, health and recreation opportunities of the Negro at the same time that we demand of him the contribution of his hands and brain in industry can we look for fundamental improvement in race relations. Organized labor as well as organized capital must understand him and his human longings and both must give him justice and chance to make his contribution to the common life of our communities."

Responsible authorities—public officials, professionals, the media, and others—had an obligation to "bring to bear the forces of public opinion to rectify the abuses which produce conditions of distrust and almost of despair." [8] As for the League, Hollingsworth Wood said, it was "doing its utmost to turn this raw, ignorant labor from a possible danger into a civic and industrial asset." It was eager to help other cities avoid a repetition of East St. Louis, but it needed "the cooperation of the best white and colored elements in the communities" [9] to substitute "the rule of reason, even-handed justice, and cooperative endeavor" for "the rule of the bayonet and the machine gun." [10] When a riot broke out in Tulsa in 1921, the League immediately sent its St. Louis executive "to inaugurate a social welfare program . . . to remove the causes of friction, enlarge the Negro's industrial opportunity and secure for him a square deal in all phases of community life." [11]

The race riots set much of the context for race relations in the postwar era. The decade that followed was a time of contradiction: an age of normalcy, yet an age of change; an era of progress and prosperity, yet an era of great divisiveness and hatred. The popular portrait of America between World War I and the Great Depression is one of a complacent country experimenting in manners and morals while reaping an economic bonanza. But the well-known images of the Jazz Age and the Roaring Twenties have little relevance to the problems of Afro-Americans in this period. It was the other face of postwar America—intolerance, prejudice, fear—that impinged most heavily on the efforts of racial reformers and the lives of the men and women they sought to uplift.

Pushed by national crisis, white Americans during World War I had been forced to face up to the problems and potential of their black neighbors. The small measure of economic progress suddenly accessible to blacks came not because of any revolution in racial attitudes, but because of white self-interest. Whites paid positive attention to blacks when they filled an economic need; they also paid heed to them when pressures of migration brought the racial question from the plantations into the cities.

Once the wartime emergency had ended, the economic and social standing of blacks was once again up for reconsideration. For example, how would white factory owners feel about black workers when white veterans were seeking jobs? How would communities react to the need for social services for blacks once the pressures of the migration slacked off? The war had created many problems for blacks, but it had also given them undeniable advantages. In an age of normalcy, what kinds of reactions could black men expect from whites?

Blacks ranked very low on the roster of absorbing national issues in the 1920s. The return of Republican administrations to Washington disappointed those blacks who expected the party of Lincoln to heed their concerns. The Republicans seemed more interested in cultivating a lily-white constituency in the South than in courting the black vote. The Harding and Coolidge administrations appointed few blacks to federal posts and failed to reverse the policies of civil service segregation that had begun under Woodrow Wilson. During the Coolidge administration, there were fewer blacks holding presidential appointments than there had been in the Roosevelt-Taft era; seven months before Coolidge left office, there were only 77 more blacks working for the federal government than there had been when he became president in 1923. While Harding and Coolidge both spoke out against lynching, the NAACP's battle to secure federal antilynching legislation found little support in the White House. Proponents of the legislation scored their greatest victory of the decade in 1922, when the Dyer antilynching bill passed the House, but the measure failed to pass the Senate, thanks to a determined southern Democratic filibuster in defense of states' rights. After 1922 the bill never got beyond committee.[12]

Nor did a bill to create a Negro Industrial Commission make any legislative progress. Introduced in 1921, 1923, and again repeatedly into the 1930s, the bill would have established a nonpartisan, interracial commission to investigate social and economic conditions among blacks in the United States and to recommend appropriate legislative remedies. It would have put federal money and authority behind the kinds of investigative tasks that the Urban League had begun to perform. But the bill never won a full committee hearing. And while Harding and Coolidge spoke favorably of the idea, neither chose to establish by executive order the commission that Congress had failed to create.[13]

Except for a handful of congressmen and senators, few public

figures in the 1920s cared very much about black rights. The
Senate could still debate whether the colored races were inferior
to Caucasians.[14] Neither the Congress nor the Justice Department
took any action against the Ku Klux Klan, and President Coolidge found it too delicate a political issue to mention publicly
during the 1924 presidential campaign. Although he finally denounced the Klan in 1925, he took no steps toward curbing its ex-
cesses. In fact, the only significant federal action in behalf of
blacks during the 1920s came from the Supreme Court. In January 1927, in *Nixon* v. *Herndon*, the Court said that the State of
Texas was acting unconstitutionally when it attempted to disfran-
chise black voters by prohibiting them from participating in
Democratic primaries. That same month, it struck down a New
Orleans segregation ordinance. But it was decades before voting
rights and desegregation actually became law.[15]

Even racial violence had receded from the forefront of the national consciousness. Lynchings of blacks, which had increased
from 36 in 1917 to 76 in 1919, leveled off after 1922 to an average
of 17 for each of the remaining years of the decade.[16] Probably
the most dramatic instance of racial strife was the shoot-out that
followed Dr. Ossian Sweet's purchase of a new home in a white
Detroit neighborhood in 1925. But the Sweet case, despite the appearance of Clarence Darrow for the defense, drew scarcely a notice in *The New York Times*.[17]

That black rights were so rarely a matter of national discussion
in the 1920s suggests the handicap under which racial reformers
had to work. Clearer clues, however, come from the divisive
themes that set the political temper of the decade. The war had
been a time of expansiveness, idealism, and hope; the disillusion-
ment and failures of the postwar world brought closedminded-
ness, intolerance, and fear. Frightened by the complexities of
an urban, industrial civilization, and searching for scapegoats,
many Americans retreated to nativism of the most virulent kind.
Immigration restriction was one expression of a growing unwill-

ingness to accommodate complexity and diversity. The resurgence of the Ku Klux Klan provided a vehicle for venting hatreds of all kinds—against foreigners, modernists, city dwellers, Catholics, Jews, and, of course, blacks. In 1920 America for the first time found itself with a population more urban than rural; but the country resisted the rise of the city with fierce battles in behalf of fundamentalism and prohibition. Every political issue of the decade seemed to frame itself in a paradigm of controversy: old stock versus immigrants, drys versus wets, Protestants versus Catholics, fundamentalists versus modernists, rural versus urban, white versus black.

Given this climate of divisiveness, blacks could scarcely hold out much hope for racial progress. An earlier period of adversity —the decades after Reconstruction—had called forth an emphasis on self-help and racial solidarity. Now again blacks had reason to reconsider strategies for racial reform. At a time when one United States Senator labeled the NAACP "an association for the promotion of revolution and inciting to riots," [18] was it best to pursue direct paths to political and economic justice? or to emphasize "safe," "low profile" activities better suited to the mood of antagonism? or perhaps to withdraw completely, recognizing the impossibility of coexistence in a demonstrably hostile environment?

II

Under these pressures of intolerance and uncertainty, thousands, possibly millions, of black Americans found a prophet in Marcus Garvey. Garvey preached black pride and a return to Africa, but the latter part of his message was much less important than the sense of identity and meaning he infused into the lives of so many blacks. While estimates of membership in his Universal Negro Improvement Association vary tremendously, he apparently succeeded in what no other leadership—not the NAACP, nor the

Urban League, nor black politicians, nor even black churches—
had been able to accomplish: building a mass movement among
the rank and file of American blacks.

Established black leadership had little use for Garvey. While
the NAACP "never officially endorsed or disapproved the Marcus Garvey movement," [19] W. E. B. Du Bois in his angriest mo-
ments called the Garveyites "scoundrels and bubble-blowers,"
and their prophet "dictatorial, domineering, inordinately vain and
very suspicious"—in fact, "the most dangerous enemy of the
Negro race." [20]

The Urban League recognized Garvey only in the pages of
Opportunity, and there he received scant attention. The Garvey
that emerged from the pages of *Opportunity* was a posturer and a
charlatan, at once a "dynamic, blundering, temerarious visionary"
and the master manipulator of the black masses.[21] His programs
seemed unrealistic and his methods downright dishonest; "his financial exploits were ridiculously unsound, his plans for the redemption of Africa absurdly visionary and impossible, his methods injudicious and bunglesome, and the grand result, a fleecing
of hundreds of thousands of poor and ignorant Negroes." [22] From
the perspective of the Urban League, "the Garvey bubble" [23] was
a "gigantic swindle." [24] But in scorning the "flambouyant, fantastic
and emotionally militant" Garvey movement, writers in *Opportunity* also pinpointed its larger significance.[25] Garvey's schemes
may have been preposterous, but all the pomp and pageantry and
talk of "Back to Africa" struck a responsive chord among the
black masses. Garveyism provided "an asylum" for the dissatisfied,[26] an outlet for the "balked desires" and "repressed longings"
of men and women thwarted at every turn by American society.[27] Despite its tone of condescension, the Urban League's analysis was remarkably perceptive; Garveyism, as *Opportunity*
portrayed it, "was a dream-world escape for the 'illiterati' from
the eternal curse on their racial status in this country." [28] Garvey's followers, in the eyes of the League, were "dark, dumb
masses" to whom the black evangelist held out "an opiate for their

hopeless helplessness,—a fantastic world beyond the cold grasp of logic and reason in which they might slake cravings never in this social order to be realized." [29]

Garvey's followers agreed with these views. Few of them really expected to return to Africa; what Garvey gave them, they explained, was a racial consciousness, an identity, a sense of pride.[30] While the Urban League disdained Garvey's methods, it recognized the value of these goals. It never argued that its own approach could fully heal the raw nerves Garvey soothed. When Garvey went to jail for fraud, the League supported the sentence, but it lamented the fate of the millions he had moved. With Garvey behind bars, *Opportunity* wondered, what would become "of that miserable group which now has neither its full life nor a compensation for what is denied in the intoxication of irrational hope, and in its dreams?" [31] The League worried about the black proletariat, but it also looked down on it and, in a sense, despaired of ever ameliorating its plight.

What upset the League about Garvey was not so much that he was duping the masses, but that his movement was playing into the hands of white racists. For decades whites had advocated deportation and social as well as cultural separatism as solutions to the racial problem. When Garvey preached that blacks should build their own country in Africa and that they should refuse to accept and imitate white standards, he found himself with curious allies. He even went so far as to cooperate deliberately with the Ku Klux Klan. To the Urban League, dedicated as it was to realizing racial harmony within the American system, such pandering to the prejudices of white America seemed dangerously destructive.[32]

Frowning upon the Messiah of the black masses put the Urban League against the mainstream of black popular thought. Why should it have failed to embrace such a successful leader? First of all, Garvey argued that it was impossible for blacks to achieve equality in America: "So long as there is a black and white population, when the majority is on the side of the white race, you and I will never get political justice or get political equality in this country." [33] Garvey had given up on the United States; racial reformers in the Urban League were working to integrate blacks into the American system. Garvey maintained that whites would never voluntarily relinquish one iota of their supremacy over blacks; the Urban League proceeded on the assumption that the key to changing racial injustices was to educate whites to their existence.

These differences in outlook were fundamental to the gap between Garvey and the League. Moreover, the Black Moses and the blacks who sat on the Urban League board during the 1920s could not have been more dissimilar.[34] Garvey was born in Jamaica; all of the Urban Leaguers were native Americans, nearly nine-tenths of them from the seaboard states of the South.* Garvey dropped out of school at the age of fourteen; two-thirds of the Urban Leaguers had gone to college, more than half had attended graduate school, and fully a third had earned graduate degrees. Garvey came from the working class; the Urban Leaguers represented the black bourgeoisie. Half of them were educators, and a quarter were doctors or ministers; only one was a printer, the trade in which Garvey was apprenticed as a child and later began his union organizing carrer.

The League's black staff members, too, were the antithesis of Garvey in background and personality. During the 1920s the day-to-day operations of the organization were in the hands of six men—executive secretary Eugene Kinckle Jones; industrial relations director T. Arnold Hill; directors of research and investigations Charles S. Johnson (who also edited *Opportunity*) and Ira De Augustine Reid; southern field director Jesse O. Thomas; and Johnson's successor as *Opportunity* editor, Elmer Anderson Carter. All of them were black, and, with the exception of Reid (who was born in 1901), all had been born in the last two decades of the nineteenth century in southern states ranging from Vir-

* Among fourteen black board members whose birthplaces are known, only one was born in the North.

ginia to Mississippi. Their family backgrounds were quite different from Garvey's; for example, Jones's father was a professor of
homiletics and church history at Virginia Union University, and
his mother taught music at Hartshorn College in Richmond.
Reid's father was a Baptist minister, and his mother had been
graduated from college. Johnson's parents were born into slavery,
but his father, too, became a minister.

All six National Urban League staff executives were college
graduates, and five had done graduate work in sociology or economics. While Garvey had begun his career as a printer's appren-
tice, the League staff members gained their early experience in
teaching. A career in education had long offered professional stat-
ure and social prestige to the young Negro college graduate.
Charles Johnson and Arnold Hill joined the Urban League movement directly upon completion of their academic education, but
the other four had previously taught in a variety of educational
institutions.[35]

Like their National Urban League counterparts, the staffs of
the League's affiliates had little in common with Marcus Garvey.
Three-quarters of the 25 men and 3 women who have been identified as local executives in the 1920s came from the South;
among the others were natives of Pennsylvania, Ohio, and Massachusetts. Their ages matched the youthfulness of the organization
they served; of the 19 for whom information is available, 10 were
in their twenties when they became executive secretaries and
only two were over thirty-five. Like the leaders of the National
League, they were exceptionally well-educated; all of them were
college graduates (three-fourths attended black colleges and the
remainder white universities), and all but four had gone on for
further study. Fully half held graduate degrees in the social sciences or other fields.

Their employment experiences were more diverse than those of
their National Urban League colleagues; among them were a
nurse, a minister, an architect, an advertising manager, and a
newspaper editor. Sixteen, however, had had teaching experience,

ranging from one to twenty years on the high school and college level; included among these were three school principals and an acting dean at Morehouse.

These men and women came to their positions with more grass-roots social work experience than the National League executives. A quarter of them had held other jobs in the Urban League movement before being named executive secretaries, and nearly two-fifths had served as boys' workers, YMCA secretaries, or staff members of other social agencies.[36]

On every level the blacks associated with the Urban League movement stood squarely among the elite of their race—and poles apart from Marcus Garvey. Such radical differences in background help to account for the failure of the Urban League to embrace a man idolized by the black masses. Garvey's personality made matters that much worse. He was a flamboyant showman who captured disciples through pomp, pageantry, and promises. By contrast, Eugene Kinckle Jones was "a man of quiet temper, with an almost exasperating fondness for facts." He was "no orator," according to Mary White Ovington. "He does not make a striking impression on a great audience; but give him an hour with a group of men whom he wishes to interest, and he pours out facts and shows possible results and determines to a nicety necessary costs, until his hearers are compelled to pull out their check books and meet his demands." [37]

What made the gulf unbridgeable, however, was the fact that the Urban Leaguers were the very blacks Garvey sneered at and lampooned. These were the men and women whom W. E. B. Du Bois had applauded as the Talented Tenth; for Garvey, "The Negro who has had the benefit of an education of forty, thirty and twenty years ago, is the greatest fraud and stumbling block to the real progress of the race. . . . This old school of Negro 'intellectuals' is crafty, unpatriotic and vicious. They cannot be trusted. . . . They are barnacles around the necks of a struggling virile people." [38] The Urban Leaguers were prime representatives of the black bourgeoisie—just the group, Garvey felt, in which one could find the traitors to the race, "among the men highest placed in education and society, the fellows who call themselves leaders." [39] By contemporary standards of educational background and professional status, the Urban Leaguers were leaders of the race; for Garvey, these race leaders were "the biggest crooks in the world," who could easily be bribed "to hang [their] race and block every effort of self-help." [40]

Garvey made fun especially of those blacks who tried to make themselves as white as possible in values, behavior, and appearance. The black bourgeoisie were known for their imitation of white middle-class manners and morals. And in a world where Negroid features connoted lower status, many blacks tried to soften the most visible traces of racial identification. Garvey had nothing but contempt for "the bleaching processes and the hair straightening escapades" of such men and women.[41] Mulattoes, especially those who tried to capitalize on their light skins and refined features, were one of Garvey's favorite targets; he equated "race amalgamation and miscegenation" with "race suicide," and he repeatedly called for "pride and purity of race." [42] "I am conscious of the fact that slavery brought upon us the curse of many colors within the Negro race," he said on one occasion, "but that is no reason why we of ourselves should perpetuate the evil." [43] Time and again he underscored his hatred for an " 'aristocracy' based upon caste of color," dominated by the light-skinned "group that hates the Negro blood in its veins." [44] A glance at photographs of the Urban League's black leadership shows that Eugene Kinckle Jones, T. Arnold Hill, and many of the black board members were very light-skinned. And an editorial in *Opportunity* even condoned light-colored Negroes passing for white.[45] No wonder there was little common cause between Marcus Garvey and the Urban League.

Similarly, the heavy influence of whites in the affairs of the Urban League drew it inevitably away from Garvey's line. Although he himself tacitly supported the Ku Klux Klan, Garvey roundly denounced "the monkey apings of our 'so-called leading

men'" who sought "the shelter, leadership, protection and patronage of the 'master' in their organization and so-called advancement work." While the principal target of Garvey's invective
was the NAACP, his disdain for "modern Uncle Toms" who
took "pride in laboring under alien leadership" could clearly have
applied to the Urban League as well.[46] Garvey saw the white
man as the black man's "oppressor" and thus "naturally" indis-
posed "to liberate us [blacks] to the higher freedom—the truer
liberty—the truer Democracy." [47] But in the ideology of the
Urban League, whites were concerned and indispensable partners
in the work of racial advancement. Insofar as Garveyism came
to be identified as "a gospel of hate for white people," it could
scarcely command respect in a movement dedicated to the principle of interracial cooperation. Nor could antagonism toward
whites further the Urban League's practical objectives; as a
writer in *Opportunity* summed it up, "No program of permanent uplift for the Negro can successfully proceed on such an
issue." [48]

If the nature of its black leadership made it unlikely that the
Urban League would embrace a program akin to Marcus Garvey's, the composition of its white leadership made such a prospect
all the more preposterous. The chairman of the board, L. Hollingsworth Wood, was a tall, jovial Quaker who had helped found
the American Friends Service Committee and who served as president of the Friends Center in New York, clerk of the New York
Yearly Meeting of the Society of Friends, and treasurer of *World
Tomorrow*, a magazine published by the Fellowship of Reconcilia-
tion. Consistent with his Quaker beliefs, he was a dedicated pacifist who served as treasurer of the American Union Against
Militarism. Educated at Haverford College and Columbia University Law School, Wood practiced estates law in New York City.
But he devoted much of his time to his wide-ranging reform
interests. Concern for Negro welfare involved him in the Urban
League as its board chairman, the Howard Orphanage and Industrial School as its president, as a member of the committee of the

New York Colored Mission, and as vice-chairman of the board of trustees of Fisk University.[49] "It is generally conceded," the Chicago *Broad Ax* wrote, "that Mr. Wood though a white man is most sympathetic with the Negro's claim for equal opportunity and has an unusual understanding of the Negro's point of view in his efforts to attain the higher things of life." [50] "We didn't ever think of him as being white or anything of that sort," one local executive recalled. "He was just Mr. Wood." [51] Wood's white colleagues on the executive board were very much like him in background and interests. Like their predecessors of the 1910s,* they were well-educated professionals, businessmen, and philanthropist-reformers from New York and other major cities, where they were engaged in a wide range of civic and charitable activities.†

III

This leadership drew the Urban League inevitably away from the separatism and race hatred preached by Marcus Garvey. It was critical in determining the League's approach to racial problems in the 1920s. Equally critical, if not more so, was the nature of the organization's funding, for the National Urban League depended for its survival on a handful of wealthy philanthropists and foundations, while local Leagues were funded principally by community chests.[52]

Unlike the NAACP, which was financed through its branches, the National Urban League received very little support from its affiliates. Initially the League required affiliates to pay a $5.00 joining fee and $5.00 in annual dues thereafter. In December 1918

* One significant difference between the two groups is the higher proportion of Jews on the board in the 1920s, when Jews accounted for one-third of the twenty-eight members whose religious affiliations are known. (Even if all eleven unidentified Urban Leaguers were Christians, Jews would still comprise about one-quarter of the board in the 1920s, as compared to one-sixth in the 1920s.)
† For more detailed information about the educational background, place of residence, and profession of Urban League board members in the 1920s, see Tables A.6, A.7, and A.8, Appendix.

this financial obligation was revised so that each affiliate would "contribute to the National Urban League 2% of the gross amount received for its annual budget." Locals "not employ[ing] paid workers" or "not directly sustained by contributions" were to pay a minimum annual membership fee of $10.00.[53] Beginning in 1929, each executive secretary was expected to make a minimum personal contribution of $10.00 a year to the national organization. Each employed local staff member was to contribute at least $1.00, each local League president $5.00 or more, and each local board member no less than $1.00.[54]

Collecting these contributions proved to be difficult, especially during times of financial stringency. In any event, even if they had been paid in full, they would have amounted to only a tiny fraction of the national organization's annual budget. While affiliates were self-supporting, they did not support the national office. Hence it had to find its own contributors. The National Urban League raised most of its money in the New York metropolitan area, which "seem[ed] to be the most fertile field to work." [55] Most fertile of all were the offices of John D. Rockefeller, Jr. Rockefeller's personal gifts were typically small—for example, he gave $1000 a year in the early 1920s—a level of support which he justified by his conviction that organizations, once established, "should command support from other philanthropists." [56] He seemed more interested in helping projects through their experimental stages; from 1925 through 1931 he earmarked $4500 for the annual support of the Department of Industrial Relations, providing that the League raise a matching $4500.[57]

More substantial regular support came from the Laura Spelman Rockefeller Memorial, set up in 1918 by John D. Rockefeller, Sr., in memory of his wife. Managed by John D., Jr., the Memorial emphasized philanthropies "in the field of the social sciences and social technology." [58] Usually made on a proportional matching basis (for example, $14,100 in 1926 providing that the League raise $56,400 from other sources), the Memorial contribution to the

League's general budget ranged from $2500 to $15,000 a year; throughout the 1920s, with only two exceptions, it alone constituted between one-fifth and one-sixth of the League's entire annual income.[59] John D. Rockefeller, Jr., himself, plus the Memorial, or its successor, the Spelman Fund of New York (founded in 1929), accounted for more than 25 per cent of the National Urban League's annual income in 1925–29.[60]

These Rockefeller gifts may have been major in the context of the Urban League's meager budget, but they were minor in comparison to the millions devoted to various Rockefeller philanthropies. The League even ranked low among Rockefeller's racial philanthropies. During several years in the 1920s, when Rockefeller gifts to the Urban League ranged from about $4000 to $20,000 annually, pledges from John D., Jr., and the Memorial to the Commission on Interracial Cooperation amounted to $40,000 a year.[61]

The National Urban League attracted only two other regular contributors comparable to Rockefeller. One was the Carnegie Corporation of New York, which supported the Department of Research and Investigations with annual grants of $8000 for five and a half years, beginning in mid-1921, and in other years contributed upwards of $2500. The Urban League's research activities satisfied the Carnegie Corporation's intention "to promote the advancement and diffusion of knowledge and understanding among the people of the United States." [62] Such sums were small in comparison with other Carnegie benefactions for educational purposes, and infinitesimal against the millions devoted to all Carnegie philanthropies; yet for the Urban League, $8000 in any given year covered a large part of its limited budget.

The other leading source of funds was the Altman Foundation, established in 1913 by department store executive Benjamin Altman "to aid charitable and educational institutions in New York State." [63] While its contributions to the League ranged from $1500 to $10,000, the Foundation averaged an annual gift of $7500 from 1924 through 1930.

Three other regular donors gave $1000 or more each year during the period 1919–31. Julius Rosenwald contributed $2000 annually from 1919 through 1921 and eventually leveled off to $1000, his final gift in 1928. In that year the contributions were taken over by the Julius Rosenwald Fund, which made pledges up to $2500 through 1931. Agnes Brown Leach, a member of the Urban League's executive board from 1920 to 1942, donated from $1500 to $2500 through 1926, after which her gifts fell below $1000. V. Everit Macy, a director of several New York banks, gave the League between $1000 and $1500 each year until his death in 1930.

These six sources accounted for roughly half of the National Urban League's total annual income from 1920 through 1926. While the League had hundreds of benefactors each year, small contributors never sustained it, as they did the NAACP. In the decade 1921–31, contributors of $200 or more—they numbered between 19 and 34—each year accounted for at least 60 per cent of the National Urban League's total income (except in 1927, when the figure was 55 per cent).[64] Just as large donations were the financial mainstay of the organization, so did white contributors account for the greater part of its funds.

The League appointed an extension secretary in 1921 to concentrate on "stimulating interest in interracial organizations and financial support of social work for Negroes by Negroes of means." [65] Like most Urban League staff members, the new secretary, J. R. E. Lee, came from an academic background. Lee, who was a native of Texas, had taught Latin and history at his alma mater, Bishop College, in Marshall, Texas, for a decade following his graduation in 1899. Thereafter he worked closely with Booker T. Washington as director of the academic department at Tuskegee Institute until 1915. He was the first president and later secretary of the National Association of Teachers in Colored Schools, which he helped found in 1904. He came to the Urban League at the age of fifty-one after six years as a high school principal in Kansas City.[66]

Lee traveled to help local Leagues conduct financial campaigns, and he worked on fund-raising among Negroes for the national organization. Eight per cent ($3643) of the National Urban League's income in 1922 came from blacks. Some affiliates reported a better response; in 1923, in New York City, blacks contributed $6500, or almost one-third of the affiliate's budget.[67] But the experience of Boston, where blacks accounted for about 8 to 10 per cent of the yearly budget, was probably more representative. "We can't ask our white friends for more money," the executive there said, "until the colored people themselves show that they are interested in their industrial development." [68]

The argument that whites could not be expected to support the organization without some show of black backing was a familiar theme in the National Urban League. If blacks who had "met with prosperity" demonstrated their willingness "to share it with their less fortunate brothers," Eugene Kinckle Jones explained, "white friends" would be likely to increase their contributions.[69] No one expected blacks to fund the League alone, but there was continuing concern over "whether Negroes in general gave a fair proportion of financial and moral support to the organization." [70]

This financial portrait had obvious programmatic implications. The low level of black support meant that the Urban League was not effectively beholden to blacks. Of course blacks were well represented among the League's board and staff, and black problems provided the organization's *raison d'être*. But it is nevertheless true that any organization must be acutely sensitive to its sources of funding. While the black perspective was never absent from the League's deliberations, the fact remains that, whenever the organization thought about keeping its policies in line with its donors' views, those were the views of whites.

Even more important, they were the views of a small handful of very powerful—and relatively conservative—individuals and foundations. In order to keep the National Urban League afloat, the first priority lay in satisfying the Rockefeller, Rosenwald, and Carnegie interests. While there are no records of deci-

sions being taken with these influences explicitly in mind, it is
clear that, in shaping its policies, the League could never forget
where its benefactors stood.

In at least one case a key benefactor tried to use financial pressure to change the way the Urban League operated. Beginning in
the late 1920s, the Julius Rosenwald Fund worked actively to
force the League to merge with the NAACP and to oust Eugene
Kinckle Jones as executive secretary.[71] The proposed merger, the
Fund felt, would save money and "avoid duplication of effort";
"a definite union," the Fund's president, Edwin R. Embree, predicted, "would result in greater influence than is now wielded by
the two agencies acting as separate groups." [72] The merger was
conceived chiefly in terms of efficiency and economy; the Fund
never seemed to realize that there were important differences of
philosophy and methods between the two organizations that
would stand in the way of a consolidation.

Another motive for the merger was dislike for Eugene Kinckle
Jones on the part of Alfred K. Stern, Julius Rosenwald's son-in-
law, his administrative assistant in the early days of the Fund, and
a member of the board of the Chicago Urban League. "Our main
purpose in suggesting a merger of the two organizations," Stern
confessed, "was that Eugene Kinckle Jones would thereby be replaced by a man of James Weldon Johnson's caliber. If the two
organizations operate separately, which may be the best policy, a
considerable amount of reorganization is necessary in the National as well as [the] local Urban League. In the first place, Eugene Kinckle Jones should be retired." [73] Stern considered Jones
ineffective; perhaps more important, he found him personally un-
congenial and unwilling to bow automatically to Stern's advice.

The Urban League resisted the pressures for a merger, as did
the NAACP. But preserving independence and integrity resulted
in a financial loss. After making a gift of $1000 to the League in
1929, the Fund, still insisting on a fundamental reorganization of
the agency, withheld further support for almost a decade.[74]

With this one exception, the leaders of the League maintained good relations with their most important sources of funds. Following a visit by Eugene Kinckle Jones in 1921, James R. Angell, the president of the Carnegie Corporation, noted that Jones had made "a good impression" on him. "I have no question," Angell added, "that the work of the League is useful." [75] Inside the Rockefeller interests, the prevailing view was that "the National Urban League appears to be the only organization in the north, and in fact in the country outside the Inter-Racial Commission, which, in a sane and constructive way, is endeavoring to develop right and proper opportunities for Negroes and a better understanding of their problems." [76] The Urban League could not have won praise in such quarters with a radical, boat-rocking program. In the view of John D. Rockefeller, Jr., even the NAACP was too controversial.[77] The moderating influence of these sources of funding put an unmistakable imprint on the course the National Urban League would follow. A moderate policy was equally essential to the local Leagues, which had to apply to Community Chests for their financial support. But the League's course was shaped as much by its objectives as by sensitivity to its contributors. Concerned principally with opening employment opportunities for blacks—opportunities which would arise through concessions from white businessmen— the League understandably avoided policies that were likely to antagonize businessmen-philanthropists. Finally, the modest size of the League's funding * kept its programs on a small scale.[78]

These factors, in combination with the character of the Urban League's leadership, determined its response to the pressures and tensions of the postwar world. The majority of blacks in the 1920s may have rallied, albeit temporarily, to the standard of Marcus Garvey. For the Urban League, however, the direction was to be different. It responded to the climate of race and reform in the 1920s in much the same way that blacks had re-

* For the National League, $27,713 in 1920, $58,635 in 1925, $79,427 in 1929, $76,244 in 1930; for the affiliates, $117,392 in 1920, $266,149 in 1925, $404,845 in 1930.

sponded to the white retreat in the years between Reconstruction and the rise of Jim Crow. There was no use in embarking on futile campaigns in a climate heavily tinged with indifference and outright racial hostility. It was easier to tailor the organization's emphases to the times. What this dictated, first, was an encouragement of black creative talent and an emphasis on research and investigations—scientific fact-finding as a preliminary basis for subsequent racial reform. It also dictated, in much the same spirit as Booker T. Washington's prescriptions for industrial training, an emphasis on preparing blacks to take advantage of industrial opportunity. It permitted a policy of polite persuasion as the route to widening those opportunities. And it allowed the continuation of the social service programs that the League had begun in the previous decade.

11 SOCIAL SERVICES IN THE CITIES

Constrained by a climate of intolerance and complacency, the Urban League in the postwar decade continued to work for social amelioration and uplift. While it generally eschewed active reform, it strengthened and broadened the social service efforts it had begun during the 1910s. In so doing, it helped to confirm the persistence of progressivism in a period traditionally characterized by normalcy and reaction.

With special funding from philanthropists, fraternal organizations, social agencies, and others, the National Urban League expanded its fellowship program to train black social workers. It supported 19 men and 19 women during the 1920s, 20 of them at the New York School of Social Work, 8 at the University of Pittsburgh, and the remainder scattered from the University of Chicago to the Atlanta School of Social Work.[1]

I

The practical social service projects the League undertook in the 1920s were principally the province of a growing network of affiliates. In the decade following the war, when the National League's staff expanded to include southern and western field organizers, the Urban League added seventeen new affiliates including Atlanta, Baltimore, Kansas City, Los Angeles, Louisville,

Omaha, Tampa, and Minneapolis–St. Paul. Of the 27 affiliates claimed in 1918, however, only 16 survived in 1935. It is hardly surprising that some of them failed. Neither Savannah nor Augusta, for example, ever managed to raise a budget or employ a paid staff, mainly because raising money for interracial activities was a difficult assignment in the South. It was not until after Jesse O. Thomas's appointment as southern field director in 1919 that the League laid down a policy confining affiliates "to cities where a budget could be raised, making possible the employment of at least an Executive Secretary and one clerical assistant." [2] At that time, that meant a budget of several thousand dollars—not less than $1500 for an executive secretary, $1000 to $1200 for his assistant, and $900 for a stenographer. [3]

Even then the League had trouble establishing and sustaining affiliates, particularly in the South. In theory, the requirements of the work there were the same as in the North; in fact, it was hard to gain support for what seemed in the South to be more radical work. In New Orleans, whites opposed to the formation of an affiliate spread the story that Communists controlled the National Urban League! [4] Maintaining active boards in southern branches was one of his "most perplexing problems," Thomas told Eugene Kinckle Jones. [5] In Atlanta there were two boards—one black, the other white—that met separately three weeks out of each month and held one joint monthly meeting. [6] But the problem lay not only in finding whites willing to work with blacks; in 1925, for example, Thomas took Richmond's Negro board members to task for "conspicuously negligible" attendance at meetings. [7]

Part of the difficulty in the South may have been Thomas himself. A thirty-six-year-old native of Mississippi, he was a graduate of Tuskegee and the New York School of Social Work. His greatest experience had been in education; he served for four years as field secretary for Tuskegee and then for two years as principal of the Voorhees Normal and Industrial Institute in Denmark, South Carolina. During the war he had been New York State Supervisor for the Division of Negro Economics and, later, exam-

Urban League Affiliates, 1930

SOURCE: Affiliated Organizations, 1930, NUL Papers

iner in charge of the U. S. Employment Service in New York City.[8] He took on the job of field organizer for the Urban League with real enthusiasm: "I really got a chance now 'To Solve The Race Problem,' " he told a friend.[9] But his work seemed to elicit more criticism than solutions. Eugene Kinckle Jones and the National League's auditor often reprimanded him for sloppy accounting and bookkeeping practices. Jones was even more exasperated at Thomas's readiness to devote time to educational and political speechmaking at the expense of progress in affiliations. "I think that it is about time for us to be observing some actual Urban Leagues in some of the cities which you are visiting from time to time," he admonished.[10]

Thomas traveled throughout the South to spread the Urban League's message, and he corresponded and met with leaders of Negro civic, fraternal, and religious groups to encourage them to take an interest in forming a local affiliate. In other sections such salesmanship was less essential. Official League policy quickly came to discourage any attempts by the national office to promote affiliates in cities that were not ready for the responsibility of a new organization. In theory, the organization of an affiliate came in response to initiatives taken by interested local committees or individuals. Yet the National League did not hesitate "to make inquiries and observations" and "to sound out the sentiment" in communities it thought would benefit from an Urban League's presence.[11] "I took the position that I had nothing to 'sell,' " T. Arnold Hill wrote after a visit to Oakland in 1926. His point was not "to urge the founding of a branch," but to acquaint people in Oakland with its program, "so that they, knowing the needs of the city, might decide whether a branch could function effectively to meet the needs." [12]

Demonstrated Negro support was a prerequisite to seeking white sponsorship. Following local expressions of interest in the Urban League's program, the national office ascertained the community's need for an affiliate. Sometimes this was done through surveys, conducted by the Department of Research, which described problems among the city's Negroes and evaluated efforts of existing agencies to ameliorate conditions. Full-scale surveys, however, were not prerequisites for affiliates; more often, particularly in smaller cities, a national staff representative personally canvassed social agencies and leaders of both races in a more informal investigation of the community's problems and needs.[13]

The League was always happy to send Hill or Thomas to help an affiliate through the formalities of organization, but when the process stalled because of difficulties on the local level, the national office refrained from pressing the issue and left it largely to the community in question to work out its problems and mobilize its interested citizens. Frequently, this meant a lapse of several years between the initial show of interest and the actual establishment of a League.

In practice, the National Urban League gave affiliates a relatively free rein in their program activities and generally limited its supervision to instances of intraorganizational dispute. It expected and enforced at least a minimum standard of performance; and it proposed candidates for executive secretaryships subject to local approval and answered affiliates' requests for suggestions for other personnel. Hill and Thomas traveled regularly to prod somnolent affiliates into action, to mediate internal conflicts, and to keep the affiliates in touch with the national office.

In its attention to affiliates, the national staff had to draw a careful line between assistance and interference. Atlanta, which Jesse O. Thomas envisioned as "the demonstration city for the southland," complained in 1922 that "the national organization through . . . Thomas . . . exercised too much authority and was a little too much in evidence in the local work." The affiliate, Thomas countered, "had not taken sufficient interest and become sufficiently active in assuming responsibility for their local affairs to allow him to take his hands off the situation as he would like." [14] When the Los Angeles League was debating the division of its executive authority, a local leader advised T. Arnold Hill "not [to] press too freely for a reorganization as the board is a little resentful at any interference on the part of the National body." [15]

Within the broad limits of its mandate, the national office recognized local Urban Leagues as autonomous bodies that were free to shape their own specific programs. Nevertheless, the activities of the individual affiliates were, typically, very similar. In the 1920s, they fell into two principal categories: social service and employment.

II

The social services that the Urban Leagues offered aimed at improving the quality of urban life. While circumstances sometimes forced them to engage in direct relief, they mainly envisioned themselves as coordinating or administrative agencies that sponsored programs of amelioration and social uplift. In this respect they paralleled the service efforts of settlement houses in the 1920s. Since most settlement houses did not minister to blacks at that time, Urban Leagues had to duplicate the work they had pioneered.

Many of the Leagues' programs actually took place in community houses. While they were different from the settlements in that they did not have a resident staff, the community centers offered similar activities and atmospheres.[16] They sponsored an assortment of clubs, classes, and recreational and cultural activities. Girls' clubs enjoyed sewing, embroidery, needlework, crocheting, basketry, and cooking, while their mothers learned more complicated techniques of making rugs, lampshades, and dresses. The girls' handicraft class in Detroit entered Proctor & Gamble's competition for the best carving from a bar of Proctor & Gamble soap. There were classes in piano, violin, and music theory for black children, and dramatics and art clubs for adults. Members of the art clubs in Detroit, Pittsburgh, and St. Louis exhibited their works in public shows; Detroit's dramatics club performed for the Jewish Women's Club, the Young Women's Hebrew Association, and the Junior League. The community centers were hosts to troop meetings for girl and boy scouts and story telling and games for their younger brothers and sisters.

The houses were conceived as neighborhood centers in the broadest sense of the word. Black fraternal, social, and civic groups used the facilities for meetings and parties. Boys and girls competed on baseball and basketball teams and in marbles tournaments. Their parents came to the houses for community social functions.

These settlements encouraged wholesome recreation, neighborhood fellowship, and personal improvement. Some of them also operated clinics, kindergartens, and day nurseries. Roughly 1100 babies were treated each year at the Detroit Urban League's clinic between 1924 and 1928; in 1929 the clinic served more than twice that number. The average daily attendance at Kansas City's day nursery in 1929 was 24 children per school day; at Tampa's Helping Hand Day Nursery and Kindergarten, it was 37.[17] Detroit's kindergarten had an enrollment of 42 in 1927. "Hundreds of little boys and girls" who later became "useful American citizens" were first trained at Brooklyn's Lincoln Settlement Kindergarten.[18] Eventually, as the Urban League hoped, local boards of education took over the operation of some of these schools, as was the case in Brooklyn and St. Louis in the 1920s.

Encouraging public agencies to assume responsibility for the pilot projects it started was typical of the Urban League's social service efforts. The League envisioned itself as an administrative or coordinating agency; it engaged in practical social service programs only because no one else would, and it eagerly turned them over to more appropriate sponsors. In St. Louis the League ran a dental clinic for blacks from 1920 until 1929, when the local health department agreed to take it on. Since blacks were barred from public playgrounds, the League set up three of its own in 1928 to persuade the city to provide public recreational facilities.[19] In 1929, Atlanta established an infant welfare station that was taken over by the city health department.[20] Seeing to it that municipal agencies added blacks to their staffs was another part of this effort. At the urging of the Detroit Urban League, for example, the probation department of the Municipal Court hired a black worker who had previously been on the League's payroll. The League was also responsible for the appointments of a black policewoman, a black physician in the health department, and a black worker in the girls' protective league, in the recreation commission, and in the welfare department.[21] In Philadelphia, the board of education hired the Armstrong Association's long-time home and school visitor, "thus justifying the . . . Association in its experiment." [22] Columbus secured the appointment of a black policeman to work with newcomers to the city.[23] In Newark, the Social Service Bureau hired four black caseworkers to take over the family casework formerly conducted by the Negro Welfare League. The Jacksonville League was responsible for the appointment of a Negro supervisor for the city's Negro public schools.[24]

Urban Leagues worked in other ways to make life in the cities more bearable. Were children trapped in hot, crowded tenements? The Urban League would organize outings to ball games, picnics, or plays, and it might send a handful of lucky ones to the country for a week or two of summer camp.[25] Was the incidence of disease and infant mortality unusually high among blacks in the city? The Urban League would sponsor pageants, contests, lectures, and demonstrations to dramatize proper health care.[26] Were black neighborhoods run down? The League would organize community clean-up and beautification projects. Its "Better Lawns Contest," the Detroit League informed Eugene Kinckle Jones, was its "most outstanding accomplishment" in 1926.[27] In 1928 Chicago inaugurated a speakers' bureau on better living conditions and an essay contest on "Better Homes and Better Health." [28] Shortly before the stock market crash, Milwaukee boasted of a canning and preserving contest with entries of 113 jars and glasses.[29]

Casework, or the adjustment of individual problems, was a staple feature of every League's program. "A Day at the Urban League" brought "all sorts of human problems . . . through its doors." [30] To blacks, the League was "the panacea for every ill"; to whites, it was "the agency that [could] provide any information or service that [had] to do with the Negro." When it said that "individuals in almost every walk of life" used its services "as a means towards straightening out [their] problems," the Detroit Urban League was scarcely exaggerating.[31]

Leagues sponsored school visitors to look after black children who were prone to "irregular attendance, poor scholarship, chronic tardiness, untidiness, [and] bad behavior." [32] Such cases, the Detroit League found, typically arose in schools "where the parents [took] little or no interest in the children's appearance or behavior." [33] Urban Leagues sent visiting nurses and doctors into black homes to tend to the sick.[34] Staff members handled hundreds of cases each year.[35] A League might be called upon to trace missing relatives, to find a home for a newly dispossessed family, to adjust differences between parents and children, husbands and wives. Summing up its services in one particular case, the Detroit Urban League reported that it had "acted as sort of father-confessor to the entire family over [a] period of 7 years." [36] In such work, the organization cooperated closely with private and public agencies, including departments of public welfare, schools, churches, police departments, juvenile courts, the Red Cross, and travelers' aid societies. While they were not, officially, relief-giving agencies, some local Leagues kept a special fund to provide Christmas baskets, food, clothing, and coal for the needy.[37]

Through it all the Leagues continued to emphasize the standards and behavior they had tried to inculcate in the migrants during World War I. In St. Louis, League spokesmen gave "morale talks" to "impress upon the colored employees the necessity of holding their jobs and increasing their efficiency." The talks had made their mark, the League felt, when those in attendance made such remarks as " 'I will spend my money more carefully than I have.' 'The next time I have a job I will try to be more neat.'

'Look at my bank account since you made the talk.' " [38] Cleveland sponsored thrift campaigns and community betterment clubs.[39] The Detroit League organized an association of taxi drivers "to bring home to them a regard for traffic laws and to better their habits of speech and decency." [40]

Columbus worked "to control and improve the behavior and conduct of Negroes in the streets and other public places in the Negro community"; Detroit distributed pamphlets of "Helpful Hints" and considered ways of "raising . . . standards" and "making for better behavior on the part of the Negro group." [41] Given their rural roots, Chicago felt, black people "require[d] instruction, admonition and direction, lest their individual defects should be regarded as racial or constitutional failures." Accordingly, "in the factory, in the home, in the office, and in the church," the Urban League "preach[ed] the gospel of punctuality, regularity, and general efficiency." [42] The continuing influx of newcomers, particularly during the upsurge of migration in 1923–24, made "the need for the promotion of programs of civic betterment . . . almost as great now as it was at the time when the [wartime] migration was at its height." At mid-decade the Chicago League still saw an "urgent" need "for cleaner streets, well kept houses, more attention to personal hygiene and stricter conformity to other civic requirements." Hence it taught "habits of thrift, cleanliness, health and general good behaviour." In a campaign to encourage thrift, for example, it scheduled classes in budget-making and a special Thrift Sunday with sermons on "the value of saving." [43] Notices in the black press reminded parents, in a slightly patronizing tone, that Chicago, unlike the South, required school attendance.[44] Unsubtle parables taught the importance of proper behavior. "Once upon a time," a typical Urban League story went, "there lived a young man on a farm in the South. . . . There was no need to think about what kind of clothes to wear and how to act because there was no one there to see." But when he came to Chicago to work in a steel mill, "he was the same young man" who wore "his dirty, smelly overalls" and shouted and sprawled in streetcars. People shrank away from him, and he wondered about the "meanness and prejudice of the white folks in Chicago." The moral? "Wake up. . . . It might be your fault." [45] By such efforts, the white Chicago *Daily News* felt, the Urban League was "doing important work not only for the individual but for the community." [46]

III

This whole range of services was identical to those that settlement houses were providing in immigrant neighborhoods in the 1920s.[47] They help to illustrate that the decade was not merely a wasteland of complacency and reaction, but that concerned men and women continued to seek ways to ameliorate the condition of the less fortunate in American society. We know that important strands of progressivism persisted in the 1920s in the campaigns for women's rights, social insurance, and the protection of children, as well as in the services that settlement houses sought to provide. The activities of Urban Leagues in the 1920s show that the spirit of progressivism also survived in the field of racial advancement. Progressivism survived in the Urban League's leadership, both in the individuals whose service bridged the war years, and in the composite profile of board members in the 1920s. It survived, too, in the programs the Urban League pursued.

There continued to be a major difference between the Urban League and other voluntary agencies seeking social amelioration. Whether the vehicle was the National Consumers League, the National Child Labor Committee, or the settlement houses, the emphasis on social service in the 1920s typically went hand in hand with a campaign for social reform. Most voluntary agencies had come to recognize that their objectives could not be met on a piecemeal, private basis. The social reordering that they anticipated required state and federal action. And so they fought for the enactment of welfare programs, old age pension systems, laws

prohibiting child labor, and a range of other reforms to rehuman-
ize an often cruel and exploitative industrial society.[48]

The Urban League still declined to engage in lobbying for legislation. In part, that decision was practical. The experience of
other voluntary agencies showed how difficult it was to accomplish real reform in the decade between the Progressive Era and
the New Deal. In the climate of intolerance that prevailed, it
would have been impossible to find support for legislation beneficial to blacks. In part, too, the decision was tactical. By leaving
the more controversial legislative arena to the NAACP, the
Urban League had a better chance of securing foundation and
community chest support for its own, milder, social service program.

There is no reason to believe that the Urban League could
have accomplished more if it had chosen to emphasize social
change instead of social service. Indeed, given the atmosphere of
the 1920s, a more aggressive program might have accomplished
less. But social services could have only modest results. As the
Kansas City League put it, in summarizing its activities during
1929, "the results have not been spectacular nor will they ever be
so." "The genius of the organization," it felt, was "its quiet, easy
manner of attacking minority group problems, and, in some cases,
solving them." [49]

In some cases. The services that the Urban Leagues provided
certainly made an important difference in the lives of the people
they touched. If, in a given year, 1500 children were taken on
outings, or the same number enrolled in classes and clubs, or 1100
babies examined at a clinic, their lives were made that much more
tolerable. Without the Urban League programs, their existence
would have been more trying. But the Urban League operated in
just 20 cities in 1920, and in only 34 by 1930; moreover, it
touched only a comparative handful of the blacks who lived in
the cities it served. With expenditures for the entire League
movement at about $145,100 in 1920, and only $582,200 a decade
later, it necessarily had a limited impact.[50] It provided examples

and set precedents, but it was a laboratory that never encompassed most blacks in urban America.

Useful services, but unspectacular results—these judgments seem to sum up the Urban League's efforts at social amelioration in the 1920s. In many ways they also apply to the League's work in seeking employment.

12 INTEGRATING WHITE CAPITALISM

Most employers who hired blacks during World War I did so not because they were trying to be fair, nor because they believed that blacks were unusually able, but because the availability of blacks happened to coincide with a special need for workers. No doubt some employers did come to be impressed by the blacks they hired, and certainly some were receptive to arguments for equal opportunity. But, over all, their motives can be explained in simple terms of economic necessity and self-interest. Given a choice, most of them would have continued to do what they had always done—hire whites.

Under such circumstances, the Urban League had a built-in advantage in its efforts to open industrial opportunities to blacks. But when those circumstances changed, the League's task became harder. When employers no longer desperately needed black workers, it was easier for them to satisfy their prejudices as well as their pocketbooks. Thus, in the postwar decade, the Urban League faced a twofold task: to help blacks hold on to jobs acquired during the war and to make inroads into new areas of employment.

I

In seeking jobs for blacks, the Urban League had to reverse traditional prejudices against integrated work forces. Sometimes employers simply refused to consider the matter; "it is not the policy of this company to employ Negro labor" became a familiar response. When they were willing to account for their reasons, a common answer was that whites would not stand for Negro co-workers, or worse yet, Negro supervisors. "Do not know that white help would care to work with colored girls under conditions in our workroom," one millinery establishment said. "Skilled employees in our line refuse to work with Negroes," an auto body shop concurred. A typical objection was that blacks were incapable of performing jobs that demanded any measure of skill or intelligence; "Negroes are not employed in our plant because of the highly technical nature of the work," a beet sugar manufacturer explained. Blacks needed "too much supervision," another firm said.[1] A clothing manufacturer in Chicago worried that hiring black factory workers "would have a tendency to lower the sales power of their clothes . . . since Negroes were looked upon as inferior workers in this particular field."[2] Companies were concerned, too, about the effect of black employees on customer relations; their "customers would object to colored salespeople," department stores told the Chicago Commission on Race Relations.[3]

Unsatisfactory experiences with individual black workers in the past reinforced employers' predispositions to write Negroes off as unfit for industrial employment. In Denver, employers dismissed black workers because of "theft," "lack of skill," "irregularity," "drinking," and "lack of interest in job."[4] One employment manager, who explained to the Urban League why 250 Negroes employed by his company had been discharged or had quit over a period of three years, handily summarized the prevailing stereotype of Negro labor. He had fired one man for "loafing on [the] job," another who "refused to hurry," and a third because he "wanted overtime for Washington's Birthday." Other men were "lazy," "very stubborn," and "absolutely no good."[5]

Views like these made the Urban League's task especially difficult. Indeed, as the decade of the 1920s opened, the prospects for black employment were particularly inauspicious. Contemporaries reported that blacks hired during the war were being laid off as white workers returned to the factories. A Women's Bureau investigator who visited 150 manufacturing and mechanical industries in nine states at the end of 1920 found that black women had been dismissed or demoted to less skilled jobs. A typical explanation from a firm that had employed hundreds of black women who performed satisfactorily was that "They were employed solely on account of the shortage of labor and it was not the intention of the management from the beginning to retain them when white girls were available." Among 57 firms that in 1918 had declared their intention of keeping their black employees, 11 had dismissed them outright; the 41 firms still in business had cut their black work force by 42 per cent over the two-year period.[6]

The most dramatic development in black employment patterns during the 1910s was the exodus from agriculture; between 1910 and 1920 over 700,000 blacks left jobs on the land.[7] While 58 per cent of the black men and 52.2 per cent of the black women who were gainfully employed in 1910 made their living in agricultural pursuits, by 1920 the figures had dropped to 48.2 and 39 per cent, respectively. The number of black men who were gainfully employed rose by almost 75,000 in the course of the decade, but the number of black women who worked for a living dropped by close to 445,000.[8] Thus many of the blacks who left the agricultural sector were women who also left the labor market—in part, no doubt, because their husbands' new jobs in northern industries provided enough money to support their families. But a large proportion of blacks moved from the land to jobs in urban industries. The biggest absolute increase in any occupational category over the decade was in manufacturing and mechanical industries, where some 255,000 blacks found new jobs in the wake of the war emergency.

While a number of blacks moved into the industrial sector, there is some evidence that blacks in nonagricultural employment were as heavily overrepresented in the lowest level jobs in 1920 as they had been in 1910. Slightly more than 83 per cent of black males who worked in nonagricultural jobs in 1910 held positions as semiskilled workers, laborers, or servants. A decade later the distribution still held to within a tenth of a percentage point. Among gainfully employed black women, 94.7 per cent held jobs in these categories in 1910, and 92.7 per cent did in 1920. Blacks may have moved from the land to the city, but the race as a whole had enjoyed very little occupational mobility.[9]

Proponents of racial advancement took different viewpoints on the best way to cope with the economic disabilities of black Americans. For Marcus Garvey, the answer lay in opting out of the white economy. "A race that is solely dependent upon another for its economic existence sooner or later dies," Garvey warned.[10] Instead, he promoted businesses owned and operated by blacks—the ill-fated Black Star shipping line, and the less well-known Negro Factories Corporation, which succeeded in developing grocery stores, a restaurant, laundry and tailoring establishments, and a publishing house. By laying a base for economic self-sufficiency and creating an object of racial pride, such ventures would, Garvey thought, be the best route to short-run racial advancement.

A different approach to black capitalism came from the National Negro Business League. Founded in 1900 by Booker T. Washington, the League was an organization of successful businessmen who encouraged other blacks to follow in their footsteps. Its rationale was that business success benefited blacks in more ways than providing material wealth; the accomplished businessman of "intelligence and high character" won the respect of whites as well as blacks. As Washington explained it, "This fact suggested that, in proportion as we could multiply these examples North and South, our problem would be solved." [11]

II

The Urban League virtually ignored black capitalism as a route to racial progress. Rarely, if ever, did it encourage independent black businesses. While it offered special courses for domestic workers and occasional instruction in salesmanship and foreman-ship, it never tried, for example, to train blacks in business meth-ods or to help them obtain credit so they could set up their own shops. The whole thrust of the League's efforts was to find niches for blacks in the existing structure of white industry.

This emphasis would have critical consequences for the League's work in the industrial sector. It might have been easier to use the influence and financial resources of white Urban Leagu-ers to develop businesses owned and operated by blacks that ca-tered to a black market. The pattern for this kind of effort al-ready existed in the relationship between black professionals and the large black communities in urban centers. But building small black enterprises was not necessarily the best route to improving the economic status of the black masses. Moreover, the Urban League believed in integration in its economic as well as its so-cio-political sense. This faith determined that the League would work to integrate American capitalism. Given white prejudices and black deficiencies in training, however, it also meant that the main focus of the League's employment efforts would be on the lowest levels of the industrial ladder.

The second premise underlying the Urban League's employ-ment efforts was that the League should try to influence private behavior rather than public policy. This focus automatically lim-ited what the organization could accomplish. Because it worked on a piecemeal basis, by direct contacts with individual private employers, the Urban League could not hope to achieve the same kind of mass impact that might have been realized by the estab-lishment of public policy prohibiting employment discrimination. Yet there is no indication that such a policy could have been adopted on a national, state, or local level even if the League had refocused its efforts in that direction. At a time when it was im-possible to secure effective legislation to protect blacks from being lynched, it would have been pointless to work for laws guaranteeing them employment opportunity. By the 1920s, gov-

ernment had taken only relatively tentative steps toward regulat-
ing employment policies in the private sector. It was not until the
New Deal that such authority was further developed; before that,
it could scarcely have been expected to be invoked in behalf of
blacks.

To conduct its industrial diplomacy in the world of white capitalism, the National Urban League established a Department of
Industrial Relations in March 1925. The League had been considering the need for a national employment program for six
years; it took that long to set up mainly because funds were so
scarce.

The Department sought to widen employment opportunities
for blacks through a variety of emphases. On the one hand, it
tried to persuade employers to hire blacks by publicizing "information on successful experiments with Negro workers," thus proving that blacks could handle jobs beyond "certain stereotyped
lines of work." On the other hand, it sought to establish "friendly
relations with labor groups" and to strike down the barriers
against black participation in the organized labor movement. At
the same time, it recognized the need for "education of the
Negro worker" through "better training . . . in trade schools"
and "better apprenticeship opportunities." [12]

The National Urban League relied heavily upon polite, painstaking, personal contacts with executives of major corporations
as a primary means of expanding employment opportunities for
blacks. Local Urban Leagues were capable of tackling employment discrimination in smaller local firms, but it required "a man
with a national viewpoint," working out of the national office, to
approach the officers of major national corporations.[13] The man
for the job was the thirty-six-year-old executive of the Chicago
Urban League, T. Arnold Hill.

Like Eugene Kinckle Jones, who was three years his senior,
Hill had been graduated from Wayland Academy and Virginia
Union University, both in his native city of Richmond. While
Jones had earned a master's degree in economics at Cornell, Hill

went to New York University for a year of graduate study in economics and sociology. Jones hired Hill as his assistant in the Urban League's New York office in 1914; in December 1916 he sent him to Chicago to handle the establishment of the League's new Chicago affiliate.[14]

While Hill's assignment in Chicago was originally a temporary one, he stayed on as the Chicago League's executive secretary until he returned to New York as director of the Department of Industrial Relations in April 1925. According to the Chicago *Broad Ax*, Hill's work in the West had been "most successful." [15] During his eight-year tenure in Chicago, he succeeded in building support for the League among influential groups and individuals. He made important friendships, especially with William C. Graves, secretary to Julius Rosenwald, who was a principal benefactor of both the National and the Chicago Urban Leagues. He was a personable man and a persuasive advocate. Horace J. Bridges, leader of the Chicago Ethical Culture Society and president of the Chicago Urban League, later recalled how impressed he had been by Hill "and the social ideal he so ably expounded." To Bridges, Hill was "most attractive and interesting" as well as "one of the most capable, indefatigable, and efficient executive personalities" he had ever encountered.[16]

The qualities Hill displayed in Chicago were perfect for launching the Department of Industrial Relations. He was a man of great tact, a proved racial diplomat who had had wide experience in dealing with white leaders and considerable success in convincing them of the rightness of his cause. He was skilled at "person-to-person contacts"—exactly the kind of approach the industrial relations work required.[17] Moreover, he looked the part of the polished racial diplomat—light-skinned, with fine features, close-cropped hair and a well-trimmed moustache, conservatively dressed in heavy-rimmed glasses and a three-piece suit. His pictures suggest a person of substance, cultivation, and self-confidence—a man easy to imagine in a bank or a company board room. He was a man with contacts in high places, and he was nationally known and respected in his field of social work. In view of the mandate of the Department of Industrial Relations, this businessman's son seemed to be the perfect ambassador to the world of white business.

III

Hill worked out a careful rationale to use in appealing for jobs for blacks. The League, he said, ran "the whole gamut of ortho-dox techniques" in trying "to persuade employers to see the ad-vantages of using Negroes." [18] Instead of basing his case on equal rights or compensation for centuries of deprivation, he generally argued on the basis of national interest—and the self-interest of employers. Give blacks good jobs, he would say, and the burden on hospitals, charitable agencies, and penal institutions would grow lighter. Their increased purchasing power would benefit business. From an employer's point of view, Negro labor was more efficient than immigrant labor; blacks spoke English, were "acquainted with American customs," and were "more easily taught than foreign born" workers. It was easier to find a well-trained black man than a white man "for an ordinary task," since "an ordinary job for a white person is a good job for a Negro." Stores in black neighborhoods would increase their sales if they hired blacks.

The League also counted on employers being reasonable men. It had a naïve faith that sitting down and explaining the injustice of discrimination would almost make it disappear. "America's reputation for fair play [is] at stake," Hill said, 'for it is obviously undemocratic, unfair and positively deteriorating to deny oppor-tunities on the basis of racial prejudice to a group that has never been unfaithful to its country." [19]

Hill used arguments like these in dealing with some of the country's largest industries. In 1926, for example, he approached Standard Oil of Indiana about hiring Negro gas station atten-dants. Hill told company officials that hiring "colored salesmen, filling station managers, and demonstrators will increase your sales among Negroes" [20]—logic that he felt "impressed" Amos Ball, general manager of Standard Oil's sales department. After a year of correspondence, meetings, and denials by Standard Oil that it had intentionally discriminated against blacks, the company agreed to work with Urban League affiliates in eight cities to find qualified black employees.[21]

The experiment was launched in Chicago, where Hill cautioned the Urban League to choose the prospective employees "with exceeding care." [22] In March 1928, two Standard Oil stations each accepted two Negro attendants "on a month's probation," and the industrial relations director of the Chicago Urban League reported them as "doing nicely." In June Hill praised the company for "making good on its promises in many parts of the country" by finding new jobs for Negroes in Springfield and Kansas City, as well as Chicago. The League hailed Standard Oil for placing Negroes "in exclusive charge" of two filling stations in Chicago (where they also operated four greasing stations) and one each in St. Louis and Minneapolis.[23]

Despite this token progress, promotions on any meaningful scale never really materialized. In 1930 two Standard Oil stations in Buffalo became the first in that city to put Negro attendants in charge of workers of both races.[24] But in that same year, a Chicago Urban League official told Hill that Standard Oil had decided to promote employees to station manager according to seniority. Hence, "Negroes who were youngest in the service were shut out of the jobs." [25]

Integrating Standard Oil's working force proved easier because Amos Ball spoke with authority for the company's operations throughout the country. The Urban League often encountered the problem of "a favorable attitude toward the employment of Negroes in a company's plant in one city, and a reverse attitude in the same company's plant in another city." [26] Thus some A & P stores employed Negro clerks while others in different cities did not. The same held true for Western Union messengers and workers in Ford Motor Company and International Harvester Company plants, among others. (Nevertheless, the Department of Industrial Relations counted even the very limited inroads by Negroes at A & P, Ford, and International Harvester among its chief accomplishments during its first three years—an indication, perhaps, of the enormity of the Urban League's task.) Thus, the Department of Industrial Relations worked to influence executives of multi-city corporations to set standardized employment policies for all their plants and subsidiaries. This was not so easily accomplished. Using contacts arranged through a member of the League's executive board, Hill tried fruitlessly to persuade the president of A & P to standardize antidiscrimination policies throughout his stores.[27] The root of the problem with such companies was that "local plants usually [had] a considerable degree of autonomy"; hence "the convictions of a headquarters man" did not "always carry through the organization." Permitting "a considerable degree of latitude in local administration" may have encouraged discrimination, but it was a good business policy; "it serve[d] to get results." [28]

Not every employer was as agreeable to hiring Negroes as Standard Oil was. In 1928, in Pittsburgh, the Bell Telephone Company employed only two Negroes, both as bootblacks. T. Arnold Hill secured an interview with W. E. Quimby, an assistant to the vice president, and based his case for Negro employment on the improving educational status of Negroes and on the fact that the telephone was a public utility (Negroes therefore provided a certain share of the telephone company's income). Explaining that Bell was "not in a position to take a step which might not be successful," Quimby stated that opposition to hiring Negro operators stemmed from the belief that "mixing colored and white girls would not work out well." Similarly, the company hesitated to risk adding Negroes to the ranks of their drivers, truck repairers, installers, or coin box collectors; these jobs required at least some skill, and Quimby "did not feel that they were able to secure Negroes who could do the type of work." [29]

IV

To counter these kinds of objections, the Urban League liked to marshal hard evidence of successful on-the-job performances by Negro employees. It used any kind of leverage it could muster. A single job placement in a previously unintegrated company could be "an enormous victory," for the League could then confront the company's competitors on a much firmer footing.[30] Employers who spoke favorably of their experiences with Negro labor were likely to receive a note thanking them for offering employment opportunities to blacks and asking for a written copy of their remarks. "I should like to have it on file," Hill told one man, "as one of the few such favorable accounts we have of Negro labor, —not that colored men are not doing the work well, but rather that employers are unwilling to give them credit publicly for the splendid work they are doing." And, he might have added, the statement would serve as useful ammunition in persuading hesitant employers to given Negroes a chance.[31]

The same held true regarding employee relations. "The almost invariable answer given by an employment manager to one seeking jobs for Negroes [was] 'Our white employees will not work with them,'" the Urban League had found. Believing this argument to be often a product of the manager's personal prejudice, or even his imagination, the Department of Industrial Relations made it its business to prove that whenever blacks had had "a fair chance . . . to demonstrate their skill," and when the management had taken "the proper attitude," there had not been "an overpowering objection on the part of white workers."[32]

In addition to examples of Negroes and whites working together in harmony, Hill's office kept records of Negro occupational advances, with special emphasis on unusual positions attained by individuals. Together with prejudice, one of the central factors impeding the Negro's progress in employment was habit; whites and Negroes alike, accustomed to thinking of Negroes in certain stereotyped jobs, needed to know that members of the race had made it in new and different occupations. "I am searching for instances of notable progress in occupations by Negroes," Hill might write. "I know Detroit must have made some achievement along this line." [33] The affiliates would respond with evidence of the slow, painful process of cracking the color line in employment: for example, jobs for Negro elevator operators at Gilchrist's department store in Boston, or Negro clerks working in A & P stores in the Negro neighborhoods of Baltimore. The evidence came in, piece by piece, voicing tentative hopes, documenting minor triumphs—and all ready to bolster Hill's case before recalcitrant employers.[34]

Another way of countering objections to hiring Negroes was to run a pilot project to show what would happen. The Chicago Urban League tried this approach in 1928 in an effort to crack the barrier against Negro employment in retail stores. Cooperating closely with store officials, the League's employment bureau screened Negro applicants who were then hired as clerks and cashiers at the South Center Department Store on Chicago's increasingly black South Side. Carefully chosen workers (not long after the experiment was launched, there were forty-four of them, representing over 40 per cent of the store's total sales force) met regularly with Urban League officials "for instruction and counsel" in techniques of salesmanship and personal behavior. At first sales declined slightly, causing the dismissal of several clerks. However, only one of these was a Negro, and she was replaced by a Negro. The experiment was particularly important, the League believed, "for the reason that if it proves successful, it can be used to illustrate that *it can be done.*" [35]

V

Personal contact with individual employers was the Urban League's way of fighting job discrimination. Actual job placements, however, were principally the work of the League's affiliates. The National Department of Industrial Relations concentrated on "creating sentiment favorable to the employment of Negroes and urging the importance of thorough preparation on the part of Negroes for opportunities as they develop." [36] In industry, as T. Arnold Hill pointed out, " 'intangible' efforts" were "frequently more productive than the direct appeal to individual employers." It was essential to sway public sentiment toward opening occupational opportunities to Negroes. "After all, the obstacles Negro workers face are due largely to a subversive public opinion which individual employers cannot ignore even though they might like to." [37] Toward this end, the Department of Industrial Relations used intensive, week-long campaigns in individual cities "to arouse public thinking on the low economic status of Negroes." [38]

These "Industrial Campaigns" or "Negro in Industry Weeks" involved addresses to service clubs, student organizations, and Chambers of Commerce; radio broadcasts; newspaper publicity; and meetings with prospective employers. To employers, the campaigns conveyed the importance of hiring Negroes and affording them opportunities for advancement. To Negro workers, they brought "advice and admonition with respect to their own responsibility for improving their economic status" [39] through "training and thorough application" to their work. By such behavior, they would better their own chances and at the same time "demonstrat[e] the capacity of the race." [40]

Measuring the results of the campaigns is difficult, but the League thought they were encouraging. In Boston, for example, 1253 blacks had applied to the Urban League for jobs in 1926; the next year, stimulated by "Negro in Industry Week," registrations jumped to 4290. Employers, too, were influenced by the industrial campaign; the League found 1157 jobs in 1927, as compared to 800 the year before.[41] The campaign was credited with the employment of Negroes as furniture finishers, glass blowers, factory workers, air compressor operators, and needlework salesmen. The secretary of the Retail Trade Board promised his efforts in furthering the employment of Negroes in retail department stores and asked for twelve to fifteen chauffeurs for whom he would find jobs driving delivery trucks. An industrial committee formed during the campaign, whose members included a white lawyer and white department store executive, began negotiations with the new Parker House management to see that Negro waiters and bell boys would be on the staff when the hotel opened. They also contacted the Statler Hilton Hotel, the Gillette Company, and the Boston branch of Ford Motor Company in the interest of Negro employment. A few months later the Urban League reported that eight Negroes, some of them mechanics, had been hired at the new Ford plant.[42]

In Chicago in 1927, the League boasted of placing two men "in responsible positions" in a real estate firm, as well as clerks "with A. & P., in two shoe stores and in numerous groceries, fruit stores etc. as a result of the week." The Kansas City industrial committee met with gas company officials in 1925 to negotiate the hiring of Negroes as meter readers.[43] Industrial campaigns during the Department's first four years brought comparable results in such cities as Philadelphia, Indianapolis, Milwaukee, St. Louis, Akron, Springfield, Illinois, St. Paul, Minneapolis, Pittsburgh, Columbus, and Canton, Ohio.

There were other ways of keeping in touch with the employment situation on the national level. T. Arnold Hill contributed articles on Negro labor to trade journals and attended industrial and business meetings to promote the work of the League. He conferred with representatives of the employment division of the Labor Department and the national Chamber of Commerce, heads of personnel management associations, and labor officials. During his trips to organize affiliates and plan industrial campaigns, he squeezed in meetings with important regional employers. On a midwestern swing in January 1928, for example, he stopped in Akron to talk with officials of five major rubber companies concerning the possibility of more Negro employment and the status of those already employed. Hill also traveled regularly to see for himself how Negro workers were faring. Unlike Negro in

Industry Weeks, these visits were devoted to fact-finding; "I am not interested in making speeches," Hill emphasized, "but in having others talk to me." [44]

It was impossible, however, for Hill to cover the field single-handedly. He therefore appointed "Industrial Associates" (some of them Urban League secretaries) in forty-eight cities to supply information on labor conditions for a departmental bulletin on the status of Negro workers. The National League had previously solicited such information from individual Urban Leagues on a more informal basis to furnish a weekly column, "Where the Negro May Find Work," for the Pittsburgh *Courier*. Beginning in June 1926, the Department compiled the Associates' reports in a monthly bulletin which it distributed to newspapers, business journals, employers of Negro labor, the Associates, and other interested parties. The information on variations in supply and demand also equipped the Department to advise job-seekers and prospective migrants on the most promising fields for employment and locations for resettlement.[45]

VI

The National Department of Industrial Relations maintained contact with local employment conditions through communications with national offices of companies with scattered local plants and through meetings with local employers during Negro in Industry Weeks. But staff, budget, and time limitations meant that the National League could not keep in close touch with each community's particular employment situation. The League therefore urged its affiliates to employ industrial secretaries of their own, men who would be effective local agents of the League's efforts in encouraging training and efficiency and broadening employment opportunities.

By 1927 Urban League affiliates in New York, Cleveland, Chicago, Brooklyn, Newark, Philadelphia, Detroit, and Kansas City had hired industrial secretaries. In Leagues without special secretaries or industrial committees, the regular staff handled industrial and employment activities. Their work differed from that of the National Department of Industrial Relations in that they were responsible for most of the actual job placements. The national office dealt with large national firms, and it worked to create a climate favorable to black employment; the affiliates functioned as employment agencies.

What kinds of people sought their help? Between August 1925 and July 1926, 201 men and 168 women applied to the Minneapolis Urban League for work. Just over half of the men were married and supporting families; "nearly two-thirds of the women were married and had been forced by economic conditions to seek work outside of the home, in addition to the care of their children." More than half of the women and close to two-thirds of the men were between the ages of twenty and forty—the optimum years for employment. Of the total applicant group, 121 had lived in Minneapolis for more than nine years; 86 claimed less than a year's residence, and 32 had been in the city for less than a month.

What kind of credentials did they bring to their job search? Five per cent had attended college, but only a quarter of those had actually been graduated. A similar number had received technical training in vocational schools. Slightly more than 10 per cent had been graduated from high school, twice that many had completed from one to three years of high school, and 63.4 per cent had only attended elementary school. Just three of the applicants were illiterate.

Their aspirations were limited. Of the 369 applicants, 198 specifically requested jobs in domestic and personal service, 11 said they wanted to be common laborers, and 33 asked for work driving, washing, or repairing cars, while only 53 sought jobs "requiring more training, as in the skilled mechanical trades and in the clerical occupations." The Urban League found jobs for 121 of the applicants, about 87 per cent of them in domestic and personal service.[46]

Measuring the Urban League's success on the employment front is a difficult task. The National League did not preserve records of annual job placements, and even if it had, "accomplishment" and "success" would still remain elusive terms. Eugene Kinckle Jones claimed 38,000 placements in 1920, 30,000 in 1921, and 40,000 in 1922.[47] Partial records from a few affiliates show that they were able to place anywhere from one-seventh to three-quarters of the blacks who applied for jobs in a given year.[48] But we do not know what proportion of job seekers in any particular city ever applied to the Urban League—nor, for that matter, whether those who applied were out of work or were simply looking for a better position. Evaluating the League's performance would be complicated even if better statistics existed. Should the formula for success be a ratio of job placements to job seekers? Of skilled to unskilled positions found? Of cracking the color line in new lines of endeavor? Of materially advancing the standard of living of the masses of black Americans? These choices are not easy to make; with only the barest fragments of evidence from the national and local offices, assigning a concrete figure to the League's job placements becomes an impossibility.

Such a figure, even if it existed, might not accurately gauge the Urban League's influence. The Chicago Urban League argued persuasively that "the initial contacts" it established with employers and "the propaganda and agitation" it "conducted unceasingly for the employment of colored workers" had made employers accustomed to thinking in terms of black employees, so that "many a young man and woman with personality, force and initiative can now make his own way without the intercession of the League or any other agency."[49] Hence placements might understate the League's actual impact.

Such logic leads to an inspection of census records. Correlating black employment advances with the Urban League's influence is a purely speculative effort; we know from individual testimonials that some employers did hire blacks because of the League's intercession and influence, but we cannot know how many others acted purely out of economic self-interest. Further, census statistics obscure fluctuations in employment patterns within a decade. We know where blacks stood in 1920 as compared with 1910, but we cannot know with any accuracy to what extent the 1920 figures may represent a slippage from a wartime high. Nor can we accurately estimate the employment status blacks may have achieved before the stock market crash as against their status in 1930. These problems are compounded by certain changes in occupational classifications and methods of inquiry from census to census. And, of course, we have learned to treat census data for blacks with a degree of caution.

Despite these difficulties, it is possible to make some meaningful judgments about the changing economic status of blacks over the decades and to make at least tentative inferences about the role the Urban League may have played in them. As Table 12.1 shows, the decade of the 1920s continued the movement, so marked in the 1910s, of blacks away from the land. While the largest numerical gains in black employment came in the manufacturing and mechanical industries, blacks in those fields in 1930 constituted the same percentage of all employed blacks as in 1920. The largest gains—in terms of both absolute numbers and percentage of employed blacks—were realized in the area of domestic and personal service. For black women, especially, the 1920s meant an acceleration of a tendency toward greater concentration in such pursuits.

Simply to look at rough census occupational categories is not especially illuminating. To say that blacks were better off or worse off because they were leaving the agricultural sector entails value judgments about rural and urban lifestyles that are impossible to quantify. Then, too, within each of the large occupational categories of the census there are marked variations among levels of jobs; a hotel keeper, though classified under domestic and personal service, has a higher status job than a laborer listed under manufacturing and mechanical industries.

If we impose categories of status and skill on the various occu-

Table 12.1

Percentage of Gainfully Employed Workers, 10 Years of Age and Over, by Occupation, 1910, 1920, 1930.

	All Blacks			All Workers			Black Women		
	1910	1920	1930	1910	1920	1930	1910	1920	1930
Agriculture, Forestry, Animal Husbandry	55.7	45.2	36.7	33.2	26.3	21.9	52.2	39.0	26.9
Extraction of Minerals	1.2	1.5	1.4	2.5	2.6	2.0	—	—	—
Manufacturing and Mechanical Industries	12.2	18.4	18.6	27.8	30.8	28.9	3.4	6.7	5.5
Transportation	4.9	6.5	7.2	6.9	7.4	7.9	.1	.2	.1
Trade	2.3	2.9	3.3	9.5	10.2	12.5	.3	.7	.8
Public Service	.4	1.0	.9	1.2	1.9	1.8	—	.1	.1
Professional Service	1.3	1.7	2.5	4.4	5.2	6.7	1.5	2.5	3.4
Domestic and Personal Service	21.6	22.1	28.6	9.9	8.2	10.1	42.4	50.3	62.6
Clerical Occupations	.4	.8	.7	4.6	7.5	8.2	.2	.5	.6

SOURCES: Bureau of the Census, *Fourteenth Census of the United States Taken in the Year 1920*, Vol. IV: *Population, 1920: Occupations* (Washington, D.C., 1923), pp. 340–41.

pations listed in the census, we can learn something about the relative standing of blacks in nonagricultural employment in the early decades of this century. As Table 12.2 shows, blacks in 1930 were still disproportionately concentrated in semiskilled, laboring, and servant jobs; in fact, while there were small gains and losses in individual categories, the general employment picture in 1930 was remarkably similar to that of 1920. Indeed, if one looks at the lowest level categories alone, as Table 12.3 indicates, blacks in 1930 were almost exactly where they were in 1920. While there was a

All Women			Black Men			All Men		
1910	1920	1930	1910	1920	1930	1910	1920	1930
22.4	12.7	8.5	58.0	48.2	41.6	36.1	29.8	25.8
—	—	—	1.9	2.2	2.0	3.2	3.3	2.6
22.5	22.6	17.5	17.7	24.0	25.2	29.3	32.9	32.1
1.3	2.5	2.6	8.0	9.5	10.8	8.4	8.6	9.4
5.8	7.8	9.0	3.5	4.0	4.6	10.5	10.8	13.4
.2	.3	.2	.7	1.5	1.3	1.5	2.3	2.2
9.1	11.9	14.2	1.2	1.3	2.0	3.2	3.4	4.5
31.3	25.6	29.6	8.5	8.4	11.6	4.1	3.7	4.7
7.3	16.7	18.5	.5	.9	.8	3.8	5.1	5.4

Bureau of the Census, *Fifteenth Census of the United States: 1930*, Vol. V: *Population: General Report on Occupations* (Washington, D.C., 1933), p. 74.

very small over-all improvement in the employment status of native-born white workers and a more significant improvement in the situation of foreign-born whites, blacks in 1930 were, if anything, slightly *more* concentrated in semiskilled, laboring, and servant positions than they had been in 1920.

In short, *in the aggregate mass*, blacks in 1930 were really no better off than they had been in 1920. Blacks were moving into trade, transportation, and industry, but not in such a way as to alter their position at the bottom of the employment ladder. Tens of thousands of blacks entered industry in the 1920s, but the per-

Table 12.2

Employment Distribution of Gainfully Employed Workers, 10 Years of Age and Over, 1920 and 1930, in Nonagricultural Occupations.

	% All Workers, 1920			% Males, 1920			% Females, 1920		
	Native-born White	Foreign-born White	Black	Native-born White	Foreign-born White	Black	Native-born White	Foreign-born White	Black
Proprietors, Officials, Managers	9.3	10.3	1.9	11.3	11.2	2.0	3.2	5.6	1.8
Clerks and Kindred Workers	23.5	8.4	2.3	18.8	7.2	2.8	37.1	14.8	1.5
Skilled Workers	16.4	19.1	5.5	21.7	22.3	8.5	.7	1.5	.2
Semiskilled Workers	21.2	24.6	14.4	20.4	22.6	14.7	23.6	35.4	14.0
Laborers	14.8	25.6	36.2	17.1	28.3	54.5	7.9	11.0	4.1
Servants	3.9	7.2	35.9	1.6	3.9	14.0	10.6	24.9	74.6
Public Officials	.7	.2	<.1	.8	.2	<.1	.3	<.1	<.1
Semiofficial Public Employees	1.8	1.2	.7	2.5	1.4	1.2	<.1	<.1	<.1
Professional Persons	8.4	3.4	2.9	5.7	2.8	2.4	16.5	6.6	3.9

	% All Workers, 1930			% Males, 1930			% Females, 1930		
	Native-born White	Foreign-born White	Black	Native-born White	Foreign-born White	Black	Native-born White	Foreign-born White	Black
Proprietors, Officials, Managers	9.6	11.9	1.9	11.8	13.2	2.0	3.4	5.6	1.7
Clerks and Kindred Workers	25.6	10.8	2.2	20.9	9.4	2.8	38.6	17.7	1.4
Skilled Workers	14.5	19.9	5.0	19.5	23.8	8.1	.5	1.0	.1
Semiskilled Workers	22.4	24.7	15.4	21.2	22.6	16.8	25.6	35.1	13.2
Laborers	11.3	17.4	31.2	14.9	20.6	49.6	1.3	1.4	1.9
Servants	4.7	9.4	40.3	1.9	5.1	17.1	12.4	30.4	77.1
Public Officials	.6	.2	<.1	.7	.2	<.1	.2	<.1	<.1
Semiofficial Public Employees	1.6	1.1	.4	2.2	1.3	.7	<.1	<.1	<.1
Professional Persons	9.7	4.6	3.4	6.6	3.8	2.8	17.9	8.6	4.5

SOURCES: Bureau of the Census, *Fourteenth Census of the United States Taken in the Year 1920*, Vol. IV: *Population, 1920: Occupations* (Washington, D.C., 1923), pp. 342–59.
Bureau of the Census, *Fifteenth Census of the United States: 1930*, Vol. V: *Population: General Report on Occupations* (Washington, D.C., 1933), pp. 76–85.
Dean Dutcher, *The Negro in Modern Industrial Society: An Analysis of Changes in the Occupations of Negro Workers, 1910–1920* (Lancaster, Pa., 1930).
Bureau of the Census, *A Social-Economic Grouping of the Gainful Workers of the United States* (Washington, D.C., 1938), esp. pp. 10, 13, 86–87.

Table 12.3
Employment Distribution of Gainfully Employed Workers, 10 Years of Age and Over, 1920 and 1930, in Semiskilled and Unskilled Positions in Nonagricultural Occupations.

% Males, 1920

	Native-born White	Foreign-born White	Black
Unskilled	18.7	32.2	68.5
Semiskilled	22.9	24.0	15.9
Total	41.6	56.2	84.4

% Females, 1920

	Native-born White	Foreign-born White	Black
Unskilled	18.5	35.9	78.7
Semiskilled	23.6	35.4	14.0
Total	42.1	71.3	92.7

% All Workers, 1920

	Native-born White	Foreign-born White	Black
Unskilled	18.7	32.8	72.1
Semiskilled	23.0	25.8	15.1
Total	41.7	58.6	87.2

% Males, 1930

	Native-born White	Foreign-born White	Black
Unskilled	16.8	25.7	66.7
Semiskilled	23.4	23.9	17.5
Total	40.2	49.6	84.2

% Females, 1930

	Native-born White	Foreign-born White	Black
Unskilled	13.7	31.8	79.0
Semiskilled	25.6	35.1	13.2
Total	39.3	66.9	92.2

% All Workers, 1930

	Native-born White	Foreign-born White	Black
Unskilled	16.0	26.8	71.5
Semiskilled	24.0	25.8	15.8
Total	40.0	52.6	87.3

SOURCES: See Table 12.2.

centage of blacks in industry who were laborers was just as large in 1930 as it had been a decade earlier.

What this implies is that the Urban League, in the largest sense, had been unable to affect the employment patterns of blacks in a truly lasting way. To be sure, the League did crack the color line at some points. The excitement over the appointment of one stenographer becomes more understandable in view of the fact that in 1920 there were only 2300 black stenographers in the entire country. It may seem pathetic in retrospect to boast about gaining jobs for elevator operators, but there were so few black elevator operators in 1920 that those jobs represented a real advance.

The sad thing is that the boasting and excitement may have fooled Urban Leaguers into ignoring what was really happening to the masses of blacks in the 1920s. In fact, it may have obscured what the Urban League itself was actually doing. The League's efforts mainly involved finding a place for blacks in the urban working class. There were many exceptions to this generalization; each year affiliates reported the placement of individual blacks in positions of special skill or responsibility. Annual figures sometimes reflected broader success in this direction. In Cleveland, for example, 925 of 3705 placements in one year were for skilled workers, while in New York the League found 337 skilled jobs, as compared to 363 semiskilled and 373 unskilled.[50] But the vast majority of the placements the League congratulated itself on making each year were on the level of unskilled and semiskilled labor.

Local Leagues testified to this in their monthly and annual reports. The employment situation among blacks in Detroit was improving in the summer of 1921, the executive there reported, mainly because "so many men" were being taken on "as common laborers with the various city departments." [51] In 1924, the work of Brooklyn's industrial department was "confined largely to placement in domestic service." [52] In 1926 the Detroit League found "only four or five avenues" for the placement of "those who have training for specialized types of work." "Ordinary placements" predominated.[53] In 1928 the League sent "many" men to automobile plants, foundries, and other factories, but "most" of them worked as moulders, machine operators, laborers, and janitors; the "goodly number" placed in department stores and businesses were porters, janitors, elevator operators, and starters.[54] Kansas City's "outstanding placements" for 1928 included two Standard Oil station helpers and a stock girl for a downtown department store.[55] In the first two months of 1929, the jobs the Detroit League found for 106 men were mainly in factories as janitors, laborers, truck drivers, elevator operators, and machine operators.[56] During the whole year, while "most of the women" were placed as domestics, "a goodly number" were "referred to the stores and apartment houses as elevator operators and maids, and a fairly large group found employment as stenographers, typists and file clerks in offices." [57] A "Special Notice" at the end of the Milwaukee Urban League's 1929 report announced: "Day workers for domestic employment given our special attention." [58]

When times were hardest, as in the depression of 1920 and 1921, at least 90 per cent of the jobs the League managed to find were for women—and this at a time when the vast majority of black women worked in domestic and personal service.[59] Even in relatively good times women were easier to place. "The demand for house maids at the Urban League cannot be met," the Chicago *Broad Ax* reported in 1923.[60] The employment record in Chicago in 1926 showed some improvement over the previous year, but "as usual the greater increases were in the female department where domestic, laundry and factory help predominated." Of some 2000 women placed, over 1500 were in laundry and domestic work. Jobs for moulders, bricklayers, and factory workers went begging because of lack of experienced applicants.[61] In 1924 Detroit found jobs for approximately 3000 women as compared to over 500 men, making the ratio almost six to one. In 1926, the ratio was more than two to one; in 1927, more than four to one; in 1928, more than two to one.[62] The reason was simple: in a time of peace and prosperity, families could easily afford to hire domestic help. Since immigration, which had slowed considerably during the war, was cut sharply by law in 1921, there was less of a competing supply of foreign-born workers for such positions. By far the majority of domestic and personal service jobs were held by women. In industry, where jobs were more commonly reserved for men, the return of peace obviated the need for black labor. The comparative difficulty of finding jobs for men was a troubling sign; the Detroit executive said that he was proud of his success in placing women, but he was "more concerned with men, who are the heads of the families and whose earnings are necessary to the adequate provision of the family." [63]

The Urban League was not altogether comfortable about the trend its employment record revealed. After Ira Reid became industrial secretary of the New York Urban League in 1925, he complained that he had to spend too much time on domestic placements. Following a "keen" discussion of where the League's industrial emphasis should lie, the affiliate's board resolved that "The future program and policy of the League would be that of creating new openings in the skilled trades and raising the standards of performance of Negro workers through educational programs." [64]

Even the Urban League's most faithful boosters saw that it was failing to fulfill its mandate. "The primal purpose of the Urban League was to find opportunities for these willing workers to enter into the industrial field in occupations suited to their various capacities," the New York *Age* pointed out. "It is not enough . . . [to] place a few workers of the race in the ordinary pursuits that were always open to them. . . . With the prestige and influence acquired by the League . . . and the moral and material influence of its backers, greater opportunities than these should be open to the ambitious and trained youth of the race." [65]

That was easier said than done. "Ideally," the Urban League believed, "people should be given work commensurate with their capacity." [66] Its "ultimate aim," the Cleveland affiliate reaffirmed, was "to enable colored men and women to follow the vocation for which each is best fitted and thus to bring about the complete assimilation of the race into the industrial life of the nation." [67] But in order to find any jobs at all for blacks, it was often necessary to begin at the bottom of the employment ladder. If the Urban League would settle for low-level placements, it would be much more likely to get results. Once blacks were in those jobs, though, it was extremely difficult for them to move upward. In the 1920s, blacks were gradually changing from a peasantry to an urban working class. Nothing the Urban League did could stop that over-all trend, and, in some ways, its efforts merely accelerated it.

13 THE URBAN LEAGUE
AND THE AFL

As the Urban League adopted a new national focus in the wake of the migrations, it began to address itself to the fundamental forces affecting black employment. During the years between World War I and the Great Depression, it started to grapple with the question of discrimination in organized labor.

The 1920s were "lean years" for American labor. Discredited by postwar strikes and identification with radical elements, labor unions entered the 1920s in popular disfavor. Conditions during the decade compounded their difficulties. The heterogeneity of the labor force made labor unity an unlikely goal. While the American working man profited less from the economic boom than his capitalist neighbors, he shared enough in the advancing prosperity to remain convinced that he could make it on his own. It was a time for individualism, not for collective action. Employers' experiments with welfare capitalism encouraged loyalty to the firm instead of the union; more explicit discouragement of unionism came through active repression. Important industries such as automobiles, utilities, chemicals, and rubber were strongly opposed to collective bargaining. And the craft system, by which most unions were structured, could not accommodate the changes brought about by mechanization and large-scale additions to the labor force.[1]

As a result, union membership fell from 5,047,800 in 1920 to

3,622,000 in 1923 and 3,442,600 in 1929. Union membership in 1930 accounted for 10.2 per cent of the country's more than 30 million nonagricultural employees; a decade earlier, the figure had been 19.4 per cent. Nevertheless, unions dominated such major industries as construction, coal, railroads, printing, clothing, street railways, water transportation, and music.[2] Insofar as blacks were moving off the land into industry, it was important not only to overcome the prejudices of major employers, but to crack the color line in organized labor.

I

In principle, the American Federation of Labor was from its earliest years committed to the organization of all workers, regardless of race, creed, or color. At its 1890 convention the Federation recorded its opposition to unions that barred black workers—a position that would be cited repeatedly in subsequent years as evidence of good faith on the race question. One of the "cardinal principles of the labor movement," the Federation declared in 1893, was that "working people must unite and organize, irrespective of creed, color, sex, nationality or politics." [3]

In fact, the policy of nondiscrimination proved to be little more than empty rhetoric. Unions with exclusion clauses in their constitutions were allowed to belong to the AFL, and in 1900 the Federation's president, Samuel Gompers, suggested that the AFL organize separate Negro unions. Accordingly, in 1902 the AFL's constitution was amended to permit the issuance of separate charters to all-black central labor unions, local unions, and federal labor unions "where, in the judgment of the Executive Council, it appears advisable and to the best interests of the trade union movement." [4] This meant that, while the AFL mouthed pieties about equality and nondiscrimination, it was actually acquiescing in, if not encouraging, the very policies it purported to oppose. On the one hand, it refused to compel its constituent unions to live up to the official policy against discrimination; at the same time, it caved in to Jim Crow by authorizing separate charters for black unions.

While the history of serious Urban League–AFL diplomacy properly begins in 1918, the initial contacts between the two organizations date to 1913, when George Haynes appeared before the executive council to urge the AFL to cooperate with the League in organizing Negro workers. Negroes, Haynes told the council, had to be disabused of the widely held notion that white labor unions did not want them; they had to be educated "in correct ideas of the under-lying principles of organized labor" and shown that their interests were "ultimately one with those of white labor." The prejudice or indifference of white labor toward blacks had to be eradicated. Concretely, Haynes wanted the AFL to bring Negroes into white unions where possible, or, if necessary, to organize them into separate locals "with full privilege and rights of representation in the central councils and in the National conventions." [5]

The meeting seemed singularly inconclusive. President Gompers told Haynes that attention to Negro workers was a routine part of the Federation's efforts "to reach those who [had] not yet adopted the ideas of organized labor," but that Negroes would not receive any special consideration. Two members of the council spoke of their own unsuccessful efforts to organize Negroes in the shipbuilding industry in Newport News and in the railway service, especially in the West, noting that they were "puzzled as to what next to do." Haynes refrained from urging the council even to make a public statement of sympathy with Negro labor; "while I saw that they were favorable to the fullest extent toward any effort to reach Negroes, they seemed somewhat disinclined to take any definite action on this our first appearance before them."

Of their own accord, however, the council issued a statement "announcing their readiness to cooperate with the National League in organizing," and, during the years 1910–14, the Federation employed three Negro organizers.[6] But the AFL felt that the organizers "made very little headway, practically none." The fault lay not with the Federation, but with the Negro workers, who "did not show a willingness nor a desire to belong to the trade union movement." Beginning in 1916, three successive AFL conventions endorsed the principle of organizing Negro workers but failed to create machinery to undertake the job; as the Federation explained, "previous experience along this line did not justify such action." [7]

II

The AFL paid relatively little attention to blacks before the First World War. Similarly, the problems of organized labor were among the Urban League's lowest priorities during those years. The wartime migrations threw the question of organizing Negro workers into a new context. Union leaders had to confront the potentially permanent substitution of large numbers of Negroes for white immigrant industrial workers. It was an opportune time to remind the AFL of its stand against discrimination.

Moreover, the role of AFL unions in the East St. Louis race riot in the spring and summer of 1917 made some agreement with the Federation imperative.[8] The seeds of the riot were planted in April, when the Aluminum Ore Company broke the strike of the AFL-affiliated Aluminum Ore Employees Protective Association and forbade its workers to belong to a union. While most of the strikebreakers were white, the company had recently been increasing its black work force, and the Protective Association blamed the loss of their jobs and the destruction of their union on blacks. Frustrated labor organizers, who had never been particularly successful in East St. Louis, sought to stop the migration of blacks into the city. For propaganda purposes, they recalled (incorrectly) that other unsuccessful strikes, particularly one the previous summer in the meatpacking industry, had been broken by the importation of black workers.

Union officials charged in the public press that employers were planning to bring thousands of blacks to the city to supplant white workers. In May the Central Trades and Labor Union, composed mainly of AFL craft unions, implored city officials to stop the migration and warned that if it continued, a race riot might erupt. When nothing happened, the union called a mass meeting for May 28 to demand action against the influx of blacks. The meeting dissolved into mob violence when a rumor spread that a black robber had intentionally killed a white man. In the intervening month, no steps were taken to prevent future disorders; indeed, labor leaders continued to blame the violence on a conspiracy by employers to flood the city with black workers. When the race riot finally erupted in all of its savage fury on July 2, white laborers led the mobs; while union leaders did not plot to cause the riot, their previous stance had certainly inflamed racial tensions. They made no effort to stop the violence, and, apparently, they even condoned the rioting.

The race riot, in the words of Eugene Debs, was "a foul blot upon the American labor movement. . . . Had the labor unions freely opened their door to the Negro instead of barring him . . . the atrocious crime at East St. Louis would never have blackened the pages of American history." [9] Debs's statement distorted and oversimplified the labor situation in East St. Louis, but he was right in pointing up the explosive potential of racial tensions. While AFL unions were not wholly responsible for the violence at East St. Louis, their role was important enough to make race leaders see some rapprochement with the Federation as essential.

At its conference on Negroes in industry in January 1918, the Urban League for the first time publicly defined its labor policy. Urging Negroes to affiliate with AFL unions, the conference adopted resolutions asking the Federation to accord Negro laborers the same rights and treatment as whites.[10] Following this, Eugene Kinckle Jones arranged for a series of meetings between the AFL executive council and a group of Negro leaders and concerned whites representing the Urban League, the NAACP, the Negro press, and philanthropic funds. Topics discussed included plans for organizing Negro workers and reducing racial friction in the labor movement.[11] The AFL thought that the meetings were a great success. When the visiting delegation learned of the AFL's "whole plan, work and desires . . . in regard to the organization of colored workers," they were "greatly impressed," and they agreed to urge blacks to join unions.[12]

When the Urban League enunciated its official labor policy the following year, it must have pleased the AFL. "We believe in the principle of collective bargaining," the League resolved in 1919, "and in the theory of cooperation between capital and labor in the settlement of industrial disputes and in the management of industry." Even its limited acceptance of strikebreaking jibed with the AFL's official view that unions should not discriminate against blacks; it advised blacks "to take jobs as strikebreakers" only when the unions involved "excluded colored men from membership," the League said. "We believe they should keep out of jobs offered in a struggle to deny labor a voice in the regulation of conditions under which it works." Negroes, it felt, "should begin to think more and more in terms of labor-group movements, so as ultimately to reap the benefit of thinking in unison." Toward that end, the League urged blacks "to organize with white men whenever conditions are favorable." "Where this is not possible," it pointed out, in a caveat that would become especially significant during the Depression, "they should band together to bargain with employers and with organized labor alike." [13]

While the AFL must have been well satisfied with the Urban League, the League was guardedly optimistic about the AFL. After the meeting in 1918 with President Gompers, the black representatives reported that Gompers had taken a stand that "was exceedingly pleasing to the delegates and was approved in full by them." He declared that he would try "to break down prejudice," and he promised to let the special committee name a black organizer who could interpret the labor movement to black workers.[14] The committee enthusiastically suggested ways of implementing Gompers's resolve. But at its convention later that year, the AFL simply voted to "give special attention to organizing the colored wage workers in the future"—with the understanding that "no fault" was to be found with what had been "done in the past." [15]

III

The AFL never took any steps to implement these pious pronouncements. The patience of black spokesmen with this record of platitudes and inaction is remarkable. Organizations like the Urban League persisted in their polite efforts to make the Federation live up to its promises. In 1920, for example, the League's executive board member, Abraham Lefkowitz of the American Federation of Teachers, joined Negro delegates to the AFL convention in presenting resolutions calling upon the Federation to undertake an educational campaign to convince white and black workers of the necessity of organizing all workers regardless of race, creed, or color; to hold periodic meetings between its executive council and "white and colored leaders who can suitably represent and express the point of view of Negro workingmen and can convey to Negro working-men the good will and sympathy felt by the American Federation of Labor towards them"; to employ in its Washington headquarters a Negro to act as liaison between the AFL and black labor; and to appoint Negro organizers to build up Negro union membership. The AFL resolved only to appoint Negro organizers where necessary—if funds permitted.[16]

Throughout the 1920s black delegates tried to put some force into the AFL conventions' supposed opposition to discrimination by pressuring the Federation to revoke the charters of offending unions. But the AFL would do no more than "recommend" or "request" that its internationals strike "whites only" provisions from their constitutions. The Federation steadfastly resisted compulsion or prohibitions on the ground that it could not "interfere with the trade autonomy of affiliated national and international unions." [17] This attentiveness to union rights, as one delegate pointed out in 1921, was reminiscent of the states' rights defense of slavery and discrimination.[18]

It should have been easy to see through what the AFL was doing. It never appointed the Negro organizers it promised, nor did it make much of a dent in its internationals' discriminatory practices. Whenever anyone raised the issue, it merely reiterated its previous statements of principle. Indeed, it did so in a way that shifted the blame from its own shoulders to those of its critics. Resolutions calling on unions to cease discrimination seemed to imply that the AFL was "not concerned in the full observance . . . of the principles and practices of non-discrimination." "To the contrary," the Federation had the gall to state, "an unbiased review of the activities of the American trade union movement will indicate that organized labor has made greater progress and has exerted a larger and more consistent effort in the elimination of all race, sex and religious discriminations and prejudices than any other group." In a not-so-gentle reprimand to those who found fault with its lack of action, the Federation pointed out that "toleration and co-operation must be practiced by all, those said to be discriminating as well as those alleged to be discriminated against." [19]

Black spokesmen could take just so much of this without beginning to bristle. When Samuel Gompers's successor, William Green, wrote the Urban League to request that it endorse the Federation and encourage Negroes to join AFL unions, the League at last began to temper its unfailing politeness with some hardheaded realism. "It is not sufficient to resolve," T. Arnold Hill wrote the AFL executive council. "Some way must be found to initiate your resolves. The Negro must know that he is wanted within the ranks of the Labor Movement and efforts must be employed to get him in." [20]

During 1925 and 1926, Hill appeared twice before the executive council and once at the AFL's annual convention with suggestions for overcoming the impasse in organizing Negro workers. Hill proposed that the AFL appoint a Negro executive adviser "to counsel with the officials of the labor movement on organization problems affecting Negroes," and "to negotiate with the National and local bodies that refuse[d] membership to Negroes." [21] The League even offered to raise half of the adviser's salary, but the executive council decided that the Federation was not able to meet the remaining expense involved.[22] Thereafter, the Urban League from time to time offered the AFL the names of prospective Negro organizers, but to no avail.

Given the record of unrelieved inaction and disappointment in the Urban League's dealings with the AFL, why did the organization persist so steadfastly in trying to change the Federation's policies? The reason is probably not that the League believed so strongly in organized labor as an end in itself. Despite its affirmation of collective bargaining, it passed no moral judgments on the value of the closed shop. Indeed, its general orientation toward businessmen and philanthropists set it at least somewhat at odds with the labor movement. Cooperation with the AFL could be justified on grounds of expediency alone. Since unions controlled access to hundreds of thousands of jobs, it made sense for the Urban League to keep lobbying the AFL, even though its efforts often seemed futile.

In 1928 and 1929, the launching of an intensive organizing effort in the South (especially in the textile industry) raised anew the matter of the AFL's intentions regarding Negro workers. Questioned by the Negro press at the Toronto convention in 1929, President Green carefully rehearsed four decades of official AFL pronouncements condemning racial discrimination and pointed out that Negro unions were eligible for separate charters where "it appear[ed] advisable and to the best interest of the trade union movements." [23] *Opportunity* thought very little of the AFL's Toronto performance, charging the Federation with failing to reach not only black workers, but the unskilled labor force in general. Editor Elmer Carter attacked the AFL's bias toward craft over industrial unionism, a foreshadowing of the League's later receptivity to the formation of the CIO.[24] President Green in turn deplored the "misleading character" of Carter's editorial and pointed out that progress in unionization would necessarily be slow because of the receptivity and understanding it required among workers.[25] The Urban League resented allegations that black workers were not organized because they were as yet unprepared to appreciate and accept doctrines and methods of organized labor; the fault, it believed, lay with the AFL.

The dialogue in *Opportunity* continued, with the League stressing the need for an organized recruiting effort to bring black workers into the union fold. T. Arnold Hill commended Green's avowal "that the Federation 'stands ready to help' the Negro 'raise his standards'"; to Hill, the AFL's ideals sounded fine, but its practices fell far short. "We are afraid," he told Green, ". . . that the word 'stands' is to be taken literally." The Urban League had "seen the Federation stand still, exerting not a single muscle to welcome Negroes into the folds of organized labor, while blaming them for not accepting the restrictions grudgingly offered." What could blacks expect from Green's latest promises? [26]

IV

The balance sheet at the end of the decade offered little encouragement. The Urban League estimated that 81,658 blacks belonged to unions in 1926–28. That meant that, at a time when slightly more than 2,500,000 blacks were working in nonagricultural pursuits, unions accounted for a much smaller proportion of black workers than of the total labor force. Those 81,658 members were clustered in a handful of unions—there were 12,381 in the Longshoremen, 10,131 in the Hod Carriers, 10,000 in the Maintenance of Way Employees, 5000 in the Mine Workers,

3000 in the Musicians, 3000 in the Sleeping Car Porters, 12,585 in independent Negro unions, and 25,561 in the balance of the labor movement.[27]

The reason for this clustering can be summed up in a single factor: racial discrimination. A study of Negroes and unions, begun in 1925 by research director Charles S. Johnson (in cooperation with the Department of Industrial Relations) and completed in 1930 by his successor, Ira De A. Reid, revealed that 22 national and international unions, 11 of them affiliated with the AFL, excluded Negro members either by constitution or by ritual. Thus, Negroes were still denied admission to such major organizations as the Machinists, Boiler Makers, Railway Mail Clerks, and at least 14 separate railroad workers' unions—an exclusion estimated to affect no less than 225,000 Negro workers in trades governed by the 11 AFL unions alone.[28]

Some unions openly defied the Federation's anti-discrimination pledges with outright constitutional prohibitions against Negro membership. Others accomplished the same end more subtly, through such devices as tacit agreements, entrance examinations, local determination of eligibility for membership, and ritual pledges binding members to propose only white workmen for admission to the union. As the American Flint Glass Workers Union put it, it prohibited Negro members "because Pipes on which Glass is Blown passes from one Man's mouth to another." [29] Some nationals and internationals, such as the Sheet Metal Workers, the Hotel and Restaurant Employees, and the Rural Letter Carriers, denied Negroes full privileges of membership but permitted affiliation through auxiliary bodies. "Our Southern membership, up to day, have objected to full membership," the International Brotherhood of Blacksmiths explained.[30] Negro local and federal unions, once a seemingly promising vehicle for organizing black workers, dropped in number from 169 in 1919 to 38 in 1929. While three Negro organizers had been employed by the AFL in 1911, there were none by 1929. Yet nearly all of the unions surveyed by the Urban League, even those denying membership to Negroes, answered that they did "regard the organization of Negroes as essential to the success of the labor movement." [31]

The persistence of union discrimination encouraged some local Urban Leagues to support strikebreaking by black workers. Publicly committed to the principle of collective bargaining, the National League never officially condoned such activities. But its position, as expressed in the League's labor policy in 1919 and subsequently reiterated by its executives, was that strikebreaking was a pragmatic tactic, an ultimate weapon to be held in reserve in the face of unbending union discrimination. Getting jobs was the Urban League's overriding objective, and union intransigence could conceivably force the use of questionable methods in pursuit of that goal.

Local Urban Leagues were free to formulate their own labor policies, independent of guidelines laid down by the national office. How actively some of them engaged in strikebreaking is a matter of controversy. Two major studies of blacks and the labor movement, Sterling D. Spero and Abram L. Harris, *The Black Worker* (1931), and Horace R. Cayton and George S. Mitchell, *Black Workers and the New Unions* (1939), accused several League affiliates of supplying black labor to plants struck by white unions.[32] Local League officials vigorously denied these allegations, and some of the charges seem overstated. Nonetheless, the Urban League acquired a reputation for engaging in strikebreaking—a reputation that could not have enhanced the credibility of its labor policy.

Strikebreaking was the only real weapon the Urban League could use against the AFL. But even if it had been disposed to promote it actively as a way of exerting pressure, the AFL's reaction would more likely have been irritation than cooperation. It was just too difficult to mobilize enough black workers at critical points to make the AFL sit up and take notice.

The Urban League's failure to effect any significant gains in its protracted negotiations with the AFL was not the League's fault.

Even if its spokesmen had been much less trusting and conciliatory in their dealings with the Federation, there is no reason to believe that different tactics would have produced more positive results. There were too few black delegates to make any real trouble at an AFL convention; nor were black workers ripe for organizing in opposition to the AFL.

The reasons for the AFL's intransigence lay beyond the Urban League's control. When unions were on the defensive, they could scarcely be expected to overcome deep-seated racial hostilities to admit blacks to equal membership. At a time when there were too few benefits for white union members, they were unreceptive to sharing what they had with blacks. For the AFL, racial discrimination was trivial compared to the bread and butter issues of union survival. The Urban League's faith in persuasion and polite diplomacy as weapons against union discrimination was certainly misplaced. But the temper of the times would have made futile almost any effort to end the color line in organized labor.

14 THE POWER OF FACTS

Believing from the first in "the theory and practice of scientific social research as the basis for the ultimate adjustment of racial difficulties in America," the National Urban League moved in the 1920s to make careful surveys of urban living and working conditions an integral part of its program.[1]

I

In 1921 the League established a Department of Research and Investigations, using an $8000 grant from the Carnegie Corporation. The Department's first director was Charles S. Johnson, a twenty-eight-year-old black who had organized a research department for the Chicago affiliate in 1917, while studying sociology at the University of Chicago. Johnson was born in 1893 in Bristol, Virginia, where his father, a former slave, had entered the Baptist ministry. During Johnson's childhood the legalization of Jim Crow turned a relatively tolerant racial climate into one of increasing segregation and discrimination. He attended a private academy for black students and was graduated in 1917 from Virginia Union University. He derived much of his philosophy of race relations from the teachings of Booker T. Washington. Johnson's work for the Chicago Urban League, he said, developed his "own first deep interest in social research," an interest that qualified him to head the investigations of the Chicago Commission on Race Relations following the 1919 riot. Johnson was the principal author of the massive report of their findings, *The Negro in Chicago*. He became director of research of the National League in July 1921, at a salary of $3600 per year.[2]

Johnson resigned from the Urban League in 1928 to head the department of social sciences at Fisk University, where he later became president. He was succeeded as director of research by Ira De Augustine Reid, a former Urban League fellow who had been serving as industrial secretary of the New York Urban League. Reid, who was born in Clifton Forge, Virginia, in 1901, grew up in Germantown, Pennsylvania, where his father, a Baptist minister, had settled. He attended private schools, was graduated from Morehouse College, took graduate courses at the University of Chicago, and received a master's degree in social economics from the University of Pittsburgh, where he wrote a thesis on "The Negro in the Major Industries and Building Trades of Pittsburgh." He earned his doctorate in sociology at Columbia University in 1939. Before joining the New York Urban League in 1924, Reid taught sociology and history at Texas College in Tyler, Texas, and high school classes in Huntington, West Virginia. At six feet, four inches, he made an imposing picture. Except for his height, no one would have guessed that the scholar also played semiprofessional basketball.[3] Reid assumed his duties as director of research and editor of *Opportunity* in 1928.

The Department of Research collected, analyzed, and published data on social and economic conditions among Negroes in cities. It usually conducted its surveys at the request of social agencies interested in inaugurating programs for blacks. Often the surveys were a first step toward the establishment of an Urban League affiliate. Sometimes they aided existing affiliates in reevaluating their programs and services. They were never prescriptive; rather, they provided the raw material with which local agencies could devise local programs to meet local needs.

The investigations touched on various facets of the lives of urban Negroes. Interracial councils in Trenton, Denver, and Worcester requested comprehensive studies of their black communities. Social agencies in Pittsburgh asked for a survey of Negroes in the Hill District to be used "as the basis for extending their programs of service to colored people." The Metropolitan Life Insurance Company wanted to know how many blacks were employed in industrial concerns having pension plans. Ira Reid's study of blacks and unions began as an inquiry under the auspices of the Department of Research.[4]

The procedures for community surveys followed basic guidelines. The director of research would spend two to six weeks in the city under study, organizing a staff (largely volunteer, though sometimes including professional social workers) and conferring with leaders in industry, labor, education, and welfare. The staff would distribute questionnaires to blacks to ascertain their family history and employment status, and to employers to learn about their experience with black workers.

Other information came through personal interviews with workingmen, questionnaires distributed to pastors, family visiting, analysis of health records and of Family Service Bureau cases, compilation of statistics on school attendance and police arrests, and meetings with playground directors, officials of social agencies, and other individuals.

Depending on his schedule, the director of research might remain to supervise the collection of information, or he might conduct only the initial interviews and leave a staff assistant in charge of assembling the data. Five to six weeks would then be devoted to tabulating and analyzing the material collected and to preparing a report with recommendations for ameliorative action. The League donated the research director's time, but the community was responsible for all other costs—his transportation and living expenses while in the field, printing, postage, and clerical services. The total cost to the community ranged from $400 to $800, at least for the earlier surveys.

These surveys provided extensive information on black city

life, much of which was unavailable elsewhere. The most thorough of the studies began with a sketch of the history of the city's black population and the circumstances under which migrants had come there. They drew a detailed portrait of the way blacks lived—the sections of the city, type and cost of housing, numbers in each household, and the proportion of home owners to renters. An economic profile showed where blacks worked, how much money they made, how local unions treated them. Interviews revealed why employers refused to hire blacks or, if they did hire them, what their experiences had been. Statistics summed up comparative rates of disease and mortality, crime and delinquency. The studies surveyed educational and recreational opportunities in the city and described the social and civic organizations active in the black community.[5]

In comparison to later community studies, these surveys were strong on description, but unsophisticated in methods and analysis. In their own terms and in their own time, however, they succeeded in creating an important body of data that, in many cases, no one else had bothered to collect. While they were much less detailed and literate than Du Bois's *Philadelphia Negro*, they were very much part of the same tradition. Invariably they took the conventional Urban League line: the most critical problems blacks faced were economic and social, rather than political or legal, and the greatest priority of all lay in finding jobs. "There is no advantage in trying to improve recreational, housing and health conditions for the Negro," the Denver survey said, "without attempting to get the race into better paying jobs."[6] Throughout, they worried more about discrimination than segregation, and they paid little or no attention to problems such as disfranchisement and racial violence.

The information obtained through these surveys enabled the Urban League to implement its conviction that social reform must be grounded on "the factual interpretation of authenticated data rather than emotional and sentimental appeal."[7] As T. Arnold Hill put it, "the League proceeds on a basis of fact and not on theory and sentiment. . . . We like to be known as an agency that has definite knowledge of the conditions and needs and that bases its programs and action upon such authentic findings." [8]

II

Gathering information was one part of the work of the Department of Research. The other was disseminating it and thereby promoting a better understanding of blacks and their problems. The League persuaded the Carnegie Corporation to give the New York Public Library $10,000 to purchase the Schomburg collection of books, prints, and other material on black history and culture.[9] From its own resources it filled requests for information about blacks for debates, lectures, articles, research papers, and classroom discussions. In order to reach a broader audience on a regular basis, the League started its own magazine.

Opportunity: Journal of Negro Life first appeared on January 1, 1923. It served as a house organ for the League movement by publishing reports of each year's accomplishments and news of personnel and programs on the national and local level. But its primary purpose was twofold: to "[give] the American people serious and authoritative articles on the social and economic problems affecting Negro life in the United States," and to "[give] Negro authors, creative writers and artists an opportunity to display their works." [10]

The idea of an official publication for the Urban League had developed some years earlier. Since its founding the League had issued a periodical bulletin reporting on work in progress and plans for new projects. In December 1921 these publications were consolidated into a more formal, bimonthly, tabloid-style *Urban League Bulletin*, edited by Charles S. Johnson, which included articles on League projects and personalities and on socioeconomic conditions. But some Urban Leaguers insisted on a full-fledged magazine, and in October 1922 the steering committee agreed to revamp the *Bulletin* into a monthly publication with a cover, advertisements, competitive subscription rates, and a new name. The result was *Opportunity*.[11]

Opportunity was never a successful business venture. Its monthly circulation rose from an initial 6000 in 1924 and 1925 to a peak of 11,000 in pre-Depression 1927 and 1928,[12] but even that readership was tiny compared to the NAACP's *Crisis*. Under the editorship of W. E. B. Du Bois, *The Crisis* had attracted more than 10,000 readers by the end of its first year of publication, and by June 1919 its circulation had climbed to 104,000.[13] Some of the difference in popularity was doubtless due to *Opportunity*'s emphasis on facts, figures, and intellectual fare, while *The Crisis* included more pictures and snappier articles on the struggle for black political and civil rights. *Opportunity*'s "scientific" approach, a Minneapolis reader said, was "not as interesting" as that of the NAACP's journal.[14] Charles Johnson's best editorials were bland compared to Du Bois's outspoken, acerbic writing. More important, *Opportunity* depended on magazine sales and subscriptions, while the NAACP sent *The Crisis* to its large dues-paying membership, a resource the Urban League did not have.

Opportunity sold for 15 cents a copy or, by subscription, $1.50 a year. Income from magazine sales never offset production costs. As a part of the Department of Research, the magazine's expenses were covered by the Carnegie Corporation grant that had made the Department possible. With the expiration of the grant, the League tried unsuccessfully to persuade Julius Rosenwald to support its research efforts. When the Department's expenses were absorbed into the League's general budget, *Opportunity*'s recurring deficits also became the full organization's responsibility.

Opportunity was directed at an interracial readership. The League estimated at one point that 40 per cent of its readers were white.[15] The black subscribers that Jesse O. Thomas signed up included teachers, professionals, and businessmen. As Charles Johnson's successor described it in the 1930s, "OPPORTUNITY . . . is read by that class of Negroes who are able to buy automobiles. More than that its reading clientele make up the leadership in the

Negro race." [16] Libraries in black schools and colleges took subscriptions, as did public libraries, Ys, settlement houses, community centers, and, in the 1930s, CCC camps. When an Urban
League investigator in Minneapolis asked "leading" whites what
black publications they read, eight replied that they saw *Opportunity*, seven *The Crisis*, three the *Journal of Negro History*, and
one each the New York *Age*, Chicago *Defender*, *Messenger*, *Fisk
University Bulletin*, and *Howard University Quarterly*. *Opportunity*, one said, was "enlightening and interesting"; another
thought it "excellent and sane." [17]

Through it whites got "an interpretation of the social problems
of the Negro population." *Opportunity*'s policy was "to present,
objectively, facts of Negro life" as "a basis of understanding" and
"a dependable guide to action"; like the Urban League, it sought
to "encourage interracial co-operation." [18]

In large part, the magazine lived up to its mandate. "*Opportunity* offers an excellent medium through which Negroes may
present the salient facts concerning themselves and their everyday
perplexing problems," the *Southern Workman* said. It was a
"first-class" vehicle "for disseminating information and winning
new friends for Negroes." [19] Under Johnson's leadership, *Opportunity* presented a reasonably balanced overview of Negro life in
the 1920s. Many of the articles were based on studies made by
the League's Department of Research. Others were the work of
outside scientific and social scientific investigators, among them
Monroe N. Work, director of the Department of Research and
Records at Tuskegee and editor of the *Negro Year Book;* Dean
Kelly Miller of Howard University; Arthur A. Schomburg, president of the American Negro Academy; Graham R. Taylor, a
staff director of the Commonwealth Fund; and the black sociologist, E. Franklin Frazier. They covered such topics as the northward migrations, the debate over Negro intelligence, the industrial adjustment of black workers, and health, housing, and
other conditions of urban life. *Opportunity* offered some insights
into the major racial developments of the decade—such as the

influence of Marcus Garvey and the resurgence of the Ku Klux Klan—but it had relatively little to say about racial violence and segregation, which were considered to be primarily the province of the NAACP.

How deeply *Opportunity* probed the dynamics of race relations and black life patterns in the 1920s is another question. That was the decade when the Harlem ghetto was transformed into a slum, when cities bursting with black migrants from the South began to institutionalize the patterns of deprivation and discrimination that still persist in urban ghettos. To be sure, the elements that went into this progressive deterioration of urban black life did not go ignored in the pages of *Opportunity*, just as they were not ignored in the investigations of the League's Department of Research. One can understand from reading *Opportunity* that blacks in the 1920s faced overcrowded, insanitary housing, serious health risks, and formidable barriers to employment. Yet one gets too little sense from the magazine of what life must have actually been like for the black man, woman, or child caught in the emerging urban slums. A sense of urgency and a sense of proportion were missing. Which was a more accurate index of the nature of black life in the 1920s—figures on the incidence of tuberculosis in Harlem or accounts of blacks who had achieved success in "unusual" occupational roles? *Opportunity* told both stories, and others like them, but it failed to offer reliable guidance as to which really ought to be given more weight. Most of the evidence was there, but Johnson and his staff rarely stopped to analyze the import of what they were printing.

It was not that other journals and writers were better at explicating, or foreseeing, the complex factors that were setting the pattern for urban black life. When men such as James Weldon Johnson wrote books about Harlem in the 1920s, it was in terms of celebration, not doom. Given its promise of "scientific" investigation, the Urban League might have done better. The optimism that pervaded *Opportunity*'s pages, though, was very much in line with other black writing of the decade. Indeed, it matched the entire spirit of the times, for the problems of white society in the 1920s generally got short shrift in the popular press in comparison to the euphoria over normalcy and economic prosperity.

The air of conscious optimism becomes apparent in the way the magazine treated subjects susceptible to different emphases. For example, articles on black employment problems painted the factory welfare worker as a virtual magician. When a cushion manufacturer appointed a black personnel director to adjust the problems it was having with its black workers, she won their "confidence and good-will" by making minor physical improvements in factory conditions. She ordered smart new uniforms for the workers and encouraged them to have "a spirit of respect for . . . authority." The result? Production went up, 97 per cent of the employees reported to work on time, and absenteeism fell to 3 to 5 per cent.[20] A black welfare worker hired by a large foundry reported confidently that he had managed to mould "a progressive little community" among its black workers. During his tenure he put a stop to gambling and created a "higher moral tone." A new recreational center helped to maintain "the tranquility of family life" and to avoid "idle loafing and indifference." His answer to the problems of his black workers? Sewing clubs and social circles, organized games and dances, contests for the best looking homes. His assessment of industrial relations between the races? "My observations have been that the white worker has about accepted the Negro as a permanent increment in northern industry, and much of the hostility against him has died out."[21]

Employers and personnel managers rhapsodized over their experiences with black workers. Was there any substance to widely held beliefs about the unreliability of Negro labor? Definitely not, these men testified: "they are loyal, industrious and steady workers"; "the Negro, by his loyalty, faithful and satisfactory performance of duties, has proved to be a desirable employee"; "when a Negro is properly supervised he works just as steady, and he does not lay off any more than any other class of help in our work."[22] And how did employers perceive the mood of their

black workers? As the personnel manager of the National Mallea-
ble Casting Company summed it up,

> We have found that the Negro workers greatly appreciate any
> thing that the Company may do in the way of improving shop
> working conditions, such as installing locker rooms, shower rooms,
> cafeterias and lunch rooms. They like to come to work wearing
> something better than their ordinary working clothes. They enjoy
> spending the noon hour mingling with their fellow workers in the
> dining room, and when the day's work is over they like to jump
> under a shower before going home. Yes, they appreciate these
> things and they show their appreciation by using the shower more
> than any other class of help in our shops.[23]

To say that these statements, taken alone, constitute a heavy
dose of optimism is to understate the case. It would be unfair to
suggest that *Opportunity* never showed the other side of the picture. But in featuring such Pollyanna-like stories, it could not
help but distort reality.

Insofar as the prospects for employment advancement were
concerned, the record was more evenly balanced. Issues of the
magazine included frequent notes of pessimism and realism, such
as the appraisal that "domestic and personal service is probably the backbone of the Negro's financial existence in St.
Louis." [24] But the other side of the story made for livelier reading. "With an education behind him, if he is a successful laborer," one employer predicted, the black worker would "have
very little trouble in prying off this so-called lid of prejudice.
. . . This lid of prejudice looks large and formidable, but the
mere weight of it makes it slip off easily if it is once started." [25]
Opportunity repeatedly gave "examples of unusual success"
among blacks to inspire and encourage other members of the
race. A black mover in Ohio had built up the largest moving
company in the state.[26] A feature on "The World's Fastest Mail
Sorter," a black postal employee in New York, assured readers
that she was "a perfectly normal, modest, hard working
individual." [27] There were black draftsmen, civil engineers,

school teachers, nurses, journalists, and public officials. *Opportunity* gave its readers glimpses of black Horatio Algers: a laborer who had become a customs clerk, a kitchen boy promoted to steward, a watchman who had risen to immigration inspector.[28] The message was obvious: these men and women have made it, and you can, too.

You can, that is, if you adhere to fundamental middle-class values. *Opportunity* also gave its readers lessons in proper behavior, sometimes explicit, sometimes implied. The way to progress was paved with traditional bourgeois values: education, hard work, thrift, sobriety, self-effacement, concern for others, and above all, self-help. "The Negro should remember," T. Arnold Hill admonished, "that the attack against the traditions of habit, custom, indifference, prejudice or whatever it is that keeps the race out of adequate employment must come from him. Lethargy must be converted into intelligent action before the condition will change." [29] An account of a poor black family that scrimped and saved to put every child through college pointed up "the profits of education . . . an example well worth pointing out." [30] An illiterate, shabbily dressed teen-aged runaway "proved very willing, apt, [and] truthful"; under the tutelage of the Urban League and a foster family, he became an "enthusiastic" student who "dressed very, very neatly" and straightened his "once kinky hair." [31] Among the unsung heroes of the race was a train porter who "sensed his individual opportunity to strike effectual blows for racial goodwill and understanding" by advising migrants on northern attitudes and the practicalities of reaching their destinations. His message was as important as his concern: "Whatever you do," he counseled the migrants, "do not go into the north to take revenge on the other race there, for what was done to you down south; for these people in the north have not done a thing to you." [32] Proper behavior was defined in strictly Puritanical terms; little morality stories recounted the triumph of good over evil when welfare workers put a stop to gambling and closed "disorderly houses" among black workers. One steel plant official reported with relief that the company's discovery of some black employees "living together as man and wife when in reality they were not married" had a happy ending: "we succeeded in rectifying these cases by insisting that the parties be legally married." [33]

Sometimes *Opportunity* sounded naïve, if not simplistic. It was all well and good to teach that "facts carry their own light. Argument for opportunities carry conviction when backed by the evidence of capacity." [34] But how could one put such faith in "the compelling influence of simple information" in light of any objective indices of deprivation and discrimination? [35] It was fine to believe that "prejudices and misunderstandings disappear when citizens of different races work together for the common good of the entire community," but that was hard to reconcile with the intense intolerance of the decade.[36] Sometimes the magazine simply missed the mark. At a time when Harlem was turning into a teeming slum, it was peripheral at best to point out that "much of the inferior feeling of Negroes is derived from surroundings which elicit none of their finer feelings. Such surroundings can influence conduct by fostering carelessness and what is worse yet, self-contempt." [37]

And yet such optimism had a function. It made sense to encourage blacks to believe that progress was possible; similarly, it was probably good policy to give whites examples of blacks making good. *Opportunity* by no means neglected the more negative aspects of Negro life, and, in many respects, it admirably fulfilled its mandate of providing important information about blacks in an objective manner. Where it fell especially short, however, was in its goal of offering "an interpretation of the social problems of the Negro population." Interpreting the data it presented was what *Opportunity* was least able to do in an informed, sophisticated manner. This flaw showed up in two main ways: first, there was inadequate analysis of the causes and implications of black problems; and second, there was a pervasive implication that things were getting better all the time. These flaws did the most damage where they helped to shield the middle classes from intimate knowledge of the plight of the black masses. Take, for example, Eugene Kinckle Jones's description, written at mid-decade, of the growing black communities of the North: "Negro cities, as it were, within the already established cities, may be seen in New York, in Pittsburgh, in Boston, in Chicago, in Cleveland, in Detroit, in Philadelphia and in many other Northern and border communities." Here were the emerging slums that later exploded as Harlem and Watts and Hough. But here Jones saw "Negro banks, theaters, hotels, restaurants, stores of all kinds, real estate offices and modern churches with social service facilities," as well as "Negro doctors, lawyers, architects, social workers and other professional men and women . . . kept constantly busy ministering to the needs of their own people." "Of course," he added, almost as an afterthought, "with the large increase in the Negro population . . . there must be attendant problems of housing and health and a decided increase in delinquency." [38] *Opportunity* might have done better by forcing blacks and whites to confront such "attendant problems" with a more objective sense of reality.

III

The other side to *Opportunity*'s task in the 1920s was to provide recognition for Negro achievement in the creative arts. At that time it was not easy for blacks to publish in established white magazines. *The Crisis* published literary and artistic works and encouraged Negro talent, but its contents usually emphasized instances of discrimination, political and legal problems, and efforts to overcome racial prejudice. Another important Negro magazine of the period, A. Philip Randolph's and Chandler Owen's Socialist *Messenger*, made it clear that "with us economics and politics take precedence to 'Music and Art.'" [39] While *Opportunity* concerned itself with the practical details of black living and working conditions, it also offered "asylum and encouragement to aspiring Negro writers and poets for whom there was then no

place in the pattern of American culture." [40] The magazine introduced the early works of some of the most famous Negro authors
in America. The March 1924 issue included a seven-line poem,
"The White Ones," by a then-unknown poet named Langston
Hughes. Two months later, Claude McKay, the Jamaica-born
writer whose volume of poetry, *Harlem Shadows*, was published
in 1922, contributed some of his works. Countee Cullen, whose
first book of poems, *Color*, appeared in 1925, when he was only
twenty-two, published regularly in *Opportunity* and served for a
time as its assistant editor. Alain Locke frequently wrote articles
for the magazine. These contributions, in addition to works by
most of the major writers of the Harlem Renaissance, make the
magazine's files an important repository of Negro culture during
the second quarter of this century.

Urban League officials brought together young Negro talent
and leaders of the white publishing world. For example, William
H. Baldwin arranged once with Frederick Lewis Allen, then editor of *Harper's*, to hold a luncheon "to bring Negro writers,
poets and artists to the attention of the big-time magazine editors
and book publishers." Allen invited a "small but representative
group from his field," and Baldwin and Charles S. Johnson "supplied an equally representative group of Negroes." [41]

On a more formal level, *Opportunity* sponsored literary contests to encourage young Negroes' creative efforts, offering prizes
for the best short stories, poems, essays, plays, and personal experience sketches. The magazine published the winning entries.
The Crisis ran similar contests, funded by some of the NAACP's
white leaders, beginning in 1924. *Opportunity*'s first contest, held
in 1924–25, drew 732 manuscripts. The winners included
Langston Hughes, Countee Cullen, and E. Franklin Frazier. The
prize money—$470, allotted among fifteen awards—was the
gift of Agnes Brown Leach, a member of the League's executive
board and one of its major benefactors.[42] In 1925 Casper Hol-
stein, a black businessman, donated $1000 to help finance the sec-
ond annual contest, which added categories of musical composi-

tion and "constructive journalism" (with $200 in prizes presented by the New York State Federation of Colored Women's Clubs), in addition to a special $100 Alexander Pushkin Poetry Prize. The third contest, in 1926–27, again offered $1000 in prizes donated by Holstein, and it attracted more than 1000 entries.[43]

Over the years, contest judges included some of the most famous names in American letters.* Each year the awards were presented at gala dinners attended by prize winners, editors, publishers, writers, and others. The *Opportunity* dinner "promises large things," Alain Locke wrote.[44] "A novel sight, that dinner," the New York *Herald Tribune* editorialized after the first one took place, "—white critics, whom 'everybody' knows, Negro writers, whom 'nobody' knew—meeting on common ground." [45]

Opportunity suspended the contests in the fall of 1927 to allow potential participants more time for careful work on their manuscripts. In fact, the regular literary contests were never resumed. Three years of competition, the editors of *Opportunity* felt, had produced "some new voices and new names for the roster of young American writers" and had made it easier for their manuscripts to get accepted by publishers.[46] Proving the point, the League published *Ebony and Topaz*, an *Opportunity* collectanea, at Christmas time that year. The anthology included the works of the leaders of the Harlem Renaissance—a group of authors who, but for *Opportunity*, would have had considerably greater difficulty in reaching the American public. The Urban League also assisted Negro artists and illustrators by opening *Opportunity* to their cover designs and illustrations and devoting several entire issues to the arts. *Opportunity*, Alain Locke declared, was "second only to *The Harmon Foundation* in its helpful sponsorship of representative Negro art." [47]

---

* For example, Robert Frost, Alain Locke, William Stanley Braithwaite, William Rose Benet, Vachel Lindsay, Jean Toomer, Van Wyck Brooks, Fannie Hurst, Robert C. Benchley, Alexander Woollcott, Henry Goddard Leach, Dorothy Canfield Fisher, Carl Van Doren, and Eugene O'Neill.

Many of the writers whom *Opportunity* introduced and encouraged went on to distinguished careers. They were central figures in the Harlem Renaissance of the 1920s, a time described by Langston Hughes, one of its leaders, as "the period when the Negro was in vogue." [48] "The American Negro is finding his artistic voice," the New York *Herald Tribune* wrote, after the first *Opportunity* prize dinner in 1925, "and . . . we are on the edge, if not already in the midst, of what might not improperly be called a Negro renaissance." What was significant was "not that people with more or less Negro blood can write . . . but that these American Negroes are expressing for the most part essentially Negro feelings and standing squarely on their racial inheritance." [49]

The writers of the Renaissance were a race-conscious group, pointing out social and economic wrongs and protesting against the way the system treated them. Their Renaissance brought forth a flowering of Negro creative effort and introduced to the American reading public not only the poets Hughes, Cullen, and McKay, but also a long list of Negro writers of distinction, including James Weldon Johnson, the poet, novelist, and anthologist of spirituals who chronicled the Renaissance in his *Black Manhattan* (1930) and *Along This Way* (1933); the French-educated Jean Toomer, author of a poetry-prose collage *Cane* (1923); and Wallace Thurman, whose novel *Infants of the Spring* (1932) satirized the Negro intellectuals and literati of the period. Other important novelists of the Harlem Renaissance were Jessie Fauset, Walter White, Eric Walrond, Zora Neal Hurston (who was also a student of anthropology and writer of folklore), and Arna Bontemps. In Washington during this period, Georgia Douglas Johnson and Angelina W. Grimké emerged as noted poets. Abram L. Harris, E. Franklin Frazier, and Benjamin Brawley broadened the scope of the Renaissance to encompass scholarship in the humanities and social sciences. Almost all of these writers published in *Opportunity*. Through his editorship of the magazine, Charles S.

Johnson "did more to encourage and develop Negro writers during the 1920's," Langston Hughes later wrote, "than anyone else in America." [50]

When Elmer Anderson Carter, a black graduate of Harvard and the former executive secretary of the Columbus, Louisville, and St. Paul Urban Leagues, took over as editor of *Opportunity* following Johnson's resignation in 1928, he announced his intention to concentrate on "presenting to the intelligent minority a new picture of the Negro—a picture which is framed in facts —adduced by trained investigators and interpreted by students of social phenomena who are unbiased and unafraid." [51] While he continued to publish the works of Negro poets and writers, Carter stressed "the sociological and economic aspects of the Negro's relation to American life" by inaugurating a monthly section on labor and offering articles analyzing the economic status of blacks.* [52] With the coming of the Depression and the New Deal, *Opportunity* provided extended commentary on Negroes and unions, Negroes and relief programs, and, later, Negroes and war industries.

In the area of research and publication, the Urban League realized, perhaps more readily than in any other, a large measure of success in a relatively brief time. Despite its limited circulation, *Opportunity* opened up new worlds for Negro writers of talent and served as a medium of communication to make white readers aware of Negroes on all levels. The black Cleveland *Gazette* justifiably called it "one of our very best publications." [53] To the chief of the circulation department of the New York Public Library, it was "invaluable." [54] The surveys and investigations undertaken by the Department of Research, despite the uneven

---

* For example, "Present Trends in the Employment of Negro Labor" (May 1929), "Negro Women in Our Economic Life" (July 1930), "The Negro in Cincinnati Industries" (December 1930), "The Economic Crisis of the Negro" (May 1931), "Some Impacts of the Depression Upon the Negro in Philadelphia" (July 1933), "Population and Occupational Trends of Negroes" (August 1933), and "Negro Workers in Skilled Crafts and Construction" (October 1933).

quality of their methods, carried on the tradition inaugurated by W. E. B. Du Bois and began to develop a solid body of knowledge on the life and needs of urban blacks.

And yet there is no evidence that, by presenting facts and reasoned analyses, the Urban League measurably improved race relations in the 1920s. At a time when conditions among blacks in cities were rapidly deteriorating, scientific studies yielded facts, but they lacked the impact of immediate action.[55] Nothing would illustrate more forcefully the importance of combining education with action than the coming of the Great Depression.

PART THREE

1929-1940

15 DEPRESSION: FIRST FIRED, LAST HIRED

For many Americans, the stock market crash of October 1929 and the ensuing economic catastrophe came as a profound surprise. The 1920s had been a time of unprecedented prosperity; the stock market spiral reflected the boom in production, construction, and land speculation that was making more and more Americans richer than they had ever been in their lives. But workers and farmers shared little in the profits of prosperity. The 1920s were not of a single economic piece; the decade had begun with a depression, and as it ended, "71 per cent of American families had incomes under $2,500, generally thought to be the minimum standard for a decent living."[1]

I

One group to miss out on the boom well before the 1929 debacle were blacks. By the spring of 1926 the Urban League was advising potential migrants to the North to think twice unless they had a concrete promise of a job, since overcrowding and unemployment were so prevalent. In March 1927, with Baltimore in the midst of "one of the worst slumps in employment . . . in many years," the League there canceled plans for a Negro in Industry Week. "It is an art to get a man a job just now," the executive secretary explained; "it would be an impossibility almost to get him a better one." [2] Similar reports came from other affiliates: the unemployment situation among blacks was so "acute" as to be "alarming." [3] As early as January 1927, local Leagues began to document cases of employers firing their Negro workers and replacing them with whites.[4] In general, "conditions for 1927 were so depressing" that T. Arnold Hill could not bring himself to write a report on the industrial status of blacks, as he had for 1926. "Month by month," he explained, "we received from our advisors in various parts of the country such dismal accounts of employment . . . that to compile them would appear too pessimistic." [5] By 1929, at least 300,000 black industrial workers were out of work, "and employment offices were able to place less than a third of the applicants." [6]

When the Depression began, the Urban League considered itself well-equipped to cope with the economic crisis. It had trained personnel, contacts among social workers, a tested fact-finding apparatus, and experience in social service and employment. As Eugene Kinckle Jones put it, "The well-rounded program of the League could not have been more efficiently planned if its work of the past twenty-one years had been designedly developed to meet just this situation." [7]

The executive board pledged full support for and cooperation in private and public emergency relief and employment activities and offered President Hoover the services of the League to help relieve the unemployment crisis.[8] The Urban League joined other organizations in successfully petitioning for the inclusion of a Negro on the President's Emergency Committee for Employment. John W. Davis, a member of the League's own executive board, was appointed to the post, and T. Arnold Hill acted as liaison officer between the committee and the black community.[9]

While Hill tried to persuade Hoover's committee "to think along the lines of Negroes," the Urban League sought a fair share of jobs and relief for blacks.[10] For the most part the Depression meant suspending regular efforts for better employment op-

portunities and, instead, seeing to it that blacks got the relief they
badly needed. Affiliates lent staff and office space to local unemployment committees and kept "the cause of Negroes . . . in
front of those handling unemployment benefits." [11] They initiated
or cooperated in the operation of emergency relief projects, including workshops, "employment bureaus, lodgings, food and
clothing distributing stations, temporary relief facilities," and even
a soup kitchen.[12] The Department of Industrial Relations tried to
persuade major employers such as the Pennsylvania Railroad,
John Wanamaker Stores, and AT & T to retain their Negro
workers during the economic emergency.[13]

Such efforts in behalf of blacks, Eugene Kinckle Jones felt, had,
by the early part of 1932, resulted "in an almost universal inclusion of the Negro in adjustment efforts." [14] Yet a press release a
few months later explained that the League had not been issuing
its regular employment bulletins "in order to avoid monotonous
statements on conditions which showed no improvement." [15] The
Urban League's own research was to prove T. Arnold Hill's
sober evaluation much nearer the truth than Jones's optimism:
"At no time in the history of the Negro since slavery has his economic and social outlook seemed so discouraging." [16]

In 1931 the Urban League undertook two major investigations
of urban Negro unemployment, the first, "How Unemployment
Affects Negroes," covering 75 cities, and the second, "Unemployment Status of Negroes," based on data from 106. These
studies, in combination with more limited periodic inquiries conducted throughout the 1930s, established a clear picture of the
Negro's plight. Blacks were unemployed in numbers far out
of proportion to their percentage of the population; in Baltimore,
for example, where Negroes formed 17 per cent of the city's population, they made up 31.5 per cent of the unemployed in March
1931. In Chicago, which was only 4 per cent black, blacks accounted for 16 per cent of those out of work. The same was true
in other cities. By 1931, displacing Negroes from their jobs "to

reduce unemployment among *whites*" seemed to be "an accepted policy." As long as whites were out of work, the chances of blacks being rehired by private employers were slim.[17]

In 1933 the Urban League reported 2,117,644 blacks (over 17 per cent of the black population) on relief, "as contrasted with 10,566,020, [or less than 10 per cent] of the total white population." Although just over 9 per cent of the American people were black, blacks accounted for more than 18 per cent of all cases on relief. In the cities the disproportion was even more striking: over 26 per cent of urban blacks, but less than 10 per cent of urban whites, were on relief in 1933. In some of the larger industrial centers half of the unemployed were black. Gary, Indiana, reported the staggering statistic of roughly half the Negro population on full relief, with another 30 per cent receiving partial relief. By 1935 the national relief rolls included 3,030,000 blacks, or more than one-quarter of the black population, "as compared with 17,140,000 'white and other racial groups,' [or less than 16 per cent] of the total remaining population." Again, in the cities the imbalance was even greater: almost 40 per cent of all blacks, as against less than 15 per cent of all whites, were on relief.[18]

As "the first . . . fired and the last hired," subject to discharge by employers favoring suffering white workers, and sometimes victims of "well-nigh criminal neglect" in unemployment relief programs, blacks felt, understandably, that "their problems should have larger place and more sympathetic treatment." [19] Insofar as government and private industry were unprepared to extend that treatment, blacks were prime candidates for radicalization. During the Depression, Communists and Socialists made a strong appeal to blacks who, they believed, should feel totally alienated from the system as it traditionally operated. The Urban League, on the other hand, had a strong stake in the capitalist system. This stake, together with the state of its finances and the character of its leadership, shaped the League's response to the economic crisis of the 1930s.

II

As a long-time promoter of Negro welfare, the Urban League moved to elevate the Negro cause on the lists of local and national priorities. The nature of the economic emergency structured the approaches the League would have to take. Before the Great Crash, the employment problem of blacks had been "chiefly one of advancement to positions commensurate with ability." The Depression, however, found them desperately "endeavoring to hold the line against advancing armies of white workers intent upon gaining and content to accept occupations which were once thought too menial for white hands." [20] With whites willingly taking the most menial positions, the Urban League's employment emphasis shifted from opening opportunities to retaining those low-level jobs blacks already held.

Insofar as the Depression cast problems peculiar to blacks into a new context, it prompted a reappraisal of the traditional approaches of the National Urban League. The "social and economic chaos" of the Depression, the League recognized, forced social welfare agencies to "reevaluate their programs and principles of operation." "Our agency," it asserted, "must change sufficiently to meet new needs." [21]

The mood of change expressed itself in the League's regional executive secretaries' conferences, which began in 1932. The sense of the first year's conferences was that "the League should adjust itself to the rapidly changing local conditions without sacrificing the basic principles of League program—emphasis might be changed, but there should be no shift in program." Local secretaries suggesting topics for discussion at the 1933 conferences sounded similar themes. "It seems to me that the attitude of the public towards social welfare organizations is changing rapidly—and only those organizations which are rendering a vital service can hope to gain support," one executive pointed out. "What have Urban League offices been doing in their local communities to make themselves secure?" Another was concerned about "the ever present question, does the Urban League need a new emphasis, and how should it function to prevent other organizations from overlapping its program?" A third summed up the general questioning of fundamentals when he suggested that "We might devote some part of the discussion to the basic philosophy of the League movement." [22]

Realizing that persuasion and conciliation had failed to convert employers and union leaders to the Negro's cause, the Urban League resolved to organize and educate Negro workers to speak for themselves in economic competition. The League began to supplement high-level economic diplomacy with mild forms of pressure—letter-writing campaigns, petitions to public officials, even "Don't Buy Where You Can't Work" campaigns. And, as the federal government entered the business of employment and relief, the League made serious efforts to influence administrative and legislative policy-making.

While the economic crisis pushed the Urban League toward more aggressive actions, other factors circumscribed what it could do. The projects it could undertake depended on the funds in its treasury; the tactics it might espouse had to be consistent with the complexion of its leadership.

The Depression nearly bankrupted the National Urban League. Money was never plentiful in the League movement during its first three decades, but during the 1930s the executive board and a few staunch contributors barely managed to save the League from financial collapse.

More than ever the League came to depend on Rockefeller and other foundation philanthropies. From 1932 through 1939 the Spelman Fund, John D. Rockefeller, Jr., himself, and the Davison Fund, which he created in 1934 to handle his personal contributions, gave the League between $12,500 and $19,500 annually, or about 20 to 30 per cent of its income in any of those years. In each year except 1932 and 1937, more than half of its annual income came from Rockefeller funding combined with gifts from the Carnegie, New York, and Friedsam Foundations.[23]

Even with such tremendously wealthy benefactors, the League barely avoided bankruptcy. The national office's yearly expenditures peaked at $77,485 in 1930 and remained in the mid-$70,000 range throughout the decade. After 1932, however, the League's annual income ranged between $55,596 and $64,377 through 1940; in 1935, for example, a budget of $76,680 had to be matched against an income of only $58,874.[24] In 1930, the League was still able to meet its annual expenses. Soon thereafter, the deficits began—the first in 1933, climbing to some $16,000 by the end of 1935, reduced to $6685 two years later, up again to $9927 the following year.[25]

Had the foundations been willing, they could certainly have spared the Urban League the agony of mounting deficits. They, too, of course, were affected by the Depression. It was not altogether surprising that the Carnegie Corporation denied the League's plea for $5000 in 1935 "due to the unusual number of proposals before the Committee and the equally unusual bareness of the cupboard."[26] Such a denial, however, inevitably reflected the low priority of racial advancement amidst the problems of the 1930s. In 1933 the Corporation had voted the League $5000 from its fund for emergency support of national social welfare organizations, but at the same time it gave $10,000 to the American Association for Labor Legislation and $17,500 to the Foreign Language Information Service.[27] Philanthropists may have had some doubts about the League: "The League's work," Carnegie's secretary told its president in 1931, ". . . is fairly effective," even though he was "not sold on Hollingsworth Wood" and felt that Eugene Kinckle Jones "tends to be assertive." But the League ranked at the top of organizations for racial advancement. "From the outside information that we get," he wrote at the end of the decade, "the consensus of opinion is that, of the interracial agencies, the National League is one of the soundest."[28] John D. Rockefeller, Jr., gave the NAACP only about 5 per cent of the Rockefeller gifts to the Urban League because he felt that its tactics and leadership were too controversial to be effective.[29] From the point of view of conservative philanthropists, the Urban League was the best of the lot; that it was in such severe financial straits testifies to the lack of importance attached to racial problems in those years.

That the League survived the Depression at all was due almost exclusively to the personal efforts of Hollingsworth Wood and Eugene Kinckle Jones. The two men had worked closely together for two decades. "They were closer than brothers," one of their local executive secretaries recalled; theirs was "one of the deepest and most wholesome friendships that I've ever seen." It is impossible to determine just how one influenced the other. Nor is it altogether clear which one took the lead in League affairs, although fragmentary evidence suggests that it was "largely Jones" who made policy decisions, while Wood and the board backed him consistently.[30]

From the earliest years of the organization, Wood and Jones had been the mainstay of the National Urban League's fund-raising efforts: "We had no professional help and very little help from other board members," Lloyd K. Garrison, who became treasurer of the League in 1928, recalls. "It was pretty much a matter of seeing people we knew, writing letters, etc., on a sort of 'catch-as-catch-can' basis." [31] Members of the staff were sometimes sent out on fund-raising trips, and the League periodically undertook mass mailings or public campaigns, but the most lucrative source of financial support continued to be direct personal appeals by its top officials to individuals and foundations.

During the Depression, pleas to the League's major benefactors took on a desperate tone. When the organization's deficit approached $14,000, Jones beseeched the president of the Carnegie Corporation for help: "I know you will think of me as the world's worst loser for I am writing you again to find out whether there is anything under heaven you can do to help me out in a most embarrassing and distressing situation." "I am aghast at the arid prospect until spring," Wood echoed the following year, "as it means such a distressing deficit and such a radical curtailment of our activities." [32]

By 1939, with foundations slow in acting on appeals, with staff salaries, rent, and bills unpaid, and with a full year's budget of $75,000 to be raised, the League was in a "dangerous situation," Wood wrote.[33] He put the problem more bluntly to his close associates: "I am in agony . . . about the National Urban League. . . . When I think of the trust that has been reposed in me to pull the organization out of impossible spots, I am unable to sleep at night." [34] With Jones hospitalized with tuberculosis, Wood had been running the organization singlehandedly. The personal strain that the financial crisis put on him was more than he could bear. "This is no 'Wolf! Wolf!' story," he wrote, "but a plea for help from a chairman who is close to losing his nerve as he thinks of the impact of his failure upon all the devoted people who have trusted him and his leadership so long." [35]

In February 1941 the Urban League was still carrying a $12,000 deficit it had accumulated during the Depression.[36] This spelled serious hardship for the League movement. Operations were curtailed: Jesse O. Thomas was notified in December 1932 that his office would be closed and much of his budget cut in order "to save as far as possible the salary schedules of the regular employees and to save the organization embarrassment," and the Department of Research slowed to a near halt after Ira De A. Reid left in 1934.[37] The League's fellowship program, which had grown from 17 recipients in the 1910s to 38 in the 1920s, sent 18 men and 16 women to graduate school in social work during the 1930s.[38] Over the course of the decade the League added only three new affiliates. During the 1920s, expenditures for the entire League movement had more than tripled; in 1939, at $526,632, they were only $20,000 greater than they had been in 1931.[39]

The demands on the Urban League during the New Deal years made it impossible to sustain any significant cutback in activity; accordingly, it was the staff that suffered most. Beginning in November 1931, and continuing for at least seven years, staff members returned a percentage of their monthly pay to the League, part of the time voluntarily, sometimes on explicit instructions

Urban League Affiliates, 1940

SOURCE: Affiliated Branches of the National Urban League (1940), NUL Papers

from the executive board.[40] These "monthly contributions" were simply a euphemism for salary cuts. Eugene Kinckle Jones, whose annual income had risen from $2500 in 1918 to $6000 in 1928, was making the same $7500 per year in 1939 that he had earned a decade earlier. Raises of $300 gave T. Arnold Hill $5300 and Jesse O. Thomas $3800 in 1931—the same sums they were paid in 1939.[41] To alleviate the strain, salaries of some League employees "were placed in whole or in part on public agencies which agreed to prosecute types of work in line with the League's program and ideals." While the national office did not dismiss any of its employees, salaries were sometimes "withheld for months." [42] The Chicago Urban League's executive secretary and stenographer-switchboard operator (the only two members of the staff who did not resign during the Depression) worked for two years without pay. T. Arnold Hill, who was voted a raise of $1000 in 1935, when he was holding down Jones's job as well as his own, was paid $500 and advised to "pray for the rest." [43]

Such constraints put practical limits on the League's operations. Other limits came from the kind of people who were running the organization. Hollingsworth Wood, who succeeded Ruth Standish Baldwin as president of the League in 1915, held that same position throughout the 1930s. Eugene Kinckle Jones remained the chief member of the executive staff; during his absences in Washington, as adviser on Negro affairs in the Commerce Department, the League's daily operations were in Arnold Hill's hands. Jesse O. Thomas stayed on as southern field director. Elmer A. Carter, who succeeded Charles S. Johnson as editor of *Opportunity* in 1928, continued to serve in that capacity. Lester B. Granger, who became secretary of the new Workers' Bureau in 1934,* was the only important addition to the executive staff in the 1930s, and his background and experience closely paralleled those of his colleagues. The National League maintained a secretarial and clerical staff of about a dozen during the decade.[44]

* See pp. 284–85.

Continuity in staff paralleled continuity on the executive board. The complexion of the League's board in the 1930s was nearly identical to what it had been in the two preceding decades: the members were well-educated professionals, centered principally in New York.* Where the board of the 1930s differed from its counterpart of the 1910s was in its inclusion of more blacks and more women. Whites accounted for three-quarters of the board members during the Progressive Era, but less than two-thirds during the New Deal. And whereas about a quarter of the whites on the board in the 1910s were women, in the 1930s almost two-fifths were. This change accounts for the high representation of philanthropist-reformers on the board of the 1930s, and it also accounts for the relatively lower percentage of highly educated whites. Racial reform had become more and more the province of the concerned, well-to-do, community-spirited white woman, or the "professional volunteer."

Perhaps most important of all, the men and women who ran the Urban League in the 1930s were in large part the same individuals who had guided it in its earliest years. Of the sixty people who sat on the League's board during the 1930s, one-quarter had also served in both the 1910s and the 1920s, and almost two-thirds were holdovers from the 1920s alone. Equally significant, the members with the longest tenure were usually the ones who were most influential in the League's deliberations. Of course, there were a few particularly active newcomers, among them Lloyd K. Garrison, a practicing lawyer in New York and, later, dean of the University of Wisconsin Law School, and Caroline B. Chapin, a white philanthropist and social reformer from Englewood, New Jersey. But leadership of the organization rested

* If anything, the white board members were becoming more concentrated in their geographical origins. Whereas in the 1910s 44 per cent were born in the Middle Atlantic states, in the 1930s 55 per cent were. However, the percentage of blacks born outside the South increased—from about 9 per cent in the 1910s to about 19 per cent in the 1930s. For more detailed information about the educational background, place of residence, and profession of Urban League board members in the 1930s, see Tables A.9, A.10, and A.11, Appendix.

mainly in the hands of League veterans.* Their names were the ones that appeared again and again on attendance records for meetings; they were the ones who became officers of the League, were appointed to the steering committee, were singled out to solve delicate problems, and could often be identified with important policy decisions.

This meant that the League had the benefit of continuity, experience, and dedicated service among its board members as well as its staff. It also meant that the organization approached the special circumstances of the Depression with a leadership whose ideas had been shaped under different conditions, and who had a personal stake in the League's traditional methods. They believed in American capitalism, and thus sought to salvage and not to replace it. Dedicated to integration and interracial cooperation, they saw the destiny of blacks as irretrievably intertwined with the destiny of the nation as a whole. They were schooled in the tactics and values of the Progressive Era, and they brought its unmistakable influence to bear on the problems of the Depression and the New Deal. These factors shaped their responses to the economic crisis and provided a conservative counterweight to the radicalizing influence of the Negro's economic plight.

* Among whites, the leaders, in addition to Hollingsworth Wood, included public relations counselor William H. Baldwin; his cousin Roger N. Baldwin, director of the American Civil Liberties Union; two Quaker reformers, Elizabeth Walton and Agnes Brown Leach; and Dorothy Straus, a New York lawyer. The black stalwarts included Fred R. Moore, publisher and editor of the New York *Age;* Eugene P. Roberts, a New York City physician; Robert R. Moton, principal of Tuskegee Institute; Charles C. Spaulding, president of the North Carolina Mutual Life Insurance Company; and Mary McLeod Bethune, president of Bethune-Cookman College.

16 VOCATIONAL OPPORTUNITY

The Depression effectively nullified the Urban League's work in industrial relations. It left the organization "holding the line against the white invasion." No longer could it plan its program "in terms of progress"; rather, it had "to think grimly of bare survival." [1] With whites out of work in overwhelming numbers, employers would scarcely listen to entreaties for employment opportunities for blacks. Affiliates lamented "the continued pressing problem of unemployment"; as Detroit put it, "it is almost impossible to place a single man on a job." [2] When there were no jobs at all, arguments for new jobs for blacks became moot; even holding onto positions blacks already filled was more than the Urban League could possibly have accomplished.

I

As the Depression progressed, local Urban Leagues reported a widening gap between the numbers who sought work and the available positions. In 1929, the Cleveland Negro Welfare Association had had 10,241 requests from employers seeking workers, and it had made 6886 placements; the next year the requests plummeted to 3442 and the placements to 2591. In 1934 the organization received only 1196 requests and managed to fill 878 of them.[3]

"Placement work for the year has reached an unprecedented low level," Pittsburgh found in 1932.[4] "The number of people handled and jobs available grew further apart in 1932," St. Louis reported. "Only 2,246 placements were made—a reduction of 33% in the jobs available under the year 1931." In 1932 the League made 2058 placements—7 per cent fewer than in 1932. In 1934 it found 1800 jobs; in 1935, 1814. The League interviewed 23,575 job-seekers in 1937 (an increase of 6 per cent over 1936), but was able to place only 2243 of them—12 per cent fewer than the year before. In 1939, and again in 1940, the St. Louis affiliate had more than 31,000 applicants for work, but in neither year was it able to secure jobs for more than 10 per cent of them.[5] As the Seattle League put it, "These truly have been 'Years of the Locust.' "[6]

The average man seeking work at the St. Louis Urban League in 1939 was about thirty-three years old, with a working wife and three small children. The family lived in a three-room house with no bath, and they probably shared an outdoor toilet with fifty other people. The applicant's credit had run out at the grocery store, his landlord was threatening eviction, and he was weeks behind on his insurance payments. "More than likely" he had been on the relief and public works rolls since 1932, and had been "cut off relief at least four times, C.W.A. once, W.P.A. once." With a fourth-grade education, "inadequate" references, and a "vague" working history, he would have been a poor candidate for a job in the best of circumstances.[7]

In a time of economic crisis, what help could the Urban League offer such a man? The St. Louis League's records indicated "more and more a leveling down from opportunities where skills are required to common labor, in spite of trade training and experience or other background."[8] "Present conditions constitute the challenge of an impossible situation so far as the Negro group in the City of Newark is concerned," the New Jersey Urban League reported in 1932. It managed to find jobs for 91 men— 35 as elevator operators, 18 as laborers, 20 as porters, and 18 as waiters. The 241 women it placed included 15 cooks, 13 elevator operators, 183 household workers, 9 laundresses, 5 department store matrons, 6 children's nurses, 6 waitresses, and 4 stenographers.[9] The same pattern emerged from the reports of other affiliates: their placements, as Buffalo put it, were "almost entirely confined to domestic service." [10] From 75 to 100 per cent of the positions found by affiliates for which records are available were in domestic and personal service. Of the remaining jobs, all but a handful were in unskilled labor.[11] In short, these Urban Leagues dealt "almost exclusively in the *underprivileged* class." [12]

In the 1920s, the Urban League's placements had helped to feed the growth of a black industrial proletariat. In the 1930s, when jobs were no longer available in industry, the League had little choice but to channel blacks into the servant classes. As Detroit put it, "with so much unemployment we have been content with almost any job given us." [13] Moreover, the League's employment work in the 1920s involved substantial numbers of black men. During the Depression, the overwhelming majority of the jobs it secured (in most cases, more than 90 per cent) were for black women. The records of local Urban Leagues document the impact of the Depression on black employment patterns: the erosion of opportunities for men, and the increasing tendency of the black woman, working in domestic service, to become the family breadwinner. In Cleveland, the Negro Welfare Association remarked that "unemployment of colored men . . . and low wages of employed colored men make it necessary that the majority of colored women seek employment not only for their own support, but also to supplement low family incomes." [14] As jobs grew harder to find, women came to appropriate more and more of them. "Month by month and year by year, the plight of St. Louis' Negro worker is steadily growing worse," the Urban League lamented. That trend was significant enough, but the distribution of jobs between the sexes had equally important implications, as the League was perceptive enough to realize. The "increasing number of Negro women who are finding their way into domestic service as a way of taking up the slack resulting from the scarcity of jobs for men" was cause for concern; "that this development portends a bad future for Negro family life and the welfare of its children, no one can deny." [15]

The Urban League could not even count on being able to fill domestic positions. Calls for help frequently outran domestic placements, often because employers offered disgracefully low wages—perhaps $2.00 to $5.00 a week, sometimes nothing but room and board.[16] As a matter of pride, if nothing else, some Leagues refused to refer applicants for these positions. But an equally significant cause of orders left unfilled was the lack of properly qualified applicants.[17] It took some training to be able to keep house efficiently or operate modern appliances—training too few blacks seemed to have. Moreover, the Depression found whites seeking the most menial positions. Without adequate training, and with newfound competition from whites, blacks had to scramble to retain the lowest positions. The Urban League had to make special efforts even to place blacks at the bottom of the economic ladder.

The Depression forced many Urban Leagues to institute training programs for waiters, janitors, maids, cooks, elevator operators, chauffeurs, and bellmen.[18] Its classes in household management taught "everything from the proper method of arranging milady's boudoir to the finest of cookery," the Los Angeles Urban League boasted.[19] In addition to providing practical training, Memphis taught black workers "the importance of Punctuality, Efficiency and Loyalty," "honesty and industry as safeguards against loss of jobs." [20] In Philadelphia, the Armstrong Association distributed little flyers of tips for chauffeurs on how to behave on the job. The good chauffeur was "polite, cool-headed and obliging"; "careful, punctual and temperate"; "dependable, steady"; "industrious, reliable and honest"; "thoughtful and capable"; "neat and clean." "Unless you equip yourself to serve best," the Association admonished, "you may lose your job to someone who can give greater satisfaction." [21] All the men in the New

York Urban League's class for superintendents and building managers came dressed in three-piece suits.[22]

These classes helped some blacks to find and hold down jobs. In St. Louis, for instance, Lillie, who "was never called back after doing one day's laundry work" because of her inability "to manage modern laundry machinery," attended laundry demonstrations at the Urban League and became "one of our most efficient day workers." [23] The classes also gave the unemployed something to do with their time. And, not incidentally, they helped keep idle blacks from despairing of their lot and turning to radical activity. In Harlem, the New York Urban League offered "everything from . . . teaching janitors better understanding of boilers, to the more cultural and relaxing atmosphere of lessons in French and art," the *Herald Tribune* reported, in order "to mitigate the frightened and desperate outlook of local citizens." [24]

This rationale applied more than ever to the social services that Urban Leagues had been providing for decades. When it was possible to find jobs, the clubs, classes, and recreational activities Urban Leagues sponsored were icing on the cake—not essential to daily existence, but a means of enrichment, of improving the quality of life. When jobs could not be found, these social services and direct relief were all some League affiliates had to offer. They were a way of keeping people occupied and taking their minds off their predicament; they were also a way of maintaining the Urban League's credibility when its ability to deliver was seriously crippled. Thus, at a time when "the long sustained depression reached a state approaching chaos," the Cleveland Urban League was organizing a garden club "to promote beautification of premises owned or operated by colored people," [25] and Urban Leagues in Chicago, Philadelphia, Omaha, Seattle, and Detroit, among others, were running contests for the most attractive, best kept homes, gardens, and lawns.[26] Improving the "health . . . happiness, and morals" of blacks in cities continued to concern affiliates.[27]

II

At best these efforts were ineffective palliatives; at worst, they were cruel evasions of the real problems of the 1930s. The Urban League had to do more than train domestics or promote community clean-ups. In a tour of the South and West, where the League was weakest, T. Arnold Hill found blacks distressed over their economic situation, with "the deepest despair among the young people who had not even had a chance to get started." [28] This despair was exactly what Communists and Socialists expected to use to win a large following during the Depression. Radical groups were counting on blacks giving up on the system. The Urban League, by contrast, had every interest in preserving the democratic, capitalist structure. At a time when promises of jobs could not be fulfilled, the League looked for other ways of channeling black aspirations in safe directions. The importance of stimulating hope among Negroes motivated the League's new emphasis on vocational opportunity.

Before the stock market collapsed, the Urban League had planned to inaugurate an annual National Negro in Industry Week, similar to National Negro Health Week and patterned after the Negro in Industry Weeks already held in several cities. But a national employment campaign made little sense in the context of the Depression. Seeking to salvage something, T. Arnold Hill and local League executives decided to shift the emphasis of the campaign to vocational opportunity through vocational training.

The Vocational Opportunity Campaign gave the Urban League a handle on the employment crisis that was consistent with its earliest principles. While 1930 was "a bad time to appeal for jobs," it was "not a bad time to put forth the achievements . . . [of blacks] in industry, professions, transportation and trades," both to educate employers and to remind blacks, by implication, that a system that had once held out the possibility of upward mobility would surely do so again.[29] Nor, the Urban

League felt, was it a bad time to encourage and equip blacks to better their employment status when the economic crisis eased. By focusing on proper training as the key to opportunity, the League reverted to the old Booker T. Washington prescription for progress in the face of adversity. By "emphasizing forcefully the Negro's own responsibility in the equation," the organization managed to shift some of the burden away from the system that was failing black Americans.[30] And in stressing training, the League could concentrate on a future of possibility rather than a present of despair.

It takes a leap of faith to imagine training for jobs when jobs are unavailable. But the League tried to turn a dismal situation to its advantage: since blacks could no longer count even on the most menial jobs, the argument ran, they would have to prepare themselves to re-enter the labor market at all levels once the Depression ended.[31]

The place to begin was in the schools and colleges, where there was still an opportunity to shape the aspirations and abilities of young Negroes. Vocational guidance among Negro youth traditionally suffered from a kind of myopia. Counselors adhered much too rigidly to William H. Baldwin, Jr.'s dictum that it was "a crime for any teacher, white or black, to educate the negro for positions which [were] not open to him." [32] Aware that Negroes had been "accepted" in certain kinds of work, they steered young people in those same directions, rarely stimulating them to challenge employment barriers.

Whereas good guidance should have led a young Negro "to develop his skills to the highest possible level," and then helped him find the right job to match his talents, guidance as generally practiced did just the reverse, bending and stunting potential skills to meet available jobs.[33] "Very little has been done by vocational guidance to help the Negro child enter upon jobs for which he has trained," T. Arnold Hill explained. "The idea has been to train Negroes only for those vocations they may enter upon." [34]

Employment barriers were unlikely to give way unless young people prepared themselves to try to crack them. The Vocational Opportunity Campaigns fell in the mainstream of traditional Urban League strategies. Rather than emphasizing protests against employment restrictions, the League stressed education and training—indeed, self-help—and tried "to discover ways by which conditions [might] be improved, training facilities enlarged, occupational capacity shaped and expanded, and the whole field of under-employment for Negroes made understandable to whites and to Negroes with the hope that there [would] be a closer correlation between performance and ability." [35]

The Vocational Opportunity Campaign involved a fourfold approach: to stimulate young people to train for future employment, to work with teachers to disseminate accurate advice about present occupational prospects and opportunities for training in new fields, to encourage employers and unions "to give qualified Negroes a chance," and to educate the white public on the "social and economic consequences" of restricting vocational opportunity for blacks. [36]

The tools for the campaign were simple methods of publicity and education: publicity through newspaper articles, radio broadcasts, and pamphlets; speakers for local professional and civic clubs, schools, churches, and lodges; public meetings with Urban League speakers from the national and local offices; and interviews with employers and union leaders, in the interest of securing Negro employment. The 1930 campaign, coordinated through steering committees organized in fifty cities by local Urban Leagues and social agencies, included employer/union/prospective-employee meetings "to make employers aware of the Negro's talents, skills, and progress, and to make Negroes aware of the additional training they must acquire in order to compete for employment." [37] Schools held vocational assemblies, and vocational guidance specialists came to advise local teachers. In 1931, 444 schools in 61 cities participated. In 1937 the campaign involved 76,000 Negro students in 170 schools and colleges in special programs and reached 72,000 people at community meetings. In 1938 it involved 72,057 students in 136 schools and colleges; the following year, 84,142 participated.[38]

Through the years, the League proudly noted "real proof of success" in the results from communities participating in the campaign. During the 1931 campaign, for example, the Albany *News* ran a series of articles on "the Negro's economic life," and the mayor of Cincinnati made a radio address entitled "Giving the Negro a Chance." Cleveland established a vocational clinic, and an interracial Chicago's businessmen's club created a permanent vocational opportunity committee. Six years later, the League pointed to similar accomplishments: the creation of a permanent vocational guidance council in Atlanta, the establishment in Winston-Salem of an experimental job counseling and placement service, the organization of an industrial study group in New York to secure jobs for Negroes with public utilities, and a follow-up conference in Baltimore between public school vocational counselors and employers.[39]

To call this "real proof of success" when millions of blacks were out of work seems a cruel irony. Yet, in the Vocational Opportunity Campaigns' own terms, they probably were moderately successful. If nothing else, they enabled the Urban League to engage in a holding action for industrial capitalism. For what the emphasis on opportunity amounted to, in fact, was an appeal to blacks not to give up hope in the system.

The Vocational Opportunity Campaigns continued on an annual basis from 1930 to 1933. In 1934, with the League's treasury nearly empty and jobs increasingly hard to come by, the campaign was suspended, as it was in 1935 and 1936. At the beginning of 1936 the League was operating with a deficit of nearly a quarter of its entire budget. At the end of the year, having managed to reduce that sum by nearly two-thirds, League officials felt justified in responding to "constant requests from student and youth groups for information and guidance" by planning the fifth Vocational Opportunity Campaign for 1937. The League continued its vocational guidance programs until 1964.[40]

When the campaigns resumed, Ann Tanneyhill, who was to become director of vocational services for the League, wrote an article on "Guiding Negro Youth" for *Occupations* magazine to explain just what the League was trying to accomplish. In it she summarized the basic theory behind the campaigns: that the difficulties of finding work "are lessened as preparation for work increases; and that handicaps against Negroes diminish in proportion to the degree of skill and occupational understanding they acquire." Realistic advice—and strongly reminiscent of Booker T. Washington's faith that opportunities would come as a matter of course to those who, by training and hard work, were qualified to take advantage of them. But there was more to vocational training than its simple utilitarian value. "We are proceeding on the premise," T. Arnold Hill explained, "that the trained individual is more of an asset to himself and the community, even though he may suffer some disappointment in employment, than an untrained individual." Moreover, the League interpreted vocational training in broader terms than the acquisition of occupational skills; also involved were "the formation of efficient work habits, the development of personality traits, and the growth of social understanding." [41]

The Urban League issued flyers and pamphlets by the thousands as informational tools during the Vocational Opportunity Campaigns. Brief, eye-catching flyers on brightly colored paper, designed to capture the attention of Negro youth, exhorted students to "Train Today for Tomorrow's Job!" (1938), to "Wake Up!" to the need for vocational training (1938), to consider the options for *My Vocation* (1931). Some of the pamphlets offered more detailed statistical fare; *Negro Workers: A Drama of 5,000,000 American Wage-Earners* (1930) discussed the lack of opportunity to engage in vocations commensurate with one's capacity, the disproportionate concentration of blacks in unskilled laboring and service jobs, and the growing unemployment crisis. A mimeographed sheet, sold in bulk to local Leagues for distribution, gave advice on "How to Hold Your Job" (including such admonitions as "Don't argue, fight, or sulk on the job," "Join your fellow workers in their organizations," "Leave your ideas about the 'race problem' at home," "Be on time.").[42]

He Crashed the Color Line! and its sequel, *They Crashed the Color Line!*, presented profiles of successful Negroes in jobs normally closed to blacks—chemist, artist, football coach, radio technician, civil engineer, and others. The message was clear: despite serious obstacles to Negroes seeking employment, "that driving spirit which impels success must be the possession of a large number of Negro young people." Training, of course, was essential, "But nothing is more helpful to Negro youth than the realization that what they want to accomplish is possible of attainment." Determined, ambitious, skilled individuals *had* overcome the color line in employment, and the Urban League published their life stories as an inspiration to Negro students.[43] These pamphlets were reminiscent of some of the League's annual meetings in the 1920s, where the chairman would introduce "his successful colored friends"—"an educator, an editor, a business man, a clergyman, a physician, a poet . . . a social worker . . . and . . . musicians"—who would "tell briefly the accomplishments of Negroes in their particular fields." [44]

III

It was no accident that the *Color Line Series* portraits of successful Negroes were drawn almost entirely from skilled artisans and professionals. At a time when it was virtually impossible to find a job for anyone, it was easier to measure achievement in terms of the progress of a single Negro in the professions or the skilled trades than in terms of thousands of low-level job placements. In its emphasis on vocational opportunity, the Urban League was really addressing itself not to the masses who were already maids and porters, but to those who had had a chance at some training. The campaigns were pitched toward Negro high school and college students, and only peripherally toward those many teenagers who might have dropped out of school to earn a living in unskilled, menial jobs. While local Leagues were dealing with instruction and placements in domestic and personal service, the National Department of Industrial Relations had begun to back away from the black masses and to concentrate on opening doors for middle-class Negroes struggling to make it in the American economy. Another piece of evidence that illustrates this emphasis on the educated, potentially skilled black middle class is the attention the League began to pay to civil service opportunities.

Helping Negroes prepare for and pass civil service examinations became an integral part of the League's vocational opportunity efforts when the annual campaigns resumed in 1937. In 1910 Negroes had comprised almost 6 per cent of all employees in the federal civil service; by 1918, Negro federal employment had declined to less than 5 per cent of the total civil service. Beginning in May 1914, the Civil Service Commission required applicants to submit photographs with their applications. This move, coupled with the discretionary authority of appointing officers to choose among the first three eligibles for a given job, made it easy to discriminate in awarding civil service appointments. Of those Negroes who won federal civil service positions, more than 90 per cent in 1934 were employed in subclerical custodial classifications. It was not until 1940 that civil service regulations explicitly forbade discrimination on the ground of race.[45]

Beginning in 1937, the National Urban League made a "special effort to have Negroes take Civil Service examinations" in order to qualify for employment in public agencies.[46] It inaugurated a publicity service to notify blacks of job opportunities, salaries, examination dates, and procedures, and to urge those who were qualified to take the exams. The National Department of Industrial Relations and many affiliates drew up reading lists and held classes to help blacks prepare for the exams. The League got qualified Negroes to serve as oral examiners on Civil Service Commissions in several states and muncipalities, thereby increasing the chances that able Negroes would pass the examinations and be chosen from successful candidates for available jobs.[47] Although the Negro's share of civil service employment remained close to 10 per cent over the decade of the Depression, the absolute number of Negro federal government workers increased from 50,000 on June 30, 1933, to 82,000 five years later.[48]

The Department of Industrial Relations broadened its vocational guidance work to include individual counseling and referrals in the field of social service. Men and women coming to the Department for interviews were matched with positions available in public and private agencies and institutions. During the first three months of 1938, national office staff conducted 44 personnel and guidance interviews; two years later, during the comparable quarter, 70 men and women came for guidance and placement assistance. "Social work agencies throughout the country requested personnel recommendations," T. Arnold Hill reported later that year; through League referrals, appointments were made to positions including housemother and summer assistants at the New York Training School for Girls, recreation worker in a children's agency, and dining hall supervisor in an orphan asylum.[49] Here again the Department was looking away from the masses and toward the middle classes.

The Urban League's vocational guidance program made important contributions in the 1930s, and it laid the foundation for decades of further service. But it did not shape employment patterns in the Depression; in fact, nothing the Urban League did could significantly improve the employment status of blacks during the economic emergency. In 1940, as Table 16.1 shows, 82.6 per cent of black men and 92.2 per cent of black women employed in nonagricultural pursuits held semiskilled or unskilled jobs; the comparable figures for whites were 39.8 per cent and 46.1 per cent, respectively. Among unskilled laborers and servants, the contrast was even more dramatic: such jobs belonged

Table 16.1

Employed Workers in Nonagricultural Occupations, 1940.[1]

	% Male		% Female		% All Workers	
	White	Black	White	Black	White	Black
Professional Persons	6.8	2.9	14.7	5.0	8.9	3.8
Proprietors, Managers, Officials [2]	13.9	2.5	3.8	.9	11.2	1.8
Clerks and Kindred Workers	19.2	4.4	34.4	1.7	23.5	3.2
Skilled Workers and Foremen	20.3	7.5	.9	.1	14.9	4.3
Semiskilled Workers	23.9	20.0	30.6	15.9	25.8	18.3
Unskilled Workers [3] (Laborers)	12.2	39.2	.9	1.0	9.0	22.7
Unskilled Workers (Servant Classes)	3.7	23.4	14.6	75.3	6.7	45.8

SOURCE: Derived from Alba M. Edwards, *Comparative Occupation Statistics for the United States, 1870 to 1940* (Washington, D.C., 1943), p. 189.

[1] Exclusive of those on public emergency work.
[2] Exclusive of farmers.
[3] Exclusive of farm laborers.

to 62.6 per cent of the employed black men and 76.3 per cent of the employed black women, but only 15.9 per cent of white men and 15.5 per cent of white women.[50] In short, despite the Urban League's most valiant efforts, blacks as a group were no better off in terms of occupational distribution, either absolutely or relatively, than they had been in 1920 or 1930.[51] Indeed, given the massive unemployment and low wages for those who held jobs, they were qualitatively behind their position of earlier years.

None of this was the fault of the Urban League. Nor, given the circumstances of the Depression, were employment and vocational opportunity its major preoccupation during the 1930s. In those years, the major challenge confronting the Department of Industrial Relations—indeed, the entire League apparatus— was to make sure that blacks would share in the promises of the New Deal.

17 THE URBAN LEAGUE
AND THE NEW DEAL

"You must be a god Sent man," a black Mississippian wrote
Franklin D. Roosevelt in 1934. "You have made a great change
since you have ben President. . . . you ben Bread for the hungry
and clothes for the naked. . . . God Save the President." [1] This
correspondent spoke for millions of other black Americans who
idolized Franklin Roosevelt. But while New Deal measures on
balance benefited blacks and cemented their allegiance to the
Democratic party, the cause of racial advancement ranked near
the bottom of the Roosevelt administration's priorities. President
Roosevelt was not indifferent to Negro problems, but he lacked
the deep moral commitment to equality and the sensitivity to racial injustice that made his wife a champion of minority rights.
The President was a pragmatic politician who refused to risk his
legislative program by pushing unpopular civil rights legislation.
During his first two administrations, the Vice President, the
Speaker of the House of Representatives, the Majority Leaders of
the House and Senate, and the chairmen of the major congressional committees were all Southerners; their support was more
important to Roosevelt than the possible disaffection of thousands
of blacks. And with the pressing economic problems of the 1930s,
many people thought that appeals for black rights were frivolous
diversions from the main order of business.

To anyone who regards civil rights as a matter of moral justice, the President's reliance on a political calculus is difficult to understand. In the extreme, he was so completely bound by political considerations as to verge on the absurd. The matter of presidential greetings to the NAACP's annual meeting is a good case in point.

It was a commonplace for organizations of every description to ask the White House for a brief message of encouragement to be read at a special meeting or annual convention. But before Stephen Early, President Roosevelt's secretary, would release a perfunctory letter to the NAACP in 1935, he sent it to the Democratic National Committee to be "checked carefully, considering the possible political reaction from the standpoint of the South." [2] The White House was willing to send "cordial greetings" and messages of "good will," but the President and his advisers scrupulously avoided even the slightest mention of "controversial issues" such as lynching and disfranchisement, on the grounds that they were "entirely too dangerous" to talk about.[3] When Walter White, executive secretary of the NAACP, flooded the President with letters and telegrams in a futile attempt to persuade him to support the Wagner-Costigan antilynching bill, Mrs. Roosevelt had to explain to Early that White did not mean "to be rude or insulting," but really had a legitimate grievance.[4]

I

The campaign against lynching was the major civil rights issue of the 1930s. The Urban League endorsed the proposed antilynching legislation in 1934, and it sent Elmer Carter to testify at Senate hearings that February.[5] When lynchings continued, the League wired its dismay to the President and members of the Senate and urged speedy federal action. It even went so far as to take a place on the program of a mass meeting against lynching at Carnegie Hall "as a means of defining its position." [6] In 1937, Eugene Kinckle Jones instructed his local executives to "BOMBARD" Senators with letters and telegrams "IN WHAT WE HOPE WILL BE THE LAST

DRIVE FOR THE ANTI-LYNCHING BILL." [7] In these actions the League departed from its traditional "hands-off" policy toward political/legal issues. But the departure was more perfunctory than real. The active agent in the fight against lynching continued to be the NAACP. The Association did the real work in the battle; the League, consistent with its emphasis on employment and social welfare, merely lent its name.

The League's participation in the other major Negro *cause célèbre* of the decade was even more perfunctory. It agreed, in December 1935, to go on record as a sponsor of the Joint Committee for the Defense of the Scottsboro Boys. But in committing its name, the Urban League was careful to eschew real involvement in the sphere of legislation and civil rights; it could not "become an active member of the Defense Committee without a serious change of policy and program"—a change it did not mean to make.[8]

Where the Urban League had a real role to play during the New Deal was in seeing to it that blacks shared fairly in programs for relief and economic recovery. Previously, private employers had been the principal target of the League's employment efforts; it had been possible to meet with them individually and to try to persuade them, on the basis of carefully accumulated evidence, to hire Negroes. When the federal government became the nation's chief employer, the League simply adjusted its traditional procedures: while it found it necessary to speak more loudly and more publicly, its efforts to persuade agency heads to treat Negroes equitably followed naturally from its earlier experience.

Before the midpoint of the Hundred Days had passed, Urban League officials were indicting federal relief and recovery programs, old and new, for failing to prohibit "gross," "wide-spread" discrimination against Negroes.[9] "The old deal is still ruling, as far as Negroes are concerned," T. Arnold Hill told a League conference in October 1933. "The South is riding in the saddle in Washington." [10] The Roosevelt administration, he charged, was "afraid to be too definitely committed to a New Deal for Negroes because of political consequences," with the result that "every phase of the program—relief, the reforestation camps, the NRA, the reemployment program, and so on—is falling short of its obligation to Negroes." And yet Hill proclaimed himself optimistic that progress would be made, because of the administration's "intelligent understanding" of the problems, and because Negroes were speaking out against discrimination.[11]

By official pronouncement, the Roosevelt administration opposed discrimination in the administration of relief and recovery programs. The President offered personal assurances that "every recovery and regular agency of the Federal Government [will] be administered with absolute equality and fairness"; the recovery program, he said, had been designed to help everyone in need, regardless of race, religion, or other special qualifications.[12] Officially, the WPA, PWA, the Department of Public Works within the Interior Department, and other federal agencies issued orders prohibiting discrimination in the allocation of jobs according to race or religion. Yet the Urban League and other organizations frequently found cause to complain about actual practice, which more often followed local laws and customs than federal pronouncements.

Still believing that an accurate understanding of racial problems was the first step to their solution, the Urban League drew upon its traditional resources to impress the federal government with the gravity of the Negro's plight. Just six weeks after President Roosevelt took office in 1933, the League sent him a careful report on the economic status of the Negro population, with special emphasis on problems of unemployment and relief. When the second Roosevelt administration began in January 1937, the League was ready with another memorandum. Using its own and other studies of Negro conditions during the 1930s, the League marshaled pertinent facts and statistics to support its appeal for administrative and legislative remedial action.[13]

In addition to providing careful studies, the Urban League

contributed its share of Negro specialists at various levels of the Roosevelt administration. As Arnold Hill explained, it had long been League policy "to permit its trained staff to serve public agencies when experienced and well-informed personnel [were] required for any particular task." [14] George Haynes had become director of the Division of Negro Economics in the Labor Department during World War I, and Hill himself had assisted President Hoover's emergency employment committee.

Beginning in October 1933, Eugene Kinckle Jones took a leave of absence (for almost four years) from his post as executive secretary to direct the Commerce Department's unit for the study of Negro problems. (Hill took over as acting executive secretary during this time.) *Opportunity* hailed Jones's appointment as a tremendous boost to "the Negro's faith in the sincerity of the Administration's attitude toward his status." [15] Praising the selection, *The New York Times* described Jones as "an institution in himself," who, "more than any one other person," had made the Urban League "an agency of national usefulness." [16]

Other Urban League officials took on more limited assignments. T. Arnold Hill went to Washington in 1939 as a consultant on Negro affairs to the WPA and NYA. Local League executives took part- or full-time leaves of absence to work on federal projects. Two of the National League's board members played important parts in Roosevelt's Black Cabinet: Robert L. Vann, editor of the Pittsburgh *Courier*, served as special assistant to the Attorney General, and Mary McLeod Bethune, founder-president of Bethune-Cookman College, directed the Division of Negro Affairs of the National Youth Aministration.

The Urban League believed that only with black advisers in Washington would blacks be likely to get fair treatment from the federal government. The sheer magnitude of the economic dislocations suffered by whites would "tax the experience, the wisdom and engineering ability of the members of their group to look after white people." [17] Under the circumstances, expecting whites to look out for Negroes, too, without any special prompting, was just unrealistic. Simply stated, there would be "no protection against discrimination being practiced upon Negroes unless some Negro is placed in a responsible capacity where he can follow up and check abuses of regulations." [18] This attitude led the League not only to lend its own personnel for federal and local service, but to use the whole League apparatus to lobby for the appointment of Negro advisers in state and local New Deal agencies.

The Urban League also tried to influence the Roosevelt administration by conferring with and winning the support of the President's wife—a novel tactic for the League, but one which became common among advocates of civil rights and social justice during the New Deal. Eleanor Roosevelt's well-known personal concern for the problems of blacks and her access to the President led racial reformers to seek her assistance. "The Negroes in America," Elmer Carter told her, "have a feeling that you can be numbered among their friends. They have taken no little pride in the fact that you . . . have retained Negro servants in your household." [19] T. Arnold Hill corresponded with Mrs. Roosevelt about the plight of impoverished blacks. "I write you," he explained, "because I feel certain that you will be moved to exert your influence to correct such practices." [20] The First Lady agreed to speak at an Urban League meeting in Baltimore in December 1935 as part of the national organization's twenty-fifth anniversary celebration. "If only different races knew each other better," she said on that occasion, "they could live peaceably together." In a message perfectly suited to her audience, she called for interracial cooperation "to wipe out . . . inequalities and injustices." [21] She and Hill met on a number of occasions to talk about Urban League projects and other matters relating to the "general welfare of Negroes in the United States." [22]

The First Lady provided a sympathetic ear at the heart of an administration otherwise not overly concerned with the problems of blacks. She was also an important advocate; whenever she learned of complaints about discrimination in New Deal programs, she would write to the administrator in charge to ask if something could be done. The message that the President's wife was "referring it to the proper authority for investigation" could have been a polite evasion of a sticky problem; in Mrs. Roosevelt's case it was a promise that she would use her considerable influence in the interests of achieving racial justice, a cause in which she firmly believed.[23]

She also tried to influence her husband. When the NAACP or the Urban League asked the President for a word of support, their requests were often accompanied by a handwritten note from his wife: "This is a great chance to say some wise things to the Negro & to the rest of the nation!" she once advised; or, on another occasion, "I think this might be a chance for you to do something valuable for the colored people. It wld be appreciated too." [24] Even in such simple matters, however, she labored under enormous constraints. The automatic reflex of the President's staff was to be wary of requests from organizations seeking racial advancement, partly because they were more concerned with the political consequences of filling them than with their moral rightness, partly also because some of the President's advisers retained the racial attitudes of their native South. Even the most innocent requests were often turned down. When Arnold Hill asked the President for "a word of greeting" in conjunction with the League's 1938 Vocational Opportunity Campaign, Stephen Early told him that the President would be unable to find the time to send it because of "very heavy pressure in connection with the public business." [25] But Hill had also asked Mrs. Roosevelt for her "assistance in getting the President to write us a letter of encouragement," and it was only her intercession that did the trick.[26] "I did not know of Mrs. Roosevelt's interest in the National Urban League," one of the President's staff members confessed to Early.[27] "I wish you all success in your efforts to be helpful to others," the President finally wrote.[28] But what a round of correspondence and negotiation it took to obtain even that innocuous message!

II

The lesson of the New Deal was that pressure was what counted. The League had always operated on the belief that polite one-to-one meetings were the best way of persuading people to pay attention to blacks. With the New Deal, though, quiet, confidential entreaties too easily got lost in the shuffle. To plead an unpopular cause with a government that responded to organized pressure, the Urban League had to go public with its protest. And to deal with a proliferation of federal agencies, instead of a handful of private employers, it needed additional vehicles to carry its message.

During the New Deal, the National Urban League began for the first time to encourage public protest. In letters, telegrams, and meetings with Washington officials, the League sought to make the administration aware of inequities in New Deal programs. "Write Harry Hopkins," "write Frances Perkins," "write Secretary Ickes"—all these were familiar refrains in intra-League correspondence. Exhortations to "ACT AT ONCE!" to support the Urban League's demand "that Negroes be given a fair deal" became increasingly common.[29] "Use every influence to encourage other organizations to swell the tide of protest," T. Arnold Hill urged, in a typical message to local executives; ". . . lose no time in bringing to bear all possible pressure of which your community is capable." [30] Write or wire immediately to the WPA in Washington, asking that special care be taken to see that Negroes get a fair and adequate proportion of these [WPA] jobs," Eugene Kinckle Jones admonished.[31]

Just as the New Deal required that the Urban League speak with a louder voice, it also brought the organization into the legislative process. Prior to that time, the problems of black workers had had to be worked out within the world of private business and organized labor. But important New Deal legislation in the areas of labor and social security gave the federal government a critical voice in the welfare of American workers. Accordingly, the Urban League moved for the first time, through petitions, mass letter-writing campaigns, and meetings with members of Congress, to influence those laws to benefit blacks.

During the New Deal, the cause of labor was "riding 'high, wide, and handsome.'" Section 7(a) of the National Industrial Recovery Act, legitimizing collective bargaining, and, later, the Wagner Labor Relations Act made the 1930s a crucial decade for the American worker. But blacks generally failed to share in labor's bonanza; "the cause of Negro workers," as T. Arnold Hill put it, "has not been one of labor's aims." [32]

Renewed entreaties to the AFL documented Hill's point. When the AFL launched a massive membership campaign in 1933, Hill offered the assistance of the Urban League in reaching Negro workers. Failing to see the need for special efforts to recruit blacks, AFL President William Green maintained that the organizing drives were not discriminatory. In the interests of "complete unity among all workers," Hill urged that Green appoint a commission to hear and adjust charges of union discrimination. It was about time, too, that the Federation use its "prestige and power . . . to bring its component units in line with its own declaration of fairness to Negro workers." The three-month correspondence ended with President Green's ironic assurance that the AFL would handle the race question "in a vigorous and satisfactory way. . . . You are appealing to sympathetic friends." [33]

This renewed evidence of AFL insensitivity to racial discrimination was all the more dangerous in light of the New Deal's boost to the labor movement. By guaranteeing the right of collective bargaining, the Wagner Labor Relations Act promised a real "new deal" for American labor. But in failing "to take note of intolerant anti-Negro policies pursued by many unions," the Act seemed to the Urban League less a panacea than a serious "threat to the job security of Negro workers." [34] The legislation "elevate[d] labor to the dominant position of an active, operating co-partner with the employer and the public, each having equal rights and authority." Unless steps were taken, this "growth of labor's influence and power" would permit the continuation, with apparent congressional sanction, of discriminatory policies toward Negro workers.[35]

In the effort to amend the Wagner Act to protect the rights of Negro labor, the major initiative came from the NAACP. But the Urban League pitched in with important support. T. Arnold Hill went to Washington in April 1934 to talk to Senator Wagner about the effect of his proposed legislation on Negroes. When the Senate Committee on Education and Labor held hearings on Wagner's bill, Hill submitted a brief, setting forth the Urban League's recommendations for revising it. The bill allowed unions to exclude Negroes from membership "and from employment in occupations under their jurisdiction"; it did not protect Negroes against other forms of union discrimination on the basis of race; it failed to stop dual unionism; and in its blanket refusal to accord strikebreakers the status of employees, it failed to make an exception for Negroes in cases where the striking unions excluded them from membership. Like the NAACP, the League proposed revisions to correct these points; their chief goal was an amendment stating that

> It shall be an unfair labor practice for a labor organization to bar from membership any worker or group of workers for reason of race or creed either by constitutional provision or by ritualistic practice.

In short, no union that persisted in denying membership and employment on the basis of race or religion would be permitted to enjoy the protection of the Wagner Act.[36] The League urged Negro workers to write or wire their congressmen in support of the amendment and to press local churches and clubs to do the same.

Despite the vigorous efforts of the NAACP, the Urban League, and others, the move to amend the Wagner Act failed.

Its proposed guarantees for organized labor were extremely controversial; and since it lacked the official backing of the Roosevelt administration, the bill faced a rough reception in the Congress. Under such circumstances the bill's sponsors needed all the support they could get, and they could not afford to risk alienating powerful Southerners by including a controversial antidiscrimination clause. Given the racial climate of the times, it is little wonder that they were reluctant to imperil their long-sought labor legislation by fighting to protect black workers. Nor is it surprising that the wishes of the well-organized, increasingly powerful labor movement, which opposed such a clause, should have weighed more heavily than the desires of the loosely organized, less influential black movement. Understandable as this may be, it soured some blacks on the New Deal; the Wagner Act, Lester Granger still insisted more than three decades later, was the worst piece of legislation ever passed by the Congress.[37]

The Urban League joined the NAACP in a similarly abortive effort to amend the Social Security Act. When Senate hearings on the bill began in January 1935, the NAACP's Walter White asked the bill's sponsor, Senator Robert F. Wagner, whether it contained "adequate safeguards against discrimination on account of race." [38] Wagner was "certain that benefits under [the] economic security bill would have to be paid without any discrimination whatsoever on the basis of race," he assured White.[39] But the Senator could not have anticipated the Roosevelt administration's effort to make the bill more palatable to the Congress by trimming its costs.[40] As it finally emerged, the Social Security program excluded agricultural and domestic employees from its provisions for unemployment compensation and old-age insurance. This exclusion, the NAACP's legal counsel asserted, was a "direct blow at Negro workers." [41] The more the NAACP "studied the bill, the more holes appeared, until from a Negro's point of view it look[ed] like a sieve with the holes just big enough for the majority of Negroes to fall through." [42] It "automatically excludes 65 per cent. of the Negroes throughout the country," the

Urban League explained to President Roosevelt. Moreover, "failure to provide for workers now unemployed through no fault of their own will eliminate a large number of the remaining Negro workers, who face no prospect in the near future of returning to permanent private employment." "Until some form of security is given to domestic and agricultural workers," the League warned, "there can be no security for the Negro population." Unemployment was not the only problem. "Complete administration of the old age pensions by state governments expose Negro beneficiaries to the same maladministration that is now practiced with respect to school funds given by the Federal Government and expended by the states."

The Urban League joined the NAACP in urging the Administration to back an amendment that would include the neglected workers under the bill, or to "create a voluntary insurance plan with federal subsidy for old age and unemployment insurance for domestic and agricultural workers." The League advised affiliates to sponsor petitions addressed to the President, Senator Wagner, and the members of the Senate Labor Committee. These efforts to reshape the legislation began while it was still in committee and continued long after it had been enacted into law. Again, the effort to amend the Act failed.[43]

III

These attempts to influence national legislation show how the New Deal had changed the framework in which the Urban League operated. Whereas in earlier years it had dealt almost exclusively with private employers and organized labor, in the 1930s it had to cope with the Congress as well as with a broad range of federal departments and agencies that had autonomous state and local subsidiaries. In facing these expanded responsibilities, the Urban League relied on its affiliates to provide evidence to substantiate charges of racial discrimination. And it enlisted their aid in pressing for the appointment of qualified Negroes to staffs, boards, and committees of New Deal agencies and employment services on the federal, state, and local level.

The affiliates, however, had their hands full with local projects; and even if their staffs had been able to devote full time to ensuring equity in the relief and recovery programs, there were scarcely enough Urban Leagues to cover the field. The New Deal's administrative decisions that affected blacks most directly were made on the state and local level; with fewer than fifty affiliates, the Urban League did not have enough manpower to oversee critical local operations.

To fill this gap, the Urban League began, in September 1933, to organize local, state, and national Emergency Advisory Councils to act as "watchdogs of the rights of Negroes." [44] Their immediate target was the National Recovery Administration. "Bitter complaints from all sections of the country" convinced League officials that the NRA was not working for Negroes—indeed, that they were "systematically excluded" from its benefits "and in many cases discharged to make room for white workers." [45] To remedy this, Negroes would have to know more about what the NRA had theoretically promised them, and NRA officials would have to know more about what it was actually delivering. Specific data on individual instances of code violations would build an impressive case in behalf of those who charged the NRA with discrimination. Only then might Negroes, who represented economic strength and purchasing power "too potent" to be ignored and exploited, benefit fairly from the various emergency relief acts.[46]

The councils, quickly given the shorthand tag of "EAC," would investigate complaints of violations of the NRA involving racial discrimination. Equally important, they would educate blacks about the workings of the various relief and recovery acts, codes, and agencies, and teach them how to secure the benefits the New Deal legislation promised.

The League launched the EAC in December, and by the end of the calendar year, some 200 councils had been organized—

nearly two-thirds of them in the South, most of these in cities without Urban League affiliates or other organizations working for Negro welfare.[47] The EAC was "AN ORGANIZATION OF NEGROES FOR NEGROES," [48] although Jesse O. Thomas, for one, suggested that it include "some liberal-minded white persons." T. Arnold Hill explained the decision to exclude whites: "I had thought of it [the EAC] as an organization that would represent a solidified public opinion among Negroes, and that with this we could make so great an impact upon Washington that the cause of Negroes could not be ignored." [49]

The councils supplied manpower and influence to supplement the Urban League's own efforts to see that the New Deal offered a fair deal for Negroes. EAC chairmen were urged to initiate letter-writing campaigns—to Labor Secretary Frances Perkins, concerning discrimination in organized labor, to the United States Employment Service, to get Negroes into CCC reforestation camps, for example—and to lobby locally for Negro representation on NRA compliance boards and other state- and community-level New Deal agencies.[50] Tallying successes in securing such representation, the League cited the appointments of an adviser on Negro affairs to the Virginia Emergency Relief Administration, an assistant to the director of the New York State TERA and CWA, a member of the NRA compliance board in St. Louis, four census takers in New Bedford, and four relief investigators in Trenton, among others. In some cases EACs expanded to fulfill functions which, normally, were the responsibility of Urban League affiliates or similar agencies; for instance, they undertook slum clearance, housing, farm subsistence, and white-collar relief projects.[51]

The viable councils, however, became more the exception than the rule. By April 1935 the Urban League was complaining that poor communications had "greatly hampered" the EAC program. "Some chairmen are very faithful; others are very lax in their reports." In any case, it was too expensive to keep in touch with all of them, so the League chartered the EACs that could "be counted upon to assist . . . in protecting the Negro's interests in the work relief program." The national office sent each EAC a questionnaire to determine whether its activities qualified for a charter. By October barely a third had replied.[52]

It became increasingly difficult to find local leaders for the EAC, and organizations on the state level were often poorly developed. Many EACs were inactive well before the demise of the NRA in May 1935. When the Workers' Bureau called a national meeting of EACs that November (to coincide with the National Urban League's twenty-fifth anniversary observance), only eight councils sent representatives, "so their program was merged into the general Urban League program." [53]

By the end of the New Deal, the record amply supported Eugene Kinckle Jones's earlier claim that the Urban League had "kept the cause of the Negro on the desks of Washington officials," not merely through protests, but by providing a constant supply of "facts, programs, and recommendations." [54] Insofar as some New Deal agencies became more attentive to equitable treatment for blacks, part of the credit must go to the League's vigilance.[55] Vigorous representations by the NAACP and the Urban League helped to make the President sensitive to the problems of blacks, and by the end of the 1930s their pressure had contributed to the fairer representation of blacks in programs like the CCC and the WPA.

But there were real limits on the progress these organizations could expect to make. As yet the voice of blacks was comparatively weak; their organization as a pressure group was in its formative stages. Had they been able to exert more political muscle, they would still have faced nearly insurmountable barriers: the decentralized operation of most New Deal agencies; the willingness to subordinate black problems to the much larger problems of relief and recovery; and the habit, in a still segregated country, of racial discrimination. Black rights had not yet emerged as a major national concern; by their protests in the 1930s, the NAACP and the Urban League were laying foundations for later, more successful assaults on American racism. When it became advantageous to their interests, white power centers would begin to respond.

18 LABOR: A NEW RADICALISM?

The intensity of the economic crisis of the early 1930s led some Americans to entertain the idea that industrial capitalism had bankrupted itself. Similarly, the severity of the Depression's impact on blacks led certain black leaders to call for an overhaul of the tactics and programs of the principal organizations for racial advancement.

Shortly after Franklin Roosevelt took office in 1933, the NAACP invited a group of young blacks to a three-day conference at Amenia, New York, to "discuss in a perfectly frank way . . . the present situation of the American Negro and just what ought to be done." The conferees readily agreed that organizations like the NAACP ought to develop "a new program suited to these times." [1] The main thrust, most of them felt, should be toward organizing the masses of blacks to wield some political and economic power. Traditional appeals for equity and justice were all well and good, but the realities of the 1930s showed that policy-makers responded to the best organized, most powerful interest groups. Since blacks were a weak minority, their best hope lay in allying with the white labor movement to exert pressure on government and industry in behalf of the working classes.

The Amenia delegates called for "a campaign to make the black worker 'conscious of his relation to white labor and the white worker conscious that the purposes of labor, immediate or ultimate, cannot be achieved without full participation from the Negro worker.' " [2]

In the early 1930s the NAACP resisted these appeals for a new economic emphasis. But the same kinds of influences that had led the Amenia delegates to advocate a reorientation for the NAACP also affected the National Urban League, and there they had more immediate structural results.

I

The Depression awakened the Urban League to the realization that "ordinary 'old-fashioned' diplomacy [would] get Negroes nowhere in their fight for jobs." This tactical lesson was one that "highly organized minorities such as trade unions and unemployed groups" had already learned, one that prompted them to "set up elaborate machinery for creating spectacular protest." [3] The Urban League's actions on the labor front remained moderate within the full spectrum of protest popular during the 1930s. And yet, for the League itself, they represented a substantial tactical, if not ideological, change. Echoing Amenia, the League called for a class alliance across racial lines. The New Deal left "unorganized workers, black and white . . . without a voice." "The only possible way out," the Urban League came to believe, was "through Organized Action." [4]

The League never abandoned "its activities with organized labor, nor did it give up its appeals to employers," as T. Arnold Hill took pains to explain. "But it did conclude that both employers and employees might be more willing to listen to the demands of 5,500,000 workers than they would to the suggestions of a social service organization." [5] In short, the League redefined the principle of advocacy to emphasize preparation of workers to act effectively as advocates of their own cause.

The Urban League had begun to think about building a biracial trade union movement well before the Depression. Not long after he became director of industrial relations (in 1925),

Hill started exploring the possibility of establishing "classes to study the principles and workings of the labor movement." His theory was that "the differences between the Negro and organized labor could be improved if more colored men and women joined trade unions"—and if blacks knew more about unions, they would be more likely to join.[6] But in the 1920s, when Urban League officials were cultivating close ties with white business, Hill's plan seemed too dangerous to some local executives who feared "the difficulties they might get into with their friends should they initiate these classes." [7] By making overtures toward organized labor, the League would run the risk of upsetting employers of Negroes who maintained open shops.

By the early 1930s it was clear that even the most careful efforts to avoid offending employers would not solve the economic problems of urban blacks. In March 1934, with Eugene Kinckle Jones on leave in Washington and T. Arnold Hill acting as executive secretary, the Urban League approved Hill's proposal for a program of education and organization among Negro workers.[8]

The point of the new labor program was to show blacks the value of collective action in solving labor problems. Through "EDUCATION and ACTION," Workers' Councils would prepare blacks to join the ranks of organized labor. The Councils would teach blacks about "the problems of workers, the objectives of labor, the principles of industrial organization"; they would take "ACTION on violations of principles and practices that make for the insecurity of the worker, on exclusion from labor bodies, on racial weaknesses that handicap effective collective action." [9]

For too long, the Urban League believed, Negro workers had been relying, with less than satisfactory results, on the efforts of others to secure concessions in their behalf. The philosophy behind the Workers' Councils was that workers would be their own best lobby—that instead of continuing to be their spokesman, the Urban League ought to be preparing them to speak effectively for themselves. "Realizing that the only hope for increasing the organizing power of the Negro workers was to increase their class consciousness and encourage them to become vocal about their situation," the Urban League set up "kindergarten[s] of labor education and organization through which the Negro worker might make his cause one with that of the masses of the American working population." [10]

"The philosophy behind the Workers' Councils is that of self-determination," T. Arnold Hill explained. "Only if Negro workers themselves realize the necessity for action can their position be strengthened." "You must organize to compel the breakdown of discriminatory barriers that keep you out of unions and, consequently, out of employment," he told Negro workers. "You must organize to prevent the passing of legislation that will be a further aid to discrimination-practicing unions and employers. You must organize to demand, with other workers, a new deal for labor." [11]

The League brought St. Louis executive John T. Clark and southern field director Jesse O. Thomas to New York on a temporary basis, Clark to aid in setting up the new program and Thomas to work principally on integrating it with the EACs. Clark stayed through early summer and helped to organize the first few Workers' Councils. In September the League created a Workers' Bureau within the Department of Industrial Relations to coordinate the Councils' activities (and those of the EACs) and Lester B. Granger was named the Bureau's director.

At thirty-eight, Granger was the youngest executive on the national staff in the 1930s, four years the junior of his immediate superior, T. Arnold Hill, and eleven years younger than Eugene Kinckle Jones. Like Jones and Hill, he was a native Virginian— he was born in Newport News—although he grew up in Newark, New Jersey. By family background and educational experience, he seemed an unlikely choice to organize black workers. He was a son of the upper classes; his father was a physician, his mother a teacher, and all five of his brothers were doctors or dentists. Four of the Granger brothers attended Dartmouth College and two the University of Pennsylvania. Lester Granger was graduated from Dartmouth in 1918, a time when few blacks were going to college, not to mention to the Ivy League. During World War I, when most blacks who saw military duty were consigned to the service corps, Granger went overseas with the Allied Expeditionary Force as a lieutenant in the field artillery. Upon his return to the United States, he served briefly as industrial secretary of the two-year-old Negro Welfare League in Newark, and he then enrolled as a graduate student at the New York School of Social Work. After two years of teaching in normal schools in North Carolina, he took a job, in 1922, as extension worker at the Bordentown, New Jersey, Manual Training and Industrial School for Colored Youth. Shortly thereafter he took charge of the boys' work at the school, and he organized the New Jersey Federation of Boys' Clubs. He stayed at Bordentown until 1934, with the exception of a year's leave of absence in 1930 to organize the Los Angeles Urban League. Before taking over the Workers' Bureau, he had also served for eight months as business manager of *Opportunity*.[12]

In addition to the Workers' Bureau, the League established the Committee of 100 for Negro Workers, to lend their prestige and influence and to provide moral and financial backing for its campaign in behalf of Negro labor. Headed by Robert S. Abbott, editor of the Chicago *Defender*, the committee invited representative Negro leaders to "engage in an active, aggressive fight in behalf of the Negro worker to the end that he shall have fair and just opportunities to earn a living wage and to participate in the recovery program under the New Deal."[13]

Within a year, 42 Workers' Councils in 17 states covered more than 30,000 workers. They drew their membership primarily from the building trades, steel mills, tobacco workers, domestic workers, longshoremen, laundry workers, and lumber mill workers, with railway trainmen, garment workers, and relief investigators representing a significant minority on some of the Councils. After four years more than 70 Councils had been organized in 21 states, although not all of those were still in existence by

1938. "Several" had become "nuclei for trade unions" in specific fields, but "some two dozen Councils" continued "in line with their original purpose." [14]

The Councils held classes in workers' education, dealing with labor history as well as contemporary labor questions, such as wages and hours legislation, relief practices, and industrial vs. craft unionism. Speakers included economists, labor leaders, government officials, and employers. Workers' Council bulletins provided up-to-date information on labor developments among black workers in different trades across the country. By the fall of 1935 the NAACP was offering some of the same services—and, although Walter White felt that "we have just got to find a better name [than] 'workers' education,'" many of the NAACP's branches were providing just that—instruction for adults in black history and culture and in legal, political, and economic problems.[15]

The Urban League carefully noted the Workers' Councils' achievements: the organization in Atlanta of fifty Negro railway employees who became affiliated with the National Association of Colored Railway Trainmen and successfully checked dismissals of Negro employees; employment of Negro carpenters and painters on a local housing project in Memphis; formal chartering of Atlanta painters by the AFL; and the organization of building trades workers, building service employees, steamfitters and others into a trade union in St. Louis.[16]

The Workers' Bureau kept the Workers' Councils informed about federal recovery programs and various means of protecting Negro labor's interests in them. For example, as the federal housing program got underway, the Bureau organized a delegation of Negro building trades mechanics to go to Washington to impress their demands on government officials. Workers' Council bulletins explained how New Deal legislation and agencies affected black workers, and the Workers' Bureau exhorted the Councils to lobby the state and federal governments in behalf of blacks.[17]

II

The Workers' Bureau assumed the direction of the Urban League's appeals against labor discrimination, giving them a more militant flavor. In July 1935, as a result of a resolution prepared by A. Philip Randolph for the AFL's convention in 1934, a special Committee of Five of the AFL convened in Washington to hear testimony regarding union treatment of Negroes. Randolph summoned the Urban League to send witnesses to present evidence of racial discrimination by AFL unions. Under the direction of Lester Granger, the Workers' Bureau prepared a statement that was presented at the hearing by Reginald A. Johnson, executive secretary of the Atlanta Urban League, who was then acting as the National League's Washington representative. Johnson recounted the long and unsuccessful efforts of the Urban League and others to move the AFL to act in behalf of blacks. The "futility of 'resolution passing,' " he pointed out, was readily indicated by the contrast between the "well-meaning resolutions" adopted by the AFL conventions since 1917 and the facts of union discrimination—against Negro building trades workers in St. Louis, painters in Atlanta, and plasterers in Richmond. And the instances he described were "only a few of the flagrant cases which flourish[ed] throughout the country—North and South—indicating ways in which the liberal policy of the American Federation of Labor [had] been consistently flouted by locals and internationals in the absence of strong means of enforcing AF of L rulings." Should the AFL fail to lower the color bar its affiliates had raised, Johnson warned, Negro workers would embrace a rival unionism that would conclusively alienate them from the AFL.[18]

Exhorting the AFL to take action more drastic than another statement of principle, the Urban League again urged it to exclude from membership any internationals practicing discrimination, and to appoint Negro organizers and launch a program of education among Negro workers. All of these steps had been suggested before, either by the Urban League, by Negro unions, or, most recently, in resolutions proposed by A. Philip Randolph at the AFL convention in 1934. The League offered the services of its Workers' Councils to aid in workers' education and recruitment.

With the Committee of Five scheduled to report at the AFL's October convention, the Urban League joined Randolph in a campaign to broaden the investigation through regional hearings on union discrimination. That way, T. Arnold Hill explained to William Green, workers would have an opportunity "to appear in person and tell of their own experiences. Because of the expense involved and the short notice of the previous hearing, nothing like a full story of the whole situation was heard by the Committee." Green agreed to submit the question of extended hearings to his executive council, but it refused the request.[19]

The Workers' Bureau was never very optimistic about the outcome of the AFL inquiry. It was "foolish" to expect "a report satisfactory to Negro workers," Lester Granger wrote. "Past experience justifies Negroes in believing that if left to themselves the officers of the AF of L will do as they have done for twenty years—compromise, pacify, promise, without taking any courageous step to bring to an end 'Jim Crow' in unions." Expecting that the facts as presented to the Committee of Five would suddenly galvanize the AFL into action was simply self-delusion; to move the Federation at all, "Councils, labor unions and unorganized workers must use the weeks between now and the AF of L convention in demonstrating, protesting, urging and employing all other means to force favorable action on the floor of the convention. . . . This is not a matter to be left to the conscience of the American Federation of Labor; but organized and continuous protest must keep that conscience alive." [20]

What Granger was saying fit the changed climate of the 1930s; polite representations by spokesmen for blacks were not securing substantial progress in industry or labor. Workers had to be mobilized to speak up for their own interests; the pressure tactic had to be added to traditional Urban League ways of operating. In the case of the AFL, these tactics dictated a massive workers' demonstration at the time of the Federation's October convention in Atlantic City.

During the week of the demonstration, Workers' Councils organized mass meetings of workers and staged parades to dramatize their demands for AFL action to end union discrimination. They invited union leaders to speak to groups of Negro workers and urged local unions to support their stance against Jim Crow.[21]

In Atlantic City, Lester Granger and other League representatives paid personal calls on union officials to gain support for a resolution to drop from AFL membership unions that persisted in policies of racial exclusion. They worked closely with delegates from the Brotherhood of Sleeping Car Porters, to avoid embarrassing their efforts on the convention floor.[22] The League covered Convention Hall with flashy labor leaflets prepared by the Workers' Bureau. "Race prejudice is a knife at the throat of American Labor. . . ," one warned. "Will Labor remove that knife —or will Labor cut its own throat?" "CLOSE RANKS!" another exhorted. "UNITE THE LABOR MOVEMENT! EXPEL JIM CROW! EXPEL TRADE UNION POLITICS THAT PUT PERSONAL PREJUDICE BEFORE THE INTERESTS OF LABOR!" [23]

These efforts did not lead to the positive action for which the Urban League had hoped. The Committee of Five had reported to the AFL executive council in August that its investigation revealed proven instances of discrimination, and it had recommended that internationals be required to eliminate restrictions on Negro membership or be dropped from affiliation with the AFL. The Committee also urged the Federation to discontinue separate Negro federal unions and transfer their members to mixed locals, where they could have an effective voice in determining labor conditions.[24] On the opening day of the convention, President Green wrote T. Arnold Hill that " 'the tolerant and broad-minded representatives' of the AFL were endeavoring to deal

with racial discrimination "in a constructive and helpful way.' " [25]
Nevertheless, in its report to the convention the executive council made no mention of the Committee of Five's recommendation,
because, Granger charged, such a report "would cause a bitter
dispute which might split the Convention wide open." [26]
Whereupon Randolph made public part of the report and incor-
porated it in a new resolution aimed at discriminatory internationals. Predictably, Randolph's resolution failed.[27]

In the words of its angry chairman, John Brophy of the United
Mine Workers, the Committee of Five was no more than "a
face-saving device." [28] On the surface, the Committee was the
AFL's most serious answer to long-standing charges of discrimination; in fact, its investigation was virtually ignored by the Federation. Subsequent convention resolutions proposing discipline
or exclusion of discriminatory AFL unions met a similar fate.
"Without a sharp change in the set-up of the American Federation of Labor," Lester Granger believed, there seemed little hope
of getting anti-Jim Crow legislation through an AFL convention
for some time to come. There was simply too much resistance on
the part of affiliated unions to any abridgement of their autonomy by the executive council. Whether seeking to expel radicals, include Negroes, or otherwise regulate a union's internal affairs, the council had to reckon with long-term hostility to
interference from above. Thus Granger concluded, on the advice
of union executives, that the more productive course for future
action would be to try to educate unions to the drawbacks of discrimination and thereby develop a force for change among union
members themselves.[29]

Repeated rebuffs by the AFL combined with an enduring suspicion of the exclusiveness of craft unionism to make the Urban
League particularly receptive to the movement toward industrial
unionism which culminated in the foundation of the Committee
for Industrial Organization in 1935. Granger immediately volunteered the aid of the Workers' Councils "in reaching the masses
of Negro workers," particularly through educational programs.

John L. Lewis's new group held out "Hope for Negroes in Industrial Unions," Granger thought.[30] He kept in close touch with the new CIO. Its constituent unions included the United Mine Workers, which had 65,000 Negro members, and it was taking a dominant role in the organization of steel workers, many of whom were black—indications, Granger predicted, that the CIO's future held "a deep importance for Negro labor." [31]

The League was justified in its optimism. All-inclusive industrial unionism was much more conducive to equalitarianism than the more selective craft unionism was. In its organizing efforts in the mass production industries, the CIO adhered to the principle that the large number of Negro workers within those industries should be organized together with whites. Needing allies for economic survival and political support for its social legislation objectives, the CIO went beyond perfunctory espousal of a policy of nondiscrimination; it actively sought Negro participation and backing.

The Urban League offered the fledgling CIO some familiar advice—to win the support of Negro workers "by going on record for complete racial equality in labor unions by appointing Negro organizers to their staff, and by putting the non-discrimination policy as a sine qua non for membership in its group." [32] Heeding the suggestions of T. Arnold Hill, among others, at its first constitutional convention in November 1938 the CIO adopted a resolution pledging "a policy of uncompromising opposition to any form of discrimination, whether political or economic, based on race, color, creed or nationality." Urban League officials promptly wrote the new officers and executive board members of the CIO, congratulating them on their elections and on the CIO's stand against discrimination, and pledging the support of the Urban League.[33]

Despite the clear advantages for black workers, particularly the unskilled, in the spread of industrial unionism through the CIO, the Urban League, through Lester Granger, cautioned Negroes not to be deluded into self-satisfied inactivity on the labor front.

The CIO was promising, to be sure, but it was still essential to court old AFL friends and to pursue old avenues of access to the trade union movement. The CIO should not be viewed as the ultimate solution to the black worker's problems, Granger pointed out. The "present conflict between industrial and craft union forces does not in the slightest degree alter the essential task for Negro leadership—which is to impress upon black labor the need for independent, worker-controlled organization, and the necessity for cooperation between white and Negro workers in the same crafts, the same industries, whether in craft or industrial unions." [34]

III

Trying to ensure racial justice in the CIO was the last important effort of the Workers' Bureau. When Lester Granger left the League, in September 1937, to become executive director of the New York State Temporary Commission on the Condition of the Urban Colored Population, the decline of the remaining Workers' Councils became all but certain. Reginald Johnson, who filled in for Granger as acting secretary of the Workers' Bureau, reported that his personal contact with the surviving Councils had been minimal; in fact, "little or no field work" had been undertaken during the last six months of 1937. Granger recalls that Johnson had other preoccupations and was unable to communicate effectively to or for Negro workers. The League had no money to hire a permanent successor to Granger. The twenty-five Councils still showing "evidence of some type of activity" in January 1938 were soon undermined by the gradual unionization of Negro workers (primarily through the CIO) and by the onset of World War II. Fearing Communist efforts to take over declining organizations, the League finally advised the remaining Councils to disband.[35]

The importance of the Workers' Councils should not be measured by their brief existence. The Councils effectively disproved allegations of Urban League hostility to organized labor. They marked a conscious decision by the League that only by disciplined, collective action would black workers achieve fair economic treatment. Their creation exemplified more precisely than any other single Urban League action the advocacy of pressure and organized protest that became dominant in the League during the 1930s.

The League's new "militancy" met with mixed reactions. The Workers' Councils were frequently misinterpreted as hotbeds of radicalism and dual unionism. (In 1934 Georgia police raided the Urban League's southern field headquarters in Atlanta and seized Workers' Council literature as possible evidence of Communist influence.[36]) The League had conceived the Councils as a potential aid to the AFL in education and organization. However, William Green and other labor leaders viewed the Councils suspiciously, as potential sources of support for dual unionism, opposed to the AFL and dominated by radicals. Lester Granger wrote Green in August 1935 to set the record straight. The Workers' Councils, he assured Green, were certainly "not anti-AF of L. On the contrary, we take the position that the American Federation of Labor is THE spokesman for workers in this country and that to make their strength effective, Negroes must link their strength with that of the American Federation of Labor." Nor were the Councils "formed to promote or encourage dual-unionism," for the dual union was "a weapon which defeats the interest of those who use it." In fact, Granger observed, "It is significant that the majority of the members of our National Advisory Committee (which is our policy-making group) are members in good standing of unions affiliated with the American Federation of Labor." Green accepted Granger's statement.[37]

For others, the League's labor program was not radical enough. Contemporary writers, white and black, still attacked the League for dealing only with the highest echelons of organized labor, instead of reaching the rank and file working masses. By failing to promote interracial solidarity and working-class unity among the masses, these critics suggested, the Urban League was bound to be unsuccessful in cracking trade union barriers.[38] E. Franklin Frazier, the black sociologist, doubted that the Workers' Councils had "had much influence upon the Negro working class." [39]

The Councils raised different reservations within the League movement. Lester Granger recalls that Hollingsworth Wood was not especially enthusiastic about the Councils, but that he trusted Eugene Kinckle Jones's judgment and leadership and was, therefore, prepared to go along with them.[40] Some affiliates refused to support the National League's labor program or cooperate with the Workers' Bureau in establishing Councils. Their resistance doubtless stemmed at least in part from a reluctance to upset their relations with local employers.[41] The Detroit League was concerned about jeopardizing "the decided advantage which Negro workers [held] in the absence of a 'closed shop' set-up" in the city's industries.[42] In 1935 the executive of the Baltimore Urban League urged that the Pittsburgh regional conference consider just "How far to the 'left' should the Urban League movement go?" "What will be the consequences of the organizations of militant Workers' Councils all over the country?" he wondered. Since the League might be in "danger of sacrificing financial support," he suggested that the conference might well ponder possible alternative sources of funds.[43] Another local executive secretary was frankly dismayed at both the strident tone and the contents of the League's labor leaflets. "The objective statement of fact might be a slower method in the long run but it is a good investment in human understanding," he wrote T. Arnold Hill, reminding him that the League had been known for "mature, logical, dispassionate and objective social thought." [44]

One long-time executive board member considered the policies of the 1930s so serious a departure from traditional Urban League methods that he sought to sever his connection with the organization. "The League has drifted considerably away from the original idea of cooperation or the finding of a common ground for mutual understanding," Irving S. Merrell, a Syracuse mechanical engineer, manufacturer, and trustee of Tuskegee lamented. "The change seems to be toward finding a method to coerce the other fellow; toward some means to make the other fellow do what the League thinks he should do." Instead of this new radicalism, he felt, the League should be striving for " 'fairness to everyone.' " [45]

There was considerably less substantive change in the Urban League than Merrell feared. As southern field director Jesse O. Thomas tried to explain to him, "while changing conditions may make necessary new technique and shifting of emphasis, [our] fundamental philosophy of life . . . remains unchanged." [46] And despite the rather short-lived, apparent radicalism of the Workers' Councils, most people continued, justifiably, to place the League at the conservative end of the spectrum of organizations working in behalf of blacks.

What was happening to the Urban League in the 1930s was simply additional evidence of the impact of the New Deal. The New Deal politicized previously mute or poorly organized special interest groups. It encouraged group solidarity among blacks, workers, farmers, and others, and it taught them the value of organizing to apply pressure in behalf of their particular goals.

Hence, in the context of the New Deal, the Workers' Councils were far from radical. They would have been radical, however, if they had been successful in forging a class alliance along ethnic lines. The Workers' Councils indicated a recognition that the problems of Negro workers were in many respects unlike those of the Negro middle class. While the workers shared the racial disabilities common to their more prosperous, better-educated fellow Negroes, they also shared class disabilities common to white workers. It was no longer realistic to assume that gains won by the middle classes would eventually filter down to and elevate the masses. There was something to be learned in terms of tactics and strategy from the experience of white workers; techniques that had served the Negro middle class on its way up were insufficient to cope with the barriers peculiar to Negro workers. [47]

The League was trying to transform the prejudices of white

and black workers into a realization of common interest. "A quarter century ago," Eugene Kinckle Jones admitted, in a speech for the Urban League's twenty-fifth anniversary dinner, "no Negro leader advocated the organization of Negro workers, together with white workers or separately, for the improvement of their wages and hours. Most Negro leaders thought that the salvation of the Negro as a wage-earner rested in his remaining out of the ranks of organized labor, to compete as a scab and strike-breaker for the jobs which white men controlled." But by 1935 these attitudes had been reversed. "Today," Jones said, "every sensible white or Negro student of labor problems recognizes the common lot of all men who work and urges that they unite for mutual protection." [48] The League saw the Workers' Councils as the beginning of "a national movement" that would "give intelligent voice against all forms of inequalities practiced against the working class"—not just Negro workers, but white workers as well.[49] Had the Councils survived and accomplished that objective, the Urban League would have virtually transformed American political alignments.

In fact, the Councils had little lasting influence, and some twenty-five years of Urban League activity on the labor front had only a minimal impact on discrimination in American trade unions. Despite its pronouncements of high principle and good will, the American Federation of Labor moved hardly at all toward more just treatment of Negro workers. While the Urban League was active in keeping the issue of Jim Crow before the Federation's executive council, it was A. Philip Randolph and his Brotherhood of Sleeping Car Porters who ultimately packed enough power to force the Federation to face up to the place of blacks in the labor movement. The CIO more closely fulfilled the Urban League's hopes for organizing Negro workers, but its receptivity toward Negroes was not the product of Urban League influence.

Hence, at the end of its third decade, the Urban League's record with respect to organized labor looked very much like its dealings with private industry: in some instances it had changed individual practices and habits in such a way as to benefit some blacks, but in terms of affecting the over-all employment patterns of blacks in the United States, its impact had not been significant.

19 CLOSING THE THIRD DECADE

The end of its third decade also ended an era in the leadership of the National Urban League. L. Hollingsworth Wood stepped down in 1941, turning over the presidency to William H. Baldwin, son of the woman whom Wood himself had succeeded in 1915. Equally important, the beginning of the fourth decade found the Urban League without its two top staff executives, T. Arnold Hill and Eugene Kinckle Jones.

I

Jones had become executive secretary in a battle for position and power with his former chief, George Edmund Haynes. Ironically, he left that post after winning a comparable contest of pride and will with Hill, his boyhood friend and onetime protégé who had risen to become the League's second most powerful staff executive. James H. Hubert, the New York executive in the 1930s, recalls Hill as "Jones's man FRIDAY" and "something of a 'whipping boy,' . . . [as] many of the League Executives often termed him." [1] Hill rightfully considered himself deserving of more recognition than Jones was willing to accord him. Although he was only four years Hill's senior, Jones thought of himself as Hill's mentor. He had brought him to New York as a young man of twenty-two and had made him his administrative assistant; he sent him to Chicago, made him director of the western field, and arranged for him to head the Department of Industrial Relations. Despite Hill's accomplishments, Jones continued to think of him as a youth, and not as a co-equal executive entitled to his share of the power.[2]

As director of industrial relations, Hill for years ran almost singlehandedly what was surely the Urban League's most ambitious and important department. But his requests for its expansion were repeatedly denied, because of the difficulty of raising money during the Depression. When Jones went to Washington in 1933 to join the Commerce Department, Hill took on the additional job of acting executive secretary. During that four-year period, however, he was given neither the financial remuneration nor the independent authority and responsibility that his position warranted. While Jones was earning $7500 a year in the 1930s, Hill's salary was only $5300.

The financial crisis of the Depression partially explained his low salary, but only Jones's unwillingness to relinquish more than a minimum of power accounted for the limitations on Hill's authority. Although he was officially on leave, Jones persisted in coming to New York Friday through Monday of each week to check up on Urban League operations—a practice Hill understandably resented.[3] "Information accumulated," Jesse O. Thomas recalled, that "made it appear that . . . Hill . . . was seeking to undermine Mr. Jones and replace him as Executive Secretary. This impression became sufficiently convincing for Mr. Jones to resign the position in Washington and return to New York."[4]

The final insult came when southern field director Jesse O. Thomas, and not Hill, was placed in charge of the national office when Jones fell ill with tuberculosis in March 1939.[5] His designation as acting executive secretary, Thomas recalled, put him in an "unenviable position" akin to that of a strikebreaker; by rights the job belonged to Hill, but his selection would have exacerbated Jones's "mistrust and suspicion." If Jones believed that "Hill was trying to take his job while he was well and giving part-time supervision to the organization," he could hardly help but think that "he would be more successful if he were put in charge while Mr. Jones was seriously and dangerously ill." [6]

No doubt Jones's mistrust of Hill figured importantly in the decision to turn to Thomas when Jones became incapacitated. Their break was certainly no secret. He was "exceedingly disturbed," the head of the New Jersey Urban League confided to a fellow executive secretary, "to note how extremely emotional" Jones had "permitted himself to become about T. Arnold." [7] Another of their colleagues recalled that the two men were "almost bitter enemies." Jones's views probably had strong support in the person of L. Hollingsworth Wood. While there is no direct record of Wood's attitude, at least one long-time local executive believes that he "was never too keen about Hill and what he may have suspected were his motives." Jones and Wood were devoted friends; in such circumstances it would be only natural for the president of the organization to back up his executive secretary when the latter felt threatened. [8]

Hill was an ambitious, able man whose plans had repeatedly been thwarted by circumstance; having once filled in for Jones with little thanks and less remuneration, he resented being passed over in favor of Thomas. [9] He finally offered an ultimatum: he would be named associate executive secretary in charge of program, or he would resign. [10] Jones turned him down, and on March 13, 1940, Hill resigned, effective June 1. Hill sent copies of his letter of resignation to members of the steering committee, which met in special session March 15 and heard Jones describe his meeting with Hill three days earlier. Hill had been "in a good mood," Jones said; "he was buoyant because of the fact that he decided to tender his resignation to the League, thus having contentment for the first time for a long period." Hill had told Jones "that he found himself in a blind alley and wanted to get into something where some promotional schemes that he had in mind could be carried out before he became too old. He said that . . . he wanted to make it clear that he was not submitting the resignation with the idea of getting any concession." With only three members present in addition to Jones and Wood, the steering committee voted to accept Hill's resignation.[11]

Executive board members and local secretaries were dismayed at Hill's resignation and the fact that it had been handled without consideration by the full board. Their protests prompted the executive board to instruct the steering committee to reconsider the matter. After several meetings, the committee decided that its original acceptance of Hill's resignation should stand, and the executive board confirmed the decision at a special June meeting. In cryptic comments to his friends, Hill hinted at what most people had already assumed: that there had been a lot more intrigue and friction involved than anyone had publicly admitted. Yet he, too, maintained official silence, deciding, "I must forget the whole thing for the welfare of the work as well as of myself." [12]

After Hill left, Jones named Lester Granger assistant executive secretary in charge of industrial relations as of October 1, 1940. In September 1937 Granger had taken a leave of absence as secretary of the Workers' Bureau (a position he had held since 1934) to go to work for the New York State Temporary Commission on the Condition of the Urban Colored Population. He left the League officially the following year to join the Welfare Council of New York as secretary of a committee on Negro welfare in a program to expand and improve services available to New York City Negroes. When Granger rejoined the League in October 1940, the still ailing Jones had been absent from the office for more than three months. When his illness continued, the League granted Jones an official leave of absence for one year beginning in December 1941, a leave subsequently extended indefinitely until such time as his health might warrant resumption of his duties. In the meantime, he was given the new title of general secretary, at half salary, and Granger became the working executive secretary as of November 25, 1941.[13] Granger recalls that Jones made it clear that any Urban Leaguer objecting to Granger's elevation over the heads of senior League staff could resign—a suggestion taken seriously by Jesse O. Thomas, who took a year's leave of absence, beginning in November 1941, to work for the Treasury Department. Thomas extended the leave for a second year (whereupon the League made plans to appoint a new southern field director) and then joined the American Red Cross as a special assistant to its director of domestic relations.[14]

Although Jones attended a few board meetings during 1943 and returned to the office as general secretary in September of that year, the effective leadership of the League was in the hands of Lester Granger after November 1941.[15] Jones's *de facto* retirement removed from the Urban League every major leader of its first three decades. George Edmund Haynes, T. Arnold Hill, Jesse O. Thomas, Ira De A. Reid, Charles S. Johnson, and Elmer A. Carter had all left the League, so that, by the beginning of the fourth decade, only Granger remained to provide any kind of continuity in national staff leadership. At the same time, the executive board, while retaining a number of veteran members, passed from the strong twenty-six-year direction of L. Hollingsworth Wood to the new leadership of its former secretary, William H. Baldwin.

Coincidentally, these internal changes in the National Urban League came just as the United States was about to enter World War II. The war created a new situation in racial attitudes and patterns of black employment; it helped to alleviate some of the problems confronting the Urban League while, at the same time, it created new ones. Defense industries opened industrial opportunities for blacks. President Roosevelt's Executive Order 8801, creating a Fair Employment Practices Committee, and, later, the passage of fair employment laws in a number of states and municipalities, thrust the Urban League's employment work into a new context. President Truman and the Supreme Court began to put the authority of the federal government behind the cause of civil rights. Before 1940, racial advancement was at the bottom of the list of national priorities. After the war, diplomatic and political considerations, together with a growing moral concern, created circumstances favorable to the emergence of a movement for civil rights.

These and other important changes after 1940 "alter[ed] in a drastic way the crucible in which the Urban League work[ed]." [16] Such substantial modifications in the climate of race relations, as well as in the internal organization and leadership of the Urban League, make it appropriate to take stock of the League's accomplishments at the end of its third decade.

II

By 1940, the Urban League had managed to win influential friends in both the white and black establishments. It had elicited praise from Presidents of the United States and executives of powerful foundations.[17] Leading white newspapers applauded its work; "There is no organization of public service for which we more gladly bespeak the support of our readers than the National Urban League," the New York *Herald Tribune* announced.[18] "The great work of such an organization," the New York *Evening Post* wrote, "lies in the amelioration of race prejudice and race envy and the development in Americans of the custom of acting together without regard to the color of one another's skins." [19] Such sentiments echoed across the country. To the Little Rock *Arkansas Democrat*, the League was making a "praiseworthy contribution towards improving the . . . conditions of Negroes and stimulating better relations between the races." [20] In ameliorating the status of blacks in Baltimore, a writer in the *Evening Sun* said, "no force has been more effective than the educated, intelligent and public spirited group within the Negro population," working "through the Urban League." [21] The *Southern Workman* often reminded its readers of the "intelligent organization and . . . workable program" of the Urban League, which it considered "an invaluable social-service force among Negroes in . . . urban centers." [22]

Professionals in the fields of education, employment, and social service also held the League in high regard. To the Commissioner of Conciliation in the Labor Department, it was an example of "philanthropic and useful organizations co-racial in nature." [23] "There certainly is no other organized group which can present so effectively the needs of the Negro before the city, state, and federal organizations as the Urban League," the assistant director of the New York School of Social Work believed.[24] The director of the American Association for Adult Education praised the Urban League's report on unemployment among blacks as "tremendously more effective than one might suppose a similar document issued by the Association for the Advancement of Colored People would be." [25] To John Hope, the Negro educator, the League was "the greatest agency" for the uplift of black people in the cities.[26]

The black press was equally supportive of the organization. The Urban League's work was "creditable, effective and practical," the Chicago *Defender* said, and it had produced "real, constructive . . . results." Thus it "merits our hearty support." [27] It was "doing such a splendid work in confederating the charities in the larger cities," the *Afro-American* wrote; "Baltimore needs the Urban League, and the sooner the better." [28] Sometimes the press waxed euphoric on the advantages an affiliate might bring; with the establishment of an Urban League in a city with racial problems, "there has been a turn for the better in a surprisingly short time," the Providence *Chronicle* said. "Bring the National Urban League here and there will follow as surely as night does day, a welcome awakening." [29] Once the Urban League became a reality in Phoenix, a columnist assured her readers, "The question of our men being unemployed will then be solved; our little neglected children cared for; our sick made comfortable, our orphans placed where love abounds." [30]

In picturing the Urban League as a panacea for racial problems, these commentators were carried away by their own rhetoric. What the League actually accomplished was considerably less spectacular than their enthusiasm suggests. To angry black critics, such as Ralph Bunche, the Urban League's policies were unrealistic, expedient, and conciliatory. The League began with the "naïve assumption that when the two races know and understand each other better, the principal incidents of the race problem will then disappear." "Too often" it was "willing to barter away the economic future of the Negro worker for an immediate, but transitory 'gain' in the form of temporary placement in industry." In many cities it was "little more than a glorified employment agency. It has placed many Negroes in jobs, to be sure, but it has rarely found it possible to bring about any significant alteration in the fundamental patterns of Negro employment in the communities in which it has operated." The League was "exclusively middle class," and it offered the working masses "no effective program." The "timidity and middle class conservatism" of its black members and the "caution and racial stereotypes" of its white supporters bred "weakness" in the organization. The League's stance was one of supplication—"it retains no real strength of its own, it can exert no significant pressure, and it never has any power to demand—locally or nationally; it must beg for its funds and it constantly suffers from lack of funds." While the League may have "rendered valuable services," Bunche concluded that "it operate[d] strictly on the periphery of the Negro problem and never [came] to grips with the fundamentals in American racial conflict." [31]

The truth about the Urban League lies between these extremes of praise and condemnation. We have seen that it created a body of professional Negro social workers and put them to work providing useful services for some blacks in the cities. It developed important information about urban black life that became the basis for ameliorative efforts. It interceded with employers, labor leaders, and public officials to create a more favorable climate for the employment of black workers, and it succeeded in making some placements in positions that blacks had never held before. Yet the bulk of its placements were in domestic service and unskilled labor, and, by the end of its third decade, it had been unable to change the concentration of black employment in such occupations.

Bunche was right in his judgment that the League was often "little more than a glorified employment agency." We should ask, however, whether, with different tactics, it might have made a dent in the basic patterns of black employment. Other approaches were available in the 1930s. The League might have embraced a radical demand for a socialized economy, but the failure of communism and socialism as radical alternatives in the 1930s suggests how unworkable such an approach would have been in the unlikely circumstance that the League's leaders would have been receptive to it. It might have worked for laws to guarantee equal employment opportunity to blacks, but at a time when legislation to outlaw lynching could not even get through the Congress, a bill affecting fundamental socioeconomic relations between the races never could have been passed. The League itself acknowledged the political problems attached to working through the legislative process. When the Fair Labor Standards Act came before the Congress in 1938, Eugene Kinckle Jones cautioned the local executives not "to press too strongly" for its passage—not because the bill was undesirable, but because outspoken support from blacks would rally Southerners against it.[32] In such a political climate, building a coalition behind legislation specifically benefiting blacks would have been next to impossible.

Another alternative to the League's reliance on conciliation, persuasion, diplomacy, and polite protest lay in the application of economic pressure through selective black patronage. The black press promoted "Don't Buy Where You Can't Work" campaigns, especially during the Depression, on the assumption that black buying power ought to be rewarded with opportunities for black employment. The Urban League generally supported "the buying-power argument," but it never made such campaigns a central part of its program.[33] The experience of other groups suggests that even if it had tried it would not have accomplished very much. Moreover, it would have encountered resistance from local executives, who shied away from active pressure. "Retaliating boycotting and discrimination on the part of the Negro group serve only to antagonize, rather than to eliminate friction," the head of the Los Angeles Urban League felt.[34] The St. Louis League praised blacks for their "patience and loyalty" in abstaining from "public disorder[s] . . . in such times as these." [35] And James H. Hubert, the executive of the New York Urban League, called "picketing" and "threatened violence" on the part of job-seekers "un-American" tactics that should be checked "by substitution of saner and more constructive measures." [36] Such tactics would also have alienated the League's conservative benefactors. "The League is not a social action group, but a social service agency for work among Negro people," a Kansas City publication explained. It did not engage in "mild agitation and militant action . . . except in some instances, because of its very program and means of support." [37]

The nature of its leadership ultimately circumscribed the courses of action the Urban League could be expected to take. It did not seek to overthrow the system, but rather to improve the standing of blacks within it. "From its inception," Charles S. Johnson wrote, "the Urban League has recognized and tentatively accepted existing social alignments and has elected to work primarily with the Negro in an effort to improve his social and economic status within the social structure." The advantages of such an approach were that the League "avoided serious clashes with the community mores . . . [attracted] the support of influential white leaders, and . . . secured the aid of industry itself, notably in the North, in improving the character and position of Negro workers." [38] However, as the lack of substantial improvement over the years between 1910 and 1940 suggests, the disadvantages of such an approach were considerable. It meant worrying much more about discrimination than about segregation; it also meant that progress would be measured by the tiny dents the League could make in a system that continued to oppress millions of blacks, rather than by the extent to which that system would be overhauled to accommodate blacks and whites on an equal basis. "I think," Roger Baldwin said, looking back on decades of service as an Urban League board member, "we tended to settle for the best possible rather than the most desirable." [39]

In a climate of intolerance and lack of national concern for racial issues, "the best possible" was not very much. The Urban League's saga in these decades reveals important white involvement in the cause of racial advancement, but it also betrays a striking national callousness on the issue of blacks. Urban Leaguers worked manfully, in the best progressive tradition, to make American society more democratic in the way it treated blacks. But without a concerned response from employers, labor unions, and public officials, the League's accomplishments had to remain limited. By 1910 white America had effectively segregated and disfranchised the race it had once enslaved. In the ensuing three decades, the nation at large heeded the pleas of the racial reformers on only two occasions—once, during World War I, when it needed blacks for their labor, and again, in the 1930s, when some groups feared their revolutionary potential. Had it not been for the catalytic effect of these emergencies, the cause of racial reform would probably have made even less headway in the years before the civil rights revolution.

Between 1910 and 1940, blacks and whites began to forge the instruments of protest and reform that sustained the modern struggle for racial advancement. The Urban League's efforts during those years constitute one approach to a complex, difficult problem. In its time it performed important services. Kenneth Clark, assessing the record of the League through the 1960s, has perceptively recognized that "its desire and efforts to aid the smooth adjustment of the Southern Negro who moved to Northern cities, while quite laudable, have not prevented the massive pathology which dominates the expanding ghettos of such cities as New York, Chicago, Philadelphia, Detroit, and Cleveland." "The fascinating paradox," Clark concludes, "is that the very areas in which the Urban League program has been most active—the blight of segregated housing, segregated and inferior education, and persistent and pernicious discrimination in employment—have been those areas in which the virulence of racism has increased in the North." The League was not responsible for this blight, but its approach, as Clark points out, "has not effectively stemmed the tide nor obscured the symptoms of Northern racism." [40] Clark's judgment applies equally to the Urban League in its first three decades. The League could not prevent the transformation of black Americans from an enslaved agricultural peasantry to an oppressed urban proletariat. Had it not existed, however, the plight of blacks in cities might well have been even worse.

BIBLIOGRAPHICAL NOTE

The main source for a study of the National Urban League is the extensive collection of Urban League Papers deposited in 1967 in the Manuscript Division of the Library of Congress. This collection, which covers the period 1910–66 (access is restricted after 1940), varies in quality for the earlier decades because considerable Urban League correspondence and printed material was destroyed indiscriminately when the League moved its headquarters office in the early 1950s. The strongest sections of the collection are the files of the Department of Industrial Relations, the Department of Public Relations, and the Southern Regional Office (although the correspondence of the latter is often distinguished by quantity rather than quality), and the minutes of the National Urban League's executive board, steering committee, and annual meetings. The Papers include reasonably complete files of Urban League publications— *Bulletins*, *Annual Reports* (each of these generally has a distinctive title, and they are cited as such in the Notes), reports from some affiliates, *Financial Statements and Lists of Contributors*, Workers' Council and Emergency Advisory Council *Bulletins*, *The Color Line Series*, *Opportunity*, materials relating to the Vocational Opportunity Campaigns, and others. Where these are not complete they can usually be supplemented by Urban League publications available in the regular collections of the Library of Congress or the New York Public Library. The Social Welfare History Archives Center at the University of Minnesota has an important collection of National and local Urban League publications, not all of which are duplicated in the National Urban League Papers at the Library of Congress. The annual reports of the Armstrong Association of Philadelphia can be consulted at the Historical Society of Pennsylvania. The Chicago Historical Society has scattered reports of the Chicago Urban League. The Moorland Foundation at Howard University and the

Arthur A. Schomburg Collection of the New York Public Library have both compiled useful folders of non-manuscript Urban League material.

In addition to the published materials cited above, the most important National Urban League publications for the purposes of this study were the following, most of which are commonly available in major libraries: *40th Anniversary Year Book, 1950* (New York, 1951); *A Quarter Century of Progress in the Field of Race Relations, 1910–1935* (New York, 1935); *The Urban League Story, 1910–1960: Golden 50th Anniversary Yearbook* (New York, 1961); *Building for the Future: The Story of the National Urban League* (New York, 1956); *Ever Widening Horizons: The Story of the Vocational Opportunity Campaigns* (New York, 1951); and *The Urban League—Its Story* (New York, 1938). Another document important for the League's antecedents is the *Annual Report* of the National League for the Protection of Colored Women for 1910, available in the New York Public Library.

Other League-related manuscript sources provide valuable supplements in rounding out the story of the National Urban League. The League itself has retained certain materials in the library of its national headquarters in New York City. The papers of its officials are scattered but well worth tracking down. Four file boxes of George Edmund Haynes Papers in the Erastus Milo Cravath Library of Fisk University add extremely significant material for the League's first decade, as do the Papers of Robert Russa Moton at Tuskegee Institute. Mrs. George Edmund Haynes has retained her husband's scrapbooks and unfinished memoirs at her home in Mount Vernon, N.Y. The L. Hollingsworth Wood Papers, which remain in the custody of Mrs. L. Hollingsworth Wood and Mr. and Mrs. James Wood in Mount Kisco, N.Y., include valuable correspondence. Guichard Parris, former public relations director of the League, has an important collection of speeches by Eugene Kinckle Jones. The Charles S. Johnson Papers, in the Amistad Research Center and Race Relations Department at Fisk University when I consulted them, but now at Dillard University, include some material relevant to his career as director of the League's Department of Research. The League's financial situation is documented in the Rockefeller Family Archives and the Carnegie Corporation Archives, both in New York City.

A few Urban Leagues have preserved papers from the years of this study. The richest collection is the Detroit Urban League Papers, deposited in the Michigan Historical Collections of the University of Michigan. In addition to documenting the development of one of the most active affiliates, the Papers include correspondence with the national office and publications and reports from other affiliates. The St. Louis Urban League has retained in its Department of Research an extensive collection of unpublished correspondence and reports relating to its early decades. The Papers of the Negro Welfare League, which later became the New Jersey Urban League, are available on microfilm in the New Jersey Reference Room of the Free Public Library, Newark, N.J. Also deposited there are the unpublished Reminiscences of the League's long-time executive secretary, William M. Ashby. The Papers of the Negro Welfare Association, later known as the Cleveland Urban League, can be consulted at the Western Reserve Historical Society in Cleveland. Fragments of the Papers of the Philadelphia Urban League (originally the Armstrong Association of Philadelphia) are available at the Urban Archives of Temple University. The Urban League of Bergen County, N.J., has some early records of the Englewood League for Social Service at its office in Englewood.

Black newspapers help to fill in details of Urban League activities and provide appraisals of the organization's effectiveness. I read most consistently in the following: Baltimore *Afro-American*, Chicago *Broad Ax*, Chicago *Defender*, New York *Age*, New York *Amsterdam News*, and Pittsburgh *Courier*. In addition, for the decade of the 1910s I used the Cleveland *Gazette*, Norfolk *Journal and Guide*, and Washington *Bee*.

Published studies of the Urban League are scarce. Arvarh E. Strickland, *History of the Chicago Urban League* (Urbana, 1966) is the only book about an Urban League affiliate. Guichard Parris and Lester Brooks, *Blacks in the City: A History of the National Urban League* (Boston, 1971) is a narrative prepared for the League's sixtieth anniversary. Only two Urban Leaguers have published memoirs: Detroit executive secretary John C. Dancy, *Sand Against the Wind: The Memoirs of John C. Dancy* (Detroit, 1966), and southern field director Jesse O. Thomas, *My Story in Black and White* (New York, 1967).

There are a number of unpublished studies of the Urban League, most of them of marginal quality: Henri Arthur Belfon, "A History of the Urban League Movement, 1910–1945" (master's thesis, Fordham University, 1947); Alexander B. Bolden, "The Evolution of the National Urban League" (master's thesis, Columbia University, 1932); Bert H. Cohen, "Not Alms But Opportunity: A History of the National Urban League, 1910–1918" (senior thesis, Princeton University, 1968); Eunice Joyner Jones, "A Study of the Urban League Movement in the United States" (master's thesis, New York University, 1939); Charles Radford Lawrence, "Negro Organizations in Crisis: Depression, New Deal, World War II" (doctoral dissertation, Columbia University, 1953); Edward S. Lewis, "The Urban League, A Dynamic Instrument in Social Change: A Study of the Changing Role of the New York Urban League, 1910–1960" (doctoral dissertation, School of Education, New York University, 1960); Raymond W. Smock, "The Rise of the National Urban League, 1894–1920" (paper read before the 53rd Annual Meeting of the Association for the Study of Negro Life and History, New York City, Oct. 4, 1968); Arthur Paul Stokes, "The National Urban League—A Study in Race Relations" (master's thesis, The Ohio State University, 1937). Jesse T. Moore, Jr., "The Urban League and the Black Revolution, 1941–1961: Its Philosophy and Its Policies" (doctoral dissertation, The Pennsylvania State University, 1971), picks up where this book ends. Unpublished biographical studies of important Urban Leaguers include Paul C. Marengo, "Frances Kellor: A Career Study, 1900–1920" (senior thesis, Princeton University, 1971); Ralph L. Pearson, "Charles S. Johnson: The Urban League Years: A Study of Race Leadership" (doctoral dissertation, The Johns Hopkins University, 1970); and Daniel Perlman, "Stirring the White Conscience: The Life of George Edmund Haynes" (doctoral dissertation, New York University, 1972).

It would be redundant to list the hundreds of books and articles that provided background for this study. The most useful among them appear in the Notes. Scholars interested in fuller documentation should consult the bibliography in my dissertation, " 'Not Alms, But Opportunity': A History of the National Urban League, 1910–1940" (1969), deposited in Widener Library, Harvard University, as well as James M. McPherson et al., *Blacks in America: Bibliographical Essays* (Garden City, N.Y., 1971), Part VI, chs. 2, 3, 6, 7, 9; Part VII, chs. 1–6, 11, 13, 14.

In my research I have supplemented the written record with interviews with William M. Ashby, Roger N. Baldwin, William H. Baldwin, Lester B. Granger, Mrs. George E. Haynes, Edward S. Lewis, Henry Lee Moon, Guichard Parris, Mrs. Ira De A. Reid, and Mrs. L. Hollingsworth Wood. Many of these men and women have corresponded extensively with me, as have Lloyd K. Garrison and the late James H. Hubert. The dates and places of the individual interviews and correspondence are cited in the Notes.

OTHER MANUSCRIPT COLLECTIONS

Baden Street Settlement Papers. Social Welfare History Archives Center, University of Minnesota.

Ray Stannard Baker Papers. Manuscript Division, Library of Congress.

William H. Baldwin Papers. Wisconsin State Historical Society.

Big Brothers of America Papers. Social Welfare History Archives Center, University of Minnesota.

W. E. B. Du Bois Papers. At the time I used them, in the custody of Herbert Aptheker, New York City; now deposited at the University of Massachusetts, Amherst.

Paul Underwood Kellogg Papers. Social Welfare History Archives Center, University of Minnesota.

Albert Joseph Kennedy Papers. Social Welfare History Archives Center, University of Minnesota.

Kelly Miller Papers. Moorland Foundation, Howard University.

National Association for the Advancement of Colored People Papers. Manuscript Division, Library of Congress.

National Association of Social Workers Papers. Social Welfare History Archives Center, University of Minnesota.

National Federation of Settlements and Neighborhood Centers Papers. Social Welfare History Archives Center, University of Minnesota.

National Social Welfare Assembly Papers. Social Welfare History Archives Center, University of Minnesota.

William Pickens Record Group. Arthur A. Schomburg Collection, New York Public Library.

Eleanor Roosevelt Papers. Franklin D. Roosevelt Library, Hyde Park, N.Y.

Franklin D. Roosevelt Papers. Franklin D. Roosevelt Library, Hyde Park, N.Y.

Julius Rosenwald Papers. University of Chicago Library.

Edwin R. A. Seligman Papers. Special Collections Room, Butler Library, Columbia University.

Arthur B. Spingarn Papers. Manuscript Division, Library of Congress.

Joel E. Spingarn Papers. Moorland Foundation, Howard University.

James G. Phelps Stokes Papers. Special Collections Room, Butler Library, Columbia University.

Survey Associates Papers. Social Welfare History Archives Center, University of Minnesota.

Travelers' Aid Society Papers. Urban Archives, Temple University.

United Neighborhood Houses Papers. Social Welfare History Archives Center, University of Minnesota.

U.S. Department of Labor Papers. National Archives.

Oswald Garrison Villard Papers. Houghton Library, Harvard University.

Booker T. Washington Papers. Manuscript Division, Library of Congress.

Carter G. Woodson Papers. Manuscript Division, Library of Congress.

NOTES

Since I used the National Urban League Papers before they were processed, it has been impossible to assign accurate series and box numbers for material from that collection. Scholars who need assistance in locating material in the Urban League Papers may wish to correlate the Register for the Papers with the descriptive locator titles in the notes to the dissertation on which this book is based.

ABBREVIATIONS

CCA	Carnegie Corporation Archives, New York City
CUL	Cleveland Urban League Papers, Western Reserve Historical Society, Cleveland
DUL	Detroit Urban League Papers, Michigan Historical Collections of the University of Michigan
ER	Eleanor Roosevelt Papers, Franklin D. Roosevelt Library, Hyde Park, N. Y.
FDR	Franklin D. Roosevelt Papers, Franklin D. Roosevelt Library, Hyde Park, N. Y.
NAACP	National Association for the Advancement of Colored People Papers, Manuscript Division, Library of Congress
NJUL	New Jersey Urban League Papers, Free Public Library, Newark, N. J.
NUL	National Urban League Papers, Manuscript Division, Library of Congress
NUL, SRO	National Urban League Papers, Southern Regional Office Files, Manuscript Division, Library of Congress
PUL	Philadelphia Urban League Papers, Urban Archives, Temple University
RFA	Rockefeller Family Archives, New York City
St. LUL	St. Louis Urban League Papers, Department of Research, St. Louis Urban League
SWHAC	Social Welfare History Archives Center, University of Minnesota

CHAPTER 1

1. Theodore Roosevelt to Owen Wister, in *The Letters of Theo-dore Roosevelt*, ed. by Elting E. Morison (8 vols., Cambridge, Mass., 1951–54), V, 226, quoted in George Sinkler, *The Racial Attitudes of American Presidents: From Abraham Lincoln to Theodore Roosevelt* (Garden City, N.Y., 1971), p. 318.

2. Woodrow Wilson to H. A. Bridgman, Sept. 8, 1913, quoted in Ray Stannard Baker, *Woodrow Wilson, Life and Letters* (8 vols., Garden City, N.Y., 1927–39), IV, 223.

3. U.S. Bureau of the Census, *Negro Population: 1790–1915* (Washington, D.C., 1918, reprinted New York, 1968), pp. 377, 404, 526, 571; Chicago Commission on Race Relations, *The Negro in Chicago: A Study of Race Relations and a Race Riot* (Chicago, 1922), p. 82; Walter White, *Rope and Faggot: A Biography of Judge Lynch* (New York, 1929), appendix.

4. New York *Freeman*, May 28, 1887.

5. New York *Age*, Jan. 25, 1890.

6. See, esp., Emma Lou Thornbrough, "The National Afro-American League, 1887–1908," *Journal of Southern History*, XXVII (Nov. 1961), 494–512; and Elliott M. Rudwick, "The Niagara Movement," *Journal of Negro History*, XLII (July 1957), 177–200.

7. Bureau of the Census, *Negro Population: 1790–1915*, pp. 24, 33, 89–90, 92.

8. George Edmund Haynes, "Conditions Among Negroes in the Cities," *Annals of the American Academy of Political and Social Science*, XLIX (Sept. 1913), 109.

9. *Ibid.* 110–17; George Edmund Haynes, *The Negro at Work in New York City: A Study in Economic Progress* (New York, 1912); W. E. Burghardt Du Bois, *The Philadelphia Negro: A Social Study* (Philadelphia, 1899); "The Negro in the Cities of the North," *Charities*, XV (Oct. 7, 1905).

10. Booker T. Washington, *Up From Slavery: An Autobiography* (Garden City, N.Y., 1901), pp. 219-22.

11. See, e.g., W. E. Burghardt Du Bois (ed.), *Efforts for Social Betterment Among Negro Americans* (Atlanta University Publications, No. 14 [Atlanta, 1909]), pp. 42–103; Allan H. Spear, *Black Chicago: The Making of a Negro Ghetto, 1890–1920* (Chicago, 1967), ch. 5.

12. Bureau of the Census, *Negro Population: 1790–1915*, pp. 320, 334, 388–89, 402, 434, 463, 471, 473; Gilbert Osofsky, *Harlem: The Making of a Ghetto; Negro New York, 1890–1930* (New York, 1966), pp. 4–5.

13. Bureau of the Census, *Negro Population: 1790–1915*, p. 93.

14. Seth M. Scheiner, *Negro Mecca: A History of the Negro in New York City, 1865-1920* (New York, 1965), pp. 58, 143-45, 147-48.

CHAPTER 2

1. "New York State to Protect Aliens," *Survey*, XXV (Nov. 5, 1910), 172; *Who's Who in America*, XXI (Chicago, 1940), 1447; Paul C. Marengo, "Frances Kellor: A Career Study, 1900-1920" (unpublished senior thesis, Princeton University, 1971), pp. 24-33.
2. "Distributing the Immigrant: An Organization to Do Well What the Padrone Does Badly," *Independent*, LXXVIII (May 18, 1914), 288; Frances A. Kellor, "Needed—A Domestic Immigration Policy," *North American Review*, CXCIII (Apr. 1911), 561-73.
3. Frances A. Kellor, "The Criminal Negro," *Arena*, XXV (Jan.–May 1901), 59-68, 190-97, 308-16, 419-28, 510-20; XXVI (Sept., Nov. 1901), 304-10, 521-27; Kellor, "Some Old Needs of the New South," *Charities*, X (May 2, 1903), 439-40.
4. Frances A. Kellor, *Out of Work: A Study of Employment Agencies: Their Treatment of the Unemployed, and Their Influence upon Homes and Business* (New York, 1904), pp. 6, 83; *New-York Tribune*, Aug. 11, 1905.
5. Frances Kellor to W. E. B. Du Bois, Feb. 10, 1905, W. E. B. Du Bois Papers, in custody of Herbert Aptheker, New York City. I am grateful to my colleague James M. McPherson for bringing this letter to my attention.
6. Frances A. Kellor, "Opportunities for Southern Negro Women in Northern Cities," *Voice of the Negro*, II (July 1905), 472-73.
7. See, e.g., Minutes of the Travelers' Aid Society of Philadelphia, Apr. 4, 25, May 30, Nov. 28, 1905; Apr. 24, 1906, in the Society's Papers, Box 1, Urban Archives, Temple University.
8. *New-York Tribune*, Aug. 11, 1905.
9. National League on Urban Conditions Among Negroes (hereafter NUL) *Bulletin*, I, 1 (1911), 6.
10. Lassalle Best, "History of the White Rose Mission and Industrial Association" (unpublished WPA Writers' Project paper, Arthur A. Schomburg Collection, New York Public Library), pp. 1-3.
11. National League for the Protection of Colored Women (hereafter NLPCW), *Annual Report* (New York, 1910), 3.
12. NUL *Bulletin*, I, 1 (1911), 6.
13. NLPCW, *Annual Report* (1910), 3.
14. *Ibid.* 3-4; Frances A. Kellor, "Assisted Emigration From the South," *Charities*, XV (Oct. 7, 1905), 14.

15. This description refers to the executive committee as constituted in 1910, the only year for which a full listing is available. The names come from NLPCW, *Annual Report* (1910). Various articles on the early local associations confirm that these men and women were likely to have been on the executive committee from the time of the NLPCW's founding. At that time there were no black women on the committee, but earlier a physician, Verina Morton Jones, had been a member. Biographical information is derived from the various editions of *Who's Who in America* and *Who's Who in Colored America*, obituaries in *The New York Times*, and other specialized biographical dictionaries.

16. Wallace Buttrick to W. E. B. Du Bois, Dec. 31, 1902, Du Bois Papers.

17. S. R. Scottron to W. E. B. Du Bois, June 13, 1907, Du Bois Papers.

18. New York *Age*, July 12, 1906.

19. William L. Bulkley, "The Industrial Condition of the Negro in New York City," *Annals*, XXVII (May 1906), 134.

20. Ralph Ellison, "William L. Bulkley" (unpublished WPA Writers' Project paper, Schomburg Collection), p. 1; "A Slave-boy; Now a Professor," *Success*, II (Apr. 8, 1899), 326; Osofsky, *Harlem*, pp. 63–64.

21. Julia Richman, quoted in New York *Age*, Apr. 6, 1905. Bulkley's school, Miss Richman told the Association of Neighborhood Workers, "perhaps more than any other does the best work for social service among its pupils."

22. William L. Bulkley, "The School as a Social Center," *Charities*, XV (Oct. 7, 1905), 77–78.

23. Charles W. Anderson to Booker T. Washington, Mar. 23, 1906, Booker T. Washington Papers, Box 2, Manuscript Division, Library of Congress.

24. Copies of these and similar testimonials have been compiled on untitled typed sheets marked 1908–9 in the George Edmund Haynes Papers, Erastus Milo Cravath Library, Fisk University.

25. Quoted in New York *Age*, May 17, 1906.

26. *Ibid*. Sept. 27, 1906.

27. *Ibid*. July 12, Apr. 26, 1906.

28. Mary White Ovington to W. E. B. Du Bois, May 20, 1906, Du Bois Papers.

29. New York *Age*, May 17, 1906.

30. "Committee for Improving Industrial Condition of the Negro in New York" (n.d., probably 1906), p. 3, Washington Papers, Box 310.

31. S. R. Scottron to W. E. B. Du Bois, June 13, 1907, Du Bois Papers.

32. Booker T. Washington to Charles W. Anderson, Oct. 1, 1907, Washington Papers, Box 35.

33. Charles W. Anderson to Booker T. Washington, May 25, 1906, Washington Papers, Box 2.

34. The names of the members of the CIICN and its various subcommittees come from three sources: "Committee for Improving Industrial Condition of the Negro in New York"; lists printed on the Committee's stationery, which appear in correspondence in the Du Bois Papers; and New York *Age*, Apr. 26, May 17, July 12, 1906. All told, 84 names appear in these lists. Of those, at least some biographical information has been located for 55 whites and 19 blacks. The ten "missing persons" might revise some of the percentages for the group as a whole if their identities were known. Since their names do not appear in any of the standard biographical sources, the chances are good that they were less distinguished professionally (or perhaps not professionals or successful businessmen at all) and less well-educated than those whose names do appear. Also, it is probable that many of the missing ten are black, since blacks were less likely to appear in biographical dictionaries or on the obituary pages of white newspapers. Thus the addition of information on these missing men and women might change the over-all complexion of the CIICN; but since they represent only 12 per cent of the Committee's membership, the changes would not be substantial. Biographical information on which the collective portrait in the text is based comes primarily from various editions of *Who's Who in America* and *Who's Who in Colored America*, from the obituary pages of *The New York Times*, and (less significantly) from other specialized biographical dictionaries.

35. "Industrial Condition of New York Negroes," *Charities*, XVI (June 23, 1906), 378.

36. William Jay Schieffelin to J. G. Phelps Stokes, May 24, 1906, James G. Phelps Stokes Papers, Box 18, Special Collections Room, Butler Library, Columbia University.

37. The information on college attendance and college graduation is for 18- to 21-year-olds and 21-year-olds, respectively, in 1880; it is compiled from U.S. Bureau of the Census, *Historical Statistics of the United States, Colonial Times to 1957* (Washington, D.C., 1960), pp. 211-12.

38. August Meier, *Negro Thought in America, 1880-1915: Racial Ideologies in the Age of Booker T. Washington* (Ann Arbor, 1963), pp. 228, 238.

39. New York *Age*, Nov. 21, 1907.

40. *Ibid.* May 14, 1908.

41. *Ibid*. May 17, July 12, 1906; Mar. 7, 1907; May 14, 1908; Nov. 25, 1909; July 7, 1910; NUL *Bulletin*, I, 1 (1911), 31–32; III, 2 (Nov. 1913), 12–13, 16.

CHAPTER 3

1. *Who Was Who in America*, III (Chicago, 1960), 383; *New York Times*, Jan. 10, 1960; interview with Mrs. George Edmund Haynes, July 19, 1968, Mt. Vernon, N.Y.; Daniel Perlman, "Stirring the White Conscience: The Life of George Edmund Haynes" (unpublished doctoral dissertation, New York University, 1972), pp. 1–31, 53–57.
2. W. E. Burghardt Du Bois, *Dusk of Dawn: An Essay Toward an Autobiography of a Race Concept* (New York, 1940), p. 61.
3. Du Bois, *The Philadelphia Negro*, p. v.
4. Du Bois, *Dusk of Dawn*, pp. 64, 66.
5. George Edmund Haynes, "The Birth and Childhood of the National Urban League," Apr. 20, 1960, p. 5 (mimeographed text), Moorland Foundation, Howard University.
6. *Ibid*. p. 3.
7. George E. Haynes, "The Movement of Negroes from the Country to the City," *Southern Workman*, XLII (Apr. 1913), 236.
8. Interview with Mrs. Haynes.
9. Haynes, "Birth and Childhood," p. 6; George E. Haynes to the Executive Committee of the Committee on Improving Industrial Conditions Among Negroes, Nov. 3, 1909, Haynes Papers (the quotation is from this letter).
10. Haynes, "Conditions Among Negroes in the Cities," 110, 112–13, 115–17. The quote is from Haynes to the Executive Committee of the Committee on Improving Industrial Conditions Among Negroes, Nov. 3, 1909, Haynes Papers.
11. Haynes, "Birth and Childhood," p. 3; George Edmund Haynes, "Interracial Social Work Begins," National Urban League, *40th Anniversary Year Book, 1950* (New York, 1951), p. 7.
12. Haynes, *The Negro at Work in New York City*, pp. 14, 33.
13. Interview with Mrs. Haynes.
14. Haynes, "Birth and Childhood," pp. 5–6.
15. *Ibid*. p. 6. Haynes had apparently had some contact with the work of the NLPCW; "I am glad that my tendance at your Board meeting will be of service and assure you it is always a pleasure to respond to your requests," he wrote NLPCW member Carolena M. Wood on Dec. 17, 1909 (Haynes Papers). Through her he had an opportunity to meet her brother, L. Hollingsworth Wood, who was to be his Urban League associate.

16. John Graham Brooks, *An American Citizen: The Life of William Henry Baldwin, Jr.* (Boston and New York, 1910), p. 33, n. 1.

17. Roger Nash Baldwin, *Reminiscences* (Oral History Research Office, Columbia University, 1954), Vol. I, Part I, p. 6; "The Golden Rule on Trial," *Outlook*, XCV (July 16, 1910), 553.

18. "William Henry Baldwin," *National Cyclopaedia of American Biography*, XXIV (New York, 1935), p. 64.

19. Baldwin, *Reminiscences*, Vol. I, Part I, p. 1.

20. William H. Baldwin, Jr., Memorial Fund, *William Henry Baldwin, Jr., 1863–1905* (New York, 1905), p. 6, Oswald Garrison Villard Papers, Houghton Library, Harvard University.

21. Louis Filler, *Crusaders for American Liberalism* (New York, 1939), pp. 286–87.

22. "William Henry Baldwin," *NCAB*, p. 64.

23. W. H. Baldwin, Jr., "The Present Problem of Negro Education," *Journal of Social Science*, XXXVII (1899), 52, 62.

24. Mary White Ovington, *The Walls Came Tumbling Down* (New York, 1947), p. 76.

25. Booker T. Washington, *My Larger Education* (Garden City, N.Y., 1911), p. 15.

26. Baldwin Memorial Fund, *William Henry Baldwin*, p. 8.

27. Baldwin, "The Present Problem of Negro Education," 56.

28. *Capon Springs Conference for Christian Education in the South, 1899* (Washington, D.C., n.d.), p. 74, quoted in Louis R. Harlan, *Separate and Unequal: Public School Campaigns and Racism in the Southern Seaboard States, 1901–1915* (Chapel Hill, 1958), p. 78.

29. Baldwin, "The Present Problem of Negro Education," 60.

30. Baldwin is quoted in Brooks, *An American Citizen*, p. 223. The argument from self-interest comes from Robert L. Factor, *The Black Response to America: Men, Ideals, and Organization from Frederick Douglass to the NAACP* (Reading, Mass., 1970), p. 199.

31. Baldwin in Boston *Guardian*, Jan. 3, 1907, quoted in Factor, *The Black Response to America*, p. 197.

32. *Capon Springs Conference*, p. 72, quoted in Harlan, *Separate and Unequal*, p. 78.

33. Baldwin, "The Present Problem of Negro Education," 60; Factor, *The Black Response to America*, p. 197.

34. Baldwin, "The Present Problem of Negro Education," 66.

35. Washington, *My Larger Education*, p. 18. Baldwin's biographer, John Graham Brooks, and other contemporary sources paint him as a strong believer in racial equality, but his public statements are much more equivocal. Unfortunately, his papers were destroyed after being used for Brooks's book, so the evidence for his

judgments cannot be evaluated. See *An American Citizen*, esp. pp. 203, 223, 226; and Baldwin Memorial Fund, *William Henry Baldwin*, p. 11, quoting tribute in New York *Evening Post*, n.d.

36. Brooks, *An American Citizen*, p. 209; Baldwin, "The Present Problem of Negro Education," 60.
37. Brooks, *An American Citizen*, p. 209.
38. New York *Age*, Jan. 12, 1905.
39. "Committee for Improving Industrial Condition of the Negro in New York," p. 6.
40. S. R. Scottron to W. E. B. Du Bois, Sept. 12, 1907, Du Bois Papers.
41. *Ibid.* July 5, 1907.
42. Springfield *Daily Republican*, Dec. 15, 1934.
43. *Smith Alumnae Quarterly*, XXIII, 4 (Aug. 1932), 434.
44. "Our Permanent Trustee," *Smith Alumnae Quarterly*, VII, 3 (Apr. 1916), 192; Ruth Standish Baldwin, "War-Time Protection of Girls," *ibid.*, IX, 3 (Apr. 1918), 241–43.
45. Baldwin, *Reminiscences*, Vol. I, Part I, p. 9.
46. The quotation comes from the school's letterhead, William H. Baldwin Papers (Ruth Standish Baldwin's son), Box 1, Wisconsin State Historical Society.
47. Oswald Garrison Villard to William H. Baldwin, Dec. 24, 1934, Villard Papers.
48. William Allan Neilson, quoted in "The Retirement of Mrs. Baldwin," *Smith Alumnae Quarterly*, XVII, 4 (July 1926), 428.
49. Remarks of President William A. Neilson at Chapel, Smith College, Dec. 17, 1934, Baldwin Papers, Box 1.
50. Ruth Standish Baldwin to Myles Horton, Feb. 3, 1933, Baldwin Papers, Box 1.
51. Haynes, "Birth and Childhood," p. 7.
52. *Ibid.*
53. "National League on Urban Conditions Among Negroes," *Crisis*, VIII (Sept. 1914), 243.
54. The names of the members come from an undated, typed list, "Committee on Urban Conditions Among Negroes," in the Haynes Papers and from the Urban League's Executive Board Minutes for Sept. 29, 1910, in the National Urban League Papers (hereafter NUL), Manuscript Division, Library of Congress. Only one of the members remains unidentified. Biographical information on the members of the Committee is derived from the various editions of *Who's Who in America* and *Who's Who in Colored America*, from the obituary pages of *The New York Times*, and from other specialized biographical dictionaries.
55. Haynes, "Birth and Childhood," p. 8.
56. *Ibid.* pp. 8–10. The most thorough account of Haynes's

appointment at Fisk is Perlman, "Stirring the White Conscience," pp. 83–91.

57. James H. Hubert form in "Survey of National Urban League Fellows," Jan. 1960, NUL Papers.

58. "Secretariat," *Opportunity*, VI (Mar. 1928), 84; Mary White Ovington, *Portraits in Color* (New York, 1927), pp. 135–36.

59. W. F. Willcox, quoted in Committee on Urban Conditions, Executive Committee Minutes, Mar. 31, 1911, Haynes Papers.

60. NUL *Bulletin*, I, 1 (1911), 6, 13, 15–16; Cleveland *Gazette*, Nov. 18, 1911.

61. Committee on Urban Conditions, Executive Committee Minutes, Apr. 24, 1911, Haynes Papers.

62. George E. Haynes to Samuel H. Bishop, Aug. 17, 1911, Haynes Papers.

63. George E. Haynes to Fred R. Moore, Aug. 25, 1911; Constitution, National League on Urban Conditions Among Negroes, n.d., Haynes Papers.

64. George E. Haynes to Samuel H. Bishop, Sept. 9, 1911, Haynes Papers.

65. Samuel H. Bishop to George E. Haynes, Sept. 13, 1911, Haynes Papers.

66. Committee on Urban Conditions, Executive Committee Minutes, Sept. 26, 1911, L. Hollingsworth Wood Papers, in custody of Mrs. L. Hollingsworth Wood and Mr. and Mrs. James Wood, Mt. Kisco, New York.

67. Pittsburgh *Courier*, Dec. 30, 1911.

68. "National League on Negro Urban Conditions," *Southern Workman*, XL (Nov. 1911), 599.

69. Cleveland *Gazette*, Nov. 18, 1911.

70. Baltimore *Afro-American Ledger*, Dec. 30, 1911; "Consolidation of Negro Agencies," *Survey*, XXVII (Oct. 28, 1911), 1080.

71. Cleveland *Gazette*, Nov. 18, 1911.

CHAPTER 4

1. The names of the board members of the Urban League and the NAACP during the 1910s have been compiled from annual notices of elections to the boards in *Crisis* and in the minutes of the League's annual meetings, NUL Papers. Charles Flint Kellogg, *NAACP: A History of the National Association for the Advancement of Colored People*, Vol. I: *1909–1920* (Baltimore, 1967), pp. 304, 306, lists the NAACP's boards for 1910 and 1912. In all, these lists total 49 members (11 blacks, 36 whites, 2 race unknown) for the Urban League's board in the 1910s, and 52 (22 blacks, 29 whites, 1 race unknown) for that of the NAACP. Of

these, 47 Urban Leaguers and 50 members of the NAACP have been positively identified and comprise the group on which the collective portrait in the text above is based. The effect on such portraits of the "missing persons" among the board members is discussed in ch. 2, n. 34.

Biographical information on which the collective portrait is based came primarily from various editions of *Who's Who in America* and *Who's Who in Colored America*, as well as from obituaries in *The New York Times*. In addition, some information was obtained from specialized biographical dictionaries and from correspondence with relatives and business associates of the board members.

It is important to qualify the progressive comparison that follows. Progressives were generally men and women of wealth, education, and high social status, but recent scholarship has demonstrated that conservatives shared the same characteristics. As critics of the Hofstadter-Chandler-Mowry interpretation have shown, it is impossible to use those characteristics as sufficient explanation for the behavior of a group of reformers. Since many people who were not racial reformers shared the characteristics of the racial reformers depicted in this chapter, one cannot use those traits to account for their interest in the NAACP or the Urban League. Hence this portrait is intended more to describe the racial reformers in comparison to other reformers of their day than it is to explain their behavior. In order to do the latter, one needs to examine the life experiences of each man and woman involved, but the evidence is too fragmentary to permit such a study.

2. Cleveland *Gazette*, Jan. 10, 1914.

3. Compiled from U.S. Census Office, *Compendium of the Tenth Census (June 1, 1880)*, Part I (Washington, D.C., 1883), p. 333.

4. U.S. Bureau of the Census, *Thirteenth Census of the United States Taken in the Year 1910*, Vol. I: *Population* (Washington, D.C., 1913), p. 140.

5. *Ibid.* p. 86. The NAACP deliberately concentrated its board members in the New York area so that they could attend meetings easily, but there is no indication that the Urban League followed a similar policy.

6. "Who's Who in the Urban League Movement," *Urban League Bulletin* (May 1922), 7, Robert R. Moton Papers, National Urban League File, Tuskegee Institute.

7. Oswald Garrison Villard to Francis Jackson Garrison, Apr. 28, 1898; Villard to J. C. Hemphill, Nov. 6, 1913, Villard Papers, both quoted in James M. McPherson, "The Antislavery Legacy: From Reconstruction to the NAACP," in Barton J. Bernstein

(ed.), *Towards a New Past: Dissenting Essays in American History* (New York, 1968), pp. 148, 151.

8. Mary White Ovington to Oswald Garrison Villard, May 6, 1908, Villard Papers, quoted in McPherson, "The Antislavery Legacy," p. 149.

9. William H. Baldwin III to Oswald Garrison Villard, Apr. 27, 1914, Villard Papers.

10. James M. McPherson *et al.*, *Blacks in America: Bibliographical Essays* (Garden City, N.Y., 1971), pp. 78–81; Charles Howard Hopkins, *The Rise of the Social Gospel in American Protestantism* (New Haven, 1940); David M. Reimers, *White Protestantism and the Negro* (New York, 1965); Willis D. Weatherford, *American Churches and the Negro* (Boston, 1957).

11. Interview with William M. Ashby, former executive secretary of the New Jersey and Springfield (Ill.) Urban Leagues, Jan. 24, 1973, Newark, N.J.

12. John T. Emlen to Albert J. Kennedy, June 18, 1945, Albert J. Kennedy Papers, Folder 55, Social Welfare History Archives Center, University of Minnesota (hereafter SWHAC).

13. Nathan Glazer, *American Judaism* (Chicago, 1957); Stephen Birmingham, *"Our Crowd": The Great Jewish Families of New York* (New York, 1967).

14. Quoted in *Urban League Bulletin* (May 1922), 8.

15. Felix Adler, *The Ethical Culture Society: What It Means* (n.d., probably 1917 or 1918), Survey Associates Papers, Folder 340, SWHAC.

16. R. Laurence Moore, "Flawed Fraternity—American Socialist Response to the Negro, 1901–1912," *Historian*, XXXII (Nov. 1969), 1–18; James Weinstein, *The Decline of Socialism in America, 1912–1925* (New York, 1967), pp. 63–74. The quote is from Mary White Ovington to Ray Stannard Baker, Nov. 12, 1906, Ray Stannard Baker Papers, Box 89, Manuscript Division, Library of Congress.

17. Jane Addams, "The Subjective Necessity for Social Settlements," *Philanthropy and Social Progress* (New York, 1893), p. 15, quoted in Allen F. Davis, *Spearheads for Reform: The Social Settlements and the Progressive Movement, 1890–1914* (New York, 1967), pp. 36–37.

18. Vida Scudder, "The Relation of College Women to Social Need," paper presented at the Association of Collegiate Alumnae, Oct. 24, 1900, Boston Public Library, quoted in Davis, *Spearheads for Reform*, p. 37.

19. Three out of every four California progressives went to college. See George E. Mowry, *The California Progressives* (Berkeley, 1951), p. 87.

20. Homer Folks, *Reminiscences*, p. 41, Oral History Project, Columbia University; Frederick C. Howe, *The Confessions of a Reformer* (New York, 1925), p. 1, both quoted in Davis, *Spearheads for Reform*, p. 38.

21. Baldwin, *Reminiscences*, Vol. I, Part II, p. 315.

22. Compiled from Charles S. Johnson, *The Negro College Graduate* (Chapel Hill, 1938), p. 8.

23. E. Franklin Frazier, *Black Bourgeoisie* (Glencoe, Ill., 1957), p. 91.

24. Meier, *Negro Thought in America*, ch. 12; Richard Bardolph, *The Negro Vanguard* (New York, 1959), pt. 2.

25. The identification of the ideological stance of the black board members is based on Meier, *Negro Thought in America*.

26. Ruth Standish Baldwin to Oswald Garrison Villard, July 29, 1906, Villard Papers.

27. Eugene Kinckle Jones, "The Urban League—Yesterday and Today," notes for speech to 25th Anniversary Annual Conference, Nov. 26, 1935, consulted through the courtesy of Guichard Parris.

28. Executive Board Minutes, Apr. 9, 1931, NUL Papers.

29. Eugene Kinckle Jones, "The Urban League," notes for speech to Urban League dinner, May 8, 1929, consulted through the courtesy of Guichard Parris.

30. Ruth Standish Baldwin to George E. Haynes, Feb. 13, 1914, Haynes Papers.

31. George E. Haynes to Ruth Standish Baldwin, Feb. 18, 1914, Haynes Papers.

32. Booker T. Washington to Ruth Standish Baldwin, Feb. 11, 1911, Washington Papers, Box 417.

33. Ruth Standish Baldwin to George E. Haynes, Feb. 13, 1914, Haynes Papers.

34. Executive Board Minutes, Sept. 10, 1914, NUL Papers.

35. Quoted in New York *Age*, May 20, 1915.

36. Annual Conference Minutes, Oct. 16, 1919, NUL Papers.

37. *Urban League Bulletin* (Mar. 1922), 4, Moton Papers, NUL File.

38. Washington, *Up from Slavery*, p. 208.

39. Haynes, "Birth and Childhood," pp. 8–9.

40. Ruth Standish Baldwin to L. Hollingsworth Wood, June 1, 1915, in Executive Board Minutes, June 8, 1915, NUL Papers.

41. Booker T. Washington to George Washington Cable, Apr. 7, 1890, quoted in Philip Butcher, "George W. Cable and Booker T. Washington," *Journal of Negro Education*, XVII (Fall 1948), 465.

42. Booker T. Washington to L. Hollingsworth Wood, May 25, 1915, Wood Papers.

43. This appraisal comes from Mrs. George Edmund Haynes, who

suggests that Washington was neither an advocate nor an opponent of the League since his chief responsibilities lay elsewhere.

44. Ovington, *The Walls Came Tumbling Down*, p. 112.

45. George E. Haynes, Substance of an Interview with Dr. W. E. B. Du Bois, which includes text of Du Bois to Haynes, Nov. 22, 1910, Wood Papers.

46. Committee on Urban Conditions, Minutes, Feb. 6, 1911, Wood Papers; Minutes, Mar. 31, 1911, Haynes Papers (source of the quotations).

47. Ovington, *The Walls Came Tumbling Down*, pp. 111-12.

48. "Urban League's Line: Bias is Bad Business," *Business Week* (Oct. 9, 1954), 181.

49. Joel E. Spingarn to L. Hollingsworth Wood, Jan. 27, 1917, Wood Papers; Annual Conference Minutes, Nov. 26, 1918, NUL Papers.

50. Robert L. Zangrando, "The 'Organized Negro': The National Association for the Advancement of Colored People and Civil Rights," in James C. Curtis and Lewis L. Gould (eds.), *The Black Experience in America* (Austin, Tex., 1970), pp. 153-58.

51. Robert H. Bremner, *From the Depths: The Discovery of Poverty in the United States* (New York, 1956), p. 140; Davis, *Spearheads for Reform*, pp. xii, 96. The Baker quote, in Bremner, is from *American Chronicle* (New York, 1945), p. 183.

52. Haynes, *The Negro at Work in New York City*, p. 8.

53. Quoted in Memphis *Evening Scimitar*, Apr. 17, 1893, clipping in William Lloyd Garrison, Jr., Papers, Sophia Smith Collection, Smith College. (I am indebted to my colleague James M. McPherson for this citation.)

54. Quoted in National Urban League, *Annual Report, 1966* (New York, 1967), p. 7.

55. George Edmund Haynes, "The Basis of Race Adjustment," *Survey*, XXIX (Feb. 1, 1913), 569.

56. Ruth Standish Baldwin to L. Hollingsworth Wood, June 1, 1915, in Executive Board Minutes, June 8, 1915, NUL Papers.

57. Ray Stannard Baker, "Progressivism and the Negro," in Gilbert Osofsky (ed.), *The Burden of Race: A Documentary History of Negro-White Relations in America* (New York, 1967), p. 242.

CHAPTER 5

1. Constitution, National League on Urban Conditions Among Negroes (n.d.), NUL Papers.

2. The material in these paragraphs is based on Bremner, *From the Depths*, pp. 16-56, 125-38 (the quote is from p. 56), and Roy Lubove, *The Professional Altruist: The Emergence of Social*

Work as a Career, 1880–1930 (Cambridge, Mass., 1965), pp. 1–23.

3. Lubove, *The Professional Altruist*, pp. 140–41; Frank J. Bruno, *Trends in Social Work, 1874–1956: A History Based on the Proceedings of the National Conference of Social Work* (New York, 1957), p. 142.

4. Bruno, *Trends in Social Work*, pp. 331, 336. As evidence of the lack of concern among social workers for racial problems, the Papers of the National Association of Social Workers, SWHAC, have no listing for blacks or race relations before 1940. The National Social Work Council, which consisted of executives of leading national social work organizations, in 1920 began regular monthly conferences to exchange information and discuss common problems. The Papers of the National Social Welfare Assembly, SWHAC, contain records of the topics discussed at these monthly meetings from 1925 on. Not until 1939 did the Council first mention minority problems.

5. The editors of *Charities* were consciously pioneering in this respect; see carbon of unsigned, unaddressed letter, June 14, 1905, Paul U. Kellogg Papers, Folder 101, SWHAC.

6. Eugene Kinckle Jones, "Social Work Among Negroes," *Annals*, CXL (Nov. 1928), 287; Haynes, "Birth and Childhood," p. 3. Mary White Ovington, *Half a Man: The Status of the Negro in New York* (New York, 1911), p. 87, shows that black women were active in important social service capacities in New York by 1910, but few if any of them had been trained professionally.

7. George Edmund Haynes, "Co-operation with Colleges in Securing and Training Negro Social Workers for Urban Centers," National Conference of Charities and Correction, *Proceedings, 1911* (Fort Wayne, Ind., 1911), 387; Ovington, *Half a Man*, p. 87.

8. Haynes, "Co-operation with Colleges," 387.

9. Quoted in Detroit Urban League board minutes, Jan. 8, 1920, Detroit Urban League Papers (hereafter DUL), Box 11, Michigan Historical Collections of the University of Michigan.

10. John T. Clark, "Report in re the Bush Terminal," Sept. 8, 1917, NUL Papers.

11. Robert C. Dexter, "The Negro in Social Work," *Survey*, XLVI (June 25, 1921), 439.

12. Haynes, "Conditions Among Negroes in the Cities," 118.

13. George E. Haynes to President George Gates, Apr. 12, 1910, Student File of George Edmund Haynes, Registrar's Office, Fisk University, quoted in Perlman, "Stirring the White Conscience," p. 83.

14. Committee on Urban Conditions, Minutes, Sept. 29, 1910, NUL Papers; George E. Haynes to Roger N. Baldwin, Jan. 10, 1911, etc., Haynes Papers.

15. Baltimore *Afro-American Ledger*, June 14, 1913.
16. James R. Anderson, "Co-operation for Community Betterment," *Southern Workman*, XLVI (Feb. 1917), 77–78.
17. NUL *Bulletin*, II, 9 (July 1916).
18. Haynes, "Co-operation with Colleges," 384.
19. D. Butler Pratt to George E. Haynes, July 15, 1911, Haynes Papers.
20. Clarence A. Bacote, *The Story of Atlanta University: A Century of Service, 1865–1965* (Atlanta, 1969), pp. 135–36.
21. Guichard Parris and Lester Brooks, *Blacks in the City: A History of the National Urban League* (Boston, 1971), p. 23.
22. Haynes, "Co-operation with Colleges," 384.
23. Warren Waterman to President George Gates, Apr. 12, 1910, Student File of George Edmund Haynes, Registrar's Office, Fisk University, quoted in Perlman, "Stirring the White Conscience," p. 86.
24. Haynes, "Co-operation with Colleges," 384–86.
25. George E. Haynes to D. Butler Pratt, Nov. 13, 1911; Haynes, Director's Report, Sept. 22-Oct. 20, 1913, Haynes Papers.
26. Committee of Chairmen, Minutes, Dec. 15, 1913, Wood Papers; Minutes, Jan. 13, 1914; George E. Haynes, Director's Report, Dec. 4, 1913-Jan. 27, 1914, both in Haynes Papers.
27. Eugene Kinckle Jones, "The Fellowship Program of the National Urban League," Sept. 12, 1949, NUL Papers.
28. Baltimore *Afro-American*, Feb. 12, 1916.
29. George E. Haynes to Ellie A. Walls, June 6, 1911; Haynes to H. Clay Preston, July 24, 1911 (the quotation comes from this letter); Haynes to Allen G. Brown, Sept. 11, 1911, Haynes Papers; Ellie A. Walls form in "Survey of National Urban League Fellows," Jan. 1960, NUL Papers.
30. L. Hollingsworth Wood, "The Urban League Movement," *Journal of Negro History*, IX (Apr. 1924), 120; "Training Negro Social Workers: The Story of the Urban League Fellowships," *Opportunity*, XIII (Nov. 1935), 334. The quote comes from Eugene Kinckle Jones, "The National Urban League," *Opportunity*, III (Jan. 1925), 14.
31. NUL *Bulletin*, X, 2 (Mar. 1921), Moton Papers, General Correspondence, Box 24.
32. Ellie A. Walls and Forrester B. Washington forms in "Survey of National Urban League Fellows," Jan. 1960, NUL Papers.

CHAPTER 6

1. The financial records for this period are very sparse. This financial portrait has been pieced together chiefly from scattered doc-

uments in the Wood Papers and the Rockefeller Family Archives, Record Group 2, New York City (hereafter RFA).

2. Wood, "The Urban League Movement," 120.

3. NUL Executive Board Minutes, Mar. 6, 1912, Wood Papers.

4. William H. Baldwin to Nancy Weiss, Feb. 28, 1969.

5. Florence Matilda Read, *The Story of Spelman College* (Atlanta, 1961), esp. ch. 12; Raymond B. Fosdick, *John D. Rockefeller, Jr.; A Portrait* (New York, 1956), pp. 369–77.

6. John D. Rockefeller, Jr., to Ruth Standish Baldwin, Feb. 15, 1912; L. Hollingsworth Wood to Starr J. Murphy, Dec. 6, 1912; Jerome D. Greene to Ruth Standish Baldwin, Dec. 16, 1914; National League on Urban Conditions Among Negroes, Contributions—Year 1915–16; W. S. Richardson to Wood, Jan. 9, 1918, RFA; Rockefeller to Wood, May 19, 1916; Richardson to Wood, Feb. 5, 1917, Wood Papers.

7. Edwin R. Embree and Julia Waxman, *Investment in People: The Story of the Julius Rosenwald Fund* (New York, 1949), pp. 25, 179–80; M. R. Werner, *Julius Rosenwald: The Life of A Practical Humanitarian* (New York, 1939), pp. 115–16.

8. Interviewed in Chicago *Broad Ax*, Dec. 20, 1919.

9. Rosenwald's annual contributions are listed on an undated sheet marked "National Urban League," Julius Rosenwald Papers, Box 75, University of Chicago Library.

10. *Who Was Who in America*, I (Chicago, 1942), 1332.

11. Quoted in Chicago *Broad Ax*, Feb. 19, 1921.

12. National League on Urban Conditions Among Negroes, Receipts—Oct. 1, 1911-Feb. 19, 1912; [L. Hollingsworth Wood?] to Alfred T. White, Oct. 1, 1915; White to Wood, Aug. 9, 1917, Wood Papers; National League on Urban Conditions Among Negroes, Contributions—Year 1915–16, RFA.

13. Kellogg, *NAACP*, pp. 106–7; NUL, *Financial Statement and List of Contributors* (1919), NUL Papers. In 1914 the League received gifts from 272 sources; in 1915, from 274. See NUL memo, attached to W. S. Richardson to Starr J. Murphy, Mar. 20, 1916, RFA.

14. Paul J. Sachs to Julius Rosenwald, June 27, 1914, Rosenwald Papers, Box 18.

15. Annual Meeting Minutes, Dec. 2, 1914, NUL Papers.

16. Eugene Kinckle Jones to Ella B. Harrison, Dec. 23, 1920, Wood Papers.

17. Eugene Kinckle Jones to the Members of the Executive Board, Oct. 8, 1913, NUL Papers.

18. Protective Committee Minutes, Dec. 15, 1913; Jan. 26, 1914, NUL Papers.

19. NUL Executive Board Minutes, Feb. 7, 1912, Haynes Papers; Eu-

gene Kinckle Jones to the Members of the Executive Board, Oct. 8, 1913, NUL Papers.

20. Robert L. Buroker, "From Voluntary Association to Welfare State: The Illinois Immigrants' Protective League, 1908–1926," *Journal of American History*, LVIII (Dec. 1971), 655.

21. Eugene Kinckle Jones to L. Hollingsworth Wood, Jan. 19, 1917, Wood Papers.

22. NUL *Bulletin*, III, 3 (Nov. 1913), Haynes Papers.

23. *Ibid.* V, 8 (July 1916), Moton Papers, General Correspondence, Box 1.

24. National League for the Protection of Colored Women, Minutes, Mar. 4, Sept. 1912, Haynes Papers; "National League on Urban Conditions Among Negroes," *Crisis*, VIII (Sept. 1914), 245.

25. National League for the Protection of Colored Women, Minutes, Mar. 4, Apr. 1, Sept. 1912, Haynes Papers; Committee for Protection of Women, Minutes, Jan. 6, Feb. 3, 1913, NUL Papers.

26. New York *Age*, Jan. 23, 1913; NUL *Bulletin*, III, 1 (Oct. 1913), Moton Papers, NUL File; Eugene Kinckle Jones to the Members of the Executive Board, Oct. 8, 1913, NUL Papers.

27. "Housing: Gateway to Better Living," NUL, *40th Anniversary Year Book, 1950*, p. 115.

28. NUL *Bulletin*, III, 3 (Nov. 1913); Bert Cohen, "Not Alms But Opportunity: A History of the National Urban League, 1910–1918" (unpublished senior thesis, Princeton University, 1968), pp. 32–33; Eugene Kinckle Jones to the Members of the Executive Board, Oct. 8, 1913, NUL Papers.

29. Eugene Kinckle Jones, "A Dream, A Quarter Century, A Reality! How the Urban League Has Served," *Opportunity*, XIII (Nov. 1935), 330.

30. Cohen, "Not Alms But Opportunity," p. 33.

31. Aug. 23, 1912.

32. Baltimore *Afro-American Ledger*, Feb. 13, 1915.

33. "National League on Urban Conditions," *Southern Workman*, XLV (Feb. 1916), 76–77.

34. Eugene Kinckle Jones, "The First Forty Years of Service to the American People," NUL, *40th Anniversary Year Book*, p. 1.

35. See, e.g., Davis, *Spearheads for Reform*, pp. 93–94; Ruth Gay, *Jews in America: A Short History* (New York and London, 1965), pp. 87, 97, 101–2.

36. Jane Addams, *Twenty Years at Hull-House* (New York, 1910), chs. 10, 13–16; Davis, *Spearheads for Reform*, pp. 43–54, 60–83.

37. Addams, *Twenty Years at Hull-House*, p. 112.

38. Davis, *Spearheads for Reform*, p. 58.

39. NUL Executive Board Minutes, Feb. 7, 1912, Haynes Papers; Eugene Kinckle Jones to the Members of the Executive Board, Oct.

8, 1913, NUL Papers; NUL *Bulletin*, III, 1 (Oct. 1913), Moton Papers, General Correspondence, Box 1; Baltimore *Afro-American Ledger*, May 1, 1915.

40. Eugene Kinckle Jones to the Members of the Executive Board, Oct. 8, 1913, NUL Papers; Committee on Industrial Conditions, Minutes, Feb. 4, 1913, Haynes Papers.

41. Armstrong Association of Philadelphia, *Annual Report* (Philadelphia, 1912–15), Historical Society of Pennsylvania.

42. See, e.g., H. A. V. Proctor to George E. Haynes, Sept. 26, 1912, Haynes Papers.

43. Pittsburgh *Courier*, Aug. 9, 1912; Baltimore *Afro-American Ledger*, May 9, 1914; NUL *Bulletin*, IV, 5 (June 1915).

44. George E. Haynes to Roger N. Baldwin, Oct. 28, 1911, Haynes Papers.

45. Ruth Standish Baldwin to George E. Haynes, Dec. 29, 1913, Haynes Papers.

46. Dec. 18, 1915.

47. Aug. 12, 1916.

CHAPTER 7

1. Louise Venable Kennedy, *The Negro Peasant Turns Cityward: Effects of Recent Migrations to Northern Centers* (New York, 1930), pp. 27, 30 (quotation from p. 30); William O. Scroggs, "Interstate Migration of Negro Population," *Journal of Political Economy*, XXV (Dec. 1917), 1035.

2. Joseph A. Hill, "The Recent Northward Migration of the Negro," *Opportunity*, II (Apr. 1924), 102.

3. Bureau of the Census, *Negro Population: 1790–1915*, pp. 24, 73–74, 88.

4. Derived from Bureau of the Census, *Historical Statistics of the United States*, pp. 8–9, and Chicago Commission on Race Relations, *The Negro in Chicago*, p. 80, Table II. Of course the black population in these cities was much smaller than the white population, so its percentage increase was more dramatic.

5. V. D. Johnston, "The Migration and the Census of 1920," *Opportunity*, I (Aug. 1923), 237.

6. Kennedy, *The Negro Peasant*, p. 135; George E. Haynes, "Negro Migration—Its Effect on Family and Community Life in the North," National Conference of Social Work, *Proceedings, 1924* (Chicago, 1924), 69–70.

7. "Letters of Negro Migrants of 1916-1918," *Journal of Negro History*, IV (July and Oct. 1919), 291, 294, 300. The spelling and punctuation in these letters have not been corrected.

8. *Christian Recorder*, Aug. 31, 1916, in "Attitude Northern Negroes" (copies of newspaper articles on migration), Carter G.

Woodson Papers, Folder 148, Manuscript Division, Library of Congress.

9. "Letters of Negro Migrants," 294, 305, 320, 324.
10. *Ibid.* 452.
11. Quoted in Chicago Commission on Race Relations, *The Negro in Chicago*, pp. 82–83.
12. "Letters of Negro Migrants," 434, 304.
13. *Ibid.* 448, 329.
14. Montgomery *Advertiser*, Sept. 21, 1916, quoted in Chicago Commission on Race Relations, *The Negro in Chicago*, p. 85.
15. "Letters of Negro Migrants," 450, 438, 443.
16. *Southwestern Christian Advocate*, Apr. 26, 1917, quoted in Chicago Commission on Race Relations, *The Negro in Chicago*, p. 85.
17. Emmett J. Scott, *Negro Migration During the War* (New York, 1920), pp. 14–15; John Hope Franklin, *From Slavery to Freedom: A History of Negro Americans* (New York, 3rd ed., 1967), p. 472.
18. "Letters of Negro Migrants," 423, 419–20, 305, 319.
19. Bureau of the Census, *Historical Statistics of the United States*, p. 56.
20. Quoted in Chicago *Broad Ax*, Sept. 28, 1918.
21. Scott, *Negro Migration*, p. 55; Sadie Tanner Mossell, "The Standard of Living Among One Hundred Negro Migrant Families in Philadelphia," *Annals*, XCVIII (Nov. 1921), 174.
22. Chicago *Defender*, Aug. 12, 1916, in "Attitude Northern Negroes," Woodson Papers, Folder 148.
23. Chicago Commission on Race Relations, *The Negro in Chicago*, pp. 88–90.
24. For a sample of typical *Defender* ads, see Scott, *Negro Migration*, pp. 17–18, n. 1.
25. Chicago Commission on Race Relations, *The Negro in Chicago*, p. 87; Scott, *Negro Migration*, p. 30.
26. "Beginning of the Exodus of 1916–1917" (n.d.), typescript, NUL Papers.
27. William H. Baldwin to the Members of the Executive Board, Apr. 4, 1916, Moton Papers, General Correspondence, Box 1.
28. National Urban League News-Letter, Aug. 9, 1916, Moton Papers, General Correspondence, Box 2; New York *Age*, June 8, Aug. 10, Sept. 14, 1916 (quoting Tobacco Association); Eugene Kinckle Jones to Joel E. Spingarn, Sept. 12, 1916, Kelly Miller Papers, Moorland Foundation, Howard University; Jones to L. Hollingsworth Wood, Aug. 7, 1916, Wood Papers.
29. Robert R. Moton to Eugene Kinckle Jones, May 23, 1917, Moton Papers, General Correspondence, Box 9; NUL News-Letter, Aug.

9, 1916; John E. Luddy to National Urban League, May 20, July 5, Sept. 16, 1918; F. B. Griffin to Jones, Aug. 16, 1918; Jones to Griffin, Oct. 2, 1918 (the quote comes from this letter), NUL Papers; advertisement, Chicago *Defender*, May 25, 1918.

30. F. B. Griffin to Eugene Kinckle Jones, Aug. 16, 1918, NUL Papers.

31. John E. Luddy to National Urban League, Sept. 16, 1918, NUL Papers. There are no records of whether the League sent workers to the tobacco fields in 1919, but former public relations director Guichard Parris suggests that "it would be safe to say that this program was not carried out after 1918." Guichard Parris to Nancy Weiss, Aug. 8, 1969.

32. John E. Luddy to National Urban League, July 5, 1918, NUL Papers; New York *Age*, Sept. 14, 1916.

33. Interview with Powell in Baltimore *Afro-American*, Jan. 19, 1918. For a later endorsement of the Powell view, see Parris and Brooks, *Blacks in the City*, pp. 73–74.

34. Edw. L. Davis to Chicago Urban League, "Mr. Hill as director," Apr. 21, 1917, Woodson Papers, Folder 148; "Letters of Negro Migrants," 301; "Dear sir" from New Orleans, May 1, 1917; "My dear Sir" from Pensacola, Fla., Apr. 25, 1917; "Dear Sirs" from Houston, Apr. 27, 1917, all in "Members of the Race Should Look Out for One Another" (copies of letters from potential migrants), Woodson Papers, Folder 148.

35. Chicago *Defender*, Aug. 4, 1917; June 22, 1918.

36. See letters to Forrester B. Washington of the Detroit Urban League in Folder 168, and Washington to Will Young, June 11, 1917, Folder 170, all in Woodson Papers.

37. "Letters of Negro Migrants," 294, 298, 306, 296, 432, 300, 319, 422, 297, 309.

38. *Ibid.* 459, 458.

39. Chicago Commission on Race Relations, *The Negro in Chicago*, pp. 81, 84.

40. "Letters of Negro Migrants," 461.

41. Chicago Commission on Race Relations, *The Negro in Chicago*, pp. 385-86.

42. Armstrong Association of Philadelphia, *Annual Report* (Philadelphia, 1915–18), Historical Society of Pennsylvania.

43. Chicago Commission on Race Relations, *The Negro in Chicago*, pp. 359, 363; Spear, *Black Chicago*, pp. 152–53.

44. Abraham Epstein, *The Negro Migrant in Pittsburgh* (Pittsburgh, 1918, reprinted New York, 1969), pp. 23, 31.

45. "Letters of Negro Migrants," 461, 464.

46. Chicago Commission on Race Relations, *The Negro in Chicago*, p. 302.

47. "Letters of Negro Migrants," 459.

48. *Ibid.*
49. Mossell, "Standard of Living," 175.
50. Epstein, *The Negro Migrant in Pittsburgh*, pp. 11–17.
51. Chicago Commission on Race Relations, *The Negro in Chicago*, ch. 5 *passim.*
52. "Letters of Negro Migrants," 459–60.
53. Quoted in Chicago Commission on Race Relations, *The Negro in Chicago*, p. 177.

CHAPTER 8

1. National Urban League, *A Quarter Century of Progress in the Field of Race Relations, 1910–1935* (New York, 1935).
2. NUL *Bulletin*, VII, 1 (Nov. 1917), 3.
3. Executive Board Minutes, Oct. 27, 1916, NUL Papers. In a letter distributed to the black press, Eugene Kinckle Jones urged blacks to use the demand for black labor as a bargaining device to gain better wages and working conditions. See Norfolk *Journal and Guide*, Dec. 2, 1916.
4. *Christian Recorder*, Aug. 31, 1916; New York *News*, Sept. 11, 1916, in "Attitude Northern Negroes," Woodson Papers, Folder 148.
5. For discussion of the migration problem and the decision to call the conference, see Executive Board Minutes, Dec. 6, 1916, NUL Papers.
6. New York *Age*, Feb. 1, 1917.
7. "Migration," *Crisis*, XII (Oct. 1916), 270.
8. Editorial, Feb. 10, 1917.
9. Quoted in Norfolk *Journal and Guide*, Dec. 2, 1916.
10. The Cleveland *Gazette* reported on Sept. 15, 1917, that there were three in Philadelphia, two in New York, and one each in Chicago and Norfolk.
11. Quoted in New York *Age*, May 10, 31, 1917.
12. So Eugene Kinckle Jones told William M. Ashby when the latter applied for a job with the Urban League in 1917; see Ashby, "Some Unimportant Incidents in the Life of An Unimportant Man Who is Eighty and Still Alive" (n.d.), p. 85, Free Public Library, Newark, N.J.
13. List of Urban Affiliations, 1918, NUL Papers.
14. NAACP press release, "Negro Advancement Society Doubles Membership," Dec. 20, 1919, National Association for the Advancement of Colored People Papers, Box C-135, Manuscript Division, Library of Congress.
15. Interview with Henry Lee Moon, NAACP public relations director, Aug. 12, 1969, New York City.
16. Steering Committee Minutes, Oct. 10, 1917, NUL Papers.
17. Executive Board Minutes, May 24, 1918, NUL Papers.

18. "Program for Local Work of the National Urban League," NUL Papers. This is probably a revised version of the plan of work that Eugene Kinckle Jones submitted to L. Hollingsworth Wood in 1917. See Jones to Wood, Nov. 2, 1917, Wood Papers.
19. Quoted in Chicago Commission on Race Relations, *The Negro in Chicago*, p. 101.
20. Ashby, "Some Unimportant Incidents," p. 91.
21. Forrester B. Washington, "The Detroit Newcomers' Greeting," *Survey*, XXXVIII (July 14, 1917), 334–35; [Detroit Urban League,] "A Program of Work for the Assimilation of Negro Migrants into Northern Cities," DUL Papers, Box 1, Folder 8; Chicago Urban League, *First Annual Report* (1917), p. 11, Chicago Historical Society.
22. Negro Welfare League, Minutes, Mar. 12, 1917, New Jersey Urban League Papers (hereafter NJUL), Free Public Library, Newark, N.J.
23. Ashby interview.
24. Minutes, Jan. 18, 25, Feb. 5, May 7, Sept. 6, 1917, NJUL Papers.
25. John C. Dancy, *Sand Against the Wind: The Memoirs of John C. Dancy* (Detroit, 1966), pp. 50–51; Washington, "The Detroit Newcomers' Greeting," 334.
26. Report of the Executive Secretary, Oct. 29, 1917; Newark *Evening News*, Sept. 24, 1918, both in NJUL Papers.
27. *Dunbar Record*, II (Sept. 1931), 1, NUL Papers.
28. Chicago Urban League, *First Annual Report* (1917), p. 10.
29. See, e.g., Cleveland Negro Welfare Association board minutes, Dec. 14, 1917, Cleveland Urban League Papers (hereafter CUL), Western Reserve Historical Society.
30. Washington, "The Detroit Newcomers' Greeting," 334–35; "A Program of Work. . . ."
31. Minutes, May 7, 1917; Annual Report [1918?], NJUL Papers.
32. Urban League of the St. Louis Provident Association, *A New Day* (n.d.), SWHAC.
33. Chicago Commission on Race Relations, *The Negro in Chicago*, p. 101.
34. Untitled typescript, 1917, DUL Papers, Box 1, Folder 8.
35. Quoted in Arna Bontemps and Jack Conroy, *Anyplace But Here* (New York, 1966), p. 167.
36. Chicago *Defender*, Oct. 5, 1918.
37. Chicago Urban League, *Second Annual Report* (1918), pp. 8-9, Chicago Historical Society.
38. *Ibid.* p. 10.
39. Minutes, Oct. 18, 1917, NJUL Papers.
40. William M. Ashby, Report to Executive Committee (n.d., but following Sept. 17, 1917), Minutes, NJUL Papers.

41. Washington, "The Detroit Newcomers' Greeting," 335.
42. Chicago Urban League, *First Annual Report* (1917), p. 11.
43. Copy of Dress Well Club pamphlet, with heading "New Comers' Attention. Read Carefully," DUL Papers, Box 1, Folder 8; untitled Detroit Urban League pamphlet, with heading "Helpful Hints" on inside page, DUL Papers, Box 18, Folder 12.
44. Minutes, Nov. 20, 1917, NJUL Papers.
45. "New Comers' Attention"; "Helpful Hints."
46. Chicago Commission on Race Relations, *The Negro in Chicago*, p. 193.
47. *Ibid.* pp. 301–9.
48. *8th Annual Report, 1916*, quoted in *50th Anniversary of the Armstrong Association, 1907–1957* [Philadelphia, 1957], SWHAC.
49. "New Comers' Attention"; "Helpful Hints."
50. Minutes, Aug. 2, Sept. 13, 1917, NJUL Papers.
51. *A New Day.*
52. "Helpful Hints."
53. Report, May–Aug. 1918, CUL Papers; Report of the Executive Secretary, Oct. 29, 1917; Minutes, Sept. 13, 20, 27, Nov. 1, Dec. 6, 1917, NJUL Papers.
54. Report, May–Aug. 1918, CUL Papers.
55. *A New Day.*
56. Armstrong Association of Philadelphia, *Ninth Annual Report* (Philadelphia, 1917), p. 9, Historical Society of Pennsylvania.
57. George Edmund Haynes, *The Trend of the Races* (New York, 1922), pp. 40–41.
58. See, e.g., James M. McPherson, "The New Puritanism: Values and Goals of Freedmen's Education" (unpublished paper presented to the Davis Seminar, Princeton University, Apr. 2, 1971).
59. Haynes, "Conditions Among Negroes in the Cities," 112.
60. Chicago Commission on Race Relations, *The Negro in Chicago*, pp. 301–9.
61. Quoted in St. Clair Drake and Horace R. Cayton, *Black Metropolis: A Study of Negro Life in a Northern City* (New York, 1945), p. 74.
62. Moses Rischin, *The Promised City: New York's Jews, 1870–1914* (Cambridge, Mass., 1962), pp. 95, 101.
63. *Ibid.* pp. 258–67.
64. *Ibid.* p. 263.
65. William Pickens, "Migrating to Fuller Life," *Forum*, LXXII (Nov. 1924), 602–3.
66. Mossell, "Standard of Living," 177, 216.
67. Quoted in Drake and Cayton, *Black Metropolis*, pp. 73–74.
68. Mossell, "Standard of Living," 177.
69. See, e.g., Chicago Urban League, *First Annual Report* (1917), p.

3; *Seventh Annual Report, 1923* (Chicago, 1924), p. 4, SWHAC; Minutes, Sept. 13, 1923, DUL Papers, Box 11.

70. Haynes, "Negro Migration," 75.

71. Untitled typescript, 1917, DUL Papers, Box 1, Folder 8.

72. *A New Day*.

73. Clark, "Report in re the Bush Terminal."

74. Chicago Commission on Race Relations, *The Negro in Chicago*, p. 101.

75. Dancy, *Sand Against the Wind*, p. 101.

76. Minutes, May 17, 1917, NJUL Papers.

77. Armstrong Association of Philadelphia, *Tenth Annual Report* (Philadelphia, 1918), pp. 4–5, Historical Society of Pennsylvania; Clark, "Report in re the Bush Terminal"; Eugene Kinckle Jones, "Some Recent Accomplishments of the Urban League," notes for speech, Jan. 15, 1920, consulted through the courtesy of Guichard Parris; Accomplishments of the Negro Welfare Association from Oct. 1, 1919 to July 31, 1920, CUL Papers.

78. Chicago *Defender*, June 29, 1918.

79. Annual Report [1918?], NJUL Papers.

80. Washington, "The Detroit Newcomers' Greeting," 335.

81. Editorial, Aug. 11, 1917.

82. Annual Report, 1917, DUL Papers, Box 11.

83. Washington, "The Detroit Newcomers' Greeting," 335.

84. Annual Report, 1917, DUL Papers, Box 11.

85. Quoted in Chicago *Defender*, Nov. 23, 1918.

86. Sept. 28, 1918.

87. "National League on Urban Conditions," *Southern Workman*, XLVI (Feb. 1917), 67, 69.

88. George Edmund Haynes, *Negro New-Comers in Detroit, Michigan* (New York, 1918, reprinted 1969), p. 8; Annual Report, 1917, and Minutes, Jan. 8, 1920, DUL Papers, Box 11.

89. Chicago Commission on Race Relations, *The Negro in Chicago*, pp. 147, 357, 366; A. L. Foster, "Twenty Years of Interracial Goodwill Through Social Service," in Chicago Urban League, *Two Decades of Service, 1916–1936*, NUL Papers.

90. Report of Executive Secretary, May-Aug. 1918, Sept. and Oct. 1918, CUL Papers.

91. Reports of the Executive Secretary, June, 1918, Oct.–Nov. 3, 1919, and Nov. 1919, NJUL Papers.

92. NUL *Bulletin*, X, 1 (Jan. 1921), 4.

93. There were 2,645,263 blacks employed in nonagricultural occupations in 1920, 819,708 of them outside the South. These figures are derived from U.S. Bureau of the Census, *Fourteenth Census of the United States Taken in the Year 1920*, Vol. IV: *Population, 1920: Occupations* (Washington, D.C., 1923), pp. 341, 365,

874–1047. In all probability, all but a tiny proportion of the League's placements were outside the South.

94. Washington, "The Detroit Newcomers' Greeting," 334.
95. Derived from Armstrong Association of Philadelphia, *Annual Report* (Philadelphia, 1915–18), Historical Society of Pennsylvania.
96. NUL *Bulletin*, IX, 1 (Jan. 1920), 9.
97. Chicago Commission on Race Relations, *The Negro in Chicago*, p. 365.

CHAPTER 9

1. Roger Baldwin interview with Guichard Parris, Jan. 10, 1969, typescript, National Urban League Library.
2. George E. Haynes to L. Hollingsworth Wood, Oct. 4, 7, 19, 25, 1915; Wood to Haynes, Oct. 5, 9, 1915; Haynes to Victor H. McCutcheon, Oct. 8, 1915; McCutcheon to Haynes, Oct. 13, 22, 1915, Haynes Papers.
3. National League on Urban Conditions Among Negroes, Salaries, in Executive Board Minutes, Oct. 21, 1913; Steering Committee Minutes, Oct. 11, 1921, NUL Papers; untitled budget sheets, Haynes Papers.
4. George E. Haynes to Ruth Standish Baldwin, July 8, Nov. 20, 1913, Haynes Papers.
5. Perlman, "Stirring the White Conscience," pp. 88–89. The quote is from Warren Waterman to President George Gates, Apr. 9, 1910, Student File of George Edmund Haynes, Registrar's Office, Fisk University, cited, *ibid*. p. 89.
6. NUL Executive Board Minutes, Feb. 7, Mar. 6, 1912, Wood Papers; Ruth Standish Baldwin to George E. Haynes, Jan. 8, 17, 1914, Haynes Papers.
7. Interview with Guichard Parris, former public relations director, National Urban League, Jan. 30, 1969, Washington, D.C.
8. George E. Haynes, "Suggestions for Further Executive Organization of League Work," n.d., Moton Papers, General Correspondence, Box 2.
9. George E. Haynes to L. Hollingsworth Wood, Mar. 15, 1916, Moton Papers, General Correspondence, Box 2.
10. Untitled budget sheets, Haynes Papers.
11. George E. Haynes to L. Hollingsworth Wood, Mar. 15, 1916, Moton Papers.
12. Eugene Kinckle Jones to L. Hollingsworth Wood, Feb. 23, 1916, Wood Papers; Steering Committee Minutes, Apr. 11, 1917, NUL Papers. There is no evidence of which (if any) board members sided with Haynes.
13. Roger Baldwin to George E. Haynes, July 1, 1917, Wood Papers.

14. Memorandum of Conference Held at Educational Building, Washington, D.C., Aug. 29, 1917, attached to Executive Board Minutes, Nov. 12, 1917, NUL Papers.

15. George E. Haynes to Robert R. Moton, Apr. 10, 1918, Moton Papers, General Correspondence, Box 9.

16. NUL, Resolutions on Negro Labor in America [Jan. 31, 1918], Moton Papers, General Correspondence, Box 9; R. R. Moton, James H. Dillard, L. Hollingsworth Wood, John R. Shillady, Eugene Kinckle Jones, and Thomas Jesse Jones to William B. Wilson, Feb. 12, 1918; Eugene Kinckle Jones to William B. Wilson, Feb. 28, 1918, U.S. Department of Labor Papers, Chief Clerk's Files, Box 17, Record Group 174, National Archives.

17. Copy of undated press release [Apr. 1918] announcing the appointment, Labor Department Papers, Box 17, RG 174. The documents on Haynes's appointment are not particularly revealing of the process by which it came about. It seems reasonable to suspect that Urban Leaguers might have seized on the idea as a way of easing Haynes out of the League.

18. Eugene Kinckle Jones to William B. Wilson, June 6, 1918, Labor Department Papers, Box 17, RG 174.

19. L. Hollingsworth Wood to Robert R. Moton, Aug. 6 [1919?], Moton Papers, General Correspondence, Box 9.

20. Parris interview.

21. Editorial, May 10, 1918.

22. "Report of the Special Committee . . . to Suggest a More Effective Organization of the League's Work," Jan. 1918, NUL Papers.

23. Eugene Kinckle Jones to Robert R. Moton, Dec. 14, 1917; Feb. 6, 1918; "Report of Committee on Standardizing Work of National Urban League," Jan. 31, 1918, both in Moton Papers, General Correspondence, Box 9.

24. George E. Haynes to Roger N. Baldwin, July 21, 1911, Haynes Papers.

25. Ruth Standish Baldwin to George E. Haynes, June 12, 1914, Haynes Papers.

26. *Ibid.*; "Report of the Special Committee . . ."; Executive Board Minutes, Feb. 1, 1918, NUL Papers.

27. Executive Board Minutes, Dec. 4, 1918, NUL Papers.

28. "Report of the Special Committee . . ."; New York *Age*, Mar. 23, 1918.

CHAPTER 10

1. Ray Stannard Baker, "The Negro Goes North," *World's Work*, XXXIV (July 1917), 319.

2. Elliott M. Rudwick, *Race Riot at East St. Louis, July 2, 1917*

(Carbondale, Ill., 1964), pp. 154–56; Urban League of St. Louis, *Twentieth Anniversary, 1918 to 1938*, NUL Papers.

3. Chicago *Daily News*, Aug. 1, 2, 20, 1919; Chicago *Tribune*, Aug. 4, 1919; Chicago *Broad Ax*, June 25, 1921; Apr. 18, 1925; Chicago Commission on Race Relations, *The Negro in Chicago*, pp. xv, xviii, 45–46; Charles S. Johnson, "The Mission of the Urban League," speech to Chicago Urban League, Feb. 28, 1947, quoted in Ralph L. Pearson, "Charles S. Johnson: The Urban League Years: A Study of Race Leadership" (unpublished doctoral dissertation, The Johns Hopkins University, 1970), p. 48.

4. Quoted in Chicago Urban League, *Eighteenth Annual Report* [1932], p. 19, SWHAC.

5. Minutes, Mar. 26, 1935, DUL Papers, Box 11.

6. "Statement Given By the National Urban League on the Race Conditions at the Present Time," Aug. 5, 1919, Woodson Papers, Folder 171.

7. Quoted in New York *Evening Post*, July 14, 1917.

8. "Statement . . . on the Race Conditions at the Present Time."

9. Quoted in New York *Evening Post*, July 14, 1917.

10. "Statement . . . on the Race Conditions at the Present Time."

11. Chicago *Broad Ax*, June 25, 1921.

12. Richard B. Sherman, "Republicans and Negroes: The Lessons of Normalcy," *Phylon*, XXVII (First Quarter 1966), 63–79; Sherman, "The Harding Administration and the Negro: An Opportunity Lost," *Journal of Negro History*, XLIX (July 1964), 154–68; John L. Blair, "A Time for Parting: The Negro during the Coolidge Years," *Journal of American Studies*, III (Dec. 1969), 177–79; *Congressional Record*, LXIII, 67th Cong., 3rd sess. (Nov. 28, 1922), 332–37, (Dec. 4, 1922), 450.

13. H. R. 2895, 67th Cong., 1st sess. (Apr. 13, 1921); H. R. 3228, 68th Cong., 1st sess. (Dec. 13, 1923), copies in NUL Papers.

14. *Congressional Record*, LXIII, 67th Cong., 3rd sess. (Nov. 28, 1922), 336–37.

15. Sherman, "Republicans and Negroes," 71–73; Blair, "A Time for Parting," 193–95.

16. Arthur F. Raper, *The Tragedy of Lynching* (Chapel Hill, 1933), p. 481.

17. Ryan Lee Petty, "Debunking Black and White: The Race Question as Subject in the Writings and Publications of Emanuel Haldeman-Julius" (unpublished senior thesis, Princeton University, 1971).

18. Senator Thaddeus H. Caraway (D.-Ark.), *Congressional Record*, LVIII, 66th Cong., 1st sess. (Nov. 19, 1919), 8818.

19. James Weldon Johnson to the Rev. Franklin Jones, Oct. 11, 1921, NAACP Papers, Box C-304.

20. *Crisis*, XXII (1921), 8; XXI (1920–21), 59; XXVIII (1924), 8–9,

quoted in Elliott M. Rudwick, "DuBois versus Garvey: Race Propagandists at War," *Journal of Negro Education*, XXVIII (Fall 1959), 425, 422, 429.

21. "The Passing of Garvey," *Opportunity*, III (Mar. 1925), 66.

22. Charles S. Johnson, "After Garvey—What?" *Opportunity*, I (Aug. 1923), 232.

23. Eugene Kinckle Jones, "The Negro's Opportunity Today," *Opportunity*, VI (Jan. 1928), 10.

24. Johnson, "After Garvey," 232.

25. "The Negro Sanhedrin," *Opportunity*, II (Apr. 1924), 98.

26. E. Franklin Frazier, "The Garvey Movement," *Opportunity*, IV (Nov. 1926), 346.

27. Johnson, "After Garvey," 232.

28. "The Negro Sanhedrin," 98.

29. "The Passing of Garvey," 66.

30. Harold R. Isaacs, *The New World of Negro Americans* (New York, 1963), pp. 143–44.

31. "The Passing of Garvey," 66.

32. "Garvey and the 'Garvey Movement,'" *Opportunity*, VI (Jan. 1928), 4–5.

33. Amy Jacques-Garvey (ed.), *Philosophy and Opinions of Marcus Garvey* (2 vols., New York, 1923, 1925, reprinted New York, 1969), II, 97–98.

34. The profile of black board members is based on biographical information about fourteen black men and women who are known to have served on the board during the 1920s. This information is from *Who's Who in Colored America*, obituaries, and other biographical dictionaries. The biographical information about Garvey comes from E. David Cronon, *Black Moses: The Story of Marcus Garvey and the Universal Negro Improvement Association* (Madison, 1955), and Hollis R. Lynch, preface to Jacques-Garvey (ed.), *Philosophy and Opinions of Marcus Garvey*.

35. The profile of black staff members is based on *Opportunity*, VI (Mar., Oct., Nov. 1928), 84–85, 292, 326; *Who's Who in Colored America* (Brooklyn, 5th ed., 1940), pp. 214, 255, 284, 287, 297, 506; *Who Was Who in America*, III, 383; *New York Times*, Aug. 17, 1968; Pearson, "Charles S. Johnson," pp. 35–38.

36. This information is derived from "Secretariat," *Opportunity*, VI (Mar. 1928), 84–89, 93; NUL press release, "Appointments Made to Urban League," attached to Eugene Kinckle Jones to the Members of the Executive Board, National Urban League, July 6, 1927, Moton Papers, General Correspondence, Box 37; names compiled from lists and correspondence in the NUL Papers; and various editions of *Who's Who in Colored America* and other biographical dictionaries.

37. Ovington, *Portraits in Color*, p. 143.
38. Jacques-Garvey (ed.), *Philosophy and Opinions of Marcus Garvey*, II, 286.
39. *Ibid*. I, 29.
40. *Ibid*. II, 104.
41. *Ibid*. 311.
42. *Ibid*. 38–39; I, 17.
43. *Ibid*. I, 37.
44. *Ibid*. II, 56–57.
45. " 'Passing,' " *Opportunity*, VII (July 1929), 205–6.
46. Jacques-Garvey (ed.), *Philosophy and Opinions of Marcus Garvey*, II, 24–25.
47. *Ibid*. I, 11.
48. A. F. Elmes, "Garvey and Garveyism—An Estimate," *Opportunity*, III (May 1925), 140.
49. *New York Times*, July 23, 1956; Eugene Kinckle Jones to Carter G. Woodson, Mar. 20, 1924, published as "Communication," *Journal of Negro History*, IX (Apr. 1924), 233; Baldwin, *Reminiscences*, Vol. I, Part II, p. 305.
50. Mar. 24, 1923.
51. Ashby interview.
52. Whenever central social service financing bodies existed, as they did in nearly every city with an Urban League affiliate, the local League was a participating member agency. No League was ever dropped from its membership in a united fund or community chest. The extent of support varied, but for 17 of 31 affiliates reporting chest membership in 1935, the 1934 chest appropriation constituted more than 90 per cent of their projected 1935 expenditures. In 1935 budgets of 31 affiliates with fully operative chests totaled $252,750, "of which $205,267, or about 81 per cent was contributed from chest sources." In another year, community chest support accounted for the entire budget of 30 affiliates, while 15 more received chest appropriations covering 80 per cent or more of their expenses. Other sources of local funding included individual contributions and membership dues. In addition, both the affiliates and the national organization sometimes received funds in payment for services of personnel whom they lent to government and private agencies on special assignments. See, e.g., R. Maurice Moss, "Looking Back Over the Years," *Opportunity*, XXIII (Oct.–Dec. 1945), 179; untitled typed sheet relating to Washington Urban League [1940], NUL Papers, Southern Regional Office Files (hereafter SRO), Series A; Henri Arthur Belfon, "A History of the Urban League Movement: 1910–1945" (unpublished master's thesis, Fordham University, 1947), p. 86; "Twenty-Fifth Anniversary Celebration, Report of Study of Urban

League Set-Up: Finances," pp. 4–6, NUL Papers; NUL, *A Quarter Century of Progress*.

53. Terms of Affiliation–National Urban League, n.d.; Executive Board Minutes, Mar. 12, 1917, both in NUL Papers.

54. Executive Board Minutes, May 8, 1929, NUL Papers.

55. L. Hollingsworth Wood to Julius Rosenwald, July 1, 1926, Rosenwald Papers, Box 75.

56. Charles Heydt, Memorandum for the Special Advisory Committee, Apr. 2, 1923, RFA.

57. W. S. Richardson to Eugene Kinckle Jones, Feb. 2, 1924; Thomas B. Appleget to Jones, Jan. 21, 1927; National Urban League—Industrial Department, May 31, 1928, RFA; Jones to Jesse O. Thomas, Feb. 19, 1924; Appleget to Jones, June 1, 1928, NUL Papers, SRO, Series A.

58. Fosdick, *John D. Rockefeller, Jr.*, pp. 121–22.

59. See, e.g., excerpt from letter received by National Urban League from Laura Spelman Rockefeller Memorial, June 7, 1926, Rosenwald Papers, Box 75; Kenneth Chorley to Beardsley Ruml, Feb. 5, 1925, RFA.

60. These statistics have been computed on the basis of figures derived from the following sources: typewritten budgets and printed financial statements included in published annual reports in the NUL Papers; and the *Financial Statement and List of Contributors of the National Urban League* for the years 1919–31, printed pamphlets in NUL Papers.

61. Memorandum on Commission on Interracial Cooperation, Apr. 17, 1930; "Building Better Attitudes: Educational Work and Plans of the Commission on Interracial Cooperation" (Special Statement to John D. Rockefeller, Jr.) [1928], RFA.

62. Carnegie Endowment for International Peace, *A Manual of the Public Benefactions of Andrew Carnegie* (Washington, 1919), p. 201 and *passim*; James R. Angell to Eugene Kinckle Jones, May 31, 1921; R. M. Lester to Jones, Feb. 24, 1927, Carnegie Corporation Archives, New York City (hereafter CCA). The annual $8000 gift was discontinued in 1927, when the Corporation began devoting nearly all of its assistance to adult education, library training schools, and the fine arts. See Jones to Julius Rosenwald, May 24, Sept. 30, 1927, Rosenwald Papers, Box 75.

63. *Foundation Directory* (New York, 3rd ed., 1967), p. 499.

64. These conclusions are based on statistics from the *Financial Statement and List of Contributors* for the years 1919–31 and from budgets and financial reports in the League's annual reports.

65. *Urban League Bulletin* (Dec. 1921), p. 5, Moton Papers, NUL File.

66. *Who's Who in Colored America* (Brooklyn, 3rd ed., 1933), p. 269; Chicago *Broad Ax*, July 2, 1921.

67. Eugene Kinckle Jones to William C. Graves, Jan. 20, 1923, Rosenwald Papers, Box 75; Report of Executive Secretary to the Executive Board of the New York Urban League, Feb. 13, 1924, NUL Papers.
68. Mimeographed letter from S. A. Allen, Apr. 8, 1927, NUL Papers.
69. Eugene Kinckle Jones to "My dear M . . . ," Mar. 24, 1920, Moton Papers, General Correspondence, Box 17.
70. Minutes, Joint Meeting of Budget and Finance and Steering Committees, Mar. 24, 1941, NUL Papers.
71. A. Gilbert Belles, "The Julius Rosenwald Fund: Efforts in Race Relations, 1928–1948" (unpublished doctoral dissertation, Vanderbilt University, 1972), ch. 8. (I am indebted to Professor Belles for making part of his dissertation available to me.)
72. Edwin R. Embree to Walter White, June 24, 1935, Julius Rosenwald Fund Papers, NAACP File, Fisk University, quoted in Belles, "The Julius Rosenwald Fund," p. 152.
73. Alfred K. Stern to Raymond S. Rubinow, Nov. 20, 1929, Julius Rosenwald Fund Papers, National Urban League File, Fisk University, quoted in Belles, "The Julius Rosenwald Fund," p. 163.
74. Belles, "The Julius Rosenwald Fund," p. 164ff.
75. James R. Angell, memorandum on interview with Eugene Kinckle Jones, Feb. 1, 1921, CCA.
76. Kenneth Chorley to Beardsley Ruml, Feb. 5, 1925, RFA.
77. NAACP, Nov. 28, 1934, meeting on request for funds, RFA.
78. From the League's *Financial Statement and List of Contributors*, 1920, 1925, 1929, and from "Twenty-Fifth Anniversary Celebration, Report of Study of Urban League Set-Up: Finances," p. 6, NUL Papers.

CHAPTER 11

1. Jones, "The Fellowship Program of the National Urban League."
2. Activities of National Urban League in the South, Nov. 22, 1935, NUL Papers, SRO, Series A.
3. Jesse O. Thomas to Cyrus F. Campfield, Dec. 6, 1919, NUL Papers, SRO, Series A.
4. See, e.g., Joseph P. Rummel to Marshall Ballard, Jr., July 6, 1938, NUL Papers, SRO, Series A.
5. Jesse O. Thomas to Eugene Kinckle Jones, Feb. 29, 1928, NUL Papers, SRO, Series A.
6. Arvarh E. Strickland, *History of the Chicago Urban League* (Urbana, 1966), pp. 23–24.
7. Jesse O. Thomas to Maggie Walker, Jan. 13, 1925, NUL Papers, SRO, Series A.
8. *Who's Who in Colored America* (5th ed.), p. 506.

9. Jesse O. Thomas to Claude Barnett, Sept. 22, 1919, NUL Papers, SRO, Series A.

10. Eugene Kinckle Jones to Jesse O. Thomas, July 11, 1921 (the quotation is from this letter); Jan. 24, 1922; Oct. 8, 1928, NUL Papers, SRO, Series A.

11. Eugene Kinckle Jones, "A Practical Year of Interracial Cooperation," *Opportunity*, IV (Mar. 1926), 101; T. Arnold Hill to C. L. Peake, Sept. 20, 1926, NUL Papers.

12. T. Arnold Hill, typed report on Oakland visit, Dec. 1926, NUL Papers.

13. See, e.g., T. Arnold Hill to John Howard Butler, Jan. 7, 1927; Hill to Eugene F. Lacey, Sept. 8, 1931, NUL Papers.

14. Brief Report Made by Field Secretary Thomas to Southern Advisory Board, Apr. 7, 1921, NUL Papers, SRO, Series A; Steering Committee Minutes, Feb. 8, 1922, NUL Papers.

15. Albert Baumann to T. Arnold Hill, Feb. 8, 1930, NUL Papers.

16. Sources of the activities of the community houses include: Accomplishments of the Negro Welfare Association from Oct. 1, 1919 to July 31, 1920, CUL Papers; Chicago *Defender*, Jan. 21, 1928; *50th Anniversary of the Armstrong Association, 1907-1957* [Philadelphia, 1957], SWHAC: Brooklyn Urban League and Lincoln Settlement Association, *Annual Report, 1925*, SWHAC; Kansas City *Urban League Pilot*, IV (Jan. 1930), SWHAC; Chicago Urban League, *Seventh Annual Report, 1923* (Chicago, 1924), SWHAC; *A Quarter Century of Service by the Urban League of St. Louis, 1918-1943*, SWHAC; Urban League of the St. Louis Provident Association, *Annual Report, 1921*, NUL Papers; Englewood League for Social Service, Minutes, Sept. 23, 1928, Englewood Urban League Papers, Urban League of Bergen County, Englewood, New Jersey; Pittsburgh *Courier*, Mar. 17, 21, May 5, June 29, Nov. 17, 1928; Feb. 2, 1929; Annual Reports, 1921-29, DUL Papers, Box 11.

17. Tampa Urban League, *Somebody Cares!—do YOU?* [1930], SWHAC.

18. Brooklyn Urban League–Lincoln Settlement, Inc., *Annual Report, 1931*, DUL Papers, Box 19, Folder 26.

19. Urban League of St. Louis, *Twentieth Anniversary, 1919 to 1938*, NUL Papers.

20. Eugene Kinckle Jones, "Progress: The Eighteenth Annual Report of the Activities of the National Urban League," *Opportunity*, VII (Apr. 1929), 118.

21. Minutes, Jan. 13, 1921; Summary of Work for 1920, DUL Papers, Box 11; Eugene Kinckle Jones, " 'Not Alms, But Opportunity': The Seventeenth Annual Report of the National Urban League," *Opportunity*, VI (Mar. 1928), 78.

22. Chicago *Broad Ax*, July 9, 1921.
23. New York *Amsterdam News*, Apr. 15, 1925.
24. Jones, "Progress: The Eighteenth Annual Report . . . ," 119–20.
25. See, e.g., Annual Reports, 1923–25, 1929, DUL Papers, Box 11; Pittsburgh *Courier*, Nov. 15, 1924; [Boston Urban League,] *Help Us to Give Other Men Their Chance As We Gave Him His* [1927], SWHAC.
26. See, e.g., Pittsburgh *Courier*, June 14, 1924; May 12, 1928; May 11, 18, 1929; Chicago *Broad Ax*, July 30, 1921; Annual Reports, 1923, 1924, DUL Papers, Box 11; Chicago *Defender*, May 19, June 16, 1928.
27. John C. Dancy to E. K. Jones, Nov. 9, 1926, DUL Papers, Box 1, Folder 18.
28. Chicago *Defender*, Mar. 3, Aug. 4, 1928.
29. Milwaukee Urban League, *Seventh Annual Report* (1929), SWHAC.
30. Chicago *Broad Ax*, Apr. 15, 1922.
31. Annual Report, 1933, DUL Papers, Box 11.
32. Report of Director for Mar. 1924, DUL Papers, Box 11.
33. *Ibid*. May 1924.
34. See, e.g., Brooklyn Urban League, *Annual Report, 1925*, pp. 11–12; Pittsburgh *Courier*, June 11, 1927; June 29, 1928.
35. See, e.g., Chicago *Broad Ax*, Apr. 15, 1922; Annual Reports, 1923–24, 1929; Monthly Report, May 1924; Board Notice, Sept. 13, 1923, DUL Papers, Box 11.
36. Annual Report, 1924, DUL Papers, Box 11.
37. See, e.g., Brooklyn Urban League, *Annual Report, 1925*; Tampa Urban League, *Somebody Cares!—do YOU?*; Annual Reports, 1923–24, 1927–29, DUL Papers, Box 11.
38. Urban League of the St. Louis Provident Association, *Annual Report, 1921*, p. 3, NUL Papers.
39. Annual Report, 1924; Minutes, Mar. 31, 1925, CUL Papers.
40. Report, Sept. 16, 1920, DUL Papers, Box 11.
41. Columbus Urban League, *Twentieth Annual Report* (1938), SWHAC; Minutes, June 21, Sept. 13, 1923; Annual Report, 1923, DUL Papers, Box 11.
42. Chicago Urban League, *Seventh Annual Report* (1923), p. 9.
43. Chicago Urban League, *Tenth Annual Report* (1926), p. 16.
44. Chicago *Broad Ax*, Sept. 22, 1923.
45. *Ibid*. Sept. 8, 1923.
46. Editorial, Nov. 30, 1926, quoted in Chicago Urban League, *Two Decades of Service, 1916–1936*.
47. See, e.g., Joint Committee on Work with Adult Immigrants, Tentative Report [1924–25], United Neighborhood House Papers,

Folder 307; Ethel Richardson, untitled typescript on adult educa-
tion programs for Mexicans in California, Survey Associates
Papers, Folder 341; *Baden Street Settlement, 1910–1926*, Baden
Street Settlement Papers, Folder 37, all in SWHAC.

48. Clarke A. Chambers, *Seedtime of Reform: American Social Service and Social Action, 1918–1933* (Minneapolis, 1963).

49. Kansas City *Urban League Pilot*, IV (Jan. 1930), 4.

50. NUL, *40th Anniversary Year Book*, p. 23. These figures cover 30
affiliates in 1920 and 42 in 1930. If one considers only the affiliates
with budgets and professional staffs, the total expenditures for the
League movement would be the same for 1920, but $481,000 for
1930. See NUL, *A Quarter Century of Progress*.

CHAPTER 12

1. Quoted in Ira De A. Reid, *The Negro Population of Denver,
Colorado: A Survey of Its Economic and Social Status* (New
York, 1929), pp. 10–11, NUL Papers.

2. H. N. Robinson to T. Arnold Hill, Dec. 21, 1927, NUL Papers.

3. Chicago Commission on Race Relations, *The Negro in Chicago*, p.
392.

4. Reid, *The Negro Population of Denver*, p. 10.

5. L. S. Theordan to Charles S. Johnson, Jan. 13, 1922, NUL Papers.

6. U.S. Department of Labor, Women's Bureau, *Negro Women in
Industry*, Bulletin No. 20 (Washington, D.C., 1922), pp. 2, 11, 15.

7. This statistic may be deceptive, in that the 1910 census was taken
in April, while the 1920 census was taken in January. The difference in dates would obscure the fact that thousands of blacks
were involved in seasonal agricultural employment that would not
have shown up in a January survey.

8. Because of the discrepancy in census timing, this figure may also
be deceptive.

9. Derived from Dean Dutcher, *The Negro in Modern Industrial
Society: An Analysis of the Changes in Occupations of Negro
Workers, 1910–1920* (Lancaster, Pa., 1930), p. 90.

10. Jacques-Garvey (ed.), *Philosophy and Opinions of Marcus Garvey*,
I, 48.

11. Booker T. Washington, *The Negro in Business* (Boston and Chicago, 1907), p. 269.

12. *Occupations for Negroes: Plan and Work of the Industrial Relations Department of the National Urban League* (1928), Moton
Papers, General Correspondence, Box 37; *Opportunity*, IV (Feb.
1926), 75.

13. L. Hollingsworth Wood to William C. Graves, Mar. 17, 1924,
Rosenwald Papers, Box 75.

14. *Who's Who in Colored America* (5th ed.), p. 255.
15. Apr. 8, 1925.
16. Horace J. Bridges, "The First Urban League Family," Chicago Urban League, *Two Decades of Service, 1916–1936.*
17. *Ibid.;* Strickland, *History of the Chicago Urban League,* pp. 84, 262.
18. T. Arnold Hill, "The Urban League and Negro Labor: Yesterday—Today—Tomorrow," *Opportunity,* XIII (Nov. 1935), 340.
19. T. Arnold Hill, "Suggested Arguments to Use in Appealing to Employers for Jobs for Negroes" [1930], NUL Papers.
20. T. Arnold Hill to Allan Jackson, Nov. 3, 1926, NUL Papers.
21. T. Arnold Hill, typed Memorandum of Trip West, Oct. 12–29, 1927, NUL Papers. One might suspect that, since John D. Rockefeller, Jr., was a major benefactor of the Urban League, this would have been a factor in its choice of Standard Oil rather than another oil company, as well as an influence on the partial success of the effort. But no evidence exists to substantiate this.
22. T. Arnold Hill to H. N. Robinson, Nov. 9, 1927, NUL Papers.
23. H. N. Robinson to T. Arnold Hill, Apr. 25, 1928; Hill to Elmer A. Carter, June 8, 1928; NUL press release, "Standard Oil Employs," n.d., all in NUL Papers.
24. NUL press release, "Employment Brightens in Spots, Losses Not Serious," Oct. 18, 1930, NUL Papers.
25. Alonzo C. Thayer to T. Arnold Hill, Sept. 20, 1930, NUL Papers.
26. T. Arnold Hill to Mrs. Howard H. Spaulding, Dec. 12, 1927, NUL Papers.
27. Memorandum for Mr. Jones's Use at the Steering Committee Meeting; T. Arnold Hill to John A. Hartford, Oct. 28, Nov. 17, 1925; Sept. 23, 1926; R. M. Burger to Hill, Nov. 18, 1925; Sept. 24, 1926; Hill to Henry Bowers, Nov. 17, 1925; Bowers to Hill, Mar. 6, 1926, all in NUL Papers.
28. W. J. Donald to T. Arnold Hill, Sept. 11, 1926, NUL Papers.
29. Memorandum of Interviews Held During Week of Dec. 3, 1928, NUL Papers.
30. Ashby interview.
31. T. Arnold Hill to E. C. Otis, May 23, 1927, NUL Papers.
32. Outline of Work and Activities of the Industrial Relations Department of the National Urban League, Mar. 15, 1925–May 31, 1926, NUL Papers, SRO, Series A.
33. T. Arnold Hill to John C. Dancy, Aug. 1, 1925, NUL Papers.
34. R. Maurice Moss to T. Arnold Hill, June 23, 1927; S. A. Allen to Hill, Feb. 3, May 27, 1927, NUL Papers.
35. Report of the Executive Secretary, Chicago Urban League, Mar. 1928, NUL Papers. Italics mine.

36. Eugene Kinckle Jones, "A Practical Year of Interracial Cooperation," *Opportunity*, IV (Mar. 1926), 100.

37. T. Arnold Hill to Floyd C. Covington, Sept. 10, 1929, NUL Papers.

38. *"Clinical Analysis of Negro Labor": An All Day Conference for the Study of the Negro in Industry, April 6, 1927, City Club of Chicago,* NUL Papers.

39. T. Arnold Hill to Mrs. Howard H. Spaulding, Dec. 12, 1927, NUL Papers.

40. *"Clinical Analysis of Negro Labor."*

41. Jones, " 'Not Alms, But Opportunity'. . . ," 77.

42. Outline of Work and Activities . . . ; Memorandum on Boston Campaign, June 4, 1926; telegram, F. B. Washington to T. Arnold Hill, Oct. 20, 1926; Report of Industrial Campaign in Boston, Feb. 13–20 [1926], all in NUL Papers.

43. Summary of Negro in Industry Week, Apr. 3–10 [1927], NUL Papers (the quotations are from this report); Jones, "Progress in Racial Adjustment," 78.

44. Memorandum on Trip West, Jan. 9–Feb. 4, 1928; T. Arnold Hill to P. D. Davis, Mar. 12, 1929, NUL Papers (source of the quotation).

45. T. Arnold Hill to Jesse O. Thomas, Apr. 21, 1926, NUL Papers, SRO, Series A.

46. Abram L. Harris, *The Negro Population in Minneapolis: A Study of Race Relations* [1926], pp. 30–2, NUL Papers. (Unfortunately, this is the only information of its kind in Urban League records for the 1920s. Even it needs to be treated with some skepticism, since figures in the text and tables are not always the same.)

47. Eugene Kinckle Jones, "The National Urban League," undated notes for speech to Urban League Annual Conference, Kansas City, Mo., consulted through the courtesy of Guichard Parris.

48. The ratio of placements to applicants for the Cleveland Urban League was 872 to 5594 in 1922, 6197 to 8456 in 1923, 4072 to 9375 in 1924; in the twelve months ending Oct. 31, 1922, Chicago made 10,720 placements from 38,207 applicants; Kansas City placed 648 of its 2408 applicants in 1928; and of 11,148 applicants at the Detroit Urban League during nine months in 1920 and 1921 (since these are monthly figures, many of them were probably repeating their applications), 1755 were placed in jobs. See Annual Report, 1922, 1924; Minutes, Mar. 31, 1925, CUL Papers; William L. Evans, "The Negro in Chicago Industries," *Opportunity*, I (Feb. 1923), 15; Kansas City *Urban League Pilot*, III (Feb. 1929), 2, DUL Papers, Box 19; Director's Reports, Nov. 11, 1920; Jan. 13, 1921; Mar. 10, 1921; [Apr.] 1921; May 9, 1921; July and

Aug. [1921]; Sept. 1921; Nov. 17, 1921, DUL Papers, Box 11.

49. Chicago Urban League, *Seventh Annual Report* (1923), p. 7.

50. Accomplishments of the Negro Welfare Association from Oct. 1, 1919 to July 31, 1920, CUL Papers; New York Urban League, *Annual Report, 1927*, p. 17, NUL Papers.

51. Board Report, July and Aug. [1921], DUL Papers, Box 11.

52. Brooklyn Urban League, *Annual Report, 1925*, p. 16.

53. Annual Report, 1927, DUL Papers, Box 11.

54. Untitled report, Sept. 13, 1928; Annual Report, 1928, DUL Papers, Box 11.

55. Kansas City *Urban League Pilot*, III (Feb. 1929), 2, NUL Papers.

56. Report, Mar. 14, 1929, DUL Papers, Box 11.

57. Annual Report, 1929, DUL Papers, Box 11.

58. Milwaukee Urban League, *Seventh Annual Report* (1929).

59. See, e.g., Director's Reports, Dec. 21, 1920; Nov. 17, 1921, DUL Papers, Box 11.

60. May 19, 1923.

61. Chicago Urban League, *Tenth Annual Report* (1926), pp. 11–12.

62. Annual Reports, 1924, 1926–28, DUL Papers, Box 11.

63. Untitled report, Sept. 13, 1928, DUL Papers, Box 11.

64. New York Urban League, board minutes, Nov. 24, 1925, quoted in Edward S. Lewis, "The Urban League: A Dynamic Instrument in Social Change: A Study of the Changing Role of the New York Urban League, 1910–1960" (unpublished doctoral dissertation, School of Education, New York University, 1960), p. 65; New York *Amsterdam News*, Dec. 2, 1925.

65. Editorial, Jan. 24, 1925.

66. T. Arnold Hill to N. B. Allen, Mar. 17, 1931, NUL Papers.

67. Annual Report, 1922, CUL Papers.

CHAPTER 13

1. Irving Bernstein, *The Lean Years: A History of the American Worker, 1920–1933* (Boston, 1960), pp. 83–90; Joseph G. Rayback, *A History of American Labor* (rev. ed., New York, 1966), ch. 21.

2. Bernstein, *The Lean Years*, p. 84.

3. American Federation of Labor (hereafter AFL), *Report of Proceedings* (Washington, D.C., 1932), p. 218.

4. *Ibid.* (Washington, D.C., 1934), p. 331, quoted in Philip Taft, *The A. F. of L. from the Death of Gompers to the Merger* (New York, 1959), p. 442; also see Ray Marshall, *The Negro and Organized Labor* (New York, 1965), pp. 14–16.

5. Report of the Director to Sept. 22, 1913, Haynes Papers.

6. *Ibid.*

7. AFL, *Report* (1932), p. 219.
8. The information on the role of AFL unions in the riot comes from Rudwick, *Race Riot at East St. Louis*, esp. chs. 3–5, 11.
9. *Proceedings of the Socialist Party Convention, 1919*, p. 45, quoted in Rudwick, *Race Riot at East St. Louis*, p. 145.
10. New York *Age*, Feb. 9, 1918.
11. Synopsis of Conference Held at Office of American Federation of Labor Between Committee Representing the A. F. of L. and Committee Representing the Colored Workers, Apr. 22, 1918; untitled typed sheet on Apr. 22 [1918] conference, NUL Papers.
12. AFL, *Report of Proceedings* (Washington, D.C., 1918), p. 131.
13. "The Way Out: A Suggested Solution of the Problems of Race Relations," Oct. 15–19, 1919, NUL Papers.
14. Untitled typed sheet on Apr. 22 [1918] conference, NUL Papers.
15. AFL, *Report* (1918), p. 205.
16. AFL, *Report of Proceedings* (Washington, D.C., 1920), pp. 276–77, 311; Executive Board Minutes, June 14, 1920, NUL Papers.
17. AFL, *Report* (1920), pp. 307–10, 351–52.
18. *Ibid.* (Washington, D.C., 1921), p. 432.
19. *Ibid.* (Washington, D.C., 1926), pp. 297–98.
20. T. Arnold Hill to the Executive Council of the American Federation of Labor, May 4, 1925, NUL Papers.
21. NUL press releases, "Urges Appointment of Negro Labor Leader," Oct. 17, 1925; "A.F.L. Considers Appointment of Race Executive," Mar. 25, [1925?], NUL Papers.
22. T. Arnold Hill, "Labor: Open Letter to Mr. William Green, President, American Federation of Labor," *Opportunity*, VIII (Feb. 1930), 57.
23. Monroe N. Work (ed.), *Negro Year Book: An Annual Encyclopedia of the Negro, 1937–1938* (Tuskegee, 1937), pp. 58–59.
24. "Editorials: The A. F. of L and the Negro," *Opportunity*, VII (Nov. 1929), 335.
25. William Green to Elmer Anderson Carter, Nov. 7, 1929, in "Correspondence: American Federation of Labor," *Opportunity*, VII (Dec. 1929), 381–82.
26. Hill, "Labor: Open Letter to Mr. William Green," 56.
27. Bernstein, *The Lean Years*, pp. 107–8.
28. Ira De A. Reid, *Negro Membership in American Labor Unions* (New York, 1930), pp. 33–38, 110.
29. American Flint Glass Workers' Union, Questionnaire for Labor Unions, Jan. 25, 1926, NUL Papers.
30. International Brotherhood of Blacksmiths, Drop Forgers and Helpers, Questionnaire for Labor Unions, n.d., NUL Papers.
31. Reid, *Negro Membership in American Labor Unions*, pp. 104–5.

32. Sterling D. Spero and Abram L. Harris, *The Black Worker: The Negro and the Labor Movement* (New York, 1931), pp. 140–41; Horace R. Cayton and George S. Mitchell, *Black Workers and the New Unions* (Chapel Hill, 1939), pp. 402–7. See also Pittsburgh *Courier*, Apr. 10, 1937, for other charges of strikebreaking lodged against the Chicago Urban League.

CHAPTER 14

1. "Editorials: The Inter-Racial Conference," *Opportunity*, VII (Feb. 1929), 36.
2. "Secretariat," *Opportunity*, VI (Mar. 1928), 85; *Who's Who in Colored America* (5th ed.), pp. 284–87; Pearson, "Charles S. Johnson," pp. 35–38, 99–108. The Johnson quote, from "The Mission of the Urban League," a speech delivered to the Chicago League, Feb. 28, 1947, is cited in Pearson, p. 48.
3. *Who's Who in America*, XXXV (Chicago, 1968), 1806; Philadelphia *Evening Bulletin*, May 25, 1966, clipping in the Quaker Collection, Haverford College Library.
4. Eugene Kinckle Jones, "Progress in Racial Adjustment," *Opportunity*, V (Mar. 1927), 76–77; Jones, " 'Twenty Years After': A Record of Accomplishments of the National Urban League During 1929," *ibid*. VIII (Mar. 1930), 79 (the quote comes from this article).
5. See, e.g., Harris, *The Negro Population in Minneapolis;* Charles S. Johnson, "A Survey of the Negro Population of Fort Wayne (Indiana)" (1928); R. Maurice Moss, "A Survey of the Negro Population of Grand Rapids, Michigan" [1928]; Reid, *The Negro Population of Denver*, all in NUL Papers.
6. Reid, *The Negro Population of Denver*, p. 46.
7. T. Arnold Hill, quoted in Annual Meeting Minutes, Feb. 13, 1935, NUL Papers.
8. T. Arnold Hill to Craig Morris, Feb. 11, 1928, NUL Papers.
9. Eugene Kinckle Jones to Executive Board, National Urban League, July 30, 1926, NUL Papers, SRO, Series A.
10. "An Open Letter," *Opportunity*, XXVII (Winter 1949), cover page.
11. The League chose "Opportunity" over "Co-operation" after deliberations by a special committee of the board on possible titles for the Bulletin. "*Opportunity*—How It Began," *Opportunity*, XXV (Oct.–Dec. 1947), 184; Steering Committee Minutes, May 8, Oct. 5, 1922, NUL Papers.
12. Arthur Paul Stokes, "The National Urban League—A Study in Race Relations" (unpublished master's thesis, Ohio State University, 1937), pp. 46–47.
13. Kellogg, *NAACP*, p. 51 and n. 25.

14. Quoted in Harris, *The Negro Population in Minneapolis*, p. 67.
15. Memorandum, Eugene Kinckle Jones to the Steering Committee and Mr. Winthrop Rockefeller, Aug. 30, 1940, in Steering Committee Minutes, NUL Papers.
16. Elmer A. Carter to John Dancy, Feb. 19, 1935, DUL Papers, Box 3, Folder 15.
17. Harris, *The Negro Population in Minneapolis*, pp. 66–67.
18. "Why We Are," *Opportunity*, I (Feb. 1923), 3.
19. "The Urban League Magazine," *Southern Workman*, LII (May 1923), 213–14.
20. Helen B. Sayre, "Negro Women in Industry," *Opportunity*, II (Aug. 1924), 242–44.
21. W. P. Young, "The First Hundred Negro Workers: The Frank Story of the Experience of a Negro Welfare Worker," *Opportunity*, II (Jan. 1924), 15–19.
22. "Negroes as Workers: A Page of Comments," *Opportunity*, IV (Mar. 1926), 90; W. P. Lawall, "The Worthington Pump and Machine Works," *ibid*. IV (Feb. 1926), 58; J. O. Houze, "Negro Labor and the Industries," *ibid*. I (Jan. 1923), 21.
23. Houze, "Negro Labor and the Industries," 21.
24. William V. Kelly, "Where St. Louis Negroes Work," *Opportunity*, V (Apr. 1927), 116.
25. Edgar E. Adams, "Assimilation Into Industry: The Experience of One Plant," *Opportunity*, IV (Feb. 1926), 57.
26. Eugene Kinckle Jones, "The Negro's Opportunity Today," *Opportunity*, VI (Jan. 1928), 12.
27. *Opportunity*, I (Jan. 1923), 19.
28. Eugene Kinckle Jones, "Negro Migration in New York State," *Opportunity*, IV (Jan. 1926), 8–9.
29. T. Arnold Hill, "Labor," *Opportunity*, VI (Nov. 1928), 343.
30. "The Record of a Family," *Opportunity*, IV (Jan. 1926), 5.
31. Ethel May Ray, " 'And Along Came Ben,' " *Opportunity*, II (Jan. 1924), 23.
32. Nimrod B. Allen, " 'Doing His Bit,' " *Opportunity*, IV (Dec. 1926), 385.
33. J. W. Knapp, "An Experiment with Negro Labor," *Opportunity*, I (Feb. 1923), 19.
34. "Sympathy Without Understanding," *Opportunity*, I (Jan. 1923), 4.
35. "The Negro Year Book," *Opportunity*, I (Feb. 1923), 4.
36. A. L. Foster, "A Co-operative Adventure in the Field of Race Relations: The Chicago Urban League," *Opportunity*, VII (Mar. 1929), 98.
37. "Another Kind of Beauty Hint," *Opportunity*, V (Oct. 1927), 286.
38. Jones, "Negro Migration in New York State," 7, 9.

39. *Messenger* (Mar. 1919), 22, quoted in Harold Cruse, *The Crisis of the Negro Intellectual* (New York, 1967), p. 41.

40. William H. Baldwin, "Well Done," *Opportunity*, XXVII (Winter 1949), 3.

41. William H. Baldwin memoranda to Nancy Weiss, Apr. 30, Oct. 2, 1969.

42. *Opportunity*, III (Jan. 1925), 3; (May 1925), 130, 142–43.

43. *Ibid.* III (Oct. 1925), 292, 308; IV (Oct. 1926), 318–19; Jones, "Progress in Racial Adjustment," 77.

44. Alain Locke to Paul U. Kellogg [Apr. 1925], Survey Associates Papers, Folder 710.

45. New York *Herald Tribune*, May 7, 1925, clipping in Moton Papers, General Correspondence, Box 34.

46. *Opportunity*, V (Sept. 1927), 254.

47. Alain Locke, "A Contribution to American Culture," *Opportunity*, XXIII (Oct.–Dec. 1945), 238. William H. Baldwin recalls that Charles S. Johnson, during his editorship of *Opportunity*, "was out in front in bringing African art, both pictures and sculptures, to wider public attention. This irked many of his black brethren who felt this was caricature and put American Negroes in a bad light." Memorandum to Nancy Weiss, Oct. 2, 1969.

48. Langston Hughes, *The Big Sea: An Autobiography* (New York, 1940), p. 228.

49. New York *Herald Tribune*, May 7, 1925.

50. Hughes, *The Big Sea*, p. 218.

51. Elmer A. Carter, "A Charge to Keep I Have," *Opportunity*, VI (Oct. 1928), 293. Carter became editor August 15, thus dividing with Ira Reid the editorial and research duties that Charles Johnson had handled alone.

52. Baldwin, "Well Done," 3.

53. Dec. 22, 1923.

54. Franklin F. Hopper to L. Hollingsworth Wood, Feb. 26, 1935, CCA.

55. Charles Johnson's biographer argues that the League's reliance on education and persuasion may have been a way of avoiding more forceful action against racism, and may thereby have contributed to the intensification of black problems. See Pearson, "Charles S. Johnson," pp. 270–71, 277.

CHAPTER 15

1. William E. Leuchtenburg, *The Perils of Prosperity, 1914–32* (Chicago, 1958), p. 194.

2. R. Maurice Moss to T. Arnold Hill, Feb. 24, 1927, NUL Papers.

3. Columbus Urban League, *Tenth Annual Report, 1927*, DUL Papers, Box 20, Folder 9; Special Bulletin, Department of Industrial Relations, Chicago Urban League, Oct. 19, 1927, DUL Papers, Box 1, Folder 21; John C. Dancy to T. Arnold Hill, Apr. 27, 1927, DUL Papers, Box 1, Folder 20.

4. See, e.g., Minutes, Jan. 28, 1927, CUL Papers; H. N. Robinson to T. Arnold Hill, Dec. 21, 1927; typed sheet titled St. Paul and Minneapolis, May 26–28, 1929; Ira De A. Reid to George R. Arthur, Oct. 21, 1929, all in NUL Papers.

5. T. Arnold Hill to Andrew J. Allison, Feb. 6, 1928, NUL Papers.

6. Charles S. Johnson, "Incidence upon the Negroes," *American Journal of Sociology*, XL (May 1935), 737.

7. National Urban League, *The Urban League in the Economic Crisis: Report of Urban League Accomplishments During 1931* (New York, 1932), pp. 7–8.

8. L. Hollingsworth Wood to Jesse O. Thomas, Nov. 7, 1931, NUL Papers, SRO, Series A; NUL press release, "Urban League Offers Government Services in Negro Unemployment," n.d., NUL Papers.

9. Eugene Kinckle Jones to Jesse O. Thomas, Jan. 2, 1931; Jan. 2, 1932, NUL Papers, SRO, Series A.

10. T. Arnold Hill to Jesse O. Thomas, Dec. 2, 1930, NUL Papers, SRO, Series A.

11. NUL, Department of Industrial Relations, 1931 Report, NUL Papers.

12. NUL, *The Forgotten Tenth: An Analysis of Unemployment Among Negroes and Its Social Costs, 1932–1933* (New York, 1933), p. 56.

13. NUL press release, "Pa. R. R. Keeps Red Caps: Atterbury Writes Urban League," Dec. 5, 1931; untitled release, re John Wanamaker, Dec. 14, 1931, NUL Papers.

14. NUL, *The Urban League in the Economic Crisis*, p. 7.

15. Untitled NUL press release, July 9, 1932, NUL Papers.

16. Quoted in *New York Times*, Apr. 5, 1931.

17. NUL, Department of Industrial Relations, "How Unemployment Affects Negroes," Mar. 1931 (source of the quotations); "Unemployment Status of Negroes," Dec. 1931, NUL Papers.

18. National Urban League memorandum to Franklin D. Roosevelt, "The Negro Working Population and National Recovery," Jan. 4, 1937, pp. 3–4, NAACP Papers; Johnson, "Incidence upon the Negroes," 740; NUL, *The Forgotten Tenth*, pp. 13, 27. Quotes are from memo to FDR.

19. NUL, *The Urban League in the Economic Crisis*, pp. 7, 11.

20. T. Arnold Hill, "The Present Status of Negro Labor," *Opportunity*, VII (May 1929), 145.

21. Regional Conference Memorandum for Local Secretaries, Sept. 23, 1933, NUL Papers, SRO, Series A.
22. Findings of the Regional Conferences, Oct. 1932; Wiley A. Hall to T. Arnold Hill, Sept. 11, 1933; William L. Evans to Elmer A. Carter, Sept. 12, 1933; Edward S. Lewis to Elmer A. Carter, Sept. 8, 1933, all in NUL Papers.
23. The League stopped publishing annual lists of contributions after 1931. The information on Rockefeller and other foundation donations comes from the following sources: RFA: memoranda of meetings to discuss the National Urban League's requests for funds, Oct. 23, 1930; Mar. 4, 1936; Mar. 10, 1937; Dec. 22, 1937; Dec. 22, 1938; Apr. 23, 1940; List of 10 Largest Contribution Sources, 1932 and 1933, attached to T. Arnold Hill to Arthur W. Packard, Nov. 17, 1933; Packard to Eugene Kinckle Jones, Feb. 21, 1934; Apr. 4, 1935; Mar. 15, 1937; Jan. 14, 1938; Jan. 9, 1939; Hill to Packard, Mar. 18, 1936; CCA: Frederick P. Keppel to L. Hollingsworth Wood, Jan. 20, 1933; Wood to Robert M. Lester, Mar. 4, 1935; Eugene Kinckle Jones to Lester, Nov. 19, 1935; Lester to Jones, Nov. 4, 1936; Dec. 9, 1938.
24. Annual income and expenditure figures are derived from statements in annual reports and budgets in NUL Papers.
25. Eugene Kinckle Jones, *Economic Adjustment for the Negro: Extracts from the Twenty-Sixth Annual Report of the National Urban League* (New York, 1937), p. 5, NUL Papers, SRO, Series G; Steering Committee Minutes, Nov. 29, 1938; Executive Board Minutes, Feb. 8, 1939, NUL Papers.
26. John M. Russell to Eugene Kinckle Jones, May 18, 1934, CCA.
27. Frederick P. Keppel to L. Hollingsworth Wood, Jan. 20, 1933, CCA.
28. Memorandum, Robert M. Lester to Frederick P. Keppel, Mar. 26, 1931; Lester to Arthur W. Page, Dec. 9, 1938, CCA.
29. Memorandum on meeting to discuss NAACP request for funds, Nov. 28, 1934; typed list of contributions to NAACP, n.d. (probably 1940), RFA.
30. Ashby interview.
31. Lloyd K. Garrison to Nancy Weiss, Feb. 25, 1969.
32. Eugene Kinckle Jones to Frederick P. Keppel, Dec. 18, 1933; L. Hollingsworth Wood to Keppel, Dec. 14, 1934, CCA.
33. L. Hollingsworth Wood to Mary McLeod Bethune, Oct. 11, 1939, Wood Papers.
34. L. Hollingsworth Wood to Mrs. Vladimir G. Simkhovitch, Oct. 9, 1939, Wood Papers.
35. L. Hollingsworth Wood to W. W. Carman, Oct. 9, 1939, Wood Papers.
36. Annual Meeting Minutes, Feb. 19, 1941, NUL Papers.

37. Eugene Kinckle Jones (?) to Jesse O. Thomas, Dec. 19, 1932, NUL Papers, SRO, Series A.

38. Jones, "The Fellowship Program of the National Urban League."

39. NUL, *The Urban League in the Economic Crisis*, p. 40; Eugene Kinckle Jones, *The National Urban League's Work in 1939 for "Not Alms but Opportunity": Extracts from the Twenty-Ninth Annual Report of the National Urban League*, p. 12, NUL Papers. The League's plight was so severe that it seemed to Mary White Ovington that the organization had "gone out of the picture." Ovington to Arthur B. Spingarn, July 22, 1934, Arthur B. Spingarn Papers, Box 7, Manuscript Division, Library of Congress.

40. NUL, *The Urban League in the Economic Crisis*, p. 40; Executive Board Minutes, May 6, Dec. 16, 1932; Nov. 9, 1936; Oct. 4, 1938, NUL Papers.

41. Steering Committee Minutes, May 13, 1918; Oct. 28, 1930; Jan. 15, 1934; Mar. 27, 1936; Dec. 5, 1939; Pittsburgh *Courier*, Feb. 25, 1933.

42. Jones, *Economic Adjustment for the Negro*, p. 5.

43. Steering Committee Minutes, Apr. 12, 1935; Odessa Cave Evans, questionnaire for National Urban League Quarter Century Club Survey of Staff, 1960, both in NUL Papers.

44. Steering Committee Minutes, Oct. 28, 1930; Jan. 15, 1934; Mar. 27, 1936; Dec. 5, 1939, NUL Papers.

CHAPTER 16

1. National Urban League, *Ever Widening Horizons: The Story of the Vocational Opportunity Campaigns* (New York, 1951), p. 6.

2. Minutes, July 31, 1930, CUL Papers; Fred B. Jones to Charles Fraser, Oct. 28, 1930, DUL Papers, Box 2, Folder 5.

3. Annual Reports, 1930, 1934, CUL Papers.

4. Urban League of Pittsburgh, *Annual Report, 1932*, NUL Papers.

5. St. Louis Urban League, Annual Reports, 1932, 1933, 1935, NUL Papers; 1937, 1940, St. Louis Urban League Papers (hereafter St. LUL), Department of Research, St. Louis Urban League.

6. Seattle Urban League, *Meeting Community Needs, 1938*, p. 12, SWHAC.

7. St. Louis Urban League, Annual Report, 1939, NUL Papers. Such a portrait of job applicants is extremely rare in Urban League records, but there is no reason to think that it would not be typical of other Leagues in the same period.

8. Annual Report, 1937, St. LUL Papers.

9. New Jersey Urban League, *Annual Report, 1932*, p. 3, SWHAC.

10. Buffalo Urban League, *Tenth Annual Report* (1937), p. 5, NUL Papers.

11. Summary, Female Employer Cards, CUL Papers; New Jersey

Urban League, *Annual Report, 1932*, p. 3; Columbus Urban League, *Twentieth Annual Report* (1938), and Omaha Urban League Center, *Annual Report, 1939* [1940], all in SWHAC; Columbus Urban League, *1939 Activities;* Minneapolis Urban League, *14th Annual Report, 1939;* Brooklyn Urban League-Lincoln Settlement, Inc., *Annual Report, 1939*, p. 10, all in NUL Papers.

12. Kansas City *Urban League Pilot*, V (Mar. 1931), 2, NUL Papers.
13. Annual Report, 1930, DUL Papers, Box 11.
14. Annual Report, 1934, CUL Papers.
15. St. Louis Urban League, Annual Report, 1939.
16. See, for example, Urban League of Pittsburgh, *Annual Report, 1932*, p. 9; Buffalo Urban League, *Tenth Annual Report*, p. 5.
17. See, e.g., Reports of the Executive Secretary, Apr., May 1937, CUL Papers.
18. See, e.g., Pittsburgh *Courier*, Feb. 7, Nov. 7, 1931; Oct. 15, 22, 1932; Chicago Urban League, *Eighteenth Annual Report* [1932], p. 17, SWHAC; Minutes, Mar. 1934, Englewood Urban League Papers; Urban League of Greater Little Rock, *Annual Report, 1939*, p. 9, NUL Papers; "Information Concerning Vocational Training Courses Which Have Been Sponsored by the Armstrong Association," n.d., Philadelphia Urban League Papers (hereafter PUL), Box 9, Urban Archives, Temple University.
19. Los Angeles Urban League, *Urban Light*, I (Dec. 1931), 4, NUL Papers.
20. Memphis Community Welfare League, *Annual Report, 1939*, pp. 3, 5, NUL Papers.
21. Armstrong Association of Philadelphia, *Good Chauffeuring* (n.d., but 1930s), SWHAC.
22. New York Urban League, *The Negro in New York, 1931*, picture, p. 34. NUL Papers.
23. Urban League of St. Louis, *Bulletin*, IX (June 1, 1930), NUL Papers.
24. New York *Herald Tribune*, May 7, 1933, reprint in DUL Papers, Box 18, Folder 22.
25. Annual Report, 1933, CUL Papers.
26. See, e.g., Chicago *Defender*, Mar. 29, 1930; Omaha Urban League *Voice*, I (Oct. 1930), NUL Papers; Armstrong Association Board Minutes, Oct. 8, 1936, PUL Papers, Box 4; John C. Dancy to Mr. and Mrs. Judge Phenisee, Oct. 27, 1937, DUL Papers, Box 4, Folder 5; Seattle Urban League, *Meeting Community Needs, 1938*, p. 7.
27. Kansas City *Urban League Pilot*, V (Mar. 1931), 4.
28. NUL, *Ever Widening Horizons*, pp. 6–7.
29. "Vocational Opportunity Campaign, April 20–27, 1930: Organization Plan for Local Communities," NUL Papers.

30. T. Arnold Hill to A. L. Foster, Oct. 21, 1929, NUL Papers.
31. NUL, Department of Industrial Relations, *After the Depression —What? Statement of the Purposes and Plans of the Third Vocational Opportunity Campaign to Improve the Status of Negro Workers* (New York, [1932]), NAACP Papers.
32. Baldwin, "The Present Problem in Negro Education," 60.
33. Alphonse Heningburg, "The Future is Yours . . . ," *Opportunity*, XXIII (Oct.–Dec. 1945), 181.
34. T. Arnold Hill, "Labor: Guiding the Nation's Youth," *Opportunity*, VIII (Dec. 1930), 374.
35. T. Arnold Hill, "Labor: Is Negro Youth Ready?" *Opportunity*, XV (Apr. 1937), 116.
36. NUL, *Ever Widening Horizons*, p. 8; *Vocational Mindedness: A Statement of the Purpose and Plans of the Vocational Opportunity Campaign to Improve the Status of Negro Workers* [1931], NUL Papers, SRO, Series G.
37. "Vocational Opportunity Campaign, April 20–27, 1930: Organization Plan for Local Communities"; NUL, *Ever Widening Horizons*, p. 7.
38. NUL press release, "National Urban League Selects Vocational Campaign Dates: Week of March 20–27, 1938 Chosen," Dec. 1, 1937, NAACP Papers; Eugene Kinckle Jones, *Toward Democracy: The National Urban League in the Year 1938: Extracts from the Twenty-Eighth Annual Report of the National Urban League*, p. 8, NUL Papers; Jones, *The National Urban League's Work in 1939*, p. 7.
39. NUL, *Ever Widening Horizons*, pp. 10, 15.
40. *Ibid.* pp. 12–13; T. Arnold Hill, "Labor," *Opportunity*, XV (Mar. 1937), 88.
41. Ann Tanneyhill, "Guiding Negro Youth," carbon of article prepared for *Occupations* magazine in connection with 8th Vocational Opportunity Campaign, NUL Papers.
42. Flyers and pamphlets for Vocational Opportunity Campaigns, NUL Papers.
43. *They Crashed the Color Line!* (New York, 1937), p. 5 (source of the quotations); *He Crashed the Color Line!* (New York, 1933), p. 5.
44. Eugene Kinckle Jones to Robert R. Moton, Feb. 21, 1928, Moton Papers, General Correspondence, Box 37.
45. Paul P. Van Riper, *History of the United States Civil Service* (Evanston, 1958), pp. 161, 241–42, 438; Laurence J. W. Hayes, *The Negro Federal Government Worker: A Study of His Classification Status in the District of Columbia, 1883–1938* (Washington, D.C., 1941), pp. 46, 51, 104, 109.
46. T. Arnold Hill to Executive Secretaries of Affiliated Organizations, Jan. 26, 1937, NUL Papers, SRO, Series A.

47. Summary of the Activities of the National Urban League for the Year 1937, NUL Papers, SRO, Series A.
48. Van Riper, *History of the United States Civil Service*, p. 242; Hayes, *The Negro Federal Government Worker*, p. 73.
49. NUL, Department of Industrial Relations, Quarterly Reports, Jan. 1 to Mar. 31, 1938; Apr. 1 to June 30, 1938; Jan. 1 to Mar. 31, 1940; July 1 to Sept. 30, 1940, NUL Papers.
50. Derived from Alba M. Edwards, *Comparative Occupation Statistics for the United States, 1870 to 1940* (Washington, D.C., 1943), p. 189. These figures include small numbers of agricultural employees in the skilled and semiskilled category, but they are not large enough to have a significant effect on the percentage distribution. The 1940 census did not separate native-born and foreign-born whites. "White" includes a number of persons of "other" races, but the Census Bureau estimates that their exclusion would make very little difference (see Edwards, p. 188).
51. Differences in job categorization and methods of inquiry make it impossible to compare statistics from the 1940 census to those from 1930 and 1920 with absolute accuracy. But they are remarkably close. See Edwards, *Comparative Occupation Statistics*.

CHAPTER 17

1. S. M. Cotton to Franklin D. Rasenvelt [*sic*], Dec. 28, 1934, Franklin D. Roosevelt Papers (hereafter FDR), President's Personal File (PPF) 30, Franklin D. Roosevelt Library, Hyde Park, N.Y.
2. Stephen Early to Charles Michelson, June 21, 1935, FDR Papers, PPF 1336.
3. Memorandum, [Marvin H.] McIntyre to Mr. [William D.] Hassett, June 23, 1938; memorandum, Hassett to David Niles, June 24, 1938; memorandum, Hassett to Commissioner of Education, June 6, 1939, FDR Papers, PPF 1336.
4. Memorandum, Stephen Early to Malvina Scheider, Aug. 5, 1935, Eleanor Roosevelt Papers (hereafter ER), Box 1362, Franklin D. Roosevelt Library, Hyde Park, N.Y.; memorandum, Eleanor Roosevelt to Steve [Early], Aug. 8, 1935, FDR Papers, PPF 1336.
5. U.S. Congress, Senate, Committee on the Judiciary, *Punishment for the Crime of Lynching, Hearings . . .* , 73rd Cong., 2nd sess. (Washington, D.C., 1934), pp. 169–70.
6. Executive Board Minutes, Dec. 14, 1934, NUL Papers.
7. Eugene Kinckle Jones to the Executive Secretaries, Local Urban Leagues, Dec. 30, 1937, DUL Papers, Box 4, Folder 7.
8. Steering Committee Minutes, Dec. 26, 1935, and attached "Resolution of the National Urban League in re: THE SCOTTSBORO CASE . . . ," Dec. 26, 1935, NUL Papers.

9. Eugene Kinckle Jones to "Co-Worker," Apr. 1, 1933; Jesse O. Thomas to Frances Perkins, Apr. 6, 1933, NUL Papers, SRO, Series A.

10. Western Regional Conference, proceedings, Oct. 6–7, 1933, p. 20, NUL Papers.

11. T. Arnold Hill, "Labor: The Situation in Washington," *Opportunity*, XI (Nov. 1933), 347.

12. Franklin D. Roosevelt to C. C. Spaulding, July 5, 1935, FDR Papers, PPF 2667.

13. National Urban League memorandum to Franklin D. Roosevelt, "The Social Adjustment of Negroes in the United States," Apr. 15, 1933, National Urban League Library, New York City; NUL, Memo to FDR (1937).

14. T. Arnold Hill to Paul G. Prayer, Mar. 17, 1936, NUL Papers.

15. "A Federal Appointment," *Opportunity*, XI (Nov. 1933), 327.

16. Editorial, May 6, 1936.

17. Jesse O. Thomas to Frances Perkins, June 16, July 12, 1933, NUL Papers, SRO, Series A.

18. Emergency Advisory Council, *Bulletin*, 4 (Sept. 10, 1935), 3, NAACP Papers.

19. Elmer A. Carter to Eleanor Roosevelt, Sept. 21, 1933, FDR Papers, PPF 902.

20. T. Arnold Hill to Eleanor Roosevelt, Apr. 22, 1935, ER Papers, Box 68.

21. Eleanor Roosevelt, speech to Urban League, Dec. 12 [1935], ER Papers, Box 3031.

22. T. Arnold Hill to Eleanor Roosevelt, July 22, 1938, ER Papers, Box 1462.

23. Eleanor Roosevelt's secretary to T. Arnold Hill, Sept. 9, 193[5?], ER Papers, Box 68.

24. Handwritten note, Eleanor Roosevelt to Franklin D. Roosevelt, on envelope addressed to FDR from NAACP, n.d., FDR Papers, PPF 1336; penciled note on Memorandum re Vocational Opportunity Campaign, Mar. 20–27, 1938, attached to T. Arnold Hill to Eleanor Roosevelt, Jan. 20, 1938, ER Papers, Box 1462.

25. T. Arnold Hill to Franklin D. Roosevelt, Feb. 18, 1938; Stephen Early to Hill, Feb. 23, 1938, FDR Papers, PPF 902.

26. T. Arnold Hill to Eleanor Roosevelt, Feb. 18, 1938, FDR Papers, PPF 902.

27. Memorandum, W[illiam] D. H[assett] to Mr. [Stephen] Early, Feb. 24, 1938, FDR Papers, PPF 902.

28. Franklin D. Roosevelt to T. Arnold Hill, Feb. 24, 1938, FDR Papers, PPF 902.

29. Mimeographed memorandum from Eugene Kinckle Jones, Aug. 10, 1938, NAACP Papers.

30. T. Arnold Hill to Executive Secretaries of Affiliated Branches of National Urban League, May 21, 1935, NUL Papers, SRO, Series A.

31. Jones memorandum, Aug. 10, 1938, NAACP Papers.

32. Quoted in Lester B. Granger, "Negro Workers and Recovery" *Opportunity*, XII (May 1934), 153.

33. T. Arnold Hill to William Green, Aug. 21, Oct. 3, 1933; Green to Hill, Oct. 4, 1933, copies attached to Department of Industrial Relations Report for 1933, NUL Papers.

34. NUL, Memo to FDR (1937), p. 16.

35. T. Arnold Hill, "Labor: Labor Marches On," *Opportunity*, XII (Apr. 1934), 120–21.

36. National Labor Relations Board, *Legislative History of the National Labor Relations Act, 1935* (Washington, 1949), pp. 1058–60.

37. Talk to American Civilization 302, Princeton University, Oct. 6, 1970.

38. Telegram, Walter White to Robert F. Wagner, Jan. 22, 1935, NAACP Papers, Box C-257.

39. Telegram, Robert F. Wagner to Walter White, Jan. 29, 1935, NAACP Papers, Box C-257.

40. Memorandum, Roy Wilkins to Walter White, Feb. 2, 1935, NAACP Papers, Box C-257.

41. Telegram, Charles H. Houston to Walter White, Feb. 6, 1935, NAACP Papers, Box C-257.

42. U. S. Congress, Senate, Committee on Finance, *Economic Security Act, Hearings . . .* , 74th Cong., 1st sess. (Washington, D.C., 1935), pp. 640–41.

43. NUL, Memo to FDR (1937), pp. 15, 20; T. Arnold Hill to Executive Secretaries of Affiliated Branches of National Urban League, Mar. 18, 1935, NUL Papers, SRO, Series A.

44. C. C. Spaulding to City and State Chairmen of Emergency Advisory Council, Mar. 6, 1935, NUL Papers, SRO, Series A.

45. NUL press release, "Urban League Fights Evasion of NRA: Spaulding to Head Nation-Wide Organization for Negro Workers," Aug. 12, 1933, NUL Papers, SRO, Series A.

46. EAC: Plan of Organization for the Emergency Advisory Council for Negroes, Sept. 27, 1933, NUL Papers, SRO, Series A.

47. Conflicting estimates of the actual numbers can be found in Organization Chart for Atlanta EAC, n.d., and in A Summary of the Activities of the Southern Field Director, May 4, 1934, both in NUL Papers, SRO, Series A; and Lester B. Granger, "The Urban League in Action: Emergency Advisory Councils," *Opportunity*, XIII (May 1935), 158.

48. "Education for Recovery Week, Dec. 3–10, 1933, Promoted by

the EAC for Negroes" (proposed talk on NRA & EAC), NUL Papers.

49. T. Arnold Hill to Jesse O. Thomas, Sept. 14, 1933, NUL Papers, SRO, Series A.

50. See, e.g., T. Arnold Hill to City EAC Chairmen, Oct. 14, 1933, NUL Papers, SRO, Series A.

51. Emergency Advisory Council for Negroes, News Letter, Apr. 25, 1934, NUL Papers; Granger, "The Urban League in Action: Emergency Advisory Councils," 158; Lester B. Granger, Report on the Activities of the Workers' Bureau, Oct. 25, 1935, NUL Papers.

52. C. C. Spaulding and T. Arnold Hill to State, City, and County Chairmen of Emergency Advisory Councils for Negroes, Apr. 9, 1935, NUL Papers, SRO, Series A; Granger, Workers' Bureau Report, Oct. 25, 1935, NUL Papers.

53. Lester B. Granger, Final Report of the Workers' Bureau . . . for the period Oct. 16 to Dec. 31, 1935, NUL Papers.

54. Eugene Kinckle Jones to E. M. Martin, Oct. 2, 1933, NUL Papers, SRO, Series A.

55. For examples, see Allen Francis Kifer, "The Negro under the New Deal, 1933–1941" (unpublished doctoral dissertation, University of Wisconsin, 1961).

CHAPTER 18

1. Raymond Wolters, *Negroes and the Great Depression: The Problem of Economic Recovery* (Westport, Conn., 1970), pp. 222–23.

2. Quoted in *ibid.* p. 225.

3. Emergency Advisory Council (EAC), *Bulletin*, 3 (June 11, 1935), 4, in Workers' Bureau Report, Oct. 25, 1935, NUL Papers.

4. *Any New Deal Can Be the Same Old Deal* (Workers' Council Series No. 3, Labor Leaflet No. 1 [1936]), NUL Papers, SRO, Series A.

5. Hill, "The Urban League and Negro Labor: Yesterday—Today—Tomorrow," 342.

6. T. Arnold Hill to Gordon H. Simpson, July 1, 1925, NUL Papers.

7. *Ibid.* Aug. 10, 1925.

8. Steering Committee Minutes, Mar. 8, 1934, NUL Papers.

9. Labor Program of the National Urban League, May 10, 1934, NUL Papers, SRO, Series A.

10. *ABC of Labor Problems: A Primer for Negro Workers* (Workers' Council Series No. 1 [June 1934]), p. 3, NUL Papers, SRO, Series A.

11. T. Arnold Hill, "Labor: Workers to Lead the Way Out," *Opportunity*, XII (June 1934), 183.
12. Lester B. Granger to Harvey Leebron, Mar. 29, 1926, NUL Papers; "The Answer to the 'Negro Problem,'" *Coronet*, XXV (Apr. 1949), 132; National Urban League, *Getting Things Done: Lester B. Granger, Executive Director, 1941–1961*, Moorland Foundation, Howard University.
13. NUL press release, "More Leaders Join Committee to Aid Negro Workers," July 9, 1934, NUL Papers, SRO, Series A. (In its first year the Committee recruited 154 members.)
14. Lester B. Granger, "The Urban League in Action: Negro Workers' Councils," *Opportunity*, XIII (May 1935), 158; Workers' Council *Bulletin*, 21 (July 1, 1938), 5, NUL Papers, SRO, Series G.
15. Quoted in Wolters, *Negroes and the Great Depression*, p. 330.
16. Eugene Kinckle Jones, *The Negro—Social Barometer: Extracts from the Twenty-Seventh Annual Report of the National Urban League*, p. 10, NUL Papers.
17. Workers' Council *Bulletin*, 21 (July 1, 1938), 2.
18. AFL, *Report* (1934), pp. 331–34; "Statement Setting Forth the Position of the National Urban League on Racial Discrimination in the American Federation of Labor," July 9, 1935, NUL Papers.
19. T. Arnold Hill to William Green, July 23, 1935; Green to Hill, July 29, 1935, NUL Papers.
20. Workers' Council *Bulletin*, 4 (July 24, 1935), 3–4, NUL Papers, SRO, Series A.
21. Memorandum, Lester B. Granger to T. Arnold Hill, Oct. 21, 1935, in Workers' Bureau Report, Oct. 25, 1935, NUL Papers.
22. *Ibid.*; News Letter, T. Arnold Hill to Executive Secretaries, II, 1 (Oct. 5, 1935), NUL Papers, SRO, Series A.
23. *Fools and Cowards Cut Their Own Throats—Are American Workers Fools or Cowards?; Expel the Traitor! Kick Out Jim Crow!*, NUL Papers, SRO, Series G.
24. AFL, *Report of Proceedings* (Washington, D.C., 1935), pp. 808–9.
25. William Green to T. Arnold Hill, Oct. 7, 1935, quoted in Charles Radford Lawrence, "Negro Organizations in Crisis: Depression, New Deal, World War II" (unpublished doctoral dissertation, Columbia University, 1952), p. 278.
26. Workers' Council *Bulletin*, 6 (Oct. 30, 1935), 2, NUL Papers, SRO, Series A.
27. AFL, *Report* (1935), p. 819.
28. Quoted in Taft, *The A. F. of L.*, p. 443.
29. Memorandum, Lester B. Granger to T. Arnold Hill, Oct. 21, 1935, in Workers' Bureau Report, Oct. 25, 1935, NUL Papers.

30. Workers' Council *Bulletin*, 7 (Dec. 11, 1935), 2, National Urban League Library.

31. Lester B. Granger to John Brophy, Nov. 13, 1935; telegram, Granger to John L. Lewis, Dec. 3, 1935; Granger, Report of the Workers' Bureau, Sept. 1, 1936 (source of the quotation), all in NUL Papers.

32. Granger, Report of the Workers' Bureau, Sept. 1, 1936.

33. The quote is from NUL press release, "Urban League Asks That Positions of Importance in New CIO Organization Be Given to Negroes," Nov. 19, 1938, NUL Papers. See also memorandum, T. Arnold Hill to Clinton S. Golden, Nov. 15, 1938; telegram, Hill to John L. Lewis, Nov. 15, 1938; Reginald A. Johnson to Golden, Nov. 22, 1938, all in NUL Papers.

34. Lester B. Granger, "Industrial Unionism and the Negro," *Opportunity*, XIV (Jan. 1936), 30.

35. Reginald A. Johnson, Brief Summary of the Activities of the Workers' Bureau, Jan. 24, 1938, NUL Papers; interview with Lester B. Granger, Apr. 13, 1969, Herndon, Va.

36. NUL press release, Oct. 18, 1934, Workers' Council scrapbook, NUL Papers.

37. Lester B. Granger to William Green, Aug. 13, 1925; Green to Granger, Aug. 22, 1935, both attached to Workers' Bureau Report, Oct. 25, 1935, NUL Papers.

38. Ralph J. Bunche, "The Programs, Ideologies, Tactics and Achievements of Negro Betterment and Interracial Organizations" (unpublished manuscript, prepared for Myrdal study, June 7, 1940, 4 vols), microfilm 1135, Library of Congress, pp. 267–70; Spero and Harris, *The Black Worker*, pp. 143, 465; Cayton and Mitchell, *Black Workers and the New Unions*, p. 402.

39. Frazier to Gunnar Myrdal, Sept. 2, 1942, quoted in Myrdal, *An American Dilemma: The Negro Problem and Modern Democracy* (New York, 20th anniv. ed., 1962), p. 841 n.

40. Granger interview.

41. Lester B. Granger, Memorandum on Local Urban League–Workers' Council Cooperation, May 20, 1938, NUL Papers; Ashby interview.

42. L. B. Granger to John C. Dancy, Oct. 1, 1934, DUL Papers, Box 3, Folder 11.

43. Edward S. Lewis, quoted in memorandum, Ann E. Tanneyhill to T. Arnold Hill, Feb. 7, 1935, NUL Papers.

44. John W. Crawford to T. Arnold Hill, Nov. 13, 1935, NUL Papers.

45. Irving S. Merrell to W. R. Valentine, quoted in Merrell to Jesse

O. Thomas, Jan. 26, 1935; Merrell to Thomas, Feb. 6, 1935, NUL Papers, SRO, Series A.

46. Jesse O. Thomas to Irving S. Merrell, Feb. 11, 1935, NUL Papers, SRO, Series A.

47. Lester B. Granger, "What Objectives Shall the League Set for the Next Five-Year Period in the Field of Organization in Industry," in Digest of Papers presented at the Annual Conference of the National Urban League . . . , Nov. 26 and 27, 1935, pp. 10, 12, NUL Papers.

48. Eugene Kinckle Jones, "After Twenty-five Years, What?" speech to 25th Anniversary Dinner, Nov. 26, 1935, NUL Papers.

49. T. Arnold Hill, "Labor: A Plea for Organized Action," *Opportunity*, XII (Aug. 1934), 250.

CHAPTER 19

1. James H. Hubert to Nancy Weiss, May 2, 1969.

2. Parris interview.

3. Granger interview.

4. Jesse O. Thomas, *My Story in Black and White* (New York, 1967), p. 109.

5. Steering Committee Minutes, Mar. 21, 1939, NUL Papers.

6. Thomas, *My Story in Black and White*, p. 109.

7. H. A. Lett to John T. Clark, Jan. 10, 1940, St. LUL Papers.

8. Ashby interview.

9. On Hill's attitude, see Roger N. Baldwin to L. Hollingsworth Wood, June 29, 1939, Wood Papers.

10. Granger interview.

11. T. Arnold Hill to Eugene Kinckle Jones, Mar. 13, 1940; Steering Committee Minutes, Mar. 15, 1940, both in NUL Papers.

12. Executive Board Minutes, Apr. 12, 1940; Steering Committee Minutes, May 9, 16, 21, 1940; L. Hollingsworth Wood to T. Arnold Hill, June 14, 1940; Hill to Robert L. Vann, June 27, 1940, all in NUL Papers.

13. Memorandum, Eugene Kinckle Jones to Executive Board, National Urban League, Nov. 9, 1940, NUL Papers, SRO, Series A; Executive Board Minutes, Oct. 21, 1937; Nov. 25, 1941; Nov. 17, 1942; June 8, 1943, NUL Papers.

14. Granger interview; Executive Board Minutes, Nov. 25, 1941; Oct. 13, 1942; Jan. 12, 1943, NUL Papers.

15. Executive Board Minutes, Sept. 14, 1943, NUL Papers.

16. Background of the Call of the Kansas City Convention [1955?], St. LUL Papers.

17. Warren G. Harding to Eugene K. Jones, Apr. 25, 1921, NAACP Papers; excerpts of letter from Calvin Coolidge, *Opportunity*, I

(Nov. 1923), 323; Herbert Hoover to Eugene Kinckle Jones, Apr. 1, 1929, *ibid*. VII (May 1929), 140; comments of executives of foundations, pp. 161, 243, above.

18. May 13, 1926, quoted in *Opportunity*, IV (June 1926), 193.
19. Feb. 15, 1928, quoted in *Opportunity*, VI (Mar. 1928), 84.
20. Apr. 28, 1939, quoted in Urban League of Greater Little Rock, *Annual Report, 1939*, p. 18, NUL Papers.
21. Clark S. Hobbs, "Negroes and the Community," Baltimore *Evening Sun*, Nov. 20, 1935, clipping in ER Papers, Box 68.
22. "National Urban League," *Southern Workman*, LII (Jan. 1923), 6–7.
23. Phil H. Brown, "Negro Labor Moves Northward," *Opportunity*, I (May 1923), 5.
24. Walter W. Pettit to L. Hollingsworth Wood, Feb. 26, 1935, CCA.
25. M. A. Cartwright to Mr. [Frederick P.] Keppel, Dec. 23, 1931, CCA.
26. Quoted in New York *Amsterdam News*, Jan. 28, 1925.
27. Feb. 10, Sept. 22, 1917.
28. Baltimore *Afro-American*, Feb. 24, Aug. 25, 1917.
29. Apr. 22, 1938, clipping in NUL Papers.
30. Lottie Shirley Polk, "On With Urban League," *Gleam*, July ? [1932], attached to T. Arnold Hill to L. Shirley Polk, Sept. 20, 1932, NUL Papers.
31. Bunche, "Programs, Ideologies," pp. 265–66, 270–72, 550–51.
32. Eugene Kinckle Jones to Executive Secretaries of Affiliated Branches, Apr. 19, 1938, DUL Papers, Box 4, Folder 15.
33. T. Arnold Hill, "Labor: Picketing for Jobs," *Opportunity*, VIII (July 1930), 216.
34. Quoted in San Francisco *Spokesman*, Nov. 17, 1932, clipping in NUL Papers.
35. Urban League of St. Louis, Annual Report, 1933, NUL Papers.
36. New York Urban League, *Annual Report, 1934*, pp. 9–10, NUL Papers.
37. Urban League of Kansas City, *The New Negro* [c. 1938], SWHAC.
38. Charles S. Johnson, *A Preface to Racial Understanding* (New York, 1936), p. 166.
39. Roger Baldwin interview with Guichard Parris.
40. Kenneth B. Clark, "The Civil Rights Movement," in Talcott Parsons and Kenneth B. Clark (eds.), *The Negro American* (Boston, 1966), pp. 606–7.

APPENDIX TABLES

Table A.1
Education of CIICN Members

	% CIICN Members		% College-age Population in U.S. [3]			Number Black Graduates [4]		
	White [1]	Black [2]	1880	1890	1900	Pre-1880	1881–1890	1891–1900
High School Education [5]	17.6	41.9						
Professional Education [6]	5.9	8.3				217	823	1691
Attended College [7]	76.5	50.0	2.72	3.04	4.01			
College Graduate	66.7	50.0	c.1.0	1.14	1.89	433	782	1336
Attended Graduate School [7]	41.2	33.3						
Earned Graduate Degree(s)	33.3	33.3				46	36	4

[1] Based on 51 white members whose education is known.

[2] Based on 12 black members whose education is known.

[3] From U.S. Bureau of the Census, *Historical Statistics of the United States: Colonial Times to 1957* (Washington, D.C., 1960), pp. 210–12. Includes both races. "Attended college" refers to the percentage of 18- to 21-year-olds in each given year; "college graduate" refers to the percentage of 21-year-olds in each given year.

[4] From Charles S. Johnson, *The Negro College Graduate* (Chapel Hill, 1938), p. 8. The figures for professional degrees include graduates of medical, dental, pharmacological, theological, and law schools. A few of these students may have earned college degrees previously, so the figures may overstate the number of professional degrees and understate the number of graduate degrees. Most blacks entered professional schools from high school, however. The figures for graduate degrees are estimates (probably incomplete) of master's and doctoral degrees.

[5] Imprecise biographical information makes it impossible to differentiate those who graduated from high school from those who attended grammar school or high school. This category includes all those who did not go beyond high school.

[6] This category refers to men and women who received professional training (at seminaries, law schools, etc.) after high school without previously attending college.

[7] Biographical dictionaries and obituaries often state that someone "was educated at" or "attended" a particular institution without indicating whether he or she actually received a degree. When it has been impossible to ascertain through other sources whether the person involved actually earned a degree, he or she has been included in the category of "attended." Some of these people probably held degrees; thus the percentage of degree recipients in each category may be understated.

Table A.2
Profession of CIICN Members

	% Whites [1]	% Blacks [2]	% U.S. Population, Gainfully Employed [3]	
			Whites	Blacks
Lawyer, Judge	12.8	10.5	.35	.02
Doctor	—	15.8	.57	.07
Publicist	10.9	21.0	.12	<.01
Educator	14.6	10.5	1.77	.57
Social Worker	9.1	—	Not listed	Not listed
Minister	9.1	21.0	.31	.34
Businessman	29.1	10.5	Not listed	Not listed
Philanthropist-reformer [4]	10.9	—	Not listed	Not listed
Public Official	—	5.2	Not listed	Not listed
Architect/Civil Engineer	3.6	—	.21	<.01
Trade Union Organizer	—	5.2	Not listed	Not listed

[1] Based on 52 white members whose profession is known.

[2] Based on 19 black members whose profession is known.

[3] Compiled from U.S. Bureau of the Census, *Negro Population: 1790–1915* (Washington, D.C., 1918, reprinted New York, 1968), p. 510. The figures are from the 1910 census and are based on gainfully employed workers 10 years of age and older. In 1910, 4.8 per cent of all gainfully employed whites and 1.3 per cent of the gainfully employed blacks held professional positions. Seventy-seven per cent of all employed blacks worked in agriculture or in domestic and personal service.

[4] "Philanthropist-reformers" are men and women of wealth who are not employed in business or the professions but devote their energies to civic concerns.

Table A.3
Education of Racial Reformers, 1910s

	Urban League Board Members		NAACP Board Members		% College-age Population in U.S.[5]				Number Black Graduates[6]			
	% Whites[1]	% Blacks[2]	% Whites[3]	% Blacks[4]	1880	1890	1900	1910	Pre-1880	1881-1890	1891-1900	1901-1910
High School Education[7]	23.5	27.3	9.5	10.0								
Professional Education[8]	2.9	—	9.5	5.0					217	823	1691	2769
Attended College[9]	73.5	72.7	80.9	85.0	2.72	3.04	4.01	5.12				
College Graduate	70.6	72.7	66.7	75.0	c.1.0	1.14	1.89	2.11	433	782	1336	1697
Attended Graduate School[9]	55.9	54.5	57.1	65.0								
Earned Graduate Degree(s)	52.9	27.3	42.9	50.0					46	36	4	4

[1] Based on 34 white board members whose education is known.
[2] Based on 11 black board members whose education is known.
[3] Based on 21 white board members whose education is known.
[4] Based on 20 black board members whose education is known.
[5] See Table A.1.3.   [6] See Table A.1.4.   [7] See Table A.1.5.   [8] See Table A.1.6.   [9] See Table A.1.7.

[NOTE: About 90 per cent of settlement workers in this period attended college, over 80 per cent graduated, and more than half earned graduate degrees. See Allen F. Davis, Spearheads for Reform: The Social Settlements and the Progressive Movement, 1890–1914 (New York, 1967), pp. 33–34.]

Table A.4
Place of Residence of Racial Reformers, 1910s

	% White Board Members		% Progressive Leaders[3]	% Black Board Members		U.S. Population[6]	
	Urban League[1]	NAACP[2]		Urban League[4]	NAACP[5]	% Whites	% Blacks
New York City	80.0	77.8	39.6	45.5	28.6	23.1	4.3
New York State	—	—		45.5	—		
Other Middle Atlantic	5.7	—			9.5		
New England	2.9	11.1	16.2		9.5	7.9	.7
East North Central	5.7	11.1	32.3	9.1	14.3	21.9	3.1
West North Central	—	—			—	13.9	2.5
South Atlantic	2.9	—	14.6	45.5	33.3	9.9	41.8
East South Central	—	—			—	7.0	27.0
West South Central	2.9	—	7.3		4.8	8.2	20.2
Mountain	—	—			—	3.1	.2
Pacific	—	—			—	4.9	.3

(White Board Members bracket totals: Urban League 85.7, NAACP 77.8 for New York City / New York State / Other Middle Atlantic; Black Board NAACP bracket 38.1; U.S. Population bracket 23.1 / 4.3 for the first three regions.)

[1] Based on 35 white board members whose place of residence is known.

[2] Based on 27 white board members whose place of residence is known.

[3] Compiled from Alfred D. Chandler, Jr., "The Origins of Progressive Leadership," in David M. Kennedy (ed.), *Progressivism: The Critical Issues* (Boston, 1971), p. 75.

[4] Based on 11 black board members whose place of residence is known.

[5] Based on 21 black board members whose place of residence is known.

[6] From U.S. Bureau of the Census, *Thirteenth Census of the United States Taken in the Year 1910*, Vol. I: *Population, 1910: General Report and Analysis* (Washington, D.C., 1913). p. 139.

Table A.5
Profession of Racial Reformers, 1910s

	% White Board Members		% Progressive Leaders[3]	% Black Board Members		% U.S. Population, Gainfully Employed[6]	
	Urban League[1]	NAACP[2]		Urban League[4]	NAACP[5]	Whites	Blacks
Lawyer, Judge	23.5	28.0	28.5	—	9.5	.35	.02
Doctor	—	—		18.2	23.8	.57	.07
Publicist	—	20.0		9.1	4.8	.12	<.01
Educator	26.5 } 41.2	4.0 } 52.0	35.0	54.5	14.3	1.77 } 2.84	.57 } 2.84
Social Worker	8.8	16.0		—	—	.07[7]	—
Minister	5.9	12.0		18.2	38.1	.31	.34
Businessman	11.8	8.0	36.5	—	4.8	Not listed	Not listed
Philanthropist-reformer	20.6	8.0	—	—	4.8	Not listed	Not listed
Public Official	2.9	—	—	—	—	Not listed	Not listed
Trade Union Organizer	—	4.0	—	—	—	Not listed	Not listed

[1] Based on 34 white board members whose profession is known.

[2] Based on 25 white board members whose profession is known.

[3] Compiled from Alfred D. Chandler, Jr., "The Origins of Progressive Leadership," in David M. Kennedy (ed.), *Progressivism: The Critical Issues* (Boston, 1971), p. 75.

[4] Based on 11 black board members whose profession is known.

[5] Based on 21 black board members whose profession is known.

[6] Compiled from U.S. Bureau of the Census, *Negro Population: 1790–1915* (Washington, D.C., 1918, reprinted New York, 1968), pp. 510, 525. The figures are from the 1910 census and are based on gainfully employed workers 10 years of age and older.

[7] There is no specific category for social workers in the 1910 census. This figure refers to religious and charity workers and keepers of charitable and penal institutions. The percentage of social workers would have been smaller than .07.

Table A.6
Education of Urban League Board Members, 1920s

	Urban League Board Members		% College-age Population in U.S.[3]					Number Black Graduates[4]				
	% Whites[1]	% Blacks[2]	1880	1890	1900	1910	1920	Pre-1880	1881–1890	1891–1900	1901–1910	1911–1920
High School Education[5]	33.3	33.3										
Professional Education[6]	2.8	—										
Attended College[7]	63.9	66.7	2.72	3.04	4.01	5.12	8.09	217	823	1691	2769	2984
College Graduate	61.1	66.7	c.1.0	1.14	1.89	2.11	2.70	433	782	1336	1697	3066
Attended Graduate School[7]	44.4	33.3										
Earned Graduate Degree(s)	38.9	13.3						46	36	4	4	80

[1] Based on 38 white board members whose education is known.
[2] Based on 15 black board members whose education is known.
[3] See Table A.1.3. [4] See Table A.1.4. [5] See Table A.1.5. [6] See Table A.1.6. [7] See Table A.1.7.

Table A.7
Place of Residence of Urban League
Board Members, 1920s

	% Whites [1]	% Blacks [2]	U.S. Population [3]	
			% Whites	% Blacks
New York City	64.1	31.3	5.7	1.5
New York State	2.6	—	4.9	.4
Other Middle Atlantic	7.7	12.5	12.1	3.8
New England	7.7	—	7.7	.7
East North Central	5.1	6.2	22.1	4.9
West North Central	—	—	12.9	2.6
South Atlantic	10.3	43.8	10.2	41.3
East South Central	—	6.2	6.7	24.1
West South Central	2.6	—	8.6	19.8
Mountain	—	—	3.4	.3
Pacific	—	—	5.6	.5

[1] Based on 39 white board members whose place of residence is known.

[2] Based on 16 black board members whose place of residence is known.

[3] Derived from U.S. Bureau of the Census, *Fourteenth Census of the United States Taken in the Year 1920*, Vol. II: *Population, 1920: General Report and Analytical Tables* (Washington, D.C., 1922), p. 31.

Table A.8
Profession of Urban League Board
Members, 1920s

	% Whites [1]	% Blacks [2]	% U.S. Population, Gainfully Employed [3]	
			Whites	Blacks
Lawyer, Judge	20.5	—	.33	.02
Doctor	—	12.5	.39	.07
Publicist	2.6	6.25	.09	<.01
Educator	17.9	50.0	2.0	.76
Social Worker	12.8	—	.14	.03 [4]
Minister	—	12.5	.29	.41
Businessman	12.8	6.25	Not listed	Not listed
Philanthropist-reformer	28.2	6.25	Not listed	Not listed
Public Official	2.6	—	Not listed	Not listed
Architect	2.6	—	.05	<.01
Printer	—	6.25	Not listed	Not listed

[1] Based on 39 white board members whose profession is known.

[2] Based on 16 black board members whose profession is known.

[3] Derived from U.S. Bureau of the Census, *Fourteenth Census of the United States Taken in the Year 1920*, Vol. IV: *Population, 1920: Occupations* (Washington, D.C., 1923), pp. 342–59. The figures are based on gainfully employed workers 10 years of age and older.

[4] There is no specific category for social workers in the 1920 census. This figure refers to religious and charity workers and keepers of charitable and penal institutions. The percentage of social workers would have been smaller than .03.

Table A.9
Education of Urban League Board Members, 1930s

	Urban League Board Members		% College-age Population in U.S.[3]						Number Black Graduates[4]					
	% Whites[1]	% Blacks[2]	1880	1890	1900	1910	1920	1930	Pre-1880	1881-1890	1891-1900	1901-1910	1911-1920	1921-1930
High School Education[5]	32.4	23.8												
Professional Education[6]	—	—							217	823	1691	2769	2984	3299
Attended College[7]	67.6	76.2	2.72	3.04	4.01	5.12	8.09	12.42						
College Graduate	62.2	71.4	c.1.0	1.14	1.89	2.11	2.70	6.31	433	782	1336	1697	3066	10,184
Attended Graduate School[7]	37.8	61.9												
Earned Graduate Degree(s)	32.4	47.6							46	36	4	4	80	523

[1] Based on 36 white board members whose education is known.
[2] Based on 21 black board members whose education is known.
[3] See Table A.1.3. [4] See Table A.1.4. [5] See Table A.1.5. [6] See Table A.1.6. [7] See Table A.1.7.

Table A.10
Place of Residence of Urban League
Board Members, 1930s

| | % Whites [1] | % Blacks [2] | U.S. Population [3] | |
			% Whites	% Blacks
New York City	65.8	22.7	6.0	2.8
New York State	—	—	5.1	.7
Other Middle Atlantic	7.9	18.2	12.0	5.4
New England	2.6	4.5	7.4	.8
East North Central	5.3	9.1	22.3	7.8
West North Central	—	—	11.8	2.8
South Atlantic	13.1	27.3	10.4	37.2
East South Central	—	9.1	6.6	22.4
West South Central	2.6	—	8.4	19.2
Mountain	—	—	3.0	.3
Pacific	—	9.1	6.9	.8
Abroad	2.6	—	—	—

[1] Based on 38 white board members whose place of residence is known.

[2] Based on 22 black board members whose place of residence is known.

[3] Derived from U.S. Bureau of the Census, *Fifteenth Census of the United States Taken in the Year 1930*, Vol. II: *Population, 1930: General Report: Statistics by Subjects* (Washington, D.C., 1933), pp. 35, 70.

Table A.11
Profession of Urban League
Board Members, 1930s

	% Whites [1]	% Blacks [2]	% U.S. Population, Gainfully Employed [3]	
			Whites	Blacks
Lawyer, Judge	18.9	9.1	.37	.02
Doctor	—	18.2	.35	.07
Publicist	8.1	13.6	.15	<.01
Educator	8.1	31.8	2.46	1.0
Social Worker	10.8	—	.07	.02
Minister	—	4.5	.29	.05
Businessman	13.5	9.1	Not listed	Not listed
Philanthropist-reformer	37.8	4.5	Not listed	Not listed
Public Official	—	—	Not listed	Not listed
Architect	2.7	4.5	.05	<.01
Musician	—	4.5	.36	.19

[1] Based on 37 white board members whose profession is known.

[2] Based on 22 black board members whose profession is known.

[3] Derived from U.S. Bureau of the Census, *Fifteenth Census of the United States: 1930*, Vol. V: *Population: General Report on Occupations* (Washington, D.C., 1933), pp. 74, 83–84. The figures are based on gainfully employed workers 10 years of age and older.

INDEX

INDEX